The World of Dogs
Flatcoated
Retrievers

Brenda Phillips

Photo - Y Jaussi

KINGDOM

Published by Kingdom Books
PO Box 15
Waterlooville PO7 6BQ
England

Designed by Add Graphics
PO Box 15
Waterlooville PO7 6BQ
England

Printed in England

Cover Photo - Sh Ch Exclyst Viking   Photo - Liz Phillips

Contents

introduction

The person who influenced my life more than anyone else was Patience Lock of the Halstock Flatcoated Retrievers. She was the first person in the breed whom I got to know. She became my surrogate mother, and in those 12+ years she taught me so much about the breed and life. I had the great pleasure of knowing her and her husband, John, very well.

A group of us in this country and Scandinavia (Lena Hagglund, Claus Sørensen and myself) all felt we were part of her family, and I am sure that Helen Beckwith, Peggy Miller and Audrey and Peter Forster all feel the same.

Patience wrote this in 1968:

I am just completing 10 years in Flatcoats and I look back with much interest over those years. An average of 30 shows attended each year, always with a Flatcoat in tow, though not always with Flatcoat classes scheduled. One got used at first to the inevitable remark 'What is that black dog?' and also to being accosted by delighted elderly folk seeing again their favourite breed after many years.

Ten years ago the classes were smaller and type varied as recovery slowly took place after the war years. Now, with over 200 registrations, the breed is again taking its rightful place among the gundog breeds, and rings with interested novice owners handling promising puppies and juniors are becoming a feature of the bigger shows, and are a cheering sight indeed to the lovers of our breed. These newcomers will inevitably suffer the disappointments and set-backs that are the lot of all who aspire to breed dogs; but they have the effect of sorting the wheat from the chaff; the really determined pick themselves up and dust themselves off and start again, and these are the folk the breed needs and fortunately has in pretty good measure. They become the stalwarts of the shows and training classes and later may aspire to Field Trials via the `picking-up` that the active and fortunate may be able to get on local shoots.

A small boy once said to me: 'There are two ways of enjoying your bicycle, you can either ride it or take it to pieces!' Fortunately there are many more than two ways of enjoying our Flatcoats - work and show are the obvious ones, but the joy of owning loving, faithful dogs that are utterly devoted, and of watching a litter of puppies growing day by day and learning to follow with wagging little tails, and growing like their parents and grand-parents in a hundred ways; these are the true breeders' rewards and the more precious for having taken long to achieve. Out of our loved and carefully reared litters there may be only one or two who become well-known, but the others will be doing good to the reputation of the breed in many homes as loved companions and happy assistants to quiet, one-dog, shooting people.

Dogs have much to teach as well as to learn, and it is the owner who is willing to learn from the dog as well as to teach him who derives the most satisfaction. I would say to all new-comers to the breed, 'Make your dog your partner'.

Patience Lock

acknowledgements

This book would not have been possible without the support of my good friends within the breed. It has been written (or should I say typed with one finger!) with love and a big 'thank you' to this unique breed of dog: the Flatcoated Retriever. Personally, I could not imagine my life without the dogs themselves and my good friends within the breed world-wide.

My hope is that this book will help a few new people to understand and look after the Flatcoated Retriever, giving it the life that a Flatcoated Retriever would wish to live. I also hope that people will come to understand the uniqueness of our breed. We must continue to breed our dogs to the blueprint of the Breed Standard laid down so many years ago. It would be so easy to lose this and just have 'black dogs'.

To me, the overall health of our beautiful breed is of the greatest importance. They are so brave when in pain and suffering. No breeder now needs to take even the smallest chance of producing a Flatcoat with the possibility of a genetic fault as such great strides have been made by the veterinary profession.

Many people have helped me with this book, but I should like to tender my special thanks to the following:

Rona Dixon and Sandra Candler, for many hours' help in checking proofs. The knowledge that I had their support and backing helped me enormously. In addition to this, I should like to thank Rona for her help with pedigrees, and Sandra for her line drawings;

Jane Alexandra, BVet Med, Cert VA, MRCVS for veterinary advice;

Sheila Neary and Shena Wells for their help;

My special friends who said 'Yes you **can** do it' and who have supported me in every way;

Dr Nancy Laughton for her support and kind permission to use quotations from *The Review of the Flat-coated Retriever*;

Rachel Page Elliott of the USA. She has influenced my view and understanding of dogs and their movement with her book *Dogsteps*, her lectures and her personal help;

All my friends from abroad who have so kindly put time and effort into writing about our breed in their own country;

Last but not least, my daughter Liz and my good friend Yvonne Jaussi for their special photographs.

Brenda Phillips, picking up with Viking and Watchman
Photo - Liz Phillips

Chapter 1

Origins and History
of the Flatcoated Retriever

Pre-1900

It is no coincidence that the Retriever came along at the same time as the black powder shotgun; there was no point in shooting game unless it could be located and retrieved when it had been hit. From the earliest times sportsmen had trained their dogs to work alongside them, performing the tasks for which they were better equipped than their masters. The Pointers, Setters and Spaniels of our forefathers were trained to find, flush and retrieve game, and this is still the case among the continental Hunt-Point-Retrieve and Spaniel breeds today.

In about 1850 all the different breeds were gradually being developed and established. At this time, exceptional retriever potential was recognised in a black-coated dog discovered in Labrador. This dog, which must have originated in Europe, was re-introduced into Great Britain. A natural water dog with a good constitution, the newcomer was impervious to chills, and free from the susceptibility to ear canker common in Spaniels. These dogs had a reputation for outstanding retrieving skills and remarkable intelligence. The importers called them Spaniels, a breed name which at one time was also applied to the Newfoundland, a relative. There were said to be very few in England, although this is not explicitly confirmed by contemporary records. It is thought that these dogs from Labrador were crossed with the English Setter or a Black Setter to produce the Wavy-coated Retriever, later re-named Flat-coated Retriever and now known as the Flatcoated Retriever.

One very remarkable fact about the Flatcoated Retriever is that, although the parent stock was mongrel and the setter type predominated in the early days, the ultimate result has favoured the 'Retriever' cross distinctly and prominently. This proves the potency of a pure breed and what a great influence it has in fixing type and character over the other less vital elements with which it is blended. For instance, a Mr L Shuter from Horton Kirby in Kent once bought a bitch in the streets of Bristol. She had no pedigree and her ancestors were unknown, but when she was mated to Darenth the puppies were so good that they won prizes against strong competition. It is interesting to note that these dogs without pedigrees were breeding true to type and continued to do so. In some Flatcoats the 'Setting' on game is still seen, however.

Both as a worker and as a show dog the Flatcoated Retriever soon reached something very near to the ideal standard of perfection, and this has been upheld consistently. Careful selection and systematic breeding, backed up by enthusiasm, have resulted in the production of a dog combining useful working qualities with the highest degree of beauty.

The first introduction of the Flatcoated Retriever to the show bench was at Birmingham in 1864. There were two classes, the winners being Mr T Meyrick's Wyndham and Lord Paget's Music. It is worth noting that there were other dogs named Wyndham.

Mr S E Shirley, of the Ettington affix, the President of The Kennel Club, was a very prominent admirer and breeder of Flatcoats who owned many outstanding dual-purpose dogs. He was considered to have done more for the breed than anyone else in his generation. Mr Harding Cox, another great enthusiast, continued on the same lines as Mr Shirley, his dogs being well-known for their similarity of type and improved heads. Colonel Cornwall-Leigh also played his part in bringing the Flatcoated Retriever (or Wavy-coated Retriever as it was then sometimes known) to perfection.

Whatever its original breeding base, by the latter part of the nineteenth century the Flatcoated Retriever was established as a quality breed with a great family likeness and character. The dogs were known for their beauty and for breeding true to standard. They were mainly black or liver, although other colours were permitted in the early days.

A full detailed history of the Flatcoated Retriever can be found in Dr Nancy Laughton's *The Review of the Flat-coated Retriever.*

1900-1969

At the turn of the century Flatcoats were of high quality and noted for their pleasing expression. They were favourites in the show ring and on field trials. The breeders working at the end of the nineteenth century and the beginning of the present century certainly produced dogs of high quality. Colonel Cornwall-Leigh's High Leigh Blarney was one of the leading dogs of his time. On Colonel Cornwall-Leigh's death in 1905 his dogs were auctioned at Aldridge's, and High Leigh Blarney was considered of such high quality that Mr Cooke of the Riverside affix, another eminent breeder, gave his agent a blank cheque with the instruction to buy Blarney. He was bought for 200 guineas.

High Leigh Blarney's reputation was such that Mr Cooke had recovered his cost in stud fees in less than two years. Blarney died at the age of 11 in 1913. He was never beaten in the show ring and his influence as a sire was considered unequalled.

High prices were also paid for Champion (Ch) Black Quilt (£200 by Mr Cooke) and Ch Black Queen (145 guineas by Lord Redesdale). However it was during this time that this beautiful breed sadly became less popular, and this was to some extent a direct result of large kennels inflating the prices, thus discouraging the small breeder from taking an active role in developing the breed.

At the beginning of this century it was recorded that for every first class Flatcoat dog there were at least three first class bitches. It was considered that the bitches had superior constitutions to the dogs, and that the death-rate from distemper was 50 per cent higher in dogs than in bitches, especially among puppies exceeding nine months of age. This was observed by breeders, but no reason could be given.

After the First World War Flatcoat registrations rose gradually to 438 in 1924, but Labrador registrations were three times that number. Flatcoat numbers then started to fall, and this continued up to the start of the Second World War. Flatcoats were owned mainly by wealthy sportsmen, although they were also popular with gamekeepers. A dual-purpose dog was therefore the norm.

Mr Phizacklea with some Atherbram Flatcoats.

Dr Nancy Laughton and Miss Knight at the Flatcoated Retriever Society Field Trial with Claverdon Ladybird.

Ch Atherbram Nobbie.
Copyright - Mrs Hilary Hughes.

Flatcoated Retrievers

The Flatcoated Retriever population was decimated by the Second World War; it had hardly had time to recover from the First World War. In the intermediate years there had been considerable growth in popularity among Labradors and Golden Retrievers, and this also had affected Flatcoat numbers. However breed numbers started to increase in 1946 when 94 Flatcoats were bred.

The first post-war gathering of Flatcoats was at an open show in Leeds in July 1946, arranged by The Flatcoated Retriever Club. Mr Birch was the judge. The first set of Challenge Certificates (CCs) were awarded to the dog Atherbram Nobbie owned by Mr Phizacklea and the bitch Claverdon Jet owned by Dr Nancy Laughton.

In 1947, 74 Flatcoats were registered. Waterman won two CCs. Claverdon Jet won another two, and became the first post-war champion bitch. The first post-war field trial was an All-Aged Stake held by The Flatcoated Retriever Association. It was won by Greenfield June. The first post-war Crufts was in 1948. The Flatcoated Retriever breed was judged by Mr E Turner. The dog CC was awarded to Ch Atherbram Nobbie and the bitch CC to Ch Claverdon Jet. The Flatcoated Retriever Society held its first All-Aged Field Trial Stake the same year. The winner was Maesmynan Patricia.

The breed was slowly emerging with the help of kennels such as Atherbram owned by Mr Phizacklea and his wife. This kennel was established in the early 1920s, its lines resting on a broad basis, and it was very successful. One of the Phizackleas' most outstanding early bitches, Ch Atherbram Jet, produced some outstanding progeny when mated to Ch Dancer of Riverside. Mr and Mrs Phizacklea were wise breeders who brought in outcrosses from time to time. One such was the bitch Rettendon Dido who, bred to Atherbram Prince, produced Atherbram Gunner, a much used and important stud dog.

During the Second World War Mr Phizacklea had had the good fortune to acquire the bitch Cemlyn, whose sire and dam both came from the best field trial stock. Her sire Windle Don, a field trial winner, line bred back to Field Trial (FT) Ch Elwy Mary on his male side. Her dam Windle Peggy was also a Field Trial Winner (FTW), and daughter of FT Ch Windle Popular.

This new blood combined with established blood lines to produce such Flatcoats as Ch Claverdon Jet and her brother Atherbram Monty. The kennel bred blacks and livers, and they developed a line of liver bitches which they bred to blacks.

The kennel was able to continue through the war and this was fortunate for the breed in general, as the majority of Flatcoats acquired by post war breeders in the late 1940s and 1950s came from this kennel. After the deaths of Mr and Mrs Phizacklea the affix was transferred to Mrs Phizacklea's niece, Mrs Peggy Payne, who then dropped her own affix, Sharpthorne. She continued until her untimely death in the early 1970s. The affix is continued by the family in Mrs Hilary Hughes, although the Atherbram breeding line has now been swallowed up by other lines.

Other breeders who struggled to keep their lines going during the war were: Mr Cooke, Mr Birch, Mrs Hemm, Mrs Barwise, Miss Meeson, Mr Allen, Mr Spencer and Mr S Guy. Later they were joined by others returning from service duties, including Mr S O'Neill, Major H Wilson, and Mr Colin Wells.

None of us today can really begin to understand the daunting task of picking up the threads of disappearing lines, and the hard work and dedication needed in this post-war period. There was also a shortage of food, and communication and travel were difficult. Disease in dogs was rampant.

Stanley O'Neill must be given credit for his painstaking research into lines that should be used, and for the advice and information he gave to other breeders. He and his wife were well known for their selfless devotion to the Flatcoat. The breed was very low in numbers, and all stock had to be used, some not of the best quality. The priority was to save the breed; breeding to type had to come later.

Their Pewcroft kennel was founded in the late 1930s, with the foundation bitch Pewcroft Pest *(Ch Specialist ex Towerwood Flo)*. Just before the war they produced Pewcroft Peg *(Atherbram Warrior ex Pewcroft Plague)*, a typy bitch with good quality and substance, but because of the circumstances she was not shown until later in life. She had three litters, the first of them to Ponsbourne Peter. Her next two litters played an important role in Flatcoat history. The first of them, to Bryn of Adlington (*Rastus of Adlington ex Gwyneth of Adlington*), produced Ch Pewcroft Plug and Pewcroft Pitch; the next, to Sweep of Riverside (*Dusk of Riverside ex Brynasaph Fair Trade*), produced Pewcroft Page, Claverdon Pewcroft Pieman, Ch Pewcroft Picture and Pewcroft Peep. Later Pewcroft Peep was mated to Gaff of Riverside (*Nobby of Riverside ex Waaf of Riverside*), strengthening the Bryn Asaph blood, which also came from the mating of Sweep of Riverside and Pewcroft Peg. Mr O'Neill then outcrossed his line to Denmere Prince (*Patch of Sauch ex Dot of Sauch*) and this litter produced four important puppies who were foundation stock for future breeders. Pewcroft Proper went to Mr Reed Flowers;

Ch Monarch of Leurbost.
Photo - F E Garwood, *Dog World.*

the bitch Pewcroft Prim went to Miss Hall's Blakeholme kennel; the dog Pewcroft Praetor went to Miss Meeson's Rettendon kennel; and Pewcroft Perfect went to America to Mr Homer Downing's Bramcroft kennel.

Mr O'Neill also wrote extensively on the breed and for many years was the breed correspondent for the dog papers.

There were many dedicated breeders in this period, several of them gamekeepers. I remember meeting Jimmy Boyd late in his life at a Championship Show in Glasgow. I just wish the hall had been quieter so that I could have understood his wonderful Scottish brogue! He bought Claxton Cadet and bred him to Zoë of Adlington (*Kale Rat of Adlington ex Burbage Peggy*). This produced a line of excellent and tireless workers. He is remembered for one of his final dogs, Ch Monarch of Leurbost (*Braden of Longforgan ex Halstock Louisa*), who was campaigned by Dr and Mrs McComb after his death.

Mr E Bryant founded his Ponsbourne kennel in the early 1930s. He bred mainly for work, but his dogs were considered to be of good quality. He bred well into the 1960s, but sadly his line died out with him. I remember trying to use a very old dog of this line in the early 1970s without success.

Miss Meeson's Rettendon stock sank to a very low number during the war, but she bought in several dogs afterwards and bred extensively. She believed in outcrossing and produced useful stock until her death in 1961.

Another lady, Mrs P Barwise, began breeding Flatcoats in the 1930s. Her kennel name was Forestholm and it was founded mainly on Atherbram stock. She liked livers and produced some useful stock. Forestholm Coppercoat, a liver dog, was used by Margaret Izzard. One of her last dogs, Forestholm Rufus (*Forestholm Donard ex Forestholme Brown Beauty*), was used in 1971 by Ed Atkins and myself on Wood Lass, producing the Wyndhamian 'D' litter which had a strong influence on Flatcoats in America.

Reginald Cooke of the Riverside affix was born in 1860 and died in 1951. He was considered in his time the great patron of the Flatcoated Retriever. He studied the breed, and kept detailed records which still exist today. He was determined to have the best in his own kennels, and the quality of his stock was unique in any breed of dog. In 60 years of showing Flatcoats he won 349 CCs and 130 Reserve Challenge Certificates (RCCs), and he made up many champions including two dual champions (a dog who is a Field Trial Champion and a Champion in the Show Ring), Toby of Riverside and Grouse of Riverside. His dogs also won 15 Firsts, 10 Seconds, 11 Reserves, and 21 Certificates of Merit (COMs) in field trials. Sadly this enthusiasm monopolised the Flatcoat breed and therefore encouraged others, who were not so well off, to stop competing in the breed, selling their best stock to him. In hindsight this certainly had a detrimental effect on the breed overall. In 1941, at 80 years of age, Mr Cooke decided not to show his dogs, but after the war he continued to work them and to win with them in field trials. Mr Tansy was well-known as his trainer and kennel man.

Mr Cooke's preference was for a medium size dog which he considered the best for work. 'A larger size retriever is a great mistake, for not only do his proportions hinder him in his work, but he will very quickly tire, and as a rule, a big dog is a slow dog.' (Quotation from *Dogs since 1900*, by A Croxton Smith, published by Dakers.)

Mr Cooke wrote three little pamphlets on the breed, which occasionally can be found in rare book shops. Quoting one of these: 'Pick out a medium sized puppy with a long but not weak head, small ears, dark eyes, straight coat, short stern, straight legs, small feet and plenty of bone. Give preference to a puppy which takes much notice of you, which shows no fear when you clap your hands loudly, and which you observe carrying around mouthfuls of straw and other things. This shows natural aptitude for work which will always remain.'

Various other owners took up the breed when they returned from active service. Dr Nancy Laughton of the Claverdon affix was one of these. She bought Ch Claverdon Jet, who proved to be one of the best dual-purpose bitches of her day, as a foundation bitch in 1944. She also bought Revival of Ettington *(Technician ex Miss Celeste)* who was a strong, rugged type with substance. These two were mated together in 1948, producing quality foundation stock for many important kennels. The Claverdon bitch line continued with clever breeding, outcrossing to correct faults as much as possible, and selecting the best of the progeny for future breeding. She also brought in older breeding lines which had concentrated on work. Her prime aim was always to produce working Flatcoats which proved themselves in the field but were true to breed type, hoping that these traits would be accompanied by an impeccable temperament. Dr Nancy continues with her bitch line, and still enjoys working her dogs with her friend and companion Gwen Knight.

Left to Right: Ch Waternymph, Ch Waterman, Ch Workman and Ch Waterboy.

Dr Nancy Laughton wrote the definitive book on the Flatcoated Retriever, *The Review of the Flat-coated Retriever*. This is a 'must' for every serious owner or breeder; no other book will ever come close to the detailed history of the breed. It is available as a private publication from the Secretary of the Flatcoated Retriever Society.

Mr Colin Wells' 'W' Kennel was originally founded in 1933, but the war came and it had to be disbanded when he entered the services. When he was demobbed in 1945 he bought Waterman *(Atherbram Simon ex Atherbram Meg)* and Claverdon Faith *(Revival of Ettington ex Claverdon Jet)* whose breeding brought back some of his pre-war lines. Waterman became an outstanding champion, winning 12 CCs and Best of Breed (BOB) at Crufts four times, and he also ran well in field trials.

Mr Wells was head gamekeeper to His Grace The Duke of Rutland on the Belvoir Estate. He was one of the top exponents of the dual-purpose Flatcoat. His stock was of the highest quality in type and working ability and he was a man who had an eye for a truly typical Flatcoat. He worked his dogs hard, but showed and field trialled them for his enjoyment. Many of us at home and abroad were fortunate enough to have founded our kennels on his stock.

I am sure many of us remember with pride the awards won by our stock when he was judging. He stated many years ago: 'My aim has always been to have really dual-purpose stock, good enough to win in the best company in the ring, and capable of doing really hard work with soundness, stamina and trainability'. He achieved this.

Miss Barbara Hall of the Blakeholme affix bred her first Flatcoat in 1922. She had hoped to establish her kennel in the mid-1930s, but the war prevented this. She was unable to start until 1953, when she acquired the bitch Pewcroft Prim, who had litters by the two brothers Ch Waterboy and Ch Workman *(Ch Waterman ex Claverdon Faith)*.

Miss Hall bred dogs of good quality, winning awards in the show ring and in field trials. One of her best known champions was Ch Collyers Blakeholme Brewster FTW *(Blakeholme Jem ex Rettendon Spoonbill)*. Later she bred the bitch Ch Blakeholme Just So *(Ch Fenrivers Golden Rod ex Blakeholme Jenet)*. Miss Hall had strong opinions on the breeding of Flatcoats and worried at one time that they were becoming 'little black dogs'.

Brigadier Clowes was a great patron of the breed. He was a keen sportsman and field trial judge who appreciated good workers. He was President of The Flatcoated Retriever Society for many years. His first dogs after the war were Hark of Lingwood and Breeze of Lingwood. He bred a little, but preferred to buy in dogs from different kennels.

Major Harry Wilson, who lived in Northern Ireland, bought his first Flatcoat in 1926. He had a very good working line, but sadly this died out as did so many during the war. He bought Claverdon Miss Tinker *(Ch Atherbram Nobbie ex Claverdon Celeste)* in 1950, then in 1952 Pewcroft Page *(Sweep of Riverside ex Pewcroft Peg)*, whom he described as the most wonderful Flatcoat he had ever known. Pewcroft Page was a classical example of the breed. He was trialled a little, but sadly died at six years of age, just after winning The Ulster Retrievers Open Stake in 1958. Pewcroft Page and Miss Tinker were mated, and a bitch from this litter, Nesfield Stratton, was sold to Mr Wilson Stephens. Later Major Wilson bought back two of her daughters, Hartshorn Midnight by Ch Woodlark and Hartshorn Sorrel by Teal of Hawks Nest.

Major Wilson's ability as a trainer was well known; he could get the best out of Flatcoats. Hartshorn Sorrel, a bitch of outstanding working ability, became a field trial champion, going on to win the Irish Field Trial Championship Stake, thereby becoming an **International Field Trial Champion.** Her half-sister Hartshorn Midnight had some success in trials, and when she had a litter by Blakeholme Joiner her son Nesfield Michael also became a **Field Trial Champion**.

There were many new kennels in the 1950s. Mrs Fletcher and Mr Davis (father of Peggy Miller of the Emanon Flatcoats and Curly Coated Retrievers) originally had Curly Coated Retrievers. They bought their first Flatcoat, Happy Wanderer *(Watchman ex Sooty of Castlepark)*, in 1955 from Warwick Park, where

Ch Happy Wanderer.

Mr Davis worked. Their joint affix was Rungles, with Mr Davis working the dogs, and Mrs Fletcher showing them. Happy Wanderer was mated to Waterboy of Springon *(Waterboy ex Springon Renza)*, producing quality stock, including Ch Rungles Wag, Show Champion (Sh Ch) Rungles Lady Barbara, Rungles Witch and Sh Ch Fredwell Rungles Happy Wendy. This partnership had only lasted for a short time when Mrs Fletcher died. Mr Davis died in the ring at Crufts in 1969, after winning Limit Dog with Rungles Trewinnard Cornish Miner.

At about the same time The Hon Mrs Amelia Jessel of the Collyers affix bought Asperula *(Waterboy ex Pewcroft Proper)* who became her first champion. Asperula was a very special bitch to the whole family. In 1958 The Hon Mrs Amelia Jessel bought Claverdon Skipper *(Bob of Riverglade ex Claverdon Turtledove)*, who did well in field trials. In 1962, she bought Collyers Blakeholme Brewster. He also became a champion and did well in field trials. Asperula had three litters and her line continued within the kennel. In 1973 Mrs Jessel's daughter bred a litter from her bitch Collyers Juno to Ch Wizardwood Sandpiper *(Ch Tonggreen Sparrowboy ex Halstock Jemima of Wizardwood)*. In this litter ·vas the very successful FT Ch Werrion Redwing of Collyers. The Collyers line continues today mainly through the male line.

Mrs Jessel has a great interest in field trials, being an 'A' judge and a member of the Field Trial Committee at The Kennel Club. Her main concern has always been to prove the working ability of the Flatcoat in the shooting field. To this end, she was instrumental in setting up the Shooting Dog Certificate for Flatcoats (see **Appendix C**). She has worked tirelessly, organising and running events leading to this qualification, and they are supervised by accredited 'A' field trial judges. A qualified Flatcoat Retriever is a dog or bitch who has proved its worth as a retriever and who, while taking the test, was quiet on a drive, who retrieved well with a soft mouth from land or water, and who hunted cover well for game. From personal expérience I know that this is a tough test for dog and owner, and anyone who has gained this qualification with their dogs should certainly be proud of them.

Mr Read Flowers (Fenrivers), Patron of the Flatcoated Retriever Society. Picking up At Ryston: 'one of my favourite pictures of a special dog, doing what we did best'. Dog featured: Downstream Nimble.

Mr Reed Flowers also started his kennel in the 1950s by buying Pewcroft Proper *(Denmere Prince ex Pewcroft Pitch)*. This bitch was mated to Ch Waterboy. The first litter were all 'A's: Ch Asperula, Alyssum, Ch Adonis. The later litters carried the affix 'Fenrivers'.

Alyssum was kept by Mr Flowers and she was entered in field trials with success, winning the Flatcoated Retriever Open Stake in 1957. Her second litter, to Ch Atherbram Pedro, produced Fenrivers Evergreen, who was the mother of Ch Fenrivers Golden Rod.

Ch Fenrivers Golden Rod was an outstanding dog who had a great influence on the breed. A high quality dog with great presence, size and substance, he was still within the 'medium size' mould. One of the bitches to whom he was mated was Tonggreen Swift, and this produced Ch Tonggreen Sparrowboy whom Mr Flowers brought back into his kennel. This dog had a great influence on the breed, being mated to a large number of the bitches of his time.

Mr Flowers, a keen shooting man, was able to work his dogs. Unfortunately, ill health has restricted his activities for the last few years. He has always had good quality Flatcoats from his own breeding, or progeny from his stud dogs. He

Ch Atherbram Pedro.

Origins and History of the Flatcoated Retriever

Mrs Patience Lock at home with her dogs.

is a past President of The Flatcoated Retriever Society; a very kindly man, whose advice is sound and balanced, and a much revered elder statesman of our breed.

Patience Lock of the Halstock affix grew up with Flatcoats. She had happy memories of her father's kennel of Flatcoats at the beginning of the century, but it was not until 1958 that she was able to start her own kennel where, with her husband John, she bred other high quality gundogs. They bought two sisters, Halstock Dinah and Halstock Salote *(Ch Adonis ex Pewcroft Pretty Print)*. Dinah was mated to two different dogs, the first being Ryshot Rungles Trademark *(Waterboy of Springon ex Happy Wanderer)*. One of the bitch pups was Halstock Black Jewel who produced quality stock from her three litters, including American (Am) Ch Halstock Javelin, owned by Ed Atkins, Halstock Juliette owned by George Lancaster and Sh Ch Halstock Joanna owned by Miss Helen Beckwith.

Over the years there were Halstock bitches from many different lines, but Patience's ability was to blend these lines together, producing many foundation bitches at home and abroad over a period of 20 years. Sadly Patience died in 1981 and John passed away soon afterwards. She is still greatly missed by many of us who grew up in Flatcoats with this wonderful lady's sound guidance. She took great joy in encouraging novice owners with promising puppies, supporting us through the setbacks and disappointments which beset those aspiring to breed dogs, and she also loved to share our victories. Her dogs were totally devoted to her: in the latter part of her life Patience was unsteady on her feet and often landed on the ground, and I remember how Daniel would position himself to assist her. He was always there to help her get up, and also to save her from falling. Certainly she was a very special Flatcoat person!

Two Flatcoat enthusiasts, Peter Johnson and Shirley Dickson, met in 1958. They married in 1963 and founded their kennel under the affix of Downstream. Peter was a gamekeeper, so he and Shirley enjoyed working their dogs. They also enjoyed showing, but work and bringing up a family prevented them from breeding their dogs for a time. Their line was founded on Fenrivers Erica and Wish. They subsequently bought Woodway from Mr Colin Wells and made him up to champion. Their breeding policy was to produce dual-purpose dogs, eager to work and with good noses and kind temperaments, using dogs who had proved themselves in the shooting field. Peter and Shirley have been associated with the Flatcoated Retriever Society for many years; Peter is the Field Trial Secretary and Shirley the Litter Recorder. Both are international breed championship judges.

Mr and Mrs Wilson Stephens of the Hartshorn affix founded their kennel in 1958 with the bitch Nesfield Stratton who was bred by Major Harry Wilson in Ireland. They bred three very successful litters from her, including Int FT Ch Hartshorn Sorrel, who returned to Major Wilson as a youngster and was then successful in field trials. Mr Wilson Stephens was a very popular field trial judge and also a championship show judge.

At about the same time Air Commodore Hutton's wife bought him a Flatcoat bitch, Pewcroft Prop of Yarlaw, who joined their Golden Retrievers. Pewcroft Prop of Yarlaw was an outstanding bitch who won well in field trials and also became a champion. She was a stylish worker with a typical Flatcoat character. She had three outstanding litters. The first litter was by Claverdon Sweep, and the outstanding dog of this litter was Black Friar of Yarlaw, who was later mated to Claverdon Cindy, producing the outstanding brood bitch Claverdon Rhapsody. The second litter, by Woodlark, produced a notable son, Black Prince of Yarlaw. The third litter was by Claverdon Jorrocks Junior, a dog of quality who, though injured when young, was a good worker. Their bitch line continued down Black Lass of Yarlaw and her sister Black Bell of Yarlaw, who was Joan Mason's Heronsflight foundation bitch.

Flatcoated Retrievers

Ch Elizabeth of Exclyst.
Photo - F E Garwood, *Dog World.*

Ch Midnight Star of Exclyst.

Margaret and Dennis Izzard of the Ryshot affix founded their kennel on the bitch Ryshot Starshine, born in 1944, but did not seriously start breeding until 1955. They were interested in liver Flatcoats, and founded part of their line on livers from the dog Forestholm Coppercoat of Ryshot bred by Mrs Barwise. All livers bred by them had the word 'Copper' in their name, as with Ch Ryshot Copper Bracken, their first liver champion bitch. Their first black champion was Ryshot Misty Dawn, a grand-daughter of Starshine. The most outstanding champion in their kennel was Ch Ryshot Velvet, a bitch I knew and admired. I was lucky enough to acquire as puppies Ch Elizabeth of Exclyst and Ch Midnight Star of Exclyst, her great grand-daughters.

Margaret and Dennis enjoyed working all their retrievers: Golden, Labrador, Chesapeake Bay and Flatcoated, They were well known in Hampshire and surrounding areas for their teams of picking-up retrievers worked by either Dennis or Margaret, but the Flatcoats were their special dogs. Margaret was also very active within the breed society, and was the organiser of the first Flatcoated Retriever Society Open Show on 12 April 1969. Both were well-known and respected international breed judges.

Margaret was a pioneer in her concern for health problems specific to Flatcoats. She had their eyes tested for hereditary diseases and their hips X-rayed for hip dysplasia.

Sadly, Margaret became ill and died in 1974, just after her last liver bitch, Ch Ryshot Copper Ring O'Fire, gained her third CC. Dennis continued to work his dogs until prevented by ill-health. He gained two CCs with his favourite dog, Fusillier of Ryshot.

Mrs Peggy Robinson of the Stolford affix bought Stolford Hartshorn Memory (*Woodlark ex Nesfield Stratton*) from Mr Wilson Stephens, and she also bought Stolford Whinchat (*Blakeholme Jem ex Ch Claverdon Tawney Pippet*). Mrs Robertson is best known for her Stolford Golden Retrievers. Two of her most notable Flatcoats were Ch Stolford Missis Mop, who in her latter years was shown by Mrs Rosalie Brady, and Ch Bordercot Stolford Doonigan (*Int Ch Donovan ex Ch Stolford Wychmere Blackseal*). Doonigan was owned by Mrs Brady and was for many years the breed record holder, with 22 CCs. This was an achievement for a dog born in 1969.

Many of you may wonder at the change of names in dogs. After the war you could go out, buy a dog, and change its name completely. You were permitted by The Kennel Club to add your own affix in front of the breeder's, as in **Bordercot** Stolford Doonigan. You could also buy puppies from the breeder and put your own affix at the beginning of their names. Today you can only add it on behind (for instance Stolford Doonigan **of Bordercot**). There again, up to about 1969, if you found a nice Flatcoat type dog or bitch without papers you could go to a championship show judge who awarded Challenge Certificates in the breed; if your dog was considered typical for the breed they would sign

Origins and History of the Flatcoated Retriever

a Kennel Club form, and your dog/ bitch would be issued with a Second Class Registration Certificate. If it were subsequently mated to a Registered dog or bitch, their puppies would have a First Class Registration. At the time this was an important way to collect and bring back bloodlines that were known to be pure bred. Due to circumstances during the war and afterwards, papers had been lost through such misfortunes as bombing of homes and deaths of owners. Without this many breeds would never have survived after the war. You are still allowed to add your affix after the puppy's name (for instance **Elizabeth of Exclyst**) up to the dog qualifying for the Stud Book, unless the breeder has signed the registration certificate 'Name Unchanged'.

Mrs Wells-Meecham of the Fredwell affix was one of the many notable newcomers to the Flatcoat breed in the 1950s and 1960s. Her first Flatcoat was Shiner of Fredwell who was third in an All-Aged Stake. She later bought Fredwell Rungles Happy Wendy *(Waterboy of Springon ex Ch. Happy Wanderer)*, making her up to show champion. Fredwell Rungles Happy Wendy was mated to Black Prince of Yarlaw. One of the bitch puppies, Fredwell Wave, was kept and mated to Ch Fenrivers Golden Rod, and later to Glidesdown Aristocratic *(Rungles Wag ex Glidesdown Rungles Raine)*, Bill Garrod keeping Fredwell Ferryman of Glidesdown.

Mrs Wells-Meecham is best known for her hounds. She is a Gundog Group judge, and also judges Flatcoats at championship level.

Mrs Gwen Broadly of the famous Sandylands Labradors also had Flatcoats in the late 1950s and early 1960s. She started with a bitch from the same litter as Rungles Happy Wendy, Sh Ch Sandylands Rungles Witch, who had a litter by Ch Claverdon Comet, producing Sandylands Charmer, Sandylands Challenge and Sandylands Cloud.

Tony Pascoe of the Trewinnard affix owned Sh Ch Sandylands Challenge, who won BOB under Mrs Bilton at Crufts in 1965. Trewinnard Cornish Flora *(Ch Downstream Hercules ex Sh Ch Sandylands Rungles Witch)* was later exported to Don and Nancy Kerns in the USA in about 1966.

Many small kennels that I have not mentioned by name have contributed to the breeding of quality Flatcoats. Without these enthusiastic people the breed would not have developed the way it has since the war.

Many kennels started in the 1960s. Mrs Joan Mason's Heronsflight was founded in 1964; Mary Grimes's Belsud in 1960, with a liver bitch, Brown Bella of White Rails, given to her by her husband; Helen Beckwith's Courtbeck in 1964 with the bitch Sh Ch Halstock Joanna; Georgie Buchanan of Hallbent introduced Flatcoats into her kennel in 1962 with Strathendrick Dawn; the late Paddy Petch of the Rase affix started with Tomani Bittern: Joan Chester Perks of the Tonggreen affix had owned Retrievers since 1947 but bought her first Flatcoat in 1959; Denise and Neil Jury, of Torwood, bought their Flatcoat, Ebony Reliance, in 1967; the late Velma Ogilvy Shepherd, of Vbos, who started with Cocker Spaniels in 1935, bought her first Flatcoat, Stolford Inkspot, in 1966; I started my own Exclyst kennel in 1966 with the purchase of Collyers Albertine, but today's line is directly descended from Wood Lass; and George Lancaster of Oakmoss came into the breed with the purchase of Halstock Juliette in around 1964. Another newcomer to Flatcoats in the 1960s was Rosalie Brady of the Bordercot affix, who had grown up with her mother's Papillons. She bought Bordercot Stolford Doonigan for her husband as his gundog, and he was subsequently shown and became a champion. Mr Philip Whittaker's Stonemeade line started with the purchase of Hallbent New Novel in 1969. Dr Tom and Sally McCombe of Glendaruel took on their affix in 1968; their first bitch was Kilbucho Honeybee.

In the West Country, Trevor and Kath Pennington started their kennel in 1969 with Marlcot Nicks Badger and Marlcot Nicks Jade. Trevor always had a great interest in working his dogs and developed his kennel on a dual-purpose line, as did many others. At about the same time Peter and Audrey Forster of Wizardwood, who had bred Red Setters for many years, bought their first Flatcoat, Windgather Delia, bred by Miss Margaret Mothersill. George and Joan Snape of Yonday also

Peter and Shirley Johnson and some
Downstream Flatcoats.

came into Flatcoats from another breed, having owned Golden Retrievers since 1952. After the death of their last Golden Retriever they bought Claverdon Flapper *(Teal of Hawk's Nest ex Claverdon Rhapsody)* as an older bitch. She was mated three times, her most famous daughter being Ch Yonday Willow Warbler of Shargleam, whose sire was Woodland Whipster.

As you can see, there was quite an influx of new breeders in the 1960s. Many are still breeding and more detailed information can be found in the Chapter 2: **Kennels and Personalities.** Although many were show-oriented, most of these new kennels developed along the dual-purpose lines, field trialling talented youngsters when time and commitments allowed. A large number of breeders pick up with their dogs, a job at which Flatcoats excel.

In ownership there was certainly a move away from the affluent upper and middle classes and their gamekeepers to younger enthusiasts. A balance had to be struck between the time necessary for the dogs and the pressures of earning one's living and bringing up a family. Sometimes, often for many years, family commitments had to come first. Later one saw these families coming back, still breeding good Flatcoats. The big kennels of Flatcoats have gone forever. Knowing Flatcoats as I do, I think the dogs themselves enjoy life better now, being part of their beloved families.

The first Flatcoated Retriever Society Open Show was held on Saturday 12 April 1969 at the Village Hall, Ropley, Hampshire. The Acting Secretary was Mrs Margaret Izzard, who had worked hard and long against strong opposition for the Society to have an Open Show. The entry fee was 5/- to Members, 7/6 to Non-members. Prize money was First: £1.00, Second: 10/- and Third: 5/-. Mrs Wells-Meecham of Fredwell was the judge, and 81 Flatcoats were entered. The list of winners was as follows:

Dogs:
Puppy: Mrs Lock's Halstock Echo *(Hallstock Downstream Daniel ex Halstock Jade)*. He also won Junior and Maiden.
Novice: Mrs Town-Jones's Black Magic of Yarlaw *(Hartshorn Samphire ex Black Lass of Yarlaw)*.
Post Graduate: Mr C Norris's Cleeve Trademark *(Halstock Othello ex Downstream Dinah)*.
Limit: Mr Peacock's Chastawood Majestic of Glenridge *(Wychmere Black Rod ex Tina of Glenridge)*.
Open: Hon Mrs Jessel's Ch Collyers Blakeholm Brewster *(Blakeholm Jem ex Rettendon Spoonbill)*.

Bitches:
Puppy: Mrs Garriod's Glidesdown Romance *(Ch Rungles Wag ex Glidesdown Rungles Raine)*.
Junior: Dr Nancy Laughton's Claverdon Fidelity *(Teal of Hawk's Nest ex Claverdon Rhaposdy)*. She also won Novice and Post Graduate Bitch.
Limit: Mrs Stephens's Hartshorn Moonshine *(Ch Woodlark ex Nestfield Statton)*.
Open: Mrs Izzard's Ch Ryshot Velvet *(Ryshot Mascot ex Ryshot Copper Jacynth)*.

The 1970s

This was when Flatcoated Retriever registrations started to rise again. Here was an attractive dog with a happy personality, and people started to take notice. In 1970 there was still a strong contingent of gamekeepers showing their Flatcoats, and even more were still buying well-bred working dogs for their own use. Sadly many of these useful dogs were never used for breeding; shooting men preferred to buy a replacement when they needed it.

In 1970 Nesfield Michael became a field trial champion. This was the second in three years for Harry Wilson, the first having been Int FT Ch Hartshorn Sorrel. It was also the time of the great dog Ch Fenrivers Golden Rod and his son Ch Tonggreen Sparrowboy.

The outstanding litter of the time (Ch Claverdon Comet ex Sh Ch Halstock Joanna) was bred by Helen Beckwith, the best remembered offspring being Ch Courtbeck Mercury, Ch Belsud Courtbeck Taurus and Ch Tonggreen Courtbeck Venus.

Ch Halstock Primula of Ravenscrest, 1975.
Photo - F E Garwood, *Dog World.*

At this time there were three outstanding bitches: Ch Ryshot Velvet, Ch Woodpoppy and Ch Heronsflight Black Bell of Yarlaw. Lucky were those who were able to combine all three bitches in their breeding programme; in my opinion, all three were prepotent. They still have strong lines going through the breed world-wide.

Another outstanding dual-purpose litter came from the Claverdon kennel (Teal of Hawk's Nest ex Claverdon Rhapsody), the best known offspring being Swedish Ch Claverdon Fantasia FTW, Ch Claverdon Fidelity FTW and Claverdon Flapper.

In 1972 Ch Hallbent Gipsy Lad, the first Hallbent male to be made up, won the Dog CC and Best of Breed (BOB) at Crufts. The bitch CC went to Blakeholme Just So.

There were various notable exports at this time. Ch Fenrivers Kalmia, a good dog, went to the United States of America and was lost to the breeding pool. Ch Woodman went to Sweden and his blood line continued there. Earlier Ch Donovan was exported to Italy. It is interesting to speculate on the effect on the breed if such blood lines had not been lost to us. Unfortunately FT Ch Nesfield Michael is another example of an outstanding dog with no living descendants.

Ch Damases Tarquol of Ryshot
Photo - F E Garwood, *Dog World*

In 1972 a young dog, Wizardwood Sandpiper, who later became a champion, won his Junior Warrant, and his sister, Wizardwood Whimbrell, became a field trial winner. They both had a strong influence on the breed, in the show ring, and also in the field trial world. Sandpiper's daughter, FT Ch Werrion Redwing, became the third Flatcoat field trial champion in 10 years.

Ch Bordercot Stolford Doonigan, shown by Rosalie Brady, won well and continued until 1978. This exemplifies the length of time a good Flatcoat can continue showing at the highest level.

I hope I shall be forgiven for commenting on Wyndhamian Christopher of Exclyst, who campaigned at the same time as Wizardwood Sandpiper. He was not as 'classical', but in retrospect he can be recognised as a prepotent sire; his progeny include Ch Puhfuh Phineas Finn CDX UDX WD, Ch Halstock Primula of Ravenscrest, Ch Elizabeth of Exclyst, Ch Midnight Star of Exclyst and Int Ch Celebrity of Ryshot. A lesson can be learnt from this case: once you see quality sons and daughters coming from a dog, often better than the father, use this dog while he is still there before you consider using the sons. Because Flatcoats are slow to reach maturity, the father could be approaching the wrong side of middle age by the time he has proved himself in this respect and the sons will be there to use later.

In my experience there have been very few prepotent sires or dams in the breed. A brother and sister who come to mind are Woodman and Wood Lass, and interestingly it continued down their lines. Ch Shargleam Blackcap was a great-grandson of Woodman down the female line, so this also shows the importance of a strong female line.

In the early 1970s Sh Ch Parkburn Brandy Boy went to Canada with his owner Moira Jewel. This dog had a strong influence in North America and his line continues today in the Casuarina kennel.

In 1975 Ch Damases Tarquol of Ryshot *(Ch Tonggreen Sparrowboy ex Hallbent Contessa)* was made up by Dr June Squires. This dog was bought by June on the advice of Margaret Izzard who had an unique eye for a Flatcoat. Without her insight the breed today would be very different.

We saw Dr Tim Woodgate Jones arrive on the field trial scene with the outstanding liver dog Rum Punch of Warresmere FTW *(Dante of Clebe ex Heronsflight Tell)*. Rum Punch was one of those dogs who once you have seen you never forget: in the field he had charisma and really caught the eye! Tim continues breeding and trialling his Flatcoats.

It was about the same time that the Tarncourt affix started to be seen in the field trial awards; I remember seeing Joan Marsden showing at Manchester in the early 1970s. Over the next two decades this kennel became most dominant in the field trial world. Joan was a clever trainer, with good facilities, who gave her all in field trialling her Flatcoats. The mark of the quality of her dogs was that they consistently won awards in Any Variety Retriever Trials.

Ch Puhfuh Phineas Finn CDX UDX WD, 1974.
Judge Mr A Hall.
Photo - F E Garwood, *Dog World.*

Having been closely associated with organising field trials as a field trials secretary I feel it is obvious that however good individual Flatcoats might be they do not run and work in the same way as a Labrador. Their ability is neither understood nor appreciated by some field trial judges. In the modern field trial world I am not certain we will ever be able to overcome this obstacle. Trainers often inhibit the natural flow of a Flatcoat, trying to make it more like the field trial Labrador, with the result they fall between two stools and the Flatcoat becomes wooden.

Another person with ability to train a dog in many different ways is Joan Shore. She bought Exclyst Lucinda and Linda of Puhfuh in the early 1970s. I remember introducing her to the art of picking up on a beautiful estate near Taunton. Joan had gained experience in working trials and obedience with other breeds, and she is a very versatile lady who was able to put her knowledge and experience to good use with her Flatcoats. Mating her Linda to Wyndhamian Christopher of Exclyst she produced Ch Puhfuh Phineas Finn CDX UDX WD, one of the most outstanding dogs of his time.

It is interesting to note that at this time there were very few Junior Warrant winners. To get this show award a Flatcoat had to gain 25 points between the age of 6 and 18 months. (This has now changed to 12 to 18 months.) Three points were awarded for a first at a championship show and one point for a first at an open show within breed classes. It was very difficult to gain these points as there were very few younger classes. There was a very much smaller classification.

The numbers of Flatcoats shown at Crufts were as follows:

Year:	1970	1973	1974	1976	1978
Number:	68	74	76	98	99

This compares with the figure of 332 Flatcoats at Crufts in 1994. In the early 1970s the average number at a championship show would be about 30 to 40 dogs, and the dogs that won their Junior Warrant were usually the best of their year.

In the 1970s there were some beautiful bitches whom I admired and who in my opinion stood out for their quality and true breed type. These were: Mary Grimes's Ch Belsud Magpie; Joan Chester Perk's and the Cowleys' Ch Leahador Dusk of Tonggreen; Paddy Petch's Sh Ch Rase Pipistrelle; Miss Hall's Ch Blakeholme Just So; Miss Beckwith's Sh Ch Halstock Joanna; Mrs Janet

Smith's Ch Claverdon Fidelity; Mrs Ormsby's Ch Andromeda of Kempton; Mrs Margaret Izzard's Ch Ryshot Velvet; my own Ch Elizabeth of Exclyst; Mrs Westrop's Ch Halstock Primula of Ravenscrest; and Mr Read Flower's Ch Wizardwood Brown Owl. Perhaps it is my imagination, but I think maybe the hard work the breeders had put into the breed in those 20 years was beginning to show.

There were many good stud dogs other than the ones I have mentioned before, and these are some of my personal favourites: Ch Belsud Courtbeck Taurus; Ch Courtbeck Mercury; Ch Monarch of Leurbost; Ch Exclyst Bernard; and Ch Belsud Black Buzzard. I would also include

Ch/Ir Ch Shargleam Blackcap.   Photo - Dalton.

Kenstaff Whipster, although he did not become a champion, because he had a great influence through his daughter, Ch Yonday Willow Warbler of Shargleam.

In 1978 we first saw the rising star Shargleam Blackcap, future hero of the 1980s, win his Junior Warrant; little did we imagine what he would subsequently achieve!

The 1970s had been a decade of great progress within the breed in the field trial and show world. Certainly the entries had increased, and in my opinion the quality of dogs had improved. There were many more heavy bodied dogs in the early 1970s than at the end of the decade. Heads also improved during those 10 years. At the beginning of the decade the forequarters had improved, although the hindquarters were very lacking in angulation. This had changed by the end of the decade; the forequarters had started to show a tendency towards lack of angulation and short upper arms, while the hindquarters were greatly improved.

Sadly a lot of blood lines were not used to advantage, especially on the working side. In my opinion, if the working blood of the 1960s and 1970s had been consolidated, Flatcoats would be in a stronger position today. The weak way out is to blame other people for our mistakes!

I believe that all breeding lines must be used with an open mind. We still have a very small gene pool, despite the 1400 puppies now born each year. It follows that quality Flatcoat dogs with unique lines, be they show or field trial winners, **must** be used on a variety of bitches, and that similar bitches must be put to a variety of dogs. The sound middle ground of our breed is far more important than winning, whatever the arena. Without this sound middle ground (dogs of good type, sound character and temperament, for work and family life) there will be nothing to draw from for the top working or show Flatcoat. This is where the *Flatcoated Retriever Directories* have improved the information available to all breeders and owners, and it is hoped that this information will be used by future breeders to improve the breed.

Ch Halstock Bridget. Owner: Peggy Miller.

Ch Shargleam Kingfisher.

Sh Ch Exclyst Victoria.
Photo - Russell Fine Art.

My personal ambition has been to have the best stud dogs I can breed, (or, as in the case of Wizardwood Sea Bird of Exclyst, have entrusted to me by Peter and Audrey Forster): studs who are capable of working and carrying working lines and who will hold their own in the show ring, representing true type and temperament, and who are also available to the ordinary Flatcoat owner. In my own small way I shall be making sure that the middle ground is well established in the South West. I know I am not the only breeder who thinks this way.

The 1980s

The 1980s arrived in a blaze of glory with Ch/Ir Ch Shargleam Blackcap winning BIS at Crufts. He was from Pat Chapman's only litter out of Ch Yonday Willow Warbler of Shargleam by Ch Damases Tarquol of Ryshot. Unfortunately this was Willow Warbler's first and only litter (she had an infection afterwards and had to be spayed) but it represented the beginning of the dynasty of Shargleam Flatcoats which continued until Pat's untimely death in 1993. Pat made up 10 Shargleam Flatcoat champions herself in the 1980s.

There were some outstanding dogs and bitches in the 1980s and these are a few dogs that I knew and admired: in the first part of the decade, Ch Puhfuh Phineas Finn; Ch Tonggreen Squall; Ch Falswith Apparition; Ch Exclyst Imperial Mint; Ch Bordercot Guy; Stantilaine Rory of Branchalwood; Warresmere Woodruff FTA; Tarncourt Byron FTW; and Ch Torwood Blue FTW, who was the closest to a dual-award dog, winning both CCs and field trial awards.

There were also some very special bitches: Ch Yonday Willow Warbler of Shargleam; Ch Halstock Bridget; Ch Shargleam Water Pipit; Ch Branchalwood Whinyeon; Ch Falswift Auriga; Ch Torwood Poppet; FT Ch Werrion Redwing of Collyers; Tarncourt Charm FTW; and Ch Belsud Brown Guillemot who, in my humble opinion, was the best liver bitch ever. Creekside Dinas of

Leeglen FTA was another good bitch, well placed in trials. I often saw her working: she was the bitch with personality who started Graham West's successful field trial line.

Interestingly enough, it is noticeable that many good dogs did not get the recognition in the show ring that they deserved. I think we suffered for this in the following decade. Only six dogs won CCs in 1980, six in 1981, eight in 1982, and nine in 1983.

Flatcoats, as I have said before, are good lasters. These same top dogs and bitches continued to dominate the breed in the second half of the 1980s, but certainly more dogs were winning CCs. Ch Heronsflight Pan's Promise, Ch Shargleam Kingfisher and Ch Bordercot Guy continued winning. Ch Wizardwood Tawny Pheasant was a good liver champion. I was very fond of Ch Belsud Black Jackdaw and Sh Ch Blue Boy of Braidwynn. Although he was not a champion, I also admired Watchingwell Foxtrot. He was a dog with an outstanding front but not such good hindquarters. It was his personality that I loved, however! Tarncourt Noteable FTW was one of our most successful trial dogs at this time.

Ch Branchalwood Whinyeon was a beautiful bitch who came from the very successful Scottish kennel of Scott and Dalziel. Ch Woolfhill Dolly Parton and the lovely Ch Halstock Bridget continued to win. A bitch whom I loved but who never became a champion was Meolswood Belle of Lacetrom. Other lovely bitches were: Pendlewych Puffin; Sh Ch Bright Star Brandysnap; Ch Glendaruel Hilarity; Sh Ch Herringstone's Little Gem; Ch Wizardwood Water Witch; and Sh Ch Exclyst Victoria.

These Flatcoats were some of my own personal favourites, though I am sure many of you would choose differently. Being a championship show judge of the breed throughout the 1980s, I was given the great honour of having these Flatcoats exhibited under me and seeing nearly all of them.

The late 1980s and early 1990s sadly saw the deaths of many notable friends of the breed. In 1987 Miss Barbara Hall passed away. She was a lady who commanded great respect and who had strong views on the breed. Sadly the Blakeholme affix ended with her. Another tragic loss occurred in 1989 when Philip Whittaker of Stonemead died at the young age of 56, but his breeding lines continue through his daughter Sarah with her Bramatha affix.

Mr Scott Dalziel, a very special Scotsman, died in March 1991. His wife and daughter now have the Branchalwood Flatcoats.

Dennis Izzard of Ryshot, a friend and mentor to many, left us in October 1991. Most people maybe saw the public face that hid that special private person to whom you could always turn for support or good companionship.

The year 1992 was another sad year for the breed, when Brigadier Clowes of Lingwood, a past President, passed away, as did our good friend Sheila Godbolt of Crackodown, a lady who worked tirelessly fund raising for the 'Cancer Tumour Survey'. Paddy Petch of Rase died tragically as the result of an accident. Paddy had a sharp tongue at times, but she had the breed at heart and she bred some beautiful Flatcoats. Many of us remember her husband George; such a nice man whom I am sure Paddy missed.

Pat Chapman of Shargleam died in 1993. This was another sad loss to the breed. Colin Wells of the 'W' affix also passed away, having suffered from ill health for many years. He was a great man who shaped our breed after the war, and so many of us have cause to be grateful for the quality stock we acquired. There is one bench mark many of us have when we produce a new hopeful: 'Can we see Colin with it?', or as we look in a ring of dogs can we say, 'Yes, we can see Colin with that dog or bitch'. To many of us it is the highest accolade we can give to a Flatcoat.

All these people and dogs have shaped our breed and ourselves. They will be hard to replace. We who are left have a difficult task in living up to their standards.

There are many good new breeders coming in and they have a long haul ahead of them. So many are impatient to reach the top by any means. There is a wise saying: 'It is better to travel hopefully than to arrive'.

1990 -1995

We are now five years into this decade, and the world of the Flatcoated Retriever has changed. As has been related, many of our foremost breeders have passed away or no longer breed. There has been a change of attitude and the gap between generations has widened, but there are some very capable new breeders with new ideas. I hope this gap is now closing and any differences will gradually disappear. Always respect your fellow breeder; remember, we all have different talents and enjoy different activities within our breed.

There is an advertisement for *The Listening Bank*. In the breed, listening has to be a two-way process. Those folk who have been privileged to play their part in the development of the Flatcoated Retriever breed must be ready to give their knowledge, gained with time and experience, to the newcomers, but the new folk must be willing to listen, not trying to run before they can walk. Mistakes made either through not asking or through not taking advice are often irreversible. It is the Flatcoat breed as a whole which will suffer. We dog breeders are the guardians of whatever breed we have at any given time. It is our responsibility to improve our breed, keeping it true to type, with good temperament and the ability to be trained.

Nowadays we have strong support from the veterinary profession; there is more of a partnership with breeders. Veterinary science has developed in the last decades and there have been considerable advances in the understanding and treatment of disease and in surgical techniques. Dog breeders encountering the Parvovirus scourge during the late 1970s and early 1980s had much better support from their vets than did their predecessors encountering Distemper and Hard Pad in the postwar period. These advances will continue, but we must not become too preoccupied with them. We must remember that the patients are dogs, and there is a point beyond which we cannot expect them to be treated for our sakes. At least we can give them the dignity of putting them to sleep to end their suffering.

The Flatcoated Retriever breed has gained in popularity. This is demonstrated to a marked degree by show entries. In 1990 these ranged from 81 to 183; in 1993, from 89 to 251. There has been a great influx of new breeders. Some of these disappear quickly, but every year there is a number who continue, becoming 'hooked' on the breed and associated activities. The ownership of the breed has been encouraged, rightly or wrongly, by the veterinary profession.

It is interesting that of the average 1200 to 1400 puppies born each year, a very small percentage is used in dog activities, maybe 25 per cent. The largest percentage are family companions or family and working dogs.

To end this history, I shall give a year-by-year summary of the awards won by Flatcoated Retrievers in the 1990s.

It is probably worth stating here that, to become a show champion, a Flatcoat must have three CCs, each from a different judge. At least one of these has to have been awarded after it is twelve months of age; in other words, if it won three CCs before it was twelve months of age, it would have to win another one after its 'birthday'. In practice, a Flatcoat would be unlikely to do so, as the breed is slow to mature.

To become a full champion, a Flatcoat will then have to qualify in the field. It can do this by gaining an award at a field trial; by being a 'special qualifier' at a field trial; or by passing a 'special show dog qualifier' judged by a field trial judge at a shooting day.

Some of the winners listed below who are not styled 'Sh Ch' or 'Ch' may therefore have become champions at a later date.

1990: The Flatcoated Retriever breed was judged at Crufts by Mr George Lancaster. He awarded the Dog CC and BOB to Brown Keston of Varingo and the Bitch CC to Wizardwood Silver Fox.

During 1990, 20 dogs won CCs, Ch Shargleam Kestrel leading with five CCs, and Sh Ch Ebony Kingsman next with four CCs. Nineteen bitches won CCs, Sh Ch Glendaruel Hilarity leading with four and Ch Wizardwood Water Witch, Sh Ch Bright Star Brandysnap and Ch Heronsflight Moss all gaining three.

The Flatcoat dogs who became champions and show champions in 1990 were: Ch Belsud Black Jackdaw; Sh Ch Ebony Kingsman; Sh Ch Exclyst Viking; and Sh Ch Falswith Black Storm. The bitches were: Ch Heronsflight Moss; Sh Ch Exclyst Victoria; Sh Ch Riversflight Lady Dee; Sh Ch Branchalwood Benvane; Ch Waverton on Julip; and Sh Ch Glendaruel Hilarity.

The Becky Trophy was won by Shargleam Sedge Warbler with 32 points. This trophy is awarded on a points system over a 12 month period; one point for a first prize at a championship show in a breed class; three points for a CC; two points for a Reserve Challenge Certificate (RCC).

In the field trial season 1989/90 Mrs Marsden's Wemdon Bright Bond of Tarncourt was the points winner for the Riverside Cup with 17 points, having won a First in the Flatcoated Retriever Society Open Stake and First in the Golden Retriever Club of Scotland All-Aged Stake. Twelve other Flatcoats featured in Field Trial Awards. Appollo of Arts and Artemis the Huntress each won an Any Variety Novice Retriever Trial.

Society Working Tests were run in different areas of the country, including the Wessex Group, South West Area, East Anglian Area, Southern Area, and Cotswold Area.

1991: This was the year of Crufts Centenary Show. The judges were The Hon Mrs Amelia Jessel and Mr Reed Flowers. There was an entry of 336 Flatcoats. Dog CC and BOB were awarded to Ch Shargleam Kingfisher; bitch CC was won by Sh Ch Bright Star Brandysnap.

Fifteen dogs won CCs, Ch Branchalwood Stroan leading with nine, followed by Sh Ch Larksdown Fire Opal with four. Eighteen bitches won CCs, Ch Wizardwood Water Witch leading with four and Ch Waverton Katinka, Ch Paddiswood Burnt Lobelia and Shargleam Wood Sorell all having three. The Becky Trophy was won by Ch Branchalwood Stroan with 44 points.

Flatcoat dogs who became champions and show champions were: Ch Branchalwood Stroan; Ch Heronsflight Magic; Sh Ch Llecan Gambit; Sh Ch Venazale Charlock at Russlare; Ch Candease A Hard Days Night; Ch Eskmill Explorer; Sh Ch Larksdown Fire Opal; Sh Ch Clowbeck Bourach; Ch Exclyst Watchman; and Sh Ch Heathland Gamekeeper. Bitches who made up to champion or show champion were: Sh Ch Shargleam Wood Sorrel; Ch Withybed Meadow Falcon at Gunmakers; Ch Paddiswood Burnt Lobelia; Ch Saucy Susie of Gayplume; Sh Ch Colona Black Satin; Sh Ch Shargleam Willet of Elvelege; and Sh Ch Shargleam Sedge Warbler.

In the field trial season of 1990/91 Mrs Marsden's Tarncourt Rejoice won the Riverside Cup with 13 points, winning second in the Flatcoated Retriever Society Open Stake and third in an Any Variety Open 24-dog Retriever Stake.

Nineteen Flatcoats featured in Field Trial Awards. Hipsley Henry won the Flatcoated Retriever Society Novice Stake; Riversflight Genil also won a Flatcoated Retriever Society Novice Stake; Jet of Staverton won the Flatcoated Retriever Society Open Stake; Shopnoller Sarah of Staverton won a Restricted Novice Trial.

Sh Ch Llecan Gambit.
Photo - Russell Fine Art.

Flatcoated Retrievers

1992: Crufts was judged by Miss Pat Chapman. There was an entry of 249 Flatcoats. The dog CC was awarded to Shiredale Magic Moments; the bitch CC and BOB to Sh Ch Gayplume Dixie.

Twenty dogs won CCs, the two leading dogs being Ch Branchalwood Stroan and Ch Shargleam Blackthorn with five CCs each. Thirteen bitches won CCs, the overall winner being Sh Ch Gayplume Dixie with 11 CCs, followed by Ch Shargleam Sedge Warbler with six CCs. The Becky Trophy was won by Sh Ch Gayplume Dixie with 58 points

Flatcoat dogs who became champions and show champions were: Ch Happy Harry; Ch Shargleam Blackthorn; Sh Ch Lacetrom Cardow of Bordercot; and Sh Ch Taranbeck Mossberg. Bitches who became champions and show champions were: Sh Ch Gayplume Dixie; Ch Waverton Madeira; Sh Ch Riversflight Inny; and Sh Ch Braemist Dusky Queen.

In the 1991/92 Field Trial Season the Riverside Cup was won by Mr Richard Beckerleg's Jet of Staverton with 14 points. He came second in the Flatcoated Retriever Society Open Stake, gained a COM in the Utility Gundog Society Open Stake, came fourth in the Flatcoated Retriever Society Open Stake and first in the Utility Gundog Open Stake.

Sixteen Flatcoats were featured in Field Trial Awards. Brown Keston of Varingo won the Flatcoated Retriever Society Novice Stake. Tarncourt Little Oak won the Flatcoated Retriever Society All-Aged Stake. Dawgil Which Wong of Staverton won the Flatcoated Retriever Society Novice Stake.

1993: Crufts was judged by Mrs R Brady, and 286 Flatcoats were entered. The dog CC and BOB was awarded to Ch Happy Harry. The bitch CC went to Ch Paddiswood Burnt Lobelia.

Seventeen dogs won CCs in 1993, Ch Pendlewych Puma leading with four and Ch Branchalwood Stroan and Ch Exclyst Watchman having three each. Eighteen Bitches won CCs, Sh Ch Gayplume Dixie leading with seven and Ch Wizardwood Water Witch, Sh Ch Braemist Dusky Queen, Wizardwood Firefly of Heronsfleet, Sh Ch Branchalwood Penwhern, Bitcon Castaspell and Foxoak Pewit of Wizardwood all following with two each. The Becky Trophy was won by Sh Ch Gayplume Dixie with 31 points.

Flatcoat dogs who became champions and show champions in 1993 were: Ch Pendlewych Puma; Ch Brown Keston of Varingo; Sh Ch Kenjo Black Mark; and Ch Kulawand Wood Nymph of Windyhollows. As far as the bitches were concerned, Sh Ch Branchalwood Penwhern became a show champion and Ch Riversflight Inny gained her qualifier.

During the 1992/93 Field Trial Season the Riverside Cup was won by Moonlight Padarn (owner/handler Mr Clive Harris) with 13 points. He won first in the Dukeries Gundog Club Any Variety Retriever Novice Stake and second in the Northern Golden Retriever Association All-Aged Any Variety Retriever Stake.

Sixteen Flatcoats featured in Field Trial Awards, Cleovine Gypsy Moth winning the Flatcoated Retriever Society Open Stake and Exclyst Wild Silk of Collarm won the Novice Stake. Kiri Leighwarren at Wolfhill won the other Flatcoated Retriever Society Novice Stake. Mystic Spirit won The Irish Water Spaniel Association Restricted Novice Stake.

1994: Crufts was judged by Mrs Phillips and Mrs McCullum. There was an entry of 331 Flatcoats. The dog CC and BOB was awarded to Ch Branchalwood Stroan, the bitch CC going to Gayplume Pirouette.

Fifteen dogs won CCs, Ch Exclyst Watchman leading with eight, followed by Sh Ch Withybed Quartermaster of Huntersdale with four. Seventeen bitches won CCs, Sh Ch Gayplume Dixie leading with seven and Ch Spera Moonlight Sapphire following with three.

Flatcoats dogs who became champions or show champions were: Sh Ch Withybed Quartermaster of Huntersdale; Sh Ch Braemist Fire Falcon; Ch Tom Thumb; and Sh Ch Kintore of Rosenburg. The bitches were: Ch Spera Moonlight Sapphire; Sh Ch Coalport Coral Skye; Ch Shargleam Wood Fern of Goldingale; Sh Ch Shiredale Magic Touch; and Sh Ch Bitcon Castaspell.

During the 1993/94 Field Trial season the Riverside Cup was won by Mr J Baker's Riversflight Irthing of Holloway with 19 points. He won fourth in the Flatcoated Retriever Society Open Stake, a COM in the Flatcoated Retriever Society Novice Stake, second in an All-Aged Any Variety Retriever Trial, and First in a Restricted Novice Trial.

Fourteen Flatcoats featured in Field Trial awards, Moonlight Padarn winning the Flatcoated Retriever Society Open Stake. Leeglen Enboy won the Flatcoated Retriever Society All-Aged Stake, Twinwood Yes Sir won the Irish Water Spaniel Restricted Novice Trial and Trioaks Raffle won the West Dartmoor Working Gundog Any Variety Novice Trial.

Cleovine Gypsy Moth FTW.   Photo - Dalton.

Chapter 2

Kennels and Personalities

Dr Ruth Barbour

Dr Ruth Barbour and her father, the Reverend Gibson Barbour, started off as Golden Retriever breeders. Ruth has been a member of the Flatcoated Retriever Society since 1970, and is one of the respected gundog all-rounders. She is also a championship show judge in our breed.

Belsud

In 1960 Mary Grimes, of the Belsud affix, was given her first Flatcoat, Brown Bella of White Rails, as a present from her husband. As can be surmised from the name, Brown Bella was a liver Flatcoat, and Mary has always had an affection for this colour; they have featured in her kennels. She bought Ryshot Minx *(Ryshot Dawn Afforest ex Rungles Happy Melody)*, with whom she won two Challenge Certificates (CCs), from the Izzards. She also bought Ch Belsud Courtbeck Taurus as a puppy from Helen Beckwith in 1968; Taurus was brother to Mercury and Venus, and Mary has a direct male line from Taurus in her kennel today. In 1974 her beautiful, black bitch, Belsud Magpie, gained her Junior Warrant, becoming a champion and Best Bitch at Crufts in 1976. Mary's next male Champion was Ch Belsud Black Buzzard, a son of Taurus and a grandson of Ryshot Minx. His sister Belsud Blackcap was mated to Ch Exclyst Bernard, producing a most outstanding liver bitch, Ch Belsud Brown Guillemot. Her sons by Tarncourt Cavalier of Casuarina were Ch Belsud Black Jackdaw and Ch Belsud Capercaille. Mary's line continues; she specialises in producing livers from black matings.

Mary picks up with her dogs on local shoots when time permits.

Bordercot

Rosalie Brady was brought up with dogs, and entered the world of showing at an early age. Her mother, Mrs Foreman, owned outstanding Papillions for many years. Rosalie bought a male Flatcoat puppy from Mrs Peggy Robertson of Stolford in 1967; he subsequently became Ch Bordercot Stolford Doonigan. His sire was the outstanding dog Int Ch Donovan who later went to Italy. Doonigan was a true dual-purpose dog, being Rosalie's show dog and Gerald's working dog. He was the breed record holder for many years.

Rosalie bred very few litters, preferring to buy in stock from others. These included Ch Stolford Missis Mopp and then Ch Bordercot Guy, who was also a Gundog Group winner. Her latest dog is a son of Guy, Sh Ch Lacetrom Cardow of Bordercot, also a Group winner.

Braemist

Val Jones had owned dogs for many years, including Golden Retrievers and German Shepherds. She bought her first Flatcoated Retriever from Pat Chapman: this was Shargleam Black Orchid, a sister of Ch/Ir Ch Shargleam Blackcap. Val showed her when family commitments permitted, and Black Orchid won the bitch CC at the 1988 National Gundog Championship Show. On the same day her brother won the Dog CC and Best Of Breed (BOB), the judge being Mr Read Flowers. Black Orchid had two litters, one to Tonggreen Storm Petrel *(Tomstan Hamlet ex Sh Ch Tonggreen Song Linnet)*,

Mrs V Jones and the Braemist Flatcoats.

Braemist Storm Witch being retained, the other to Ch Falswift Apparition *(Ch/Ir Ch Shargleam Blackcap ex Ch Halstock Primula of Ravenscrest)*, from which Val kept Braemist Lady of the Stars. This gave Val two slightly different lines from which she has continued to breed. Lady of the Stars had a successful litter to Sh Ch Exclyst Viking *(Ch/Ir Ch Shargleam Blackcap ex Exclyst Sequin)*, producing Sh Ch Braemist Fire Falcon and Sh Ch Braemist Dusky Queen.

Val is a championship show judge and also takes a keen interest in the health of the breed.

Braidwynn

Helen Winton started her Braidwynn kennel in 1960, breeding Golden Retrievers, and she still breeds these. She bought her first Flatcoat from Mrs Lock in 1967. This was Braidwynn Halstock Titania *(Halstock Dragonfly ex Halstock Homegirl)*, a beautiful bitch who went on to win two CCs and 3 RCCs. Titania was unlucky that she was being shown at the same time as Ch Ryshot Velvet. She was a laster, winning her second CC at 10 years of age. Titania was mated to Sh Ch Parkburn Brandy Boy *(Lysander of Tamara ex Leah of Tamara)*, and Helen kept Braidwynn Beau Blue, who won a CC under Valerie Foss. Helen trained her for the gun and picked up with her regularly. Unfortunately she and her litter died, which left Helen without any Flatcoats.

Some years before she had sold a Flatcoat dog, Braidwynn Chancellor *(Tweedbank Black Buck ex Braidwynn Beau Blue)*, to a Mr and Mrs Smith, who also bought a bitch, Vbos Velour *(Nortonwood Black Bart ex Vbos Vision)*, from Velma Ogilvy Shepherd. These two were mated, but there were only dog puppies in the litter. On Christmas day the Smiths presented Helen with a Flatcoat dog puppy, so Helen became the proud owner of Sh Ch Blue Boy of Braidwynn, a very special dog to her. In 1986 she bought from Jill Saville a bitch, Fossdyke Cascade of Braidwynn *(Ch Falswift Apparition ex Rase Iona of Fossdyke)*, who became the mother of the young stock which Helen is showing with success today. Braidwynn Bonnie Lad won the RCC at Crufts from Special Yearling in 1995.

While Helen's family were growing up she was unable to devote a great deal of time to her hobby, but now she is able to do more. She still enjoys training her dogs as gundogs, although she is now unable to pick up with them because of ill health. However, they enjoy a happy life walking the beautiful hills and forests of Scotland.

Helen is a well respected international judge of Golden and Flatcoated Retrievers.

Branchalwood

The Dalziels have had dogs all their married lives and before. In 1970 Mrs Dalziel was introduced to Dr McComb through her nursing at about the time that Ch Kilbucho Honeybee *(Sh Ch Strathendrick Haze ex Fenrivers Honeysuckle)* was due to have a litter by Jet of Waveman *(Ch Waveman FTA ex Black Diamond)*. She and her husband bought a bitch puppy, Glendaruel Catriona, and from then on Flatcoats became a part of their lives: the whole family was hooked!

Catriona was worked in obedience, an activity which Mrs Dalziel had enjoyed with all her previous dogs. She also did quite well in the show

Mr and Mrs Dalziel with their Branchalwood Flatcoats.

ring. She was later mated to Ch Wizardwood Sandpiper *(Ch Tonggreen Sparrowboy ex Halstock Jemima of Wizardwood)*, and from that litter Branchalwood Maree and Linnhe were both kept. The Branchalwood line was developed from these two bitches. Maree was mated to Ch Tonggreen Squall *(Tonggreen Starling ex Leahador Dusk of Tonggreen)*, producing Ch Branchalwood Frisa.

One of their most successful bitches was Ch Branchalwood Whinyeon, a daughter of Ch/Ir Ch Shargleam Blackcap and Frisa, winner of 17 CCs. Their most successful dog to date was Ch Branchalwood Stroan *(Ch/Ir Ch Shargleam Blackcap ex Sh Ch Palnure Pride of Branchalwood from the Ch Tonggreen Squall ex Branchalwood Linnhe mating)*. Stroan was the Top Flatcoat of 1991 and Top Male 1992 and 1993, winning Best of Breed at Crufts in 1994. Sadly he died later in 1994, but left his mark as a sire.

Early on the Dalziels were joined by their daughter Maureen Scott and her husband. It is Maureen who has shown the dogs over the years, and she is a championship judge at home and abroad. Sadly Scott Dalziel died in 1991; this kind Scotsman is missed. His son, Martin Dalziel, has a great interest in working gundogs and has had success with dogs in field trials.

This has certainly been the leading Scottish Kennel and has always produced typy Flatcoats.

The Misses Bruce

The Misses Bruce were three sisters, very special ladies. They lived in South Wales and were great friends of Patience Lock and of Audrey and Peter Forster. They had owned Flatcoats all their lives, and Mary Bruce was the sister who loved to show. My earliest memory of her is with Black Wave of Halstock. They were real enthusiasts for the breed; even after Mary become unable to show, her great joy was to get a lift to the Championship Shows and to be with her friends. The sisters were great supporters of the Welsh Gundog Club in its formative years. Whenever I went to the Welsh Show they greeted me with great kindness. They were a pleasure to know!

Mrs Camp of the 'Cottages'

Mrs Camp was another very special lady who enjoyed her Flatcoats. She always had some very nice dogs, including Yarlaw Black Titus. She was a member of the society for 23 years. Her Flatcoat litters all had 'Cottage' names: Ashcottage, Beechcottage, Cedar Cottage , Damson Cottage, Elm Cottage, Fir Cottage, Greengage Cottage, Hollycottage, Ivycottage. Such people are the backbone of the breed, and it is tragic that she died before her time.

Casuarina

Cyraine and Peter Dugdale have spent many years abroad. They were back in England in 1962, living in Hampshire, next door to Captain and Mrs Downing of Creekside. Captain and Mrs Downing now live in Cornwall and still have a great interest in the breed.

Cyraine's first bitch was Creekside Bubbles of Casuarina *(Berriman Beau ex Collyers Maybelle)*, who accompanied them to Canada in 1974. There were a number of Flatcoat owners in Canada, including Jean Crawley, Doug Windsor and Moira Jewell. Moira and her family had emigrated to Canada from Scotland in 1973 taking Sh Ch Parkburn Brandy Boy *(Lysander of Tamara ex Leah of Tamara)* and The Parc Dawn *(Jet of Waveman ex The Parc Princess)* with them. These two were mated and produced Parkburn Deextenzing of Casuarina, and Cyraine bought Deextenzing, making him up in Canada and America before coming home again. They settled in Hampshire and campaigned him, making him into a champion. They mated 'Tenzing' to 'Bubbles', and a dog from that litter, Casuarina Brigantes, was mated to Ebony Treasure *(Werrion Junior of Collyers ex Penmerric Pollyanna)*. They then bought back in a dog from that litter, Agra of Newbury for Casuarina.

Cyraine bought in the bitch Heronsflight Toss of Casuarina FTA *(Heronsflight Tercel ex Fenrivers Lily)*. She was later mated to Agra, and the dog Casuarina Akbar was kept. Cyraine continued breeding around these lines and going out to well known working lines. She has bred mostly blacks, but a liver bitch, Shantron Bess of Mardick *(Mardick Luke ex Shantron Kate)*, was bought in recently.

Cyraine was the Secretary and then the Chairman of the Flatcoated Retriever Society. She has an interest in the working side and is a championship show judge of the breed.

Cleevemoor

Charley Norris was a true West Country man, coming from farming stock in North Somerset; he grew up with Flatcoats. He used to talk about his father's dogs. Mrs Lock of Halstock lived nearby and he always had great respect and admiration for her.

Charley was a member of the Flatcoated Retriever Association from about 1963. When I first·knew him he was a gamekeeper/gardener ...and what a gardener! His great joy was to combine dog showing with gardening each September by going to Birmingham Championship Show, which was overshadowed by the most magnificent Flower Show. In the 1970s this Flower Show was in its heyday; I have never such seen exhibits. Charley's speciality was dahlias, and he was a wizard with them!

Charley did not take part in field trials, but he always had useful working dogs. I am not sure which was his first Flatcoat, but in the 1960s he owned Pixie of Keynsham, and also Halstock Bo'sun, in partnership with Mrs Lock. In 1969 he won the CC at Bath with Cleeve Trademark. He owned Claverdon Gossamer, the first bitch to be mated to Wyndhamian Christopher of Exclyst, in the early 1970s; Gossamer later went to America. He owned several dogs and bitches from different kennels over the years just for work. Charley also had a love of good Springer Spaniels of the show/working type.

On his retirement Charlie moved back to North Somerset. The last dog with whom I remember him with was a brother of Tonggreen Swift Lark of Shargleam. He enjoyed working his dogs until the season before his death in 1994.

Cleovine

Over the years Judy and David Showell have kept gundogs of other breeds including Irish Setters and a German Short Haired Pointer. Judy became interested in Flatcoats, basing her first breedings on Marion Ayres' Pendlewych kennel. One of her first bitches, Pendlewych Plover *(Tonggreen Storm Petrel ex Larg Linnet of Pendlewych)*, was born in 1982. When this breeding was repeated in 1984 she bought Pendlewych Pipit of that litter. In between these bitches she bought Branchalwood Skye of Cleovine *(Ch Shargleam Fieldfare ex Ch Branchalwood Frisa)*. This formed the base of her kennel, which she continues to develop.

David is interested in the working side and has a liver male, Fossdyke Bronze Justin *(Fenstorm Indi ex Paddiswood Burnt Lobelia)*.

Judy is the present Editor of *The Flatcoated Retriever Society Year Book* and *News Letter*.

Clowbeck

Bob and Sandra Kitching bought their first dog, Llecan Ambassador *(Woodland Whipcord ex Bruderkern Rozelle of Llecan)*, from Mrs Fletcher in about 1977. Two bitches were bought the following year: Souter Della *(Tonggreen Squall ex Branchalwood Linnhe)* and Exclyst Indian Mist *(Ch Belsud Black Buzzard ex Ch Elizabeth of Exclyst)*. Although much of the Kitchings' time was taken up with establishing a successful business and bringing up a family, their kennel gradually developed. Della was mated to Woodland Whipcord *(Kenstaff Whipster ex Woodlands Whinchat)* and they kept Clowbeck Black Pennel from this mating. Indian Mist was mated to Llecan Ambassador *(Woodland Whipcord ex Bruderkern Rozelle of Llecan)*, producing their good dog Clowbeck Candlestick Maker, whom they sadly lost at a young age. Black Pennel was later mated to Emanon Parkgate Boy *(Kenjo Black Knight ex Ch Halstock Bridget)*, producing brother and sister Sh Ch Clowbeck Cock Robin and Sh Ch Clowbeck Fine Feathers. They have continued breeding and showing successfully along these lines when time permits.

Courtbeck

Miss Helen Beckwith bought her first Flatcoat from Mrs Lock in 1964, thus forming a friendship which continued until Patience died in the early 1980s. Halstock Joanna became a show champion. When mated to Ch Claverdon Comet she produced an outstanding litter which included Ch Courtbeck Mercury, Ch Belsud Courtbeck Taurus and Ch Tonggreen Courtbeck Venus. Helen continues to produce Flatcoats which do well in both show and work.

Some Emanon Flatcoats.

Emanon

Peggy Miller and her husband had their first Flatcoat in 1956 after he came out of the Army. Peggy was the daughter of Tinker Davies of the Rungles affix. The dog Rungles Whistler was given to her, but family commitments kept showing and any other activities to a minimum.

When her father died of a heart attack at Crufts in 1969, Peggy acquired Rungles Brilla, who was later mated to Halstock Echo, a great favourite of mine who came to me for gundog training. A real 'gentleman' of a dog, he loved to come to Devon for his holidays. He was later exported to America. Peggy kept a bitch from this litter, Emanon Brillsgirl, but sadly Brillsgirl smashed her hip in a freak accident, so could not be used for breeding.

In 1978 Peggy was able to acquire the lovely bitch Halstock Bridget *(Ch Black Buzzard ex Halstock Magnolia)*. 'Ebby' was a very typical and beautiful bitch, a good worker who always gave of her best in the show ring. In 1981 (the first time I gave Challenge Certificates) Bridget won the bitch CC. In 1980 she was mated to Kenjo Black Knight, producing Sh Ch Emanon Parkgate Boy; in 1982 she was mated to Tarncourt Cavalier of Casuarina, producing Emanon Onyx. She also had a litter by Collyers Mannered, producing Emanon Water Starwort, the dog who won Best of Breed at Crufts; sadly he died young.

Peggy still produces her typical Emanon stock which she enjoys showing. She also picks up regularly in Hampshire. She is a well known international judge of Flatcoated and Curly Coated Retrievers, having owned Curlies before she had Bridget.

Eskmill

The Donnellys obtained their first Flatcoat in 1981. Jenny had previously owned Rough Collies and her husband Labradors which he had worked. They considered various breeds of gundogs and eventually chose the Flatcoated Retriever because the breed was relatively free from hip dysplasia and retinal atrophy. This, coupled with the Flatcoat being a dual-purpose dog, made it the ideal choice for them.

It was not easy to obtain a puppy in 1980/81; Ch/Ir Ch Shargleam Blackcap had just won Crufts, so they were very much in demand. However a young bitch, Torwood Jonquil *(Ch Puhfuh Phineas Finn ex Heronsflight Twirl of Torwood)*, had just been returned to the Jurys, as her owner was being sent to work in America. 'Pip' therefore came to live with them. Aged about two years, she had been trained for the gun and worked, and she settled with them, proving herself a tireless worker of immense natural ability. She lived until she was 14.

She was mated to Torwood Puzzle (*Torwood Percell* ex *Torwood Dazzler*) and produced Eskmill Bamboozle, who became a fast, stylish worker. Her second litter was to Ch/Ir Ch Shargleam Blackcap, producing Ch Eskmill Explorer: a super extrovert showdog, lovely to live with and a keen, indefatigable worker.

The Donnellys have no regrets about having Flatcoats; they say they have given them so much pleasure, and not a little pain in their parting. Jenny derives immense pleasure from showing and judging them. They also work them on the difficult terrain of the Lake District, retrieving across swollen rivers, long lakes or in thick ancient coppices, leaving many a spaniel or labrador standing. They are now on their fifth generation and cannot imagine life without Flatcoats; they consider them truly without equal.

Ch Exclyst Imperial Mint.
Photo - F E Garwood, *Dog World*.

Exclyst

My first Flatcoated Retriever was Collyers Albertine in 1966, but my Exclyst line is based on Wood Lass, also known as Woodlass (one word). I looked after Wood Lass and then co-owned her with Ed Atkins in 1972. Wood Lass had two litters, the first by Heronsflight Tercel, the second by Forestholm Rufus. I kept Wyndhamian Christopher of Exclyst, Wyndhamiam Carmella and Wyndhamian Claudette from her first litter. Wyndhamian Carmella was later mated to Ch Courtbeck Mercury and went to Sweden in whelp. Wyndhamiam Claudette was mated to Halstock Lone Ranger, producing my first champion, Exclyst Bernard. I kept this line separate from Christopher's line, but unfortunately I lost it from my kennel when Exclyst Timemaster died after an accident. Wyndhamian Christopher was mated several times to Shairelf of Ryshot.

I bought Ch Elizabeth of Exclyst and Ch Midnight Star of Exclyst as puppies and made them up. Elizabeth was mated to Ch Belsud Black Buzzard, producing one of my favourite dogs, Ch Exclyst Imperial Mint. Midnight Star was an outstanding natural worker; she was mated to Wizardwood Sea Bird of Exclyst, whom I bought as a puppy from the Forsters. He was a son of the field trial winner Wizardwood Whimbrell. He brought a certain style and character into my breeding which I had felt was missing up to that time. From this breeding I kept Exclyst Sequin, who was mated to Exclyst Timemaster. Her next litter, to Ch/Ir Ch Shargleam Blackcap, gave me a line to Woodman to go with my own line to Wood Lass his sister. This produced Sh Ch Exclyst Viking, Sh Ch Exclyst Victoria, Am Ch Exclyst Black Vixen and Exclyst Vandyke.

Sequin was also mated to Watchingwell Foxtrot, line breeding to Wyndhamian Christopher, also bringing in Ch Exclyst Bernard; this was a successful litter, including Ch Exclyst Watchman, Top Flatcoat and Top Sire in 1994 and 1995, and Exclyst Wild Silk of Collarm, who won a Novice field trial in 1992; sadly an accident in the shooting field cut short her field trialling. We look forward to the future with Exclyst Bristol Cream of Ravenhall and Exclyst Crackshot in this country. The Exclyst dogs at home have been part of the picking-up team in Devon and Somerset since 1969; I am sure that had my skill as handler been greater they would have shone at field trials, especially Exclyst Timemaster.

Fossdyke

Jill Saville bought Norton Royal and Regal *(Fernieburn Firecrest ex Bruderkern Rebecca)* in 1978 and Treebet Commando *(Ch/Ir Ch Shargleam Blackcap ex Kirkmabreck Mirabell)* in 1980. Soon afterwards she bought in the two bitches Shargleam Turtledove of Fossdyke *(Oakmoss Woodpecker of Shogun ex Shargleam Bunting)* and Rase Iona of Fossdyke *(Norton Royal and Regal ex Rase Lapwing)*, making them both into Champions. She acquired the liver bitch Paddiswood Burnt Lobelia *(Wizardwood Tawny Owl ex Heronsflight Burnt Sugar of Paddiswood)* on the death of her owner and campaigned her to champion. She has continued with these breeding lines today.

Jill has always shown a great interest in pedigrees and has an extensive collection.

Gayplume

Chris Murray has bred Golden Retrievers for many years. Her husband owned the Flatcoat Tokeida Midnight Mischief *(Ch/Ir Ch Shargleam Blackcap ex Hallbent Penny)*. When Mischief was mated to Ch Bordercot Guy *(Sh Ch Nortonwood Black Bart ex Sh Ch Vbos Vogue)* she produced Ch Saucy Susie of Gayplume and Ch Happy Harry. Susie in turn had a litter by Sh Ch Emanon Parkgate Boy. Their daughter, Ch Gayplume Pirouette, was kept and successfully shown; she had a litter by Ch Candease A Hard Days Night *(Ch Heronsflight Pan's Promise ex Shargleam Snow Bunting of Candease)*, producing top Flatcoat bitch Sh Ch Gayplume Dixie.

Sh Ch Gayplume Dixie.
Bred and owned by Chris Murray.
Photo - Sally Davis.

Glendaruel

Dr Tom and Sally McComb's first bitch was Sh Ch Kilbucho Honeybee *(Strathendrick Haze ex Fenrivers Honeysuckle)* from Dorothy Montgomery. She was mated to Jet of Waveman *(Ch Waveman ex Black Diamond)*, producing Glendaruel Christina, who was subsequently mated to Kenstaff Whipster *(Sh Ch Wood Man ex Birchinlee Wendy)*. Ch Stantilaine Garnet of Glendaruel was bought back in by the McCombs. A dog from that same litter, Ch Stantilaine Rory of Branchalwood, went to the Dalziel/Scotts.

Ch Monarch of Leurbost *(Braden of Longforgan ex Halstock Louisa)* came to live with Sally and Tom after the death of Jimmy Boyd in 1975. He was a lovely typy dog and I am certain that, had he been south of the border at that time, he would have left a stronger mark with his breeding. However I am equally sure he enjoyed life with them, especially with Tom on the grouse moors. Garnet was mated to him and they kept Glendaruel Gumboots.

Sally and Tom are well respected members of the Flatcoated Retriever Society, and Sally is currently Chairman.

Glidesdown

Bill and Win Garrod were country folk who had been brought up with dogs. Win's father was a head keeper. Bill and Win were already breeding Labrador Retrievers when they bought a Flatcoat bitch, Glidesdown Fredwell Wishful *(Ch Black Prince of Yarlaw ex Sh Ch Fredwell Rungles Happy Wendy)*, from Mrs Wells-Meecham, and another bitch, Glidesdown Rungles Raine. Raine was mated to Ch Woodway, and they kept from this litter Glidesdown Blackbird. She in turn was mated to Kenjo Black Knight. Tabitha was kept from this litter and mated to Ch Falswift Apparition; the litter included

Sh Ch Glidesdown Wendy, Glidesdown Bumble and Glidesdown Kingfisher, who was a notable stud. They had a strong bitch line that still continues, Lynette Irwin's Bumble line being one.

Bill is still active in the breed, hopefully showing his new youngster in 1995. He is a well-respected championship judge, with a good eye for a dog. Sadly, Win passed away in 1993.

Gunmakers

Joan and Jeremy came into Flatcoats later in life, having owned Great Danes. Despite periodic ill health they both enjoyed their Flatcoats. Joan has a special affection for liver Flatcoats; her favourite was Warresmere Serpentine at Gunmakers. They bought the black bitch Withybed Meadow Falcon at Gunmakers from Anne Kilminster and made her into a champion.

When I first met the Maudes, Jeremy was suffering from kidney failure, but this did not stop him from training Jan (Exclyst Nutmeg) for the gun and even running in field trials, picking up and making the occasional successful trip to the show ring. He lost his battle in December 1993, but Joan continues. She has been Secretary to The Flatcoated Retriever Society for about the last nine years, and is very approachable, willing to help anyone genuinely interested in Flatcoats. She has great insight and is striving to develop this society as it goes forward into the twenty-first century.

Miss Georgie Buchanon with some Hallbent Flatcoats.

Hallbent

Miss Georgie Buchanan bought her first Flatcoat, Strathendrick Dawn, in 1962. At the time she was well-known for her Cocker Spaniels, but I know she had always had a love for the Flatcoat breed. Her first Flatcoat champion was Hallbent Gipsy Lad *(Ch Fenrivers Golden Rod ex Hallbent Happy Wanderer)*, a grandson of Dawn. Gipsy Lad was owned by the Redmans. Georgie often showed him and he sired three Champions and some beautiful typy daughters. Georgie repeated this mating, producing Sh Ch Hallbent Teal and Hallbent Woodcock. Woodcock was the sire of Ch Hallbent New Novel, who was bought by Philip Whittaker as his foundation bitch.

Hallbent Dawn Patrol *(Yonday Marshal ex Hallbent Dark Dawn)* went to Norway, producing 14 Norwegian Champions.

Mrs Jean Green owned Hallbent Contessa. When this bitch was mated to Ch Tonggreen Sparrowboy she produced a quality litter, including Ch Damases Tarquol of Ryshot and Sh Ch Damases Tara. Tarquol was the sire of Ch/Ir Ch Shargleam Blackcap.

Georgie herself made up Sh Ch Hallbent Kim *(Claverdon Kim ex Hallbent Melody)*. In the last few years declining health has restricted her breeding and showing, but Pamela Stanley continues her Hallbent line.

Joan Mason with some progeny of Ch Heronsflight Pan's Promise.

Heronsflight

Joan Mason was involved with dogs from childhood with breeds including Bull Terriers, Working Terriers, Springer Spaniels and Griffons. When I first knew her in the early 1970s she had Golden Retrievers as well as her Flatcoats. Her first Flatcoat bitch in 1964 was Heronsflight Black Bell of Yarlaw (*Claverdon Jorrocks ex Ch Pewcroft Prop of Yarlaw*) whom she made up to champion. Heronsflight Black Bell of Yarlaw was one of the most beautiful bitches being shown in the late 1960s, the others being Ch Woodpoppy and Ch Ryshot Velvet. Later, when Stanley O'Neil was ill in hospital, Joan Mason took on Pert (*Pewcroft Proxy ex Pewcroft Putt*), a bitch bred by the late Kathleen O'Neil, who became Heronsflight Pert and was later mated to Rungles Jerome, producing Heronsflight Puff. Heronsflight Tercel (*Teal of Hawk's Nest ex Heronsflight Black Bell of Yarlaw*) was a dog who has had a lot of influence in breeding today. Tercel and Puff produced Heronsflight Pansy, the mother of Ch Heronsflight Pan's Promise and Int Ch Pan's Pledge. Heronsflight Black Bell of Yarlaw was later mated to Ch Tonggreen Sparrowboy, producing Read Flowers' Heronsflight Sedge.

Joan has always had strong ideas and principles to which she has kept, breeding to produce sound dogs with good temperament capable of doing a sensible day's work in the shooting field, but which are also of good type so that they can be shown with credibility. She is the Breed correspondent in *Our Dogs* and a Vice President of the Flatcoated Retriever Society. She is also an International Breed Specialist judge. Her daughter Rosemary Talbot has been in partnership with her for many years and is also a Championship judge.

Kenjo

Mr and Mrs Rudkin became members of the Society in 1975, but they probably had Flatcoats before this. One of their first Flatcoat bitches was Glidesdown Ripple (*Glidesdown Teal ex Glidesdown Fredwell Wishful*), bred by Bill Garrod. She was mated in 1977 to Ch Wizardwood Sandpiper, and they kept Kenjo Black Knight from that litter. In 1980 Black Knight was mated to Ch Halstock Bridget, and Joan Rudkin acquired Emanon Parkgate Boy from that litter and made him into a show champion. They also had the bitch Treebet Black Diamond (*Ch/Ir Ch Shargleam Blackcap ex Kikmabreck Mirabell*). She was mated twice to Sh Ch Emanon Parkgate Boy, and the Rudkins kept Kenjo Black Rose and Kenjo Krackerjack from the first litter and Kenjo Black Hyacinth from the second. Black Hyacinth had a successful litter to Ch Falswift Apparition; they kept Sh Ch Kenjo Black Mark, who won Best In Show (BIS) at the Flatcoated Retriever Society's Championship Show in 1991.

Leeglen

Graham West bought his first Flatcoat in 1980 from Captain and Mrs Downing. This was Creekside Dinas of Leeglen (*Ch Exclyst Bernard ex Casuarina Chipewyan*). There is quite a tale to this litter. Chipewyan was one of the puppies born in quarantine to the Dugdale's bitch when they came back from Canada; her mother, Canadian Ch Creekside Bubbles of Casuarina, bred by the Downings, went to Canada with them. Graham has always had other gundogs whom he has trialled with success.

Dinas started off running in Working Test and in the winter of 1982 she was third in the West Dartmoor Working Gundog Club's Non-Winner Retriever Field Trial. Graham later bought in Midnight Lad of Leeglen (*Wizardwood Sea Bird of Exclyst ex Gunstock Dark Stranger*), a dog with a strong character whom Graham worked with some success.

Dinas was mated to Warresmere Woodruff (*Rum Punch of Warresmere ex Foxoaks Redwing*), producing the useful bitch Leeglen Midnight Lady, who was second in the Flatcoat Novice stake in 1988 and fourth in the points for the Riverside Cup. Midnight Lady was mated with great success to Tarncourt Notable FTW (*Tarncourt Crofter ex Claverdon Lucretia*), producing an exciting litter of field trial award winners, including the bitches Leeglen Enboy and Leeglen Paris and the dog Leeglen Jazz, successful 1994 All Aged Stake winner.

Marlcot

Trevor and Kath Pennington bought Marlcot Nicks Badger (*Ch Donovan ex Atherbram Kate*) and Marlcot Nicks Jade (*Coulallanby Remus ex Ryclose Julie*) in 1969, through Colin Wells. If public office and work had not kept Trevor's dog activities to a minimum I am sure that these two beautiful bitches would both have been champions. Trevor has always enjoyed his dogs and he did have some field trial success, especially with Marlcot Nicks Otter (*Kenstaff Whipster ex Nicks Badger*) and Marlcot Nicks Dolphin (*Woodland Whipcord ex Nicks Jade*). Dolphin was a dog who should have become a champion.

Trevor bought in Cleesprings Chiroubles of Marlcot (*Ducksmoor Maximum ex Shargleam River Warbler*) in 1988 as his own dogs were growing older. She was mated to Ch Exclyst Watchman. Trevor has a grandson of this mating in the ring who looks very promising, and I hope he now has more time to enjoy his Flatcoats.

Oakmoss

George and Mavis Lancaster had their first Flatcoat, Halstock Black Dahlia from Mrs Lock in 1963, closely followed by Halstock Julette in 1964. Julette produced their first Flatcoat Champion, Oakmoss Ambassador, when they mated her to Ch Fenrivers Golden Rod. Their main interest was Sussex Spaniels which they bred with great success, but they have always had a Flatcoat around. George became the Chairman of the Society and Mavis was the Show Secretary for some time. George is a Gundog Group Championship Judge and he is now a Flatcoated Retriever Society Vice President.

Mr and Mrs George Peacock

Mr and Mrs George Peacock joined the society in 1965. They had their first Flatcoat, Rettendon Jane, from Miss Meeson in 1960. I remember them showing Chastawood Majestic of Glenridge, who won five RCCs, in the early 1970s. They bred a little, and were the sort of people who made showing in the early 1970s so pleasant. George continued to show until about 1985.

Percy and Dora Parsons

Percy and Dora Parsons owned two half brothers, both by Ch Claverdon Comet: Walford Black Diamond and Ch Courtbeck Mercury. They also looked after Comet after his owner, Brendan Robinson, died. Mercury was a very important sire, passing on the outstanding aptitude for work of his sire, Ch Claverdon Comet. This was continued in Sweden through his field trial champion grandson, and also through Ch Belsud Jackdaw and my own Exclyst Timemaster, to name but a few. It is certainly a line to watch out for when looking for quality biddable workers.

Percy was an engineer and gunsmith by trade, a good sportsman who loved hunting, shooting and fishing, and all aspects of country life. He enjoyed working his dogs, making Mercury up to champion by winning a third in the Non-Winner Stake in 1973. Dora was a lovely lady, who always had a cheery word for everyone. Sadly Dora died in 1975 and Percy in 1976. They were another charming couple who helped to make owning a Flatcoat very special.

Pendlewych

Marion Ayres' first notable Flatcoat was Ch Tonggreen Squall *(Tonggreen Starling ex Leahador Dusk of Tonggreen)*, born in 1974 and bred by Joan Chester Perks. Squall was mated to Branchalwood Linnhe and Marion had back Larg Linnet.

Larg Linnet became Ch Larg Linnet of Pendlewych. She was mated to Tonggreen Storm Petrel *(Tomstan Hamlet ex Sh Ch Tonggreen Long Linnet)* and one of her daughters, Pendlewych Puffin, was later mated to Branchalwood Gruinart *(Tonggreen Squall ex Branchalwood Maree)* to produce Ch Pendlewych Puma.

Marion has always been a great supporter of the breed, travelling from one end of the country to the other to show her dogs and campaign them to champions. I can remember in the 1970s Marion coming down to Devon from Scotland to run her dogs in the Show Qualifier: such dedication to the breed! She has continued to breed a typy Flatcoat and has made sure her dogs could fulfil their work in the field.

Puhfuh

Joan Shore bought Halstock Exclyst Lucinda and Linda of Puhfuh at the end of the 1960s. Joan already had an interest in dogs, doing Working Trials with other breeds. She also showed Tibetan Spaniels; hence the Puhfuh affix. When Joan came into Flatcoats she discovered the enjoyment of gundog work, including picking-up, field trials and working test. She mated Linda of Puhfuh to Wyndhamian Christopher of Exclyst, producing Ch Puhfuh Phineas Finn, Puhfuh Francesca and Puhfuh Ferdinand. As well as being an outstanding show dog, Finn won awards in working trials, gaining his CDX UDX WD. Joan continues to work her dogs although ill health in the last few years has curtailed her activities.

Rase

Paddy Petch bought a dog puppy, Tomani Bittern *(Black Prince of Yarlaw ex Halstock Dottrell)*, in 1966. Her first bitch was Woodwren *(Int Ch Donovan ex Ch Woodpoppy)*, from Colin Wells. She was the sound base on which the Rase line was founded. Having mated her to Tomami Bittern, Paddy kept Rase Sambo and Rase Susannah. Woodwren's second litter was by Ch Hallbent Gipsy Lad. Paddy kept Rase Romulus and Rumaigne, both of whom became Champions. Rumaigne, a beautiful bitch, was mated to Ch Bordercot Stolford Doonigan, producing Rase Pippistrelle. Paddy continued to breed quality, typy Flatcoats, but her breeding plan was sadly restricted by the loss of some of her dogs in an unfortunate accident.

Paddy was the author of *The Complete Flat-coated Retriever*. In 1993, Paddy accidentally walked out in front of a car and subsequently died.

Riversflight

Jean and Peter Griffiths bought their first bitch from the Jurys in 1977. This was Ch Torwood Poppet FTA *(Heronsflight Tercel ex Heronsflight Puff)*, sister to Torwood Percel. Jean was interested in showing and Peter in working their dogs.

Poppet was mated to Sh Ch Wizardwood Hawfinch *(Claverdon Jupiter ex Sh Ch Halstock Alicia of Wizardwood)*, producing Ch Riversflight Weaver. Weaver was then mated to Glidesdown Kingfisher *(Sh Ch Falswift Apparition ex Glidesdown Tabatha)*, producing Ch Riversflight Bobbin. Bobbin's first litter, to Ch Torwood Blue FTW *(Torwood Jolly ex Bowmore Traddles Girl of Torwood)*, produced Riversflight Grande at Cerismont, Riversflight Glyde of Beanit, Riversflight Finn at Riversglide and Riversflight Ginil FTA, who did well in field trials. They also bought the bitch Braemist Stormlady of Riversflight *(Tonggreen Storm Petrel ex Shargleam Black Orchid)*, who was mated to Glidesdown Kingfisher, producing Sh Ch Riversflight Lady Dee.

Over the years they developed these lines, always with an eye to the working side. They bought the dog Tom Thumb *(Larksdown Jet ex Everace Tender Seeker)*, whom they made up to champion.

Jean is a championship show judge in this country and abroad.

Rondix

Rona Dixon bought her first Flatcoated Retriever, a Hartshorn bitch, in the early 1960s, having previously been introduced to Flatcoats by Major Harry Wilson in Northern Ireland. When she and her husband went on army duties to Germany, the bitch stayed with her father and was never used for breeding. She then bought Suzy Wong *(Ch Woodlark FTA ex Hartshorn Sweetbriar)*, a sister of Woodpoppy FTA.

At this time Rona lived in Northern Ireland. She mated Suzy Wong to Ch Collyers Blakeholme Brewster FTW *(Blackholme Jem ex Rettendon Spoonbill)*. A bitch from this litter, Rondix

Rondix Green Matuka FTA, also known as 'Shenzi'.

Tsai Shin FTW, spent her first four years with Major Harry Wilson, winning a first in an Open field trial for him. She later went on to The Hon Mrs Amelia Jessel. From the first litter to Brewster, Rona kept Anna Mai Wong, who was later mated to Ch Belsud Courtbeck Taurus *(Ch Claverdon Comet ex Halstock Joanna)*. She kept the dog Rondix Shadow Wong.

Rona's main interest over the years has been picking-up with her dogs on most days of the season, but she enjoys showing as well. She developed a great interest in Flatcoat pedigrees and has on her computer a most comprehensive collection of information on all Flatcoated Retrievers from between the wars onwards. I am personally indebted to her for her help with this book and the Directories. She is very willing to help anyone researching their Flatcoat's pedigree, and we, as breeders, have to thank her for this service. She now charges a nominal price, as so much time and equipment has gone into this fascinating project.

Rona continues with her own line, breeding out into working lines when the need arises.

Ch Roland Tann   Born... 20.6.47

Pedigree

- **Atherbram Jackie 18.7.34**
  - **Atherbram Rufus 22.4.34**
    - **Atherbram Nimrod 23.2.27**
      - Leecroft Buxton 31.1.21
        - Leecroft Young Prince — NFP
        - Triumph Tess* — 27.1.16
      - Atherbram Topsy 19.2.23
        - Bank Barclay — 10.2.21
        - Atherbram Belle — 16.5.22
    - **Roland Peggy 27.6.31**
      - Atherbram Victor 19.2.23
        - Tosca Dazzler — 14.2.22
        - Trout of Riverside
      - Vale Nell* — NFP
        - NFP
        - NFP
  - **Atherbram Candy 18.6.38**
    - **Ch Atherbram Prince 13.11.30**
      - Ch Dancer of Riverside 16.5.25
        - Tosca Dazzler — 16.5.22
        - Trout of Riverside — 14.2.22
      - Atherbram Jet 3.5.25
        - Leecroft Buxton — 31.1.21
        - Atherbram Biddy — 19.2.23
    - **Atherbram Bess 11.2.33**
      - Atherbram Nimrod 23.2.27
        - Leecroft Buxton — 31.1.21
        - Atherbram Topsy — 17.2.23
      - Roland Peggy 27.6.31
        - Atherbram Victor — 8.3.30
        - Vale Nell* — NFP
- **Dorfield Judith 27.4.45**
  - **Atherbram Monty 28.7.43**
    - **Atherbram Gunner 23.11.37**
      - Ch Atherbram Prince 13.11.30
        - Ch Dancer of Riverside — 16.5.25
        - Atherbram Jet — 3.5.25
      - Rettendon Dido 13.11.30
        - Spar — 2.6.33
        - Spero — 15.2.31
    - **Cemlyn 1.7.38**
      - Windle Don 18.4.36
        - Bryn Asaph Quick Step — 20.3.34
        - Trade — 25.9.31
      - Windle Peggy 9.3.34
        - Quick of Riverside — 20.10.31
        - FT Ch Windle Popular — 19.7.31
  - **Atherbram Bridget 21.6.36**
    - **Atherbram Prince 13.11.30**
      - Ch Dancer of Riverside 16.5.25
        - Tosca Dazzler — 16.5.22
        - Trout of Riverside — 14.2.22
      - Atherbram Jet 3.5.25
        - Leecroft Buxton — 31.1.21
        - Atherbram Biddy — 19.2.23
    - **Atherbram Bess 10.36**
      - Atherbram Nimrod 23.2.27
        - Leecroft Buxton — 31.1.21
        - Atherbram Topsy — 17.2.23
      - Roland Peggy 27.6.31
        - Atherbram Victor — 8.3.30
        - Vale Nell* — NFP

NFP : No Further Pedigree

Mr Ewart Rowlands and Ch Roland Tann, the first male liver champion.   Photo - Jones

Roland

For most of his life Mr Ewart Rowlands had Flatcoated Retrievers, which he loved to work. He was closely associated with The Flatcoat Club before it amalgamated with the Flatcoated Retriever Association to become the Flatcoated Retriever Society. He was a founder member of the URC in 1948.

Mr Rowlands' depth of knowledge about the breed was invaluable after the war. He is best remembered for making up the first liver dog, Ch Roland Tann (*Atherbram Jackie* (black) ex *Dorfield Judith* (black)), on 20 June 1947. I think there were two livers in the litter: Roland Tann and Roland Bess. He had a great enthusiasm for livers, having been closely associated with the Phizackleas in Staffordshire. Tann's male line continued through Ch Claverdon Comet, Ch Courtbeck Mercury and Ch Belsud Courtbeck Taurus, to name only three. Tann was a prepotent dog as far as livers are concerned.

Sadly Ewart passed away suddenly as he came up for retirement in 1979. He was a Vice President of the Society at the time. He was a championship show judge, and was very aware of keeping correct type and good temperament within the breed. He was very much a family man and his family still show and enjoy their Flatcoats today.

Shargleam

Pat Chapman's life revolved around dogs. Having lived abroad and then in Jersey, where she started to show and breed Golden Retrievers, Pat bought a boarding kennel near Leicester in 1975. In 1974 she had bought her first Flatcoat, Ch Yonday Willow Warbler of Shargleam *(Kenstaff Whipster* ex *Claverdon Flapper)* from George Snape. After a successful show career she was mated to Ch Damases Tarquol of Ryshot, producing the successful litter which included Ch/Ir Ch Shargleam Blackcap, Ch Shargleam Black Abby of Withybed, and Ch Shargleam Black Orchid.

Blackcap went on to a meteoric show career, winning 63 CCs, 50 BOBs, 18 Groups, five Reserve Groups and three Best in Show All Breeds at Championship Shows, including BIS at Crufts 1980.

From this start Pat bred on. Willow Warbler did not have another litter; unfortunately she had an infection after her first litter and had to be spayed. She continued her successful show career, but this was curtailed by her untimely death due to suspected poisoning in 1980.

A high percentage of Pat's line developed from Shargleam Bunting. One of her best bitches was Ch Shargleam Water Pipit *(Oakmoss Woodpecker* ex *Shargleam Bunting)*; others were Ch Withybed Country Maid of Shargleam *(Tonggreen Squall* ex *Shargleam Black Abby of Withybed)* and Sh Ch Tonggreen Swift Lark of Shargleam *(Ch/Ir Ch Shargleam Blackcap* ex *Tonggreen Song Swift)*.

Shargleam only produced 28 litters in 15 years, so it certainly was not the number of litters bred that made Pat's kennel dominant. The litters were always spoken for before they were born, and the puppies that she did not keep herself were always carefully placed. She was a lady of integrity; many people here and abroad had success with their Shargleam dogs.

Pat worked her dogs and enjoyed picking up. She kept other breeds of gundog, including Golden Retrievers, English Setters and German Wire Haired Pointers, and also Kooikerhondjes in the last few years. She was a well respected championship show judge in this country and abroad. Sadly she passed away in May 1993.

Ch/Ir Shargleam Blackcap.   Photo - Dalton

The late Pat Chapman and two of her Shargleam Flatcoats.　　　　Photo - Russell Fine Art.

Four of the First Shargleam Litter. Left to Right: Ch Shargleam Black Abby, Shargleam Black Orchid, Ch Shargleam Blackcap and Shargleam Black Velvet.

Shiredale

Jenny Bird had had Irish Setters for many years. In 1979 Mike, her husband, was paving Pat Chapman's yard at her kennels. Shargleam Bunting was in whelp at the time, and Mike had always wanted a dog to pick up with and shoot over. He booked a dog puppy and came home, telling Jenny that if she would show him they could have the pick of the dogs. That is how Ch Shargleam Sparrow Hawk *(Wizardwood Tawny Owl ex Shargleam Bunting)*, otherwise known as 'Scott', came into their lives. As so often happens, they were hooked.

Later Jenny desperately wanted a Scott offspring. She received a great deal of help from Audrey and Peter Forster, who allowed her to have Wizardwood Lark *(Wizardwood Hawfinch ex Ch Wizardwood Wigeon)*. Wizardwood Lark was mated to Scott, and Jenny reared the litter. She was then given the bitch she liked, Wizardwood Black Magic of Shiredale, who was mated twice to Ch Shargleam Kestrel *(Ch/Ir Ch Shargleam Blackcap ex Ch Shargleam Water Pipit)*. Jenny kept their son, Shiredale Magic Moments, who won well, gaining the Dog CC under Pat Chapman at Crufts in 1992, but sadly she lost him with a brain tumour later that year. Sh Ch Shiredale Magic Touch was from Black Magic's second litter. She won the Bitch CC and BOB at Crufts 1995.

Jenny says that it sounds easy as she relates it: in practice it was not that easy! As with all of us, there were many mistakes and setbacks, but it was well worth it in the end. She rarely breeds except when she wants another Flatcoat herself. In her breeding programme she is looking not only for health and good looks, but also for good temperament, which to her is of the utmost importance.

Staverton

Richard Bergerleg, now a gamekeeper, started in Suffolk in 1980/81 with an English Springer Spaniel, which was used purely for beating. His first Flatcoated Retriever, Jet of Staverton *(Gunstock Dark Knight ex Stonemeade Gleaner)* came along in August 1988, closely followed by Shopnoller Sarah FTA *(Solomon of Shopnoller ex Warresmere Taffeta)* and Dawgil Which Wond of Staverton *(Whisper of Bitcom ex Bitcom Woven Blend)* in 1990. He has also developed his interest in Field Trial Cocker Spaniels.

Jet won in the 1990/91 Field Trial season. He was second in the Flatcoated Retriever Novice Stake in October, and won a Certificate of Merit (COM) in a Non-winners Stake, then first in November in the breed's Open (Qualifying) Stake. He was second with 12 points for the Riverside Cup in the 1990/91 season, and won the Riverside and Creton Cups in the 1991/91 season, Sarah coming fourth.

Jet and Kate were mated in 1992, producing a promising litter from which Richard kept Gipsy. He has now moved to Norfolk, and when he has settled in he will hopefully continue trialling.

The Reverend Steel

The Reverend Steel was Rector of Powderham. I met the Reverend and his wife in about 1965, when Christopher and I went to see his Flatcoats. We were met in the front of the house by three stately Flatcoats, all slightly overweight. I subsequently learned that these were Pewcroft Perch (winner of two CCs), Black Smoke of Yarlaw and their son, Spay of Polden. One of them took me by my sleeve for a tour of the garden. This was the first time I had come across this behaviour in any breed of dogs, but I now know that it is something many Flatcoats love to do.

The Reverend was a great Flatcoat enthusiast, and had had Flatcoats around him for most of his life. He was a great shooting man and enjoyed working his dogs. He was a long-time friend of Reginald Cooke, and after his death he went to the dispersal sale of the Riverside Flatcoats out of interest; he thought they would all go for more money than he wished to spend on a dog. He went to the house before the sale and was talking to Mr Cooke's nephew and Mr Tansey, Mr Cooke's dog handler. There was a suggestion that there was a little bitch who did not warrant going into the sale; maybe Mr Cooke would have liked the Reverend to have her. A drab little bitch was accordingly brought up to the house, and the Reverend agreed to collect her from Mr Tansey after the sale. After the sale, there she stood, all bathed and transformed to go home with the Reverend! He was never sure how Mr Tansey did it.

Out of interest, I have used Mr Cooke's Kennel Club's stud books in my research with kind permission of a friend, who bought them as the result of an advertisement in the dog papers. They still open on the Flatcoat pages and Mr Cooke's notes are in the margins.

My family and I had many happy evenings training our Flatcoats with the Reverend, together with some ladies with Golden Retrievers. The party also included a Clumber Spaniel who had us in stitches. In general, he thought retrieving was beneath his dignity. One evening we thought he had a change of heart, however. He gathered himself into a trot, went right up to the dummy, took two deep sniffs, turned sideways ... and cocked his leg over it! He then returned proudly to his patient owner. Tears were running down all our faces, including the kind, dignified face of the Reverend!

• The Reverend Steele was incredibly kind to me, introducing me to the art of picking up on the Powderham Estate. I think I am right in saying that the last dogs he owned were bred by Georgie Buchanan.

Stonemeade

Philip Whittaker bought Hallbent New Novel from Georgie Buchanan in 1970, and later acquired Hallbent Dusk, her mother. He repeated the mating of Dusk to Hallbent Woodcock which had produced New Novel, giving a dog from the litter, Stonemeade Prince Charming, to his daughter, Sarah. Dusk was mated subsequently to Ch Hallbent Gipsy Lad, producing Stonemeade Gypsy Bell, a lovely, typy bitch, like so many of Gipsy Lad's daughters.

New Novel was mated twice to Ch Wizardwood Teal. Later Atherbram Trollop was bought as an adult bitch. Her first litter was by Stonemeade Prince Charming, and her second by Ch Woodway. Stonemeade Bertram was kept, and was mated to Anabell Payne's bitch, Auriga of Hartsmeade of Atherbram. This litter produced a liver line, which he hoped to continue in both show and working.

Sadly Philip died in his fifties, but his daughter, Sarah, continues with her own **Bramatha** line. Many Bramatha dogs have gone abroad. One of the best known, Bramatha Copper Nijinsky, went to Sweden. Sarah hopes to continue breeding her Flatcoats, producing black and liver dual-purpose dogs.

The late Philip Whittaker with a Stonemeade Flatcoat

Mary Tanner

Mary Tanner was born in the village where she still lives. She was brought up on a mixed farm with an assortment of dogs, but, although her family shot, they never had a real gundog. This changed after she married, when she heard that her father's-in-law best-ever gundog was a Flatcoated Retriever; this encouraged her to look into the possibility of Flatcoats as their family dogs. They bought Downstream Leto as their first gundog, closely followed by Crest of Downstream, who was shown a few times. In 1979 they purchased Catkin of the Moor (Suzy) who lived to celebrate her sixteenth birthday on 4 July 1995. They also own Tacunshin Lisa and Emanon Duchess, both of whom are shown and used regularly for pick-up by Mary and are shot over by her husband and son.

Mary greatly enjoys being Show Secretary of The Flatcoated Retrievers Society, having taken up this post in 1990.

Tarncourt

Mr Marsden has been a member of the Society from about 1963. He is an excellent shot and sportsman of note. When he and Joan married, Joan decided to field trial her Flatcoats. The first Flatcoat with which she won awards was Bruderkern Witch Hazel of Tarncourt *(Heronsflight Tercel ex Skeldyke Arla of Bruderkern)*, who was awarded Second in a Novice Retriever Trial in 1977. In 1978 she won a Second in an All Age Stake. Witch Hazel was mated to Claverdon Jupiter, producing Tarncourt Bronte FTA and Tarncourt Bryon FTW. Tarncourt Byron trialled in 1980, winning Second in a Puppy/Non Winner Stake and First in an All Aged Stake.

Bronte was mated to Lingwood Medlar *(Lingwood Collyers Brinkman ex Hartshorn Fleck of Lingwood)*, producing Tarncourt Crofter, Charm and Cavalier of Casuarina. Charm and Crofter both won well at trials.

One of the most outstanding Tarncourt dogs was Noteable *(Tarncourt Crofter FTA ex Claverdon Lucretra FTA)*. He was the winner of 11 field trial awards and ran in the Retriever Championship in 1986, becoming the outstanding dog of the 1980s and winning the Riverside Cup in the 1985/86, 1987/88 and 1988/90 seasons. Joan won again with Wemdom Bright Bond of Tarncourt *(Bridport of Musk ex Tarncourt Peep)* and in the 1990/91 season with Tarncourt Rejoyce *(Collyers Mannered ex Tarncourt Nimbus)*.

A decade of trialling at the top with different dogs is very hard on a person, especially with a breed like Flatcoats that need such specialist handling. Mrs Marsden has stepped out of trials for the moment, and hopefully she is now enjoying working her dogs in the shooting field. We hope it is a sabbatical and she will return to field trials refreshed. It is interesting that Noteable is still well represented in the 1993/94 season with three bitches and two dogs in the final points for the Riverside and Creton Cups.

Tomstan

I first remember Mr and Mrs Stanley with their bitch Tomstan Stolford Doxey *(Ch Donovan ex Stolford Wychmere Blackseal)* in 1969 at the first Flatcoat Open Show. Doxey was mated to Ch Courtbeck Mercury FTW *(Ch Claverdon Comet ex Sh Ch Halstock Joanna)*, producing the useful dog Tomstan Hamlet. Mr Stanley developed his line by using Tonggreen Swithins Gull of Tomstan *(Pendlewych Petrel ex Elizabeth of Bronzedale)*. His son Graham also has a great interest in the Flatcoat, always having one or two for work. He developed his affix Taurgo, Mr Pip of Taurgo *(Tarncourt Cavalier of Casuarina ex Belle Blue Salmo)* being one of his best known dogs.

Tonggreen

Joan Chester Perks has had gundogs, mainly Labradors, from 1947 onwards. In 1959 she acquired her first Flatcoat, Rettendon Linnet, who was mated to Prewcroft Priam in 1962. Joan kept Tonggreen Swift who was mated to Ch Fenrivers Golden Rod in 1965 and 1966, the second mating producing the important dogs Ch Tonggreen Sparrowboy and Tonggreen Starling. Joan bought Ch Tonggreen Courtbeck Venus from Helen Beckwith. Venus was a lovely bitch, the first Flatcoat to win her Junior Warrant, and she also won the Gundog Group at Manchester.

A bitch from this kennel that I loved was Ch Leahador Dusk of Tonggreen. She and her brother were bred by Mrs Michael Innes, and were the progeny of Ch Hallbent Gipsy Lad. Dusk, mated to Tonggreen Starling, produced Ch Tonggreen Squall and Dutch Chs Tonggreen Spray and Tonggreen Sprig. Dusk came to live with Terry and Pam Cowley, who were in partnership with Joan for many years. At that time Terry and Pam lived in Devon, where Terry was in a Commercial Shoot. He gave a lot of help in establishing field trials in the Mid-Devon Area. Many societies, including the Flatcoated Retriever Society, benefitted from his support.

In 1976 the Cowleys mated Tonggreen Sparrow Girl to Leahador Wanderer of Tonggreen. In 1978 Song Linnet, a daughter of Ch Tonggreen Sparrowboy and Ch Tonggreen Courtbeck Venus, was mated to Tomstan Hamlet, and Joan kept Tonggreen Song Siskin. Two years later this mating was repeated, and from this litter Tonggreen Song Pipit went to the Cowleys and Tonggreen Storm Petrel to the Harkins. In 1979 Tonggreen Song Swift *(Leahador Wanderer of Tonggreen ex Tonggreen Song Linnet)* was mated to the then rising star, Shargleam Blackcap, producing Pat's Ch Tonggreen Swift Lark of Shargleam. The line continued through the 1980s, and Tonggreen Storm Petrel has been a strong influence. This bloodline is still producing quality stock.

Ch Tonggreen Squall has had a strong influence in Scotland where he was mated to both Branchalwood Maree and Branchalwood Linnhe. He was also the father of Ch Withybed Country Lad and Withybed Country Lass.

Joan judged dogs at Crufts 1995. She has always had a strong eye for the correct type of Flatcoat and the Tonggreen Flatcoats have had a strong influence on the breed in this country and abroad.

Mrs Denise Jury with bitches from the Torwood Kennel, 1995.

Torwood

Denise and Neil Jury bought their first Flatcoat, Ebony Reliance *(Ch Waveman ex Black Diamond)*, in 1967. She was mated first to Pegasus of Luda (Crufts BOB in 1970), and Nimrod Reliance was kept from that litter, then in 1971 to Heronsflight Tercel, Torwood Trader being kept from this litter.

The Jurys also acquired Heronsflight Puff from Joan Mason. They mated her first to Leofrick of Warwick Castle and then to Windgather Dirk. She was subsequently mated twice to Heronsflight Tercel, the second litter producing Torwood Percel and Ch Torwood Poppet (Griffith). Joan and Denise worked closely together.

In 1981 Torwood Jolly and Bowmore Traddles Girl were mated, producing Ch Torwood Blue, a dog who was shown with great success and who was also a good worker and had earned field trial awards. His owner was Clive Harris.

Denise and David Bellamy of the Lathkill affix joined in partnership and continued breeding and working their Flatcoats, bringing in Haswith Jack the Lad and Haswith Inigo Jones, a son and grandson of Lathkill Lad. The Kennel continues with a clever blending of dogs from the Kennels of Haswith, Torwood, Lathkill and Heronsflight, producing good-looking workers.

Mrs Town Jones

Mrs Town Jones became a member of the Society in 1966, and has had a Flatcoat for the past 30 years. She has always enjoyed showing them and has been on the Show Committee for many years; she is always in charge of the draw at the Championship Show. She is yet another lady who has made it a pleasure to be with Flatcoat folk. One of her best known dogs was Courtbeck Willow Wren.

The Drum Goblet was set up in memory of Collyers Drumhead, owned by her in the early 1960s.

Vbos

Miss Velma Ogilvy Shepherd started in Cocker Spaniels in 1939. In 1946 she registered the affix Vbos for which she is best known.

She and her sister had an interest in a wide range of dogs including the working breeds. In the early 1960s she met Jimmy Boyd and his Flatcoats and fell for the breed. In 1966 she bought Vbos Stolford Inkspot (Ch Stolford Whinchat ex Sh Ch Stolford Hartshorn Memory), later mating her to Ch Tonggreen Sparrowboy and keeping Vbos Velma whom she made up into a show champion. The sire of Vbos Velma's first litter was Ch Bordercot Stolford Doonigan, puppies included Sh Ch Vbos Vogue who was sold to Mr Gallaway. Vogue was mated to Sh Ch Nortonwood Black Bart, producing the winning brother and sister Ch Bordercot Guy and Ch Black Velvet of Candidacasa at Waverton. Her second litter to Nortonwood Black Bart produced Vbos Vilna, who in turn was mated to Ch Falswift Apparition, producing Vbos Velmorn and Sh Ch Vbos Vidio. Velmorn was mated to Ch Bordercot Guy to produce Sh Ch Vbos Vervine.

Vogue's litter sister Vanda was mated to Tonggreen Squall and Mr and Mrs McCullum's Sh Ch Nashville Dawn of Sedgedunum came from this litter. Other Vbos Flatcoats made their mark.

Velma herself was always good company and had an eye for a good Flatcoat. Sadly she passed away in 1994, so the Vbos Flatcoat era has come to an end.

Venazale

Judy Rolfe was for many years the hard-working Treasurer of the Society. She bought Tonggreen Starling from Joan Chester Perks and enjoyed success with him. She bought in his daughter out of Ryshot Copper Lyric, Flowerdown Ebony Sonata, and made her a champion. Sonata was mated to Magic Dive (Ch Fenrivers Kalmia ex Claverdon Felicity) and Judy kept Venazale Veronica. Her bitch line continues.

Waverton

David and Brenda Hutchinson have had Golden Retrievers for many years. In 1976 they bought Belsud Black Kestrel of Waverton from Mary Grimes. In 1978 they bought Black Velvet of Candidacasa at Waverton FTA (Sh Ch Nortonwood Black Bart ex Sh Ch Vbos Vogue), sister of Ch Bordercot Guy, as their foundation bitch. They made her into a full champion, showing and field trialling her. She was mated to Nethercrief Sandy Wagtail (Ch Bordercot Guy ex Nethercrief Tawny Pheasant) and they kept Ch Waverton Katinka, who was mated to Glidesdown Kingfisher (Ch Falswift Apparition ex Glidesdown Tabatha), producing Ch Waverton Madeira. They continue their strong bitch line with success.

Westering

Janet Smith was a Nursing Sister, who came into Flatcoats in the late 1960s when she bought Fenrivers Kalmia *(Tonggreen Sparrowboy FTA ex Blakeholme Juliette)* from Read Flowers and made him into a champion. Janet also bought as a youngster the beautiful bitch Ch Claverdon Fidelity FTA *(Teal of Hawks Nest ex Claverdon Rhapsody FTA)* from one of Claverdon's outstanding litters. She has continued breeding down this line. Westering Salute FTA *(Westering St Pete ex Casuarina Ici of Westering)*, a grand-daughter, did well in the 1980s in field trials. Her line continues today, producing quality stock with strong working potential.

Janet has also developed a good quality line of Chesapeake Bay Retrievers for which she is well-known.

Mr Albert Wilks

Mr Albert Wilks was a delightful gentleman who enjoyed his dogs and showing. He had the most wonderful east coast accent and is a person whom it would be hard to forget. Albert was a friend of Georgie Buchanan. He showed Prince of Glenridge, Hallbent Waterboy and Hallbent Black Dougal.

Withybed

Richard and Anne Adams' first Flatcoat came from the first Shargleam litter. This was Ch Shargleam Black Abby of Withybed. They mated her to Ch Tonggreen Squall *(Tonggreen Starling ex Leahador Dusk of Tonggreen)*, producing the well-known brother and sister Ch Withybed Country Lad and Withybed Country Lass. Ch Withybed Country Lad produced Ch Shargleam Field Fare, Sh Ch Shargleam Corn Bunting, Norwegian Ch Hallbent Spring Lad by Withybed, and Sh Ch Heathland Gamekeeper. Withybed Country Lass produced Ch Withybed Silent Knight, Ch Withybed Meadow Falcon at Gunmakers, Withybed Meadow Max and Sh Ch Withybed Quartermaster of Huntersdale.

Richard and Anne parted. Anne has continued with the Withybed affix and is now Mrs Kilminster. She has recently been campaigning Sh Ch Withybed Quartermaster of Huntersdale.

Anne is a talented artist, well known for her Flatcoat drawings and paintings.

Wizardwood

Peter and Audrey Forster bred English Setters under their Wizardwood affix. They bought their first Flatcoat, Windgather Delia of Wizardwood, from Miss Margaret Mothersall. In the same year they bought Halstock Jemima of Wizardwood from Patience Lock. Jemima was mother of Ch Wizardwood Sandpiper and Wizardwood Whimbrell FTW. Later in 1970 they bought from Mrs Lock Halstock Alica of Wizardwood, their first Champion, bred by Mrs Peggy Miller.

Windgather Delia was not shown but she was mated to Ch Wizardwood Sandpiper, producing Ch Wizardwood Teal and Ch Wizardwood Wigeon. Sandpiper was the outstanding dog of his day. In 1973 he was mated to Collyers Juno, producing FT Ch Werrion Redwing of Collyers, the last Flatcoat Field Trial Champion. His sister, Wizardwood Whimbrell, was a Field Trial Winner of note. Whimbrell's line continued down through her son by Bruderkern Consul, Wizardwood Sea Bird of Exclyst.

Delia was also mated to Fenrivers Ling, producing the liver line, Wizardwood Tawny Owl, Ch Wizardwood Brown Owl and Sh Ch Wizardwood Little Owl (black). The liver line continued down through Wizardwood Tawny Owl mated to Wizardwood Bilberry *(Kenstaff Mulberry ex Ch Wizardwood Wigeon)* producing a liver son Ch Wizardwood Tawny Pheasant, a dog of excellent type. The most outstanding bitch of late was Ch Wizardwood Water Witch *(Ch Shargleam Sparrow Hawk ex Ch Wizardwood Wigeon)*.

Audrey and Peter continue to have success with their lines, despite running a busy veterinary practice and bringing up a family. They have always been a dual-purpose kennel of note. Peter has always supported Audrey in showing, but he enjoys the working side, trialling his dogs when time allows. He has always been very supportive to Flatcoat breeders on health matters, which I know has been appreciated by many of us, although his professional life has been concerned mainly with horses.

Wolfhill

Stan and Jenny Morgan bought their first Flatcoat from Patience Lock in 1974. She was Halstock Leonora *(Cleavemoor Black Roberto ex Halstock Dolores)* and she went on to gain two CCs. She was mated twice to Ch Wizardwood Teal *(Ch Wizardwood Sandpiper ex Windgather Delia of Wizardwood)*, producing Ch Wolfhill Dolly Parton, Wolfhill Hawthorn and Wolfhill Box Car Willie. Their second bitch was Kempton Antigone of Wolfhill *(Ch Wizardwood Sandpiper ex Ch Andromeda of Kempton)*. These two lines were blended together to produce their dual-purpose Flatcoats.

Jenny is one of our championship show judges and Stan enjoys working his dogs and has had some success in trialling.

Major H A Wilson with FT Ch Hartshorn Sorrel, also known as 'Jay'.

RECENT AFFIXES

Approximately 400 affixes are used in connection with the Flatcoated Retriever. Many belong to new, enthusiastic owners and breeders who have come into the breed in the last 10 years and are making their mark. I was afraid of leaving people out, as these people and their kennels are important within our breed. I thought long and hard and decided that I would make a list, including people and affixes not mentioned elsewhere in this chapter or in Chapter 1. I apologise if you have been left out. These people and their dogs' activities and awards can be seen in **Appendix A**.

Affix	Name of owner
Ajays	Miss A J Holder
Alderby	Mr and Mrs D Perry
Alkhamhurst	Mr M Williams
Ambercroft	Mrs E A M Symmons
Bernicia	Mr and Mrs R S Stewart
Bitcon	Mr Murray Armstrong
Brakernwood	Mr D J Lees
Bruderkern	Mr W Core
Bryshot	Mr B Izzard
Bumblyn	Miss L Irwin
Candidacasa	Miss E M Holmes
Candease	Mr and Mrs M P Hughes
Cannimore	Mr and Mrs M Anderson
Castlerock	Mrs D Brooks
Clandrift	Mrs V Bowen
Classet	Mr and Mrs C Westlake
Cleesprings	Mrs E N Berks
Coalport	Mrs R S Maltby
Collarm	Mrs S Neary
Colona	Mr J G and Miss F McKinlay
Coulallenby	Mrs P Mathews
Crackodawn	The late Mrs S Godbolt
Creekside	Captain A B Downing
Damases	Mrs J Green
Darillens	Mr R D N Allen
Delisle	Mrs S A Innes
Dunctonwood	Mr and Mrs R Emblem
Earlsworth	Mr and Mrs D A Earl
Elmstock	Mr and Mrs R D Orme
Elvelege	Mrs S A Hill
Emacote	Mrs L S Parry
Everace	The late Mrs E M Cook
Ewlands	Mr and Mrs W Rowlands

Flatcoated Retrievers

Affix	Name of owner
Fabiennes	Mrs Fay Thomas
Falconcliffe	Mrs E Whittaker
Falswift	Mrs P Westrop
Fenfleet	Mrs E C Geogheghan
Fenstorm	Mr and Mrs A Harkin
Foxoaks	Mr and Mrs D Warner
Foxpath	Mrs P King
Gadfly	Mrs C J Perring
Glencooley	Mr D Gilpin
Glenwherry	Mr and Mrs G H A Stirling
Goldingale	Mr J D and Mrs M E Pendleton
Grangehurst	Mr and Mrs S R Dines
Greatwood	Mr and Mrs A I Wassell
Gulduffe	Mrs S J Wells
Gunstock	Mr and Mrs T Bailey
Hartshead	Mr and Mrs G Roberts
Hasweth	Mr and Mrs P Beard
Haysam	Mr and Mrs B J Balls
Hazelmere	Mr and Mrs H H Brown
Heathland	Mr and Mrs R E Dawson
Heronfleet	Mrs V Livermore
Herringstone	Mrs M Watts
Hipsley	Mr G Leedham
Hollymill	Mrs I Bennet
Holloway	Mr and Mrs J Baker
Kilbucho	Mrs D E Montgomery
Kulawand	Mr and Mrs R Lane
Kysheemy	Mrs P G L White
Lakemere	Mrs F R Heslop
Lacetrom	Mr and Mrs T Gate
Larksdown	Mr R and Mrs S Millbank
Lindcoly	Mr and Mrs C Saich
Lindisfarne	Mr and Mrs B Hills
Llecan	Mrs C J Fletcher
Lussac	Mrs S P Clarke
Lyckalotte	Mr and Mrs N Mee
Lyheholme	Mrs A Bishop
Madison	Mrs V Stibbe
Magic	Mr N E Hawthorn
Mardick	Miss F Marquis
Maybrian	Mr and Mrs B Pash
Meolswood	Mrs W Cranham
Misticmaker	Miss T Jordan

Affix	Name of owner
Nantiderri	Mrs V Rosser
Noiroche	Mr R P and Mrs A G P Brain
Nortonwood	The late Mr R Bradbury and Mrs M Bradbury
Okeford	Mr D and Mrs V Johnstone
Paddiswood	Mrs N Padley
Paraven	Mrs J Searle
Parsifal	Mrs M Ward
Parkburn	Mrs M Jewell
Penmayne	The late Dr W Reynard
Piddlevalley	Mrs J Kempe
Pythingdean	Mr and Mrs P Guthrie
Ravenhall	Mrs S Kearton
Rainscourt	Mr and Mrs R Parish
Riverglide	Mrs A Youens
Roglans	Mr and Mrs M Roe
Scheindubh	Mr and Mrs P Burr
Segedunum	Mr and the late Mrs A MaCullum
Shardik	Miss H Meenaghan
Skeetsmere	Mr and Mrs M A Gower
Solotown	Mr and Mrs P Riches
Spera	Mrs S De-Robbio
Starmoss	Mr and Mrs J Lockhart
Steelriver	Miss S Stevenson
Stranfaer	Mr and Mrs D Joyce
Taranbeck	Mrs S Oxford
Taurgo	Mr and Mrs G Stanley
Trioaks	Mrs J Seall
Tucklewell	Mrs J Whitwell
Tunnelwood	Mr and Mrs S W Ashby
Twinwood	Mr J B Grain
Varingo	Mr and Mrs C Gwilliam
Verdant	Mrs E Green
Visam	Mrs and Mrs J Kendall
Waddicombe	Miss P Whitwell
Watchingwell	Mr N Clues and Mrs G Blow
Wavendon	Mrs C Bedford
Wemdon	Mrs E M Brockes
Westbrook	Mr and Mrs R Iggledon
Windyhollows	Mr and Mrs E W Colson

Chapter 3

Flatcoated Retrievers World-Wide

The Flatcoated Retriever can now be found in many parts of the world. In the past 25 years there has been a world-wide population explosion of Flatcoats, not though as great as among Golden and Labrador Retrievers.

Before 1980 Flatcoated Retrievers could be found in many countries but in very small numbers. Now these countries have their own breed clubs and well-established breeding pools. Most are trying to maintain the breed standard and the working ability of our lovely breed. I have tried to cover as well as possible all countries where the breed has become well-established.

Flatcoats are relatively popular in all of the Scandinavian countries, and in most other European countries, although they are less numerous in Spain, Portugal and the Balkans. The breed is well established in the United States of America and Canada, but I have no information on Flatcoats in South America.

There have been small numbers of Flatcoats in New Zealand and Australia for many years, with a dedicated group of breeders and enthusiasts. There are also a number of Flatcoats in Japan, some American Champions having been imported, but I do not know whether there is an established breed club.

AUSTRALIA

Much of the following information is taken from a report by Dr Robert Pargetter on the history of the breed in Australia up to the end of the 1970s.

Prior to 1974, Flatcoated Retrievers had only a brief and intermittent history in Australia. It is known that a pair entered a show in Melbourne in the early 1930s, and there is some evidence that there may have been one or more Flatcoats in Australia around 1870. Apart from this, the history of Flatcoated Retrievers in Australia began with the arrival of the first pair from England in April 1974. From this pair and other imports we entered the 1980s knowing that there were between 80 and 90 Flatcoats in the country.

The introduction of the breed was a planned affair. Fay and Robert Pargetter imported Stonemeade Shandygaff ('Gaff') and Stonemeade Fine Lace from England in 1974, and Mrs Dorothy Sutch imported Stonemeade Wild Rose from England in 1975. Phillip Whittaker of the Stonemeade affix selected those three as giving a viable breeding trio from which the breed could be established. Wild Rose and Fine Lace both produced litters to Gaff in 1975.

Additional stock came into the country early in 1975 when the Pargetters imported Vanrose Black Jewel (*Stolford Kings Ransom ex Blackberry of Vanrose*) from New Zealand and, jointly with Mr S Allen, Dudwell Zenith of Downstream from England.

The two litters by Gaff produced in 1975 saw both the entry of new enthusiasts into the breed in Victoria, and the introduction of the breed into two other states. Peter and Helen Eley obtained Duffton Just Jo and Charlie Ball obtained Duffton Teal from the Gaff ex Wild Rose litter, and John and Carol Rushford obtained Tanton Arthur Gaff from the Gaff ex Fine Lace litter. Two Flatcoats, one from each litter, went to Queensland, but neither had any real influence in establishing the breed there. However, Duffton Grouse (*Stonemeade Shandygaff ex Stonemeade Wild Rose*) went to New South Wales and Canberra to the partnership of C & A Armstrong and C & R Jones, and was shown with considerable success in 1976 and 1977. He was also the first Flatcoated Retriever in Australia to be worked regularly at obedience.

A second mating of the New Zealand pair Stolfords Kings Ransome and Blackberry of Vanrose led to the import of three more Vanrose Flatcoats into Australia in 1976: a dog, Vanrose Black Knight, to Mrs Sutch and two bitches, Vanrose Black Beauty to the Armstrong/Jones partnership in New South Wales and Vanrose Black Seal to Mr Bill Robinson in Queensland. Four further litters were bred in Victoria in the 1976-1977 period, so by 1977 the Australian-wide situation was:

New South Wales

After an initial burst of success in the show ring and obedience with Grouse and Black Beauty by the partnership of Armstrong and Jones a lapse occurred and most of the NSW stock was sold and left the state in 1978.

Queensland

Bill Robinson was showing Tanton Jonnie Walker *(Stonemeade Shandygaff ex Dudwell Zenith of Downstream)* and Black Seal. Late in 1977 he produced a litter from Black Seal to Arthur Gaff. In addition to this, some puppies from the Eleys' Vanrose Black Knight/Duffton Just Jo litter stayed in Victoria while others went to Queensland, South Australia and Tasmania. Kim and Gary Methven came into the breed with Kellick Just Fine, Bill Thomas with Kellick Buccaneer (registered in the Eleys' name) and Paul Ashman purchased Kellick Sonya. Linda Webb in South Australia took Kellick Black Lace early in 1978. David Temple in Queensland took Kellick Just Is. These two interstates have become very involved in the breed, and have obtained more Flatcoats.

The big development in 1973 was Joy and Colin Smith's entry into the breed in West Australia. They purchased Vanrose Black Pearl (Black Jewel's litter sister) from Margaret Evans in New Zealand, Vanrose Black Beauty and Duffton Grouse from New South Wales and a pup from Bill Robinson's litter in Queensland. From this beginning Flatcoats have developed well in the West, as three litters have been produced and a number of new enthusiasts have come into the breed. Flatcoats are now being worked and shown regularly.

Victoria

This is the key state for Flatcoated Retrievers. The Pargetters had imported four dogs, and progeny from their two litters (the second being Stonemeade Shandygaff to Dudwell Zenith of Downstream) was either being shown or available for breeding. The Eleys had increased their stock; in addition to Duffton Just Jo they had obtained Stonemeade Wild Rose and Vanrose Black Knight from Mrs Sutch, who had virtually dropped out of the breed, and progeny was available from their litter (Jo to Black Knight). Charlie Ball was working a Flatcoat, initially Teal, but after Teal's untimely death in 1977 he took a bitch pup, Kellick Keeta, from the Eleys' litter. John and Carol Rushford were showing Arthur Gaff and had expressed a continuing interest in the breed.

The years 1978 and 1979 saw consolidation of the breed in Victoria. Three litters were produced, and the number of Flatcoated Retrievers being shown regularly slowly increased. Jan and Kevin Baker had two Flatcoats and bred a litter (all registered in the Pargetter's name). Carmilla Clifford and Angela Petermann started to show Flatcoat puppies in 1979.

Two further features of the 1970s should be noted for the history of the breed in Australia. The first is the success of Charles Ball of Victoria in working Flatcoats from 1976 onwards. Both Teal and Keeta were worked with great success, winning and gaining other awards in both field and retrieving trials. Flatcoats were also being worked in Western Australia and Victoria, and many others throughout Australia were being worked in obedience.

The second was the establishment of the Flatcoated Retriever Association of Victoria in 1976. The association was affiliated to the KCC Victoria from the beginning of 1977, and its object is to promote the breed throughout Australia. Its first Open Show took place in 1980.

Imports in the 1980s

Several dogs were imported to Australia during the 1980s. John Rushford imported two dogs from the United Kingdom in 1980, Stonemeade Hamish *(Ch Wizardwood Teal ex Ch Hallbent New Novel)* bred by P Whittaker and the liver bitch Bramatha Copper Narelle *(Norseman of Atherbram ex Atherbram Ability)* bred by Miss S Whittaker. The year 1981 saw the arrival of two New Zealand imports, Dunboy Flight o Fancy *(Proctors Woodhaven Pike ex NZ Ch Voyager Tiger Flower)* and Aust Ch Copsewood Nigra, imported by Mr and Mrs G Methven. In 1984, Roglands Night Raider *(Ch and Ir Ch Shargleam Black Cap ex Ewlands Yuletide of Roglands)* was imported by Mr and Mrs A Jenkins, and in 1985 Branchalwood Kyle *(Ch Stantislane Rory of Branchalwood ex Ch Branchalwood Frisa)* was imported by Mr and Mrs G Methven, both of these having been bred in the United Kingdom.

BELGIUM

I must thank Marie Noëlle Terlinden for her help with this section on the Flatcoated Retriever in Belgium.

The first Flatcoated Retriever to be imported into Belgium was Belsud Black Nightjar in 1977, and the second was Exclyst Kiss. (These were also the first two Flatcoats to be shown in France.) They were mated together and produced Fr Belgium and Int Ch Fairman Black of Glen Sheallag. Exclyst Kiss's second litter by Branchalwood Affric produced Ch B.IB.Wx.S'Tr.TR.S'89 James of Glen Sheallag. Both dogs were well known for their excellent working abilities.

After a few years Marie Noëlle Terlinden and Bernard Chauveau imported Ch.B IB.F.S'86. TR.S'TR. Ch FT :Dual Ch Branchalwood Islay and one year later Ch.B.IB.F.TR Branchalwood Alish and her litter brother CH IB.F.Lux.BW'89 & 93 TR Branchalwood Lochdubh. Branchalwood Islay and Branchalwood Lochdubh gave us several multi-champions and triallers, including Lochness of Glen Sheallag, Lindsey of Glen Sheallag, Leigh of Glen Sheallag, Pillow Talk of Glen Sheallag, Nancy Black of Glen Sheallag.

Islay produced one multi Champion to Ch B.IB.F.TR. O'Mansell of Glen Sheallag. Lochdubh produced champion sons in Holland and France, and although he has not been used very much his stock have been shown and worked with success.

There are not many Flatcoats in Belgium or France. Most are owned by people who are devoted to the breed and have the welfare of the breed at heart, but in both countries there are a few who breed only for money.

Nearly 80 per cent of the Flatcoats bred by Bernard Chauveau and Marie Noëlle Terlinden are sold for show and work. Many Flatcoats are worked behind the hunter's pointers.

It is really difficult to breed good Flatcoated Retrievers in France and Belgium as it means importing semen or travelling great distances (for example, to Sweden and Norway) to be able to maintain the desirable type.

CANADA

Moira Jewell has kindly given me the following information on Flatcoated Retrievers in Canada:

Flatcoated Retrievers were re-introduced to Canada in 1973, although a very small number had been exported to Canada as family dogs before this time. The breed was re-introduced as a viable breeding and competitive force when Moira Jewell emigrated to British Columbia from Scotland, bringing with her English Sh Ch Parkburn Brandy Boy and The Parc Dawn. In 1974 these two were mated, resulting in the first Canadian-born Flatcoat litter in over 40 years. Puppies from this litter went to homes all over Canada and the United States.

Meanwhile, on the other side of Canada, Cyraine and Peter Dugdale were living in Toronto and had with them their Flatcoat bitch Creekside Bubbles. They purchased a male from this litter (Parkburn Deextenzing of Casuarina). Both Tenzing and his father, Brandy Boy, went on to win their Canadian and American Championships, becoming the only two Flatcoats to hold Championships titles in England, Canada, and America. (Tenzing won his English title when Cyraine and Peter returned to England.)

In 1975 Creekside Bubbles was mated to Parkburn Brandy Boy and a bitch puppy from this first Casuarina litter went to the Jantel kennels, owned by Ted and Janet Levesque, and became the foundation of their Flatcoat breeding programme. This bitch, Can Am Ch Casuarina Nootka of Jantel, had the honour of being Best of Breed at the very first Flatcoated Retriever Society of America Speciality under Read Flowers. The Levesques also imported a male from the Dalziels in Scotland (Can Am Ch Branchalwood Feochan). Kathy Howland-Zavitz purchased a bitch puppy from a litter from Nootka and Feochan (Can Ch Jantel's Barnacarry, CDX) thus founding the Fleetwing kennel in Nova Scotia.

In 1975 Doug Windsor in Ontario purchased a bitch from the Athercroft kennels in America. This bitch (Amberwoods Blac Athercroft) was the foundation for the Butterblac Flatcoats. She was bred to Eng Sh Ch Can Am Ch Parkburn Brandy Boy and the first Butterblac Flatcoat litter was born in 1977. A dog from this litter (Butterblac's Cruise Control) was purchased by Frank and Elaine Bourassa in Saskatoon, Saskatchewan. Cruise earned his Championship, WCX, and was placed several times in Canadian Kennel Club licensed field trials. He was also Canada's first Best in Show Flatcoated Retriever. Another dog from the Butterblac kennels to make his presence felt was Can Am Ch Butterblac's Excalibur, Can CDX, WC, TT, Am CD. He was sired by the English import Can Am Ch Torwood Peerless, Can Am CDX, JH, WCX ex Can Am Ch Amberwood's Blac Athercroft, CD. He also won Best in Show in Canada.

The number of Flatcoat fanciers in Canada is growing steadily. Today we regularly see Flatcoated Retrievers in working certificate tests, obedience trials and the conformation (show) ring. It is also gratifying to see more sportsmen become aware of the unspoiled ability of the Flatcoat as a personal hunting dog. The number of breeders in Canada has been growing slowly since the mid-1980's and now an average of eight litters are born in Canada annually. Most of the newer Flatcoat kennels are founded on dogs descended from the original breeding stock of the five Canadian breeders of the 1970s.

One notable exception is the Prairielight Kennels of Saskatoon, Saskatchewan, owned by Hans and Margareta Berin. This kennel is founded on stock from Sweden (Balgair, O'Flanagan and Almanza) imported by the Berins. Some other kennels have been founded with American stock which has widened our gene pool. Over the years other Flatcoated Retrievers have been imported into this country, primarily from England, but many of these dogs were never bred from and as a result were lost to our gene pool.

Ch OT CH Parkburn Lachlan WCI, WCX.

Flatcoated Retrievers

The Flatcoated Retriever Society of Canada holds an annual Speciality Show. Each year the number and interest grows. This must be gratifying to Peter and Cyraine Dugdale who worked so hard in the early 1970's to help found the club. The club now has over 100 members and at least 50 per cent of the members not only show their dogs but take part in field work, obedience, agility, flyball, scent hurdling, tracking and other activities.

In 1995 OTCh, Ch Parkburn Lachlan, WCX (owned and trained by Gina Luloff in Winnipeg) has been recognised by the Club to be the first Canadian breed Flatcoated Retriever to achieve advance titles in all three areas: conformation, obedience and field. Ch Parkburn Icy Blue Lucky Charly (owned and trained by Madelaine Hamza in Calgary) has titles in conformation, obedience, flybal,l agility and scent hurdling. Charly has criss-crossed the country performing in Canada's Superdogs for a number of years. He is waiting to do his helicopter training to qualify as a Search and Rescue dog in Alberta. Parkburn Noir Raven (owned by Ginette de la Chevrotière) has started her training under the Provincial Emergency Programme to qualify as a Search and Rescue dog in British Columbia.

Flatcoats from the Tebca Kennel owned by Elsa and Christian S Pedersen.

DENMARK

I am indebted to Christian S Pedersen for his help with this section.

In 1880 the first 'Wavy-coated' Retriever was seen in a show in Copenhagen. Since then, the Flatcoated Retriever was seen only occasionally until the middle 1960s when Liboalgin Black Gold and Halstock Druid were imported. The following Flatcoats were subsequently imported from England from 1967 to 1974 and became the foundation for further breeding in Denmark: Ryshot Dusk, Halstock Dianthus, Ryshot Copper Oriel, Ryshot Jet, Halstock Huntersmoon, Black Bird of Yarlaw, Downstream Forester, Gelhams Zula, Wood Wind, Wood Worker and, from Sweden, Puhs Dam av Fjolner *(Ryshot Copper Fire ex Puhs Hestia)*.

Over the years the Flatcoat has become more and more popular, and in the last eight years it has been on the Danish Kennel Club's 'Top Twenty' list. The development has not been explosive, but probably still too fast. Although most of the puppies (450-500 a year) are sold as family dogs, the majority of the breeders are still telling the puppy buyers that a Flatcoat likes and needs to work.

Most Danish breeders are breeding dual-purpose dogs, some leaning more towards the good-looking dog with the ability to work, others towards the working dog with good looks. Our latest field trial champion has had a first prize in an open class at a show (a second is all that is needed to qualify). Most of our show champions have a first prize in a field trial open class but a second prize is acceptable for the title. The open class is more or less equivalent to a novice stake. Nowadays it is not common for a Flatcoat to receive a certificate in a field trial (1st winner in open class) one day and a show certificate the next, but it does happen.

Danish Flatcoats are fairly healthy. About 80 per cent are free of hip dysplasia and there are no severe eye diseases; cataract and PRA have not been found. The few dogs whose elbows have been X-rayed have been free of problems. A fair number of our Flatcoats have spondylosis showing up on their hip X-rays, but the majority seems to be unaffected.

The Flatcoat Breed Club is part of the Danish Retriever Club, the largest special club in Denmark, with about 6700 members. Labrador Retriever owners account for about 58 per cent of the membership, Golden Retriever owners about 24 per cent, Flatcoat owners about 14 per cent and Chesapeake and Curly Coated Retrievers about one per cent.

Dk/Br Ch Lubo *(Van Dango Panga ex Lubbe)*, born February 1989. Became field trial champion in the autumn of 1993.

The Retriever Club arranges joint shows and field trials. The breed club organises two week-ends per year: an official show and field trials (cold game test). They also arrange two or three official field trials (warm game) for novice and open dogs. The committee also organises at least two training week-ends. At other times small groups of Flatcoat owners get together or join with other retriever owners for training classes.

Some Flatcoats are trained for competitive obedience (we had an obedience champion a few years ago) and others are active in agility.

Although the popularity of the Flatcoat has increased we hope the breeders will continue to be aware of our goal: a good-tempered, healthy dog, easy to train, good as a family dog, a good partner when we go picking up and shooting and, of course, looking as a Flatcoat should.

FINLAND

The first Flatcoated Retriever came to Finland in 1967. The bitch Puhs Hera *(Blakeholme Jamie ex Downstream Hestia)*, 'Flimsan' to her friends, was imported by Kenneth Kankkunen and became the first Flatcoat champion in Finland. She was mated three times, and Marjatta Hyötyläinen bought a bitch and bred a couple of litters before turning her activities exclusively to Golden Retrievers.

Asterix i Vassen, from the second litter, which was by Stolford Sepoy, became an important dog. He was mated to Jennifer *(Puhs Herakles ex Puhs Evoe)*, bred by Kristina West, to produce SF Ch Mollyfer Tapio Takalas. Mollyfer was mated several times, and her puppies have turned out to be good, healthy gundogs. A bitch from her litter by Gunhills Gus Guy was bought by Anneli Koskinen of the Pepperment affix. Many skilful tracking dogs have come from this kennel. SF Ch Pepperment Miska competes in field trials and is the father of several litters, from Tracking Champion (SF JVA) Baggas Mimmiliisa, foundation bitch of Merja Veräjänkorva's Merjun kennel.

Mollyfers offspring by Celebrity of Ryshot have also been good field trial dogs. By 1990 three of them were the only Flatcoat Finnish field trial champions.

ITALY

There is no record of Flatcoated Retrievers in Italy until the late 1960s and early 1970s when Dr Giuseppe Benelli from Florence admired this lovely breed during his frequent visits to Great Britain and obtained from Colin Wells the great dog, Ch Donovan, and two bitches. Giuseppe Benelli, who died three years ago, was a great dog fancier, a dedicated breeder, who loved showing and hunting with gundogs: in a word, to be surrounded by his dogs.

An enthusiastic huntsman, he preferred shooting with Flatcoats and he often organised shooting parties on his big estates where his guests could share and enjoy the work of his retrievers.

Emanon Amzel, owned by Constanza Rimini.

A unique picture of a group of Flatcoats.
Photo - Guiseppe Benelli.

Donovan sired one or two litters for his Italian owner, whose Flatcoats were shown in the beginning of the 1970s, consistently winning the Best in the Gundog Group.

Constanza Rimine Calabrese and her family lived near his kennels, and she fell in love with Flatcoats as a young girl. She was not in a position to own one until eight or nine years later, however, and by then Dr Benelli had no Flatcoats in his kennels. She did not give up, but travelled to Great Britain several times, meeting Paddy Petch in the course of her visits. In 1983 she imported the puppy Rase Harlequin, who won consistently in Europe during his long and successful career, and through whom she re-introduced the breed to Italy. He was a lovely, faithful companion to Constanza until his death in August 1994.

Constanza was particularly interested in the Halstock strain, and in 1987 she imported Emanon Amzel ('Cookie'), who was a daughter of Ch Halstock Bridget. Cookie too was extremely successful, including among her successes World Champion at Copenhagen in 1989 out of 78 entries and Finnish Champion at Helsinki in 1991.

Constanza bred one litter from Cookie, and she still has a daughter and a grand-daughter of hers. Her breeding programme is very careful, as there is still no overwhelming demand for Flatcoats in Italy, and it is very difficult to find really sound sires in Europe. Her aim is to make the breed well known and respected in Italy.

NETHERLANDS

A very small number of Flatcoated Retrievers came to the Netherlands in the beginning of this century, but they were used only as gundogs. In 1960, however, the beautiful bitch Ryshot Ecstasy was imported by Mr S Jacob. As no stud dogs were available in the Netherlands, sperm was flown from England, and in 1963 this resulted in a litter of seven puppies under the appropriate kennel name Magic.

In 1972 the Dutch Flatcoated Retriever Club was founded by Mrs Marijke Borghorst, Mr Jaap Mulder and Mrs Carrie van Crevel. After the first AGM, at which there were about 45 members, Mrs Shirley Johnson judged the 25 Flatcoats who were present. This was followed by a 'working test' in Mrs van Crevel's garden. The dual-purpose breeding principle has been strongly supported ever since.

The breeding committee was inaugurated then and is still functioning today. Breeding days are organised twice a year, when the offspring of specific sires and dams are shown at the age of about 18 months. Flatcoat health is also monitored. Hips, eyes and knees are tested, and breeders are advised to attend a few shows and do some work with the stock that is to be used for breeding purposes.

The Shooting Committee organises an instructional day once a year, as well as various working tests which are also open to other Retrievers. Apart from that, Dutch Flatcoated Retrievers take part in field trials, obedience tests, and agility tests, and train as rescue dogs.

Every year the Dutch Flatcoat Society holds a championship show, inviting English judges for their expert opinion. Nowadays an entry of 350 Flatcoats can be expected at this outdoor event.

The development of the breed was and still is dependent on British imports, and various kennels from the UK have been helpful. Dogs who played an important part in the development of the breed are Ch Black Cindy of

Saskia Rathenau with her son and puppy

Yarlaw, Ch Yarlaw Black Mask, Ch Wizardwood Snowy Owl, Ch Tonggreen Spray and her litter sister Sprig, Ch Heronsflight Trust, Heronsflight Jinx and Heronsflight Pan's Pledge, and Ch Westering Warcry.

Many Dutch kennels have been active since 1972, including: Britannic, v Driehoksland, Fan it Wâd, Flatcastle's, Flatholmes, Freewills Farm (Spokendam), Ginnesder, v Menninge, Viewpoints, Quail's, Questions Flight, Quiet Wood's, Rushwood's, Wagging Tails.

Saskia Rathenau, of the Wagging Tails affix, writes that about 18 years ago one of her school-friends (accidentally!) became the owner of a litter of Flatcoated Retrievers. For Saskia, it was love at first sight. After Kincardine v d Tafelronde made her entrance, Warresmere Clearwing, Paddiswood Amber Chocolate and Lindcoly Bel Rheana followed. All Saskia's Flatcoats live in the house as members of the family, together with a few smooth-haired dachshunds. Her two champions are Ch Jinks and her daughter Ch Wagging Tails Hole in One. The hope for the future is Wagging Tails Backspin, now just over 12 months of age. Apart from showing, working and breeding flatcoats, Saskia judges the breed in many European countries.

The breed has gained immensely in popularity since the 1970s. Membership of the Dutch Flatcoat Society has risen to over 1300, over 600 puppies are registered every year, and the Flatcoat has gone up to nineteenth place in the Top Twenty of pedigree dogs. Could the TV commercials be to blame?

NEW ZEALAND

Doreen Ridley of the Copsewood affix has given me the following information on the Flatcoated Retrievers in New Zealand:

The first Flatcoated Retriever recorded in New Zealand was a Ryshot dog who arrived in 1967, but no doubt there were others before this, accompanying their immigrant owners. In 1970 and 1974 respectively Mrs Margaret Evans imported Blackberry of Vanrose and Stolford Kings Ransom from the United Kingdom, and from a mating of these came Vanrose Black Jewel, who was exported to the Pargetters in Victoria, Australia.

Flatcoated Retrievers

Doreen Ridley: 'My three present Flatcoats'.

The breed in New Zealand has been slow to develop, which has been all to the good, as there are so few blood lines in the country. Currently the number of Flatcoat owners is around 140. The majority of dogs are pets, but there are also some rough shooting dogs, quite a few show dogs, a couple of field trial dogs who compete at the open level and some obedience and agility dogs. One Flatcoat is being used as a guide dog for the blind, and another as a hearing dog. One was also used in the conservation area for seeking out rare, endangered bird species, such as the Kakapo (ground parrot), in the native bush for transfer to out-lying islands in the hope that these birds will breed if undisturbed.

Over the years a few dogs have been imported from the UK and Australia. In the last couple of years three batches of frozen semen have also been imported and used with success. These we hope will prove to be an asset for the breed here.

The most notable New Zealand bred show dog was Aust Ch Copsewood Nigra, who was exported to Australia in 1981. He had several group wins and also won three BISs.

The highest qualifier in obedience working trials was NZ Ch Torlum Tombane CDX UDX, an import from Australia. In Obedience Ch Copsewood Egret CDX has qualified for and is working in Test C.

In field trials the following dogs have won trials at the Open Level:
NZ Ch Heronsflight Tipster (a UK import) - 1 Challenge Point
Copsewood Plumosa - 2 Challenge Points
Copsewood Opus - 2 Challenge Points

Another dog who did well at Trials was Ch Dunboy Fenian Pride. Although he did not win a trial, he was certainly knocking on the door.

New Zealand trials are like the UK cold game test, and one has to win a trial at open level to gain a much sought-after challenge point. One requires 6 challenge points for the title Field Trial Champion.

Copsewood Quail was the dog owned by the Conservation Officer, and she ended up a very experienced helicopter passenger in her work, travelling to the remote areas of New Zealand.

Doreen Ridley has three Flatcoats in her Copsewood kennels at the moment, all of whom have FT Awards and are shot over. She thoroughly enjoys going out shooting with a good working Flatcoat and has wonderful memories of superb gundog work. She only shows her dogs occasionally, and they are all her constant companions.

Present Day Kennels:

Anaglyn	Robyn Annard
Brookton	Sally Nettleton
Copsewood	Doreen Ridley
Maplehurst	Ruth Chapman and Lois Causer (formerly Proctors)
Stratharran	Robin Fraser
Voyager	Carol Kearns
Willowood	Heather Menzies

NORWAY

Norway has taken the Flatcoated Retriever to its heart. At the beginning of the century a few Flatcoats were brought over from Britain, one of the first being imported in 1912. This was Tar of Glendaruel, owned by Lorenz Bruun from Tonsberg.

Norwegian breed history really started in 1970, when Ninni Thurman-Moe imported the bitch Apport's Shimmy from Sweden. She was the breed's first Norwegian-owned Champion (Norwegian Ch). Her grandson, Chatoharos Mac Spencer, became the first International Nordic Champion. Another grandson, Norwegian Ch C-Black Spot, is the maternal grandfather of this year's World Winner Int Norwegian and Swedish Ch Black Bowie. Bowie followed in the footsteps of his father, Norwegian Ch GSW-91 Piek (*Norwegian Ch Exclyst Kestrel ex Ki-Ro-Ma's Estelle*).

The first Norwegian litter was born in Vestfold Country in 1972, under the affix Fla-Go-Line. The breeder was Bjoerg Haldis Flatin (former Lie). Her foundation bitch was Halstock Michaela. She is the breeder of the first and only Flatcoat field trial champion in Norway,

Per Iversen - One of Norway's top Flatcoat breeders and considered by many to be one of their top all-round international judges.

Norwegian/Swedish FT Ch Fla-Go-Line's Bamby, owned by Mr and Mrs Oestensen. Mrs Flatin is still an active breeder, but she is best known for her very good imported British males such as Norwegian Ch Cambourne Tango, Norwegian Ch Exclyst Iceman, Norwegian Ch Hallbent Dawn Patrol and Norwegian Ch Hallbent Spring Lad by Withybed.

The leading kennel in the 1970s and early 1980s was the Brenna Kennel, belonging to Hjoerdis Espeland and Per Iversen. Per Iversen had been to England to study the breed and he imported from Colin Wells the bitch Norwegian Ch Kenstaff Whip in 1973. She was a beautiful bitch, who was a great success in the ring, winning Best of Breed (BOB) four times at the annual Retriever Club Championship Show. In 1974 Mrs Espeland bought Norwegian Ch Woodland Wagtail who produced six champions out of two litters, two of whom were the first liver Norwegian-born champions. In 1980 Norwegian Ch Woodland Whipper-in and Norwegian Ch Torwood Plague were imported. These dogs were to be a very positive influence on the breed.

In 1973 Jenny Hamremoen imported Halstock Lone Ranger, born in 1971. He had already sired two litters in England, his most outstanding son being Ch Exclyst Bernard out of Wyndhamian Claudette. At the same time she imported the bitch Fairleigh Stop-N-Stare. Out of this combination came the outstanding bitch Norwegian Ch Sol-Ham-Na'a Black and White Spot, who went to Kristin og Olav Riste and became the foundation bitch of their successful Fjell-Bjoern Kennel.

During the next few years several important dogs were imported. Kari and Kjell Haug, of the Cariena kennel, imported Woodland's Woodcock, the litter brother of Wagtail, and went to Sweden for a bitch, Norwegian Ch Bess (*Justice of Klevagaard ex Puhs Elissa*). These two were bred together in 1976, and the Haugs kept the female line from this mating and bred quality stock ever since. In 1985 they mated the bitch Norwegian Ch Cariena's Seven-Ten, daughter of Woodlands Whipper-In, to Ch/Ir Ch Shargleam Blackcap (by artificial insemination) and acquired a very successful litter. The sons

Flatcoated Retrievers

Cariena's Fifteen-Four, Fifteen-Eight, and Fifteen-Nine, all became champions and important stud dogs. Shargleam Treecreeper was imported in 1986, and also became an important stud dog. The Carinena kennel is considered the leading Norwegian kennel of the last ten years.

Norwegian Ch Beaty, litter sister to Norwegian Ch Bess, was imported by Bjoerg Aaby. Mated to Norwegian Ch Hallbent Dawn Patrol she produced two show champions and one international champion, Bjoergs Asarja. In 1981 his litter sister Bjoergs Afrodite produced the outstanding bitch Norwegian Ch Black Beth who took Best In Show (BIS) at The Kennel Club's International Championship Show at Sjølyst in 1982. With Norwegian Ch Caymosa's Veni Vidi Vici she was the foundation of the Crazy Couple kennel owned by Ann Kathrin Halvorsen and Pia Paulsen, who by a tragic accident in 1993 lost their two very good young bitches. They have managed to keep up the Black Beth line through two one-year-old granddaughters, and it is hoped they will be able to continue their quality line through these.

Other important dogs of the 1970s are Norwegian Ch Rase Patricia and Norwegian Ch Rase Pierrot. The combination of Pierrot and Woodland Wagtail produced Norwegian Ch Brenna's Basato, and the combination of Eng Int and Nordic Ch Woodman and Rase Patricia produced Alvaasens Black Atcha. A mating between Basato and Atcha in 1979 produced Norwegian Ch Gitle's Daughter Atcha, the foundation bitch of Mrs Yttervold's Agrebo kennel. Later she imported from Sweden the bitch Gunhill's Easter Love and from the United States of America Meadowrue Faiance. With these three bitches and their offspring Mrs Yttervold has had great success in the show ring, and if you ever come to Norway and see a tiny dark-haired lady crying big tears outside the ring, then you know an Agrebo dog has taken a ticket again.

In 1979 Barbro Lundstrøm moved from Sweden to Norway. She brought with her Norwegian Ch Mimosa of Halstock, born in 1972 *(Exclyst Shane ex Alisa Craig of Halkshill)*. Mimosa's offspring under the Caymosa affix have had a great influence on today's Flatcoats in both countries. Best known was her Swedish grandson, the famous Int Nordic Ch Snobben. Mrs Lundstrøm took back a Snobben daughter Norwegian Ch Nord V-84 Denise. Mated to Woodlands Whipper-In, she produced Norwegian Ch Caymosa's Oenskedroem, owned by Berit Skullestad of the Klokkeraasen Kennel. The combination of Norwegian Ch Klokkeraasen's Bonzo and Norwegian Ch Caymosa's Oenskedroem produced the outstanding bitch Norwegian Ch NV-90 Klokkeraasen's Gardenia.

It is impossible to list all the important breeders and dogs, but some must be mentioned. Amongst these are the top winning Flatcoat in 1994, Norwegian Ch Lussac Crusader, or 'Win', *(Ch Exclyst Imperial Mint ex Exclyst Rebecca of Lussac)* owned by Signy and Knut Skjelbred. Win is a clever police dog, a 'sniffer-dog', and ever since his first successful litter with Agrebo's Cara he has also been one of the most popular stud dogs in Norway.

Working Flatcoats in Norway

The number of Flatcoats in Norway has grown. From just a few in the 1970s registration has now increased to 500 to 600 puppies every year. Nearly all of them are pet or show dogs, but a small number of breeders are trying to keep them as gundogs.

Hans Ole Stenbro of the Stormy affix has good-looking working stock.

Grete and Arild Engedal of the Gledill kennel are the owners of the first Norwegian International champion bitch, Int Norwegian Swedish and Finnish Ch Gledill Algera, and also the well-known stud dog, Norwegian Swedish and Finnish Ch Shargleam Sandpiper, both of whom successfully participate in field trials.

Another Shargleam stud dog, Norwegian Ch Shargleam Woodcock, owned by Bjarne Sørensen of the Pintail affix, is successful in the field.

Kjersti Haugen of the Bunyan affix had a litter out of Norwegian Swedish FT Ch Fla-go-line's Bramby and Paddiswood Burnt Willow (*Wizardwood Tawny Owl* ex *Heronsflight Burnt Sugar*), producing a number of promising working dogs. She is also trying to keep a liver line from her liver Norwegian and Finnish Ch Brenna's Bunyan and the imported liver Paddiswood bitches.

In Norway you are forbidden by law to hunt deer or elk without having immediate access to an officially registered tracking dog. Many Flatcoats are trained for this purpose and successfully gain their title Tracking Champion (NV Ch). Some owners enjoy working their Flatcoats in obedience, training and competing until they have an Obedience champion (N Ob Ch). Some enjoy agility and work towards them becoming Agility champions. Others train their dogs to find mushrooms in the woods, a tasty supplement for your dinner.

As you probably know, there is a considerable amount of snow in Norway during the winter. In cases of accidents or avalanches there is a great need for dogs who are trained to find people buried under the snow. Traditionally the German Shepherd was trained for this purpose, but then some smart people tried the Flatcoat. Now a growing number of Flatcoats from different lines are trained successfully and are officially registered as rescue dogs. To the writer's knowledge the first Flatcoat dog in Norway to be trained for this purpose was Norwegian Ch Exclyst Kestrel.

Flatcoats also pull sledges through the snow. The children just love to be passengers and the dogs enjoy it even more.

Norwegian Ch Lussac Crusader ('Win') has already been mentioned as a police dog. Several Flatcoats have been and are used as sniffer dogs by the police and custom officers and they are doing an excellent job. The following is an extract from an article by Knut Skjelbred, Win's owner and handler: *Flatcoated Retrievers in Norway: in the service of Humanity*. Knut Skjelbred introduced the Flatcoated Retriever to sceptical colleagues in the police force in 1984 (the Labrador having been the traditional breed for this purpose), and Win was his second Flatcoat sniffer dog. His first one, Sheik, unfortunately died young, and when the time came for replacement:

> My conclusion was that I'd be more than willing to try another Flatcoat, hopefully one that would be more careful with himself. When the family got its third dog, our second Flatcoated Retriever, these were things worth noticing.
>
> Norwegian Ch Lussac Crusader (*Ch Exclyst Imperial Mint* ex *Exclyst Rebecca of Lussac*), bred by Mrs Sue Clarke, is a direct opposite of his predecessor. He is not big; he is elegant, lithe, calm and careful. He is made for the job, and proved this to us at an early stage.
>
> Working with Win is different in a lot of ways. It is relaxing having a dog who can work without knocking down coffee mugs and flowerpots, yet I sometimes miss Sheik's spirit and stamina which was always present in him. These facts show the span within the breed, and it also proves that Flatcoats are not necessarily absent-minded scatterbrains, something which has been claimed from time to time in certain circles over here.
>
> Since 1984 the number of Flatcoated Retrievers in the service of the Norwegian police has increased steadily, and one must say that the breed has reached a peak in popularity. We have national championship competitions every year, and I am proud to tell you the 1990 winner was a Flatcoat (I believe this dog goes back to Norwegian Ch Exclyst Iceman, brother to Ch Exclyst Imperial Mint). When this dog passed his tests, he was a hyperactive dog that could almost make you lose your breath. Just one year later he works with great care and concentration and is a superb sniffer dog. He can still show a very high level of activity, but this is where we see the value of a good relationship between the dog and the handler. Working with sniffer dogs is very much like all other work with dogs, it is a teamwork.

Third in the same competition was another Flatcoat, a dog we bred ourselves, whereas my own dog in his first official competition was eighth.

The average Flatcoat is close to hyperactive, but even this is a quality. If you manage to give it concrete, limited problems to solve, then you may have a worker of excellent quality. The police in Norway today have a total of around 30 approved sniffer dogs. Seven of these are Flatcoated Retrievers.

It is no aim in itself to get as many Flatcoats as possible for this important task, even if the numbers are impressive. What means a lot to me is that a breed that I am fond of and have faith in, but in my opinion has been overlooked in certain circles, really proves to be a breed in which the working abilities have been well preserved, thanks to the breed enthusiasts of Great Britain.

It is my wish that we will keep going in the right direction, but let resist any signs of an explosion of puppies bred, something which will pose a threat to the versatility we still have in this dual-purpose dog.

Knut Skjelbred. Sandeford, Norway: 1995.

SWEDEN

Lena Hagglund has given me the following information about the Flatcoated Retriever in Sweden:

The establishment of the modern lines of Flatcoated Retrievers in Sweden started in 1962-1963, but about 75 years earlier at the very first dog show in Sweden a 'Black Retriever' was entered. During the years that followed a small number of Flatcoated and Curlycoated Retrievers were entered in dog shows in Sweden. It is recorded that between 1910 and 1915 a few Flatcoated Retrievers were registered by the Swedish Kennel Club.

From 1985 the breed started to increase in popularity, and there was an increase in the number of dogs and litters registered. Between 1985 and 1995, 700 to 900 individuals including imported dogs were registered by the Swedish Kennel Club per year. This has put the breed on the list of the 20 most popular breeds in Sweden, though this does not compare with 2700 to 3200 Golden Retrievers and 2200 to 2500 Labrador Retrievers bred each year during the same period of time.

Many breeders enthusiastically strive to maintain a dual-purpose Flatcoat. The Flatcoat has become a very successful show dog in Sweden, winning the Gundog Group and has even won Best in Show (BIS) on several occasions, but at the same time you can see an increasing interest in entering Swedish field trials. There are many successful Swedish field trial winners in the breed, even an International and Scandinavian Field Trial Champion.

When a litter of Flatcoated Retrievers is registered in Sweden, both parents must have a known hip dysplasia (HD) status. During the last 10 to 15 years there have been only 4.7 per cent with hip dysplasia, and most of these are only borderline.

Most dogs and bitches used for breeding have also had their eyes tested for cataract and PRA. It is required that stud dogs have their eyes tested once a year. Ten to twelve per cent have been diagnosed as having cataract in the last 10 to 15 years, most of these cases occurring in dogs aged between five and six years.

The only other veterinary problem among Flatcoats in general is that a fair number are found to be suffering from cancer of the intestines as they get older. Otherwise the breed is considered to be healthy.

SWITZERLAND

The end of 1975 saw the arrival of the first Swiss-born Flatcoated Retriever litter, comprising five black bitches (*Heronsflight Trust* ex *Ryshot Copper Elation*). In 1976 there were three more litters by Heronsflight Trust, all blacks; the first livers were born in August 1979. The number of annual registrations increased very quickly and, in 1994, 46 litters were registered in this small country.

A number of good dogs have been imported, some of whom have become champions:

Steiner's Belsud Golden Eagle (UK)
Shargleam Eagle Owl (UK)
Joller's Swallowsflight Black Oberon (Netherlands)
Swallowsflight Promising Pioneer (Netherlands)
Gmür's Woodstar Linnet (Denmark)
Vuille's Firelight Black of Funday Bays Naid
(France), who became a Show and Field trial Champion.
Jaussi's Exclyst Acclaim (UK)

The first Swiss-bred champion was Joller's Doll v Felsbach *(Ruff d'Aikoo ex Moor v Felsbach)*. Her daughter Daisy v Schauensee, sired by Black Jewel of the Moor, also gained her title.

Schori's Mona v Felsbach *(Oakmoss Zest ex Cina v Felsbach)* was the first Swiss-bred liver champion. Her daughter Amoi Bright Star of Blackberry Forest, sired by Lardo v Felsbach, also gained her title.

The most successful Swiss-bred bitch is certainly Danja v Felsbach. Her dam, Erla v Felsbach *(Heronsflight Pan's Pledge ex Björshult's Petit Marron)* was unfortunately rarely shown. Nevertheless she was Junior World Champion in 1985. Danja, whose sire was Black Jewel of Moor, won six CCs and five RCCs in Switzerland. She was Top Puppy in 1987, Top Opposite Sex in 1990, Top Flatcoat in 1992 and Top Brood Bitch in 1991 and 1992. Her daughter, Neala's Fireflame, whose sire was Swallowsflight Dashing Dynamite, is also a champion. 'Flame's' son by Heronsflight Pan's Pledge, Neala's Handsome Hawk, is the first Swiss-bred international show champion. For this title the dog must also qualify in the field, and this is not easy as opportunities are few and far between. There are at present only five international champions in Switzerland: Swallowsflight Black Oberon, Promising Pioneer, Woodstar Linnet, Firelight Black of Fundy Bays and Neala's Handsome Hawk.

Swiss Champion Exclyst Acclaim

Neala's Fireflame
Owner - Christian Joun

Flatcoated Retrievers

Neala's Handsome Hawk,
the first Swiss-bred international champion.
Owner - Yvonne Jaussi

It is difficult to work Flatcoats as gundogs in Switzerland but there are many who do other forms of work. I would especially like to mention homebred Aika v Chigga, owned by Hans Dick, who qualified for the European agility Championships, and H P Marending's Italian-bred dog P as in Peter, a fully-qualified rescue dog who recently went to Japan to help find people after the earthquake in Kobe. There are also Flatcoats doing search and rescue in the woods and mountains, and some are trained to seek out narcotics and explosives.

For the future well-being of the Flatcoat in Switzerland I feel that it is most important for all breeders to keep in contact and be frank about their experiences, good and bad. No breeder is alone in having difficulties and it can be only as the result of a joint effort, with the good of this wonderful breed at heart, that we can maintain the high standards which have been given to us by our friends abroad.

Yvoune Jaussi of the Neala's affix bought her first Flatcoat in 1984. At that time Franz Steiner was the only breeder of Flatcoats in Switzerland, and she bought Cedor v Felsbach *(Belsud Golden Eagle ex Ulla v Felsbach)* from him. She went on to buy Danja v Felsbach, already mentioned as the most successful Flatcoat bitch in Switzerland, and bred Danja's daughter, Flame, who also became a champion. She subsequently imported from England her third champion, Exclyst Acclaim. She writes as follows:

I think the big problem in Switzerland at present is that there are a great many litters (45 in 1994). Thanks to their appearances in advertisements, the puppies are easily sold at good prices. Many breeders are not very interested in the standard of the breed or in improving or maintaining its quality.

The Swiss Retriever Club has minimal requirements before dogs can be used for breeding purposes. The hips have to be X-rayed (maximum allowed grade C, formerly grade 1), the eyes must be clear of hereditary diseases and the certificate not more than 15 months old. Retrievers have to pass a so-called 'selection test' in which we check whether they have the typical characteristics of their breed. We want to see whether they are friendly, like to retrieve and go into water. Dogs who are gun-shy, aggressive, or not interested in anything at all cannot be bred from. The selection also includes judging the dog's conformation and it must be graded at least 'very good' to pass.

For a few years requirements were even less than this: the only compulsory elements were hips, eyes and a correct bite. A possible result of this relaxing of criteria is that we are now seeing quite a few dogs that are not of correct Flatcoat type.

I think we need the help of experienced English judges who will tell us sincerely what improvements we need to make. We are glad when our dogs are judged fairly and we are told their faults. It does not help when every average dog gets graded 'excellent' and those who are really below average 'very good'. The grade 'very good' means that a dog can be bred from, so it should be of genuinely good quality. We try to persuade our breeders that breeding means responsibility and is not just a hobby or a pleasure for the children ...

Yvoune Jaussi, 1995

UNITED STATES OF AMERICA

History of Flatcoated Retrievers in the USA

One of the first recorded post-war Flatcoated Retrievers to be imported into America was Pewcroft Prefect *(Denmere Prince ex Ch Pewcroft Pitch)*, otherwise known as 'Doc', who was exported by Stanley O'Neill in 1953. Homer Downing and Stanley O'Neill had been corresponding for several years before this. 'Doc' became the breed's first UDT. In 1955 Homer Downing imported a liver bitch, Atherbram Stella, who gave birth in 1957 to the first litter of Flatcoats to be born in America for over 10 years.

There were other imports in the mid-1950s, and with this and another litter the population grew to 22. Very few Flatcoats were registered between 1960 and 1970, but by 1969 there had been an increase to 69 registrations. Then there was a sudden interest, and 35 litters were registered between 1968 and 1972. There was also an increase in showing and 41 champions were made up as well as 52 obedience champions.

The Flat-coated Retriever Society of America was formed in 1960. It had a membership of 15 in 1968, increasing to 44 in 1973, and today it has a membership of 800. The breed has made significant advances in quality and quantity since 1973.

Dr Nancy Laughton (Claverdon) exported dogs that were to have a big influence in the breed, such as Rab of Morinda and Ch Claverdon Gamble CD, who was one of the most important sires of his time. Another important export from the UK was Sally Terroux's Ch Claverdon Duchess CDX (1958-1972). She was a very important producer, being the dam of 14 champions and three qualifiers for the All Aged Retrievers Stake.

Dr Nancy Laughton in 1958, shipping Claverdon Duchess to Sally Terroux

Read Flowers judging the first annual National Speciality of the Flatcoated Retriever Society of America, awarding Best of Opposite Sex to Best of Breed to Ch Mantayo Briarwood Jester CD, bred, owned and handled by Sally Terroux.

Edward and Dorothy Moroff's Rab of Morinda was the first Flatcoat to impress the field trial enthusiasts. Rab won a Qualifying Stake at the Wisconsin Amateur Trial in April 1958. He was placed in many stakes, including an Open All Aged Stake in October 1959, becoming the first and only Flatcoat up to 1982 to do this.

The most coveted award offered by the Flatcoated Society of America, The Bramcroft Obedience Trophy, was established in 1972. It is in honour of Homer Downing and Doc's early obedience awards, and the Field Trial Trophy established in 1975 marks their important achievements in the field.

Flatcoated Retrievers

Many dogs contributed to the success of the Flatcoat in the show ring in the 1960s and 1970s, including Sally Terroux's Ch Bramcroft Dandy UD *(Pewcroft Prefect ex Atherbram Stella)*, who won the breed several times at the prestigious Chicago Kennel Club Show. He was also an outstanding obedience dog; he averaged 195.5 in 92 obedience trials with 50 first placings in Open B or Utility and four perfect 200 scores. He won 61 of the 63 breed shows entered and won the Sporting Group three times.

In 1962 Ed Atkins imported Halstock Javelin *(Pewcroft Perch ex Ch Halstock Black Jewel)*. 'Laddie' went to America on board one of the great ocean liners (The Queen Mary, I think). All these early dogs must have travelled this way. Laddie earned his championship from points accumulated in Group competition. He was the first Flatcoat to win a Sporting Group.

Other dogs winning well at this period were Don and Florence Shiell's Mr Chips, Sally Terroux's Ch Mantayo Bronze Clipper CD and Grace Lambert's Ch and Am Ch Fenrivers Kalmia.

Sally Terroux's Mantayo Black Watch Glory *(Ch Witham ex Ch Mantayo Reb's Dixie CD)* was the first successful bitch in the show ring. Then in the 1970s came Ch Athercroft Blac is Beautiful *(Atherbram Inky ex Ch Sassacus Arr Rolla)* bred and owned by Glenn and Barbara Conner. She was the first Flatcoated Retriever to win an All Breeds BIS in 1973. She won four groups and was placed in many others and was the top winning Flatcoat of either sex. She was also a good producer.

Pauline Jones and Barbara Conner's Ch Sassacus Arr Rolla, *(Ch Clavercroft Kite CD ex Ch Arrogance of Wyndham CDX)* was from the famous 'Arr' litter. Six of the eight litter-mates became champions. The litter was bred by Pauline Jones.

Ed Atkins imported Black Jet of Wyndhamian in 1972. Other dogs were imported by Ed from the 'C' and 'D' litters out of Wood Lass and these have greatly influenced today's stock. The most outstanding was possibly Ch Wyndhamian Dash.

This is a very short account of the breed in America, taken from historic information in the article *Significant Flat-Coated Retrievers 1953-1978* by the late Vernon W Vogel, Historian, published by The Flat-Coated Retriever Society of America, Inc, 31 March 1982.

I am sure there are many important people and dogs who have not been mentioned. This is a salute to you all, the unsung heroes, people and dogs. You have all worked so hard to develop our beloved breed to the standard it is today in America.

Flatcoated Retriever Activities in the USA

Elizabeth 'Bunny' Millikin is my kind informant about the breed and its activities in America. There could no one better; Bunny has put so much time and energy into the breed from the 1960s onward. She is a special friend.

Flatcoated Retrievers, being generally very active dogs physically and mentally, are well suited to the many performance competitions events and activities offered by various dog organisations. However, they did not have the opportunity to shine for some time, as there was almost no market for this unknown breed so the more fashionable breeds went off with the honours. Gradually, the beauty, uniqueness and working ability of Flatcoats attracted attention and they were featured in articles in various dog and sporting publications. As people became aware of Flatcoats, interest and demand increased. In spite of this very moderate growth the breed has consistently ranked about 105th in the American Kennel Club's popularity list of all 137 AKC recognised breeds, allowing the Flatcoat to remain the truly multipurpose dog which the FCRSA strongly encourages. As a result Flatcoats are not divided into specialists (that is show type and working type) as are Sporting breeds with large numbers of registered dogs. Most of our top working dogs, in obedience or field, are also show (conformation) champions, and most of our show champions are also titled in other canine events.

Bunny and friend at a Junior Hunting Test. The judges are standing.
Photo - Elizabeth P Millikin.

Our Flatcoated Retrievers, being very active both physically and mentally, are well suited to the many performance competitions, events and activities offered by various dog organisations. The best known are the **Obedience** trials with three levels of competition: novice, open and utility. These are usually combined with conformation shows which offer many classes for all ages and stages of maturity but are judged on looks and movement only. A high percentage of Flatcoats participate in shows. Other dog sports enjoyed by Flatcoats and their owners are as follows:

* **Tracking** is a popular sport for outdoor people. The dog is taught to follow a human trail to the end, where an article, usually a glove, is found. There are several levels of difficulty and titles for each level.
* **Agility** is a new dog activity for the USA. It is a timed event that requires the dog to complete a varied course of obstacles ranging from going along narrow walks to climbing and jumping hazards, negotiating tunnels or weaving through poles. Agility also has several levels of difficulty and titles for successes.
* **Flyball**, offered by many obedience clubs, is a relay race game involving ball catching and jumps. Flatcoats love this type of activity.
* Many have proved themselves excellent service dogs such as **Search and Rescue** dogs and **Therapy** dogs.
* The true purpose of the Flatcoated Retriever was to be a **Working Gundog,** retrieving game from land or water. While there is far less hunting now than when he was first bred he still possesses very strong hunting instincts and is an excellent marker of fallen game. He is an outstanding personal hunting dog and is very successful in our Hunting Tests and other types of working test.

On 31 March 1978 the first Flat-coated Retriever Society of America, Inc Specialty Show and Obedience Trial was held. The breed was judged by Mr Read Flowers from England. The FCRSA still sponsors this show annually as a national speciality for Flatcoated Retrievers only. Included in our Speciality are Conformation and Obedience trial classes, working Certificates and AKC Hunting Retriever Tests and when possible Agility, Tracking and Flyball Fun. Also offered are educational seminars and the opportunity to meet other Flatcoat enthusiasts at all the events as well seeing many of the Flatcoats they may have read about in the Society's quarterly Newsletter. Each year the Specialty is held in a different part of the country and many members come together for almost a week: a veritable feast for any Flatcoated Retriever lover.

There are several dog registries in the USA but The American Kennel Club is the largest by far and responsible for most events: conformation shows, herding trials and field trials, obedience trials, tracking, versatility and many more. Titles earned at AKC events are either prefixes or suffixes. Prefixes are titles earned in competition, such as Champion, Obedience Trial Champion, Field Trial Champion. Suffixes are earned in non-competitive events where the dog performs against a standard for a pass-fail score. Examples are obedience titles, hunt test titles and tracking titles where a minimum score must be achieved.

To become an AKC Show Champion a dog must win 15 points which are accumulated according to the number of dogs defeated at each show. The dog must win at least two 'majors', that is two victories over enough dogs to earn three points under two different judges. Five points is the maximum number of points that can be won at any one time. Most points are won from the classes which exclude champions, thus diminishing the competition.

The basic obedience titles, Companion Dog (CD), Companion Dog Excellent (CDX) and Utility Dog (UD) require three passes at each level starting with Novice for CD, Open for CDX and Utility for a UD, each title earned in succession. A new title has been added, UDX, which requires 10 passes of both Open and Utility at the same trial. An Obedience Trial Championship (OT Ch) is earned by winning 100 points in Utility and Open B competition. The dog must have three wins, one in Open B, one in Utility and the third in either class. Points won depend on the number of dogs defeated.

Field Trials offer two Championships. A Field Champion is made up by winning a total of 10 points. These may be acquired in Open, Limited or Special All Aged Stakes in which there are at least 12 qualified starters. Not more than 5 points of the required 10 may be acquired in Specialty trials (trials open to only one breed of retriever) and 5 points must come from a win in an all breed competition. First place is 5 points, second is 3 points, third is 1 point and fourth is 0.5 points.

An Amateur Field Championship is earned by winning a total of 15 points in Amateur All Aged and Open, Limited or Special All-Age when handled by an amateur, including a win in all breed competition. An amateur fulfilling the requirement for a Field Championship also becomes an Amateur Field Champion. All points and other requirements are the same.

At the time of writing no Flatcoat has earned a Field Championship and only one, Ch AFC Jon-Lee's Spring Valley Atari, has earned an Amateur Field Championship. These are very difficult titles to acquire, only about 35 a year being made up. For the record there were over 125,000 Labrador Retrievers and almost 65,000 Golden Retrievers registered in 1994 though only about 5,000 retrievers compete in trials.

More within reach of most Flatcoats are the hunting retriever tests. There are three levels:

Junior Hunter: Requiring single marked retrieves, two on land and two in water under hunting conditions.

Senior Hunter: Land and water double marked retrieves, land and water blind retrieves (unseen) and honouring another dog's work.

Master Hunter: Land and water triple marked retrieves, land and water blind retrieves, honour another dog's work and diversions. Extreme steadiness is required in this test.

Hunt test work is usually not longer than 100 yards. These tests are non-competitive and are judged against a standard of work as opposed to field trials which are judged dog against dog. Hunting retriever tests are created to resemble actual hunting situations as nearly as possible.

Sassacus Rastus FTA ('Kale').   Photo - Elizabeth P Millikin.

Search and Rescue in America

Flatcoated Retrievers have been used in many countries of the world as Search and Rescue dogs. A Flatcoat from Switzerland went to Japan to help in the earthquake disaster in 1995.

We can think of no better honour for a breed than to be recognised for its versatility. I know Debbie and Steve Porter are very proud of the achievement of Sharon Kyle of Tulsa, Oklahoma and Raven, more properly SR Ruffwood's Search n Seizure JH CGC *(Spring Valley Skyflier MH UD WCX X ex Wingmaster Dyamic Damsel JH WC CGC TDI)*. A short article by Bill Swindell in *Tulsa World* 21 April 1995 describes the search and rescue work carried out by a team of dogs and handlers from Tulsa, Sharon and Raven among them. The team searched the ruined building from the basement to the top of the rubble for victims, riding 'cherry pickers' (elevated platforms) to search the upper levels. Once the dogs registered a human scent, the handlers sprayed the area with red paint to guide the rescuers. Sharon Kyle is quoted in this article as saying she was 'ready to go all day' in an effort to find someone. Sharon herself writes:

> I have been involved in search and rescue as a volunteer using a K-9 partner for about four years. My first search dog is Penny, a seven-year-old Airedale Terrier. She has been trained in area search (find any person in a specific area by air scenting), trailing (find a specific person by following their scent left on the ground), and cadaver search on land (for buried victims of homicide and drowning victims). We have participated in more than 20 searches for local and state law enforcement agencies: searches for alzheimer's patients that

Raven and Sharon getting used to being in and around helicoptors.

Raven wearing the rescue vest.

wandered off from rural homes, victims of boating accidents, bodies in collapsed structures, buried remains of homicide victims, missing hunters, victims trapped in buildings/rubble of tornadoes.

Several years ago I wanted to get a new dog for search and rescue. I wanted a very people-friendly dog, one with a lot of curiosity, drive, one that wanted to do things with its person. I shopped and I learned about other breeds and was intrigued by what I learned about the Flatcoated Retriever. I purchased Raven, from Debbie and Steve Porter in Chicago, Illinois.

Raven is now two years old. She has had preliminary search training in area search, trailing, agility work for disaster search and some water search training. Her first search was the bombed federal building in Oklahoma City (4-95). She worked very well and was not intimidated by what was often a stressful/fearful situation. She has a lot of potential as a search dog. The three factors that I feel make her a good search dog are:

1. She wants to do things with and for me.
2. She has good natural hunting skills.
3. She loves people, at times to the point of being obnoxious. (I mean this in the most affectionate term.)

She has also completed two junior level titles in field work and we are working on the next levels. This fall we are going duck hunting, the first time for both of us. She also is a Canine Good Citizen, and is ready to test for her Companion Dog title.

Sharon Kyle, 1995

Chapter 4

The Flatcoated Retriever Breed Standard

In this chapter I start by quoting in full, by kind permission of The Kennel Club, the British Breed Standard for the Flatcoated Retriever. This is followed by the American Breed Standard. In conclusion I have attempted to give my own interpretation of these standards

The Kennel Club Breed Standard

General appearance: A bright, active dog of medium size with an intelligent expression, showing power without lumber, and raciness without weediness.

Characteristics: Generously endowed with natural gundog ability, optimism and friendliness demonstrated by enthusiastic tail action.

Temperament: Confident and kindly.

Head and skull: Head, long and nicely moulded. Skull, flat and moderately broad with a slight stop between eyes, in no way accentuated, avoiding a down or dish-faced appearance. Nose of good size, with open nostrils. Jaws long and strong, capable of carrying a hare or pheasant.

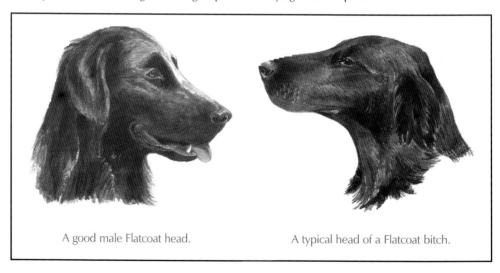

A good male Flatcoat head.   A typical head of a Flatcoat bitch.

Eyes: Medium size, dark brown or hazel, with a very intelligent expression (a round prominent eye highly undesirable). Not obliquely placed.

Ears: Small and well set on, close to side of head.

Mouth: Jaws strong with perfect, regular and complete scissor bite, ie upper teeth closely overlapping lower teeth and set square to the jaws. Teeth sound and strong.

The Flatcoated Retriever Breed Standard

Neck: Head well set in neck, the latter reasonably long and free from throatiness, symmetrically set and obliquely placed in shoulders, running well into the back to allow for easy seeking of trail.

Forequarters: Chest deep and fairly broad, with well defined brisket, on which elbows should move cleanly and evenly. Forelegs straight, with bone of good quality throughout.

Body: Foreribs fairly flat. Body well ribbed up showing a gradual spring and well arched in centre but rather lighter towards quarters. Loin short and square. Open couplings highly undesirable.

Hindquarters: Muscular. Moderate bend of stifle and hock, latter well let down. Should stand true all round. Cowhocks highly undesirable.

Feet: Round and strong with toes close and well arched. Soles thick and strong.

Tail: Short, straight and well set on, gaily carried, but never much above level of back.

Gait/Movement: Free and flowing, straight and true as seen from front and rear.

Coat: Dense, of fine to medium texture and good quality, as flat as possible. Legs and tail well feathered. Full furnishings on maturity complete the elegance of a good dog.

Colour: Black or liver only.

Size: Preferred height: dogs: 58-61cm (23-24in); bitches: 56-59cm (22-23in).
Preferred weight in hard condition: dogs 25-35kg (60-80lb);bitches 25-34kg (55-70lb)

Faults: Any departure from the foregoing points should be considered a fault and the seriousness with which the fault should be regarded should be in exact proportion to its degree.

Note: Male animals should have two apparently normal testicles fully descended into the scrotum.

Well-balanced male head. Note the smooth skull which is well-filled between the eyes, with just a slight stop. Good length of muzzle, a kind eye and a good-sized nose.

The Kennel Club © March 1994

Flatcoated Retrievers

The American Breed Standard

General Appearance. The Flat Coated Retriever is a versatile family companion hunting retriever with a happy and active demeanor, intelligent expression, and clean lines. The Flat Coat has been traditionally described as showing 'power without lumber and raciness without weediness'.

The distinctive and most important features of the Flat Coat are the silhouette (both moving and standing), smooth effortless movement, head type, coat and character. In silhouette the Flat Coat has a long, strong, clean, 'one-piece' head, which is unique to the breed. Free from exaggeration of stop or cheek, the head is set well into a moderately long neck which flows smoothly into well laid back shoulders. A level topline combined with a deep, long rib cage tapering to a moderate tuck-up create the impression of a blunted triangle. The brisket is well developed and the forechest forms a prominent prow. This utilitarian retriever is well balanced, strong, but elegant; never cobby, short legged or rangy. The coat is thick and flat lying, and the legs and tail are well feathered. A proud carriage, responsive attitude, waving tail and overall look of quality, strength, style and symmetry complete the picture of a typical Flat Coat.

Judging the Flat Coat moving freely on a loose lead and standing naturally is more important then judging him posed. Honourable scars should not count against the dog.

Size. Individuals varying more than an inch either way from the preferred height should be considered not practical for the types of work for which the Flat-Coat was developed. Preferred height is 23 to 24½ inches at the withers for dogs, 22 to 23½ inches for bitches. Since the Flat Coat is a working hunting retriever he should be shown in lean hard condition, free of excess weight. **Proportion:** The Flat Coat is not cobby in build. The length of the body from the point of the shoulder to the rearmost projection of the upper thigh is slightly more than the height at the withers. The female may be slightly longer to better accommodate the carrying of puppies. **Substance:** Moderate. Medium bone is flat or oval rather than round; strong but never massive, coarse, weedy or find. This applies throughout the dog.

Head. The long clean, well moulded head is adequate in size and strength to retrieve large pheasant, duck or hare with ease. **Skull and Muzzle:** The impression of the skull and muzzle being cast in one piece is created by the fairly flat skull of moderate breadth and flat, clean cheeks, combined with the long, strong, deep muzzle which is well filled in before, between and beneath the eyes. Viewed from above, the muzzle is nearly equal in length and breadth to the skull. **Stop:** There is a gradual, slight, barely perceptible stop, avoiding a down or dish-faced appearance. Brows are slightly raised and mobile, giving life to the expression. Stop must be evaluated in profile so that it will not be confused with the raised brow. **Occiput:** Not accentuated, the skull forming a gentle curve where it fits well into the neck. **Expression:** Alert, intelligent and kind. **Eyes:** Eyes are set widely apart. Medium sized, almond shaped, dark brown or hazel; not large, round or yellow. Eye rims are self colored and tight. **Ears:** relatively small, well set on, lying close to the side of the head and thickly feathered. Not low set (houndlike or setterish). **Nose:** Large open nostrils. Black on black dogs, brown on liver dogs. **Lips:** Fairly tight, clean and dry to minimize the retention of feathers. **Jaws:** Long and strong, capable of carrying a hare or a pheasant. **Bite:** Scissors bite preferred, level bite acceptable. **Severe Faults:** Wry and undershot or overshot bites with a noticeable gap must be severely penalised.

Neck, Topline, Body. Neck: Strong and slightly arched for retrieving strength. Moderately long to allow for easy seeking of the trail. Free from throatiness. Coat on neck is untrimmed. **Topline:** Strong and level. **Body: Chest** (Brisket) Deep, reaching to the elbow and only moderately broad. **Forechest:** Prow prominent and well developed. **Rib cage:** Deep, showing good length from forechest to back rib (to allow plenty of space for all body organs) and only moderately broad. The foreribs fairly flat showing

Some head faults

Too much stop.

Roman nose.

Domed head, ears set too low.

Ears too large.

Throaty.

Dish face.

a gradual spring, well arched in the centre of the body but rather lighter towards the loin. **Underline:** Deep chest tapering to a moderate tuck-up. **Loin:** Strong, well muscled and long enough to allow for agility, freedom of movement and length of stride, but never weak or loosely coupled. **Croup:** Slopes very slightly; rump moderately broad and well muscled. **Tail:** Fairly straight, well set on, with bone reaching approximately to the hock joint. When the dog is in motion, the tail is carried happily but without curl as a smooth extension of the topline, never much above the level of the back. **Forequarters. Shoulders:** Long, well laid back with **upper arm** of approximately equal length to allow for efficient reach. Musculature wiry rather than bulky. **Elbows:** Clean, close to the body and set well back under the withers. **Forelegs:** Straight and strong with medium bone of good quality. **Pasterns:** Slightly sloping and strong. **Dewclaws:** Removal of dewclaws is optional. **Feet:** Oval or round. Medium sized and tight with well arched toes and thick pads.

Hindquarters. Powerful with angulation in balance with the front assembly. **Upper thighs:** Powerful and well muscled. **Stifle:** Good turn of stifle with sound, strong joint. **Second thighs:** (stifle to hock joint) Second or lower thigh as long as or only slightly longer than upper thigh. **Hock:** Hock joint strong, well let down. **Dewclaws:** There are no hind dewclaws. **Feet:** Oval or round. Medium sized and tight with well arched toes and thick pads.

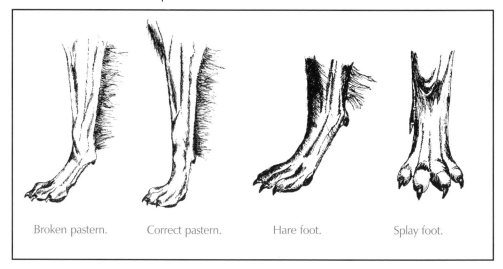

Broken pastern.   Correct pastern.   Hare foot.   Splay foot.

Coat. Coat is of moderate length, density and fullness, with a high lustre. The ideal coat is straight and flat lying. A slight waviness is permissible but the coat is not curly, woolly, short, silky or fluffy. The Flat Coat is a working retriever and the coat must provide protection from all types of weather, water and ground cover. This requires a coat of sufficient texture, length and fullness to allow for adequate insulation. When the dog is in full coat the ears, front, chest, back of forelegs, thighs and underside of tail are thickly feathered without being bushy, silky or stringy. Mane of longer heavier coat on neck extending over the withers and shoulders is considered typical especially in the male and can cause the neck to appear thicker and the withers higher, sometimes causing the appearance of a dip behind the withers. Since the Flat Coat is a hunting dog, the feathering is not excessively long.

Trimming. The Flat Coat is shown with as natural a coat as possible and must not be penalized for lack of trimming as long as the coat is clean and well brushed. Tidying of ears, feet, underline and tip of tail is acceptable. Whiskers serve a specific function and it is preferred that they not be trimmed. Shaving or barbering of the head, neck or body coat must be severely penalized.

Color. Solid black or solid liver. **Disqualification:** Yellow, cream or any color other than black or liver.

Gait. Sound, efficient movement is of critical importance to a hunting retriever. The Flat Coat viewed from the side covers ground efficiently and movement appears balanced, free flowing and well co-ordinated, never choppy, mincing or ponderous. Front and rear legs reach well forward and extend well back achieving long clean strides. Topline appears level, strong and supple while dog is in motion. **Summary.** The Flat Coat is a strong but elegant, cheerful hunting retriever. Quality of structure, balance and harmony of all parts both standing and in motion are essential. As a breed whose purpose is of a utilitarian nature - structure, condition and attitude should give every indication of being suited for hard work.

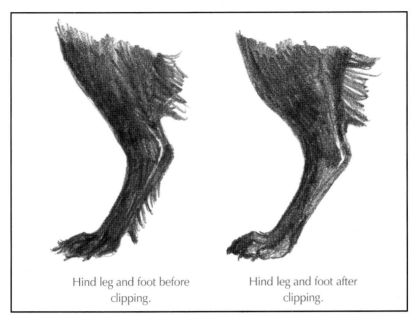

Hind leg and foot before clipping.

Hind leg and foot after clipping.

Temperament. Character is a primary and outstanding asset of the Flat Coat. He is a responsive, loving member of the family, a versatile working dog, multi-talented, sensible, bright and tractable. In competition the Flat Coat demonstrates stability and a desire to please with a confident, happy and outgoing attitude characterised by a wagging tail. Nervous, hyperactive, apathetic, shy or obstinate behaviors are undesirable. **Severe Fault:** Unprovoked aggressive behavior toward people or animals is totally unacceptable.

Character. Character is as important to the evaluation of stock by a potential breeder as any other aspect of the breed standard. The Flat Coat is primarily a family companion hunting retriever. He is keen and birdy flushing within gun range as well as a determined, resourceful retriever on land and water. He has a great desire to hunt with self-reliance and an uncanny ability to adapt to changing circumstances on a variety of upland game and waterfowl.

As a family companion he is sensible, alert and highly intelligent; a lighthearted, affectionate and adaptable friend. He retains these qualities as well as his youthfully good-humoured outlook on life into old age. The adult Flat Coat is usually an adequate alarm dog to give warning, but is a good-natured, optimistic dog; basically inclined to be friendly to all.

The Flat Coat is a cheerful, devoted companion who requires and appreciates living with and interacting as a member of his family. To reach full potential in any endeavor he absolutely must have a strong personal bond and affectionate individual attention.

DISQUALIFICATION. Yellow, cream or any color other than black or liver.

© **Flat Coated Retriever Society of America, 1995**

Explanation of the Breed Standards

I shall now give my own evaluation of the Flatcoated Retriever's Breed Standards. I shall try to explain it as it has been explained to me by the senior members of our breed over the years. Yes, this is a personal interpretation. However, I hope it brings the dog to life and helps you understand a little better why and how our dogs relate to the Breed Standard.

For historical interest, I have included in Appendix C the full text of Stanley O'Neal's article *Type in Flatcoats*, written in 1955. This gives some indications of how the Breed Standard of today evolved.

General Appearance: The Flatcoated Retriever is a versatile family companion, with a happy and active character, who was developed as a working retriever. His expression is kind and intelligent. All body lines are clean and he has substance and strength combined with elegance and refinement. The words 'power without lumber and raciness without weediness' paint a true picture of this unique Retriever.

If you study all other Retriever breeds, none fits the structural pattern of the Flatcoat. One very similar dog is the Curly Coated Retriever, whose body construction is similar although the long bones in the leg are much longer. It is totally different in head construction, however. This is why it is so important that **no** tendency towards another Retriever breed is permitted. The American Breed Standard on General Appearance and Size, Proportion and Substance says it all!

A well-developed puppy dog head of the correct type.

Head: Must be correct in its proportion. Look for a long, clean, well moulded head of good size with strength and balance, which is adequate in size and strength. Remember that the Flatcoat has a specific task to do: that of retrieving pheasant, duck, rabbit or hare with ease. The strength, depth and breadth of the muzzle are very important therefore.

The muzzle has another important function; it holds the nasal bones, and the surfaces and mucous membrane that line them contain the nerve endings which register scent. The end of the muzzle should have depth as well as breadth for this reason. The nose has large open nostrils which are black on black dogs, brown on liver dogs.

The Flatcoat should have reasonably tight lips. Too much flesh here will prevent the clean pickup of game, and feathers will have a tendency to be retained, to the dog's discomfort. Also, when there is a tendency to flews, there is a tendency to loose eyes (with possible Ectropia) and throatiness, which often gives a setter type look to the dog. These tendencies also go with a coarse or Borzoi type skull.

Ideally the impression should be of skull and muzzle being cast in one piece, an impression created by the combination of a fairly flat skull of moderate breadth and flat, clean cheeks, together with long, strong, deep muzzle well filled in before, between and beneath the eyes. As we have said before the muzzle is nearly equal in length and breadth to the skull with a gradual, barely perceptible stop, avoiding a down or dish-faced appearance. Brows are slightly raised and mobile, giving life to the expression. The stop must be looked at in profile so that it will not be confused with the raised brow.

At the back of the head, the occiput is not accentuated, the skull forming a gentle curve where it fits well into the neck. Any excessive width or roundness of skull, depth of stop, snipiness or narrowness of muzzle destroy the unique moulding of a Flatcoat's head. Without a true breed head you only have a 'black dog'. In Dr Nancy Laughton's *The Review of the Flat-coated Retriever* she includes 'Smyth's' explanation: that the width of the skull is largely determined by the conformation of the bones known as the 'Zygomatic Arch', which varies greatly in different breeds:

> The ring made by the two zygomata varies quite a lot, even within the long headed group of dogs, not only in its outward curvature, but in its depth and arch. The width of the skull and the fullness of the cheeks depend upon its overall conformation. The shape of this bone obviously figures a good deal in the characteristic moulding of the Flatcoat head. The cheeks or `flews' have no outward curvature. This is in contrast to those of the Labrador and Golden Retriever which have more pronounced cheeks.

Eyes: Eyes are set widely apart, medium sized, almond shaped, dark brown or hazel; not large, round or yellow. An over-black eye does detract from the kind expression. Livers often have lighter eyes than blacks. Eye rims are self coloured and tight, neither tight enough to encourage entropion nor loose enough to encourage ectropion. (Both these conditions are multi-genetic, caused by the shape of the bones of the head, the depth of the eye socket, and the tension or laxity of muscles around the face, head and eye.) The eyes are almost horizontally placed, not oblique as in a collie. They are set more laterally than in the other retriever breeds, giving a wider but flatter field of vision. They are oval in shape and should be neither sunk into the orbit nor prominent. A round prominent eye in a Flatcoat is totally foreign to the breed.

LIvers sometimes have a lighter eye colour than the average black.

Flatcoated Retrievers

Ears: Relatively small, well set on, lying close to the side of the head and thickly feathered, not low set (hound-like or setterish). They are 11-14cm (4½-5½in) in length. They have to be in proportion with the whole: ears that are too small and high-set detract from the overall picture. A straight-headed Flatcoat will appear to have a higher ear set than those showing a stop and head some elevation in the skull. Whatever the ear set, the ear canal will be in the same position. A pricked-up ear in a Flatcoat also detracts from the outline of the head. It is important that the ears blend well into the neck. In essence a Flatcoat's ears must not be intrusive to the eye.

Bite: A scissors bite is preferred, although a level bite is acceptable. However a level bite should be a cause for concern in a young Flatcoat, as there is a great possibility of this becoming undershot. Many young dogs have a tendency to be overshot as puppies, but this often corrects itself as the puppy grows. There is a tendency towards movement of the jaw in young Flatcoats as the length of head often matures slowly. A puppy with a narrow underjaw is best removed from your breeding programme. Broken teeth should not count against the dog, but the size of the teeth are of concern. Although we do not count teeth in Great Britain, it is important that the incisors and premolars are all present .

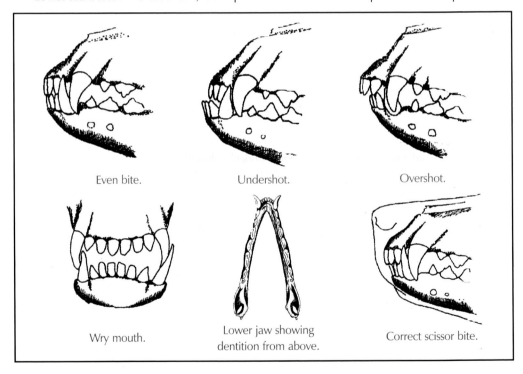

Even bite.

Undershot.

Overshot.

Wry mouth.

Lower jaw showing dentition from above.

Correct scissor bite.

Neck, Topline and Body: The head is well set into the neck. The neck is strong and slightly arched for retrieving strength. It should be moderately long to allow for easy seeking of the trial and free from throatiness. The coat on the neck is left untrimmed, only tidied.

   The conformation of the spine as a whole and the size of its vertebrae are important in determining the size and balance of the overall dog from head to tail. An overlong neck in a Flatcoat is incorrect, as it relates to weakness overall, but a short neck is just as undesirable. To some extent it is the balance and make-up of the forequarters that determine the visual length of neck. The neck must carry the head well and there must be a good angle and slope and balance into the shoulders.

The neck of a typical Flatcoat arches slightly upwards of the neck just beyond the occiput, forming a crest, and in a well-coated animal, especially a male, the hair is long and mane-like. Great care must be taken when judging not to let this influence you into thinking that the dog is overloaded on the shoulders. This is where your hands will tell you the answer.

The neck front and forequarters must be taken as a one unit. As I have said before each relates to one another. The line from the lower jaw should be free of excess throatiness. It is connected to the overall shape of the head: when there is a coarse, down-faced or convex skull (Borzoi shape) the cheeks are affected and seem to fall away without filling. Such dogs are predisposed to loose flews and throatiness.

Brisket: Below the front of the chest the bones and cartilage stand out in a prow to form the brisket Stanley O'Neill wrote on the subject of the brisket or prow in *The Flatcoated Retriever Society Yearbook*:

> This term in Flatcoats is understood to mean the effect of a breast bone jutting prominently forward beyond the junction of the shoulder and upper arm. Of itself it would just seem to be a breed characteristic inherited from the element of which the breed was built and without any practical significance.

Here I would beg to differ, and he might now agree with me. Over the last 20 years we have seen the disappearance of this feature to a large degree in Flatcoats, to the detriment of our breed. In my opinion it is strongly connected with the formation of a correct forequarter.

Dogs today often lack a brisket that one can feel because of the decline of a correct shoulder and upper arm, mainly in length of upper arm, but also in the lack of angulation. Not having measured the length of upper arm in the dogs of the 1960s and 1970s, I cannot be certain on this point. In dogs of equal size an extra half inch length of upper arm does improve its appearance, but the strongest adverse effect is produced by poor angulation of the point of the shoulder.

The Standard says that the elbow should work cleanly and evenly on the brisket. Prominent brisket is associated with a long, well laid back upper arm, which in turn is needed for clean and easy movement of the elbow.

One must always remember the importance of the quality of the muscle sheets which anchor the whole forequarters to the chest wall.

Faults in the construction of the forequarters lead to bad movement, but more important is the wasted energy used in bad movement and the stress put on joints from feet to elbow and shoulder joint. Undue stress put here predisposes the dog to OCD and arthritis in later life. A dog with incorrect forequarters will not be able to work long hours without stress and tiredness. Jumping will not be as clean and there will be stress to joints, tendons and ligaments on landing. A straight upper arm will give the dog less freedom of stride, causing a short, pattering, terrier-like movement, while a well angulated shoulder with a short upper arm gives the exaggerated thrust of a hackney action.

A correct shoulder still has to be assessed. Sometimes the chest is too narrow and lacking in depth, causing the elbows to turn in and the feet to turn out; the opposite will happen when the rib cage is wide and too well sprung, giving an exaggerated picture of width and inhibiting the free flow of the forequarters when the dog is moving.

As I have said before, quality of muscle sheets and tendons also plays an important part. When there is a lack of depth of the ribcage together with looseness, the dog is predisposed to be out at elbow, as can be seen as he comes towards you. Relate this to yourself by rounding your own shoulders: the dog's feet will pin inwards to a large degree.

It has been a long-standing concern of mine that many people do not understand the mechanics of front movement. There are so many gundogs with a short upper arm who move in a terrier fashion. Many people mistakenly take the wording 'forelegs straight' to indicate this terrier type movement.

Flatcoated Retrievers

A dog with a correct forequarter will move forward with total ease, using the minimum of energy. It is a smooth action, but remember: the faster the movement, the more the feet will come into a middle line, especially on a slippery surface. Because of the make-up of a correct forequarters in a Flatcoat there will always be a slight turning of the pad into the central line. As long as there is no weakness at the elbow or pastern, this has always been acceptable within the breed, especially on the lead leg in a working dog. This view was discussed in detail in a Breed Forum in *Dog World* in the 1970s and confirmed by the expert panel of Flatcoat breed specialists of the time.

We are looking for a good neck, pronounced brisket and a shoulder and upper arm that are both well laid back. The shoulder blade (Scapula) slopes upwards and backwards from the point of the shoulder to the withers. The upper arm slopes backwards and slightly downwards from the point of the shoulder (B) to the withers (A). The upper arm slopes backwards and slightly downwards from the point of the shoulder (B) to the point of the elbow (C). The angle of these lines should be about 80 degrees.

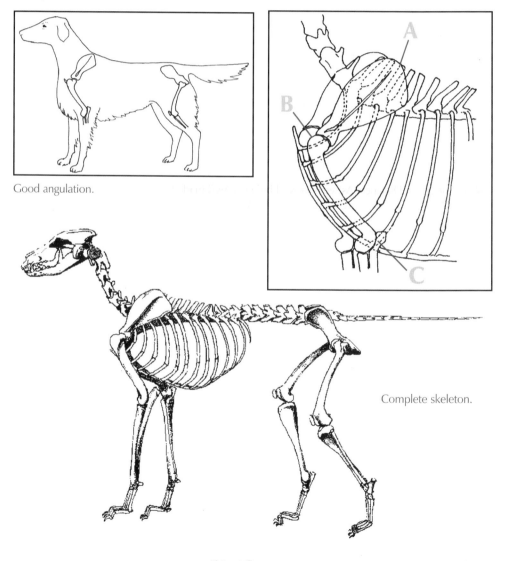

Good angulation.

Complete skeleton.

This position puts the elbows well under the body, particularly if the upper arm (Humerus) is long. This structure produces a good front action with a minimum of concussion on the spine through the front legs and easy movement of the elbows. The elbows should look directly backwards.

The best way to understand all these points is to run your fingers over your dogs every time you are grooming them, telling yourself what you can feel. The more you use your fingers in this way the easier it will become to recognise each part and the difference in these parts in each of your dogs. Write it down, then find a diagram of the skeleton of a dog and compare your notes. Do not be afraid to ask. We all are learning each day, but it takes time to understand what we have learnt.

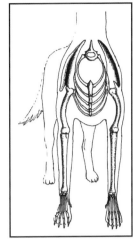
Front skeleton.

Front Legs: These should be uniformly well boned, straight down to a strong, well developed pastern, with a slight slope down into medium sized feet with well arched toes and thick pads. The quality of bone of the legs is flat rather than round, the width being seen rather from the side than in front. Because of its active work the Flatcoat needs good shock absorbers on rough ground or where a sudden change of direction is needed. Poor quality feet on a quality specimen detracts strongly in this working breed - thin loose pads that splay are vulnerable to damage and do not stand up to hard work, especially on wet plough-land or bogs. A dog in good condition and well exercised (including road work) will stand well up on his feet. Illness and lack of correct exercise have a detrimental effect on a dog's feet and pasterns.

Body: The body of a Flatcoat is unique among the Retrievers because of shape, depth and balance. As we have said before, a well made brisket goes with a depth of chest, which provides plenty of heart room. There is flatness where the forequarters lie against the ribcage. Just after the elbows the ribs show a 'gradual spring', being well arched in the centre of the body but lighter towards the loin.

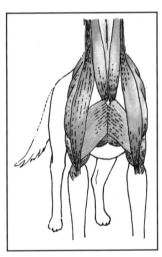
Front musculature.

Rib Cage: The rib cage is fairly wide but not as wide as a Labrador's, the emphasis being on length and depth. This, together with quality muscled shoulders, gives the Flatcoat his racy appearance. The correct spring of rib as you run your hands over the rib cage from the elbow will take you upwards and backwards.

The word 'Weediness' is used to describe one type of undesirable rib structure, indicating a narrow, 'slab-sided' chest, lacking in brisket and depth and giving the impression that the forelegs come out of one hole. Such a dog will lack stamina. 'Lumber' is the opposite, where the dog is heavy in depth and width of body. If the foreribs are sprung, the shoulder is coarse and often steep or short. The clean elbow is thrown out of line and the body looks as if it is slung between the legs instead of being poised well over them. Such an animal will often have heavy bone and a coarse head.

Back and Topline: These extend from the withers where the point of the shoulder blades come towards each other to the last lumbar vertebra, and the tail continues. All through the back there should be strong, well-defined muscles. The topline will reflect the quality of the structure and muscles beneath it.

Between the point where the last rib is attached to the spine and the last lumbar vertebra is the area called the loin. The continuation of the spine with loin and flank is the 'coupling'. This must be strong, well muscled and at least as long as it is wide, allowing for freedom of movement and length of stride. Long, weak 'open coupling' means structural weakness and must be detrimental to the breed. Too short a coupling will also be detrimental, as the dog will lose freedom of movement and its body will be short. One of the worse faults gradually creeping into the breed arises from the mistaken belief that a Flatcoat should be short in the body as a whole and have short coupling. The words 'cobby' and 'compact' are totally wrong when applied to the Flatcoat and totally against the Breed Standard.

Croup: This is the part of the spine between the last lumbar vertebra and the tail bone, occupied by the sacrum, and the expanded bone that forms the roof of the pelvis. It must be well muscled, sloping downwards towards the tail. This varies to a degree in individual dogs. The steeper the angle, the lower the tail set. A low tail set destroys the lines of a dog; more importantly it hinders hind action by bringing about lack of propulsion from the limbs. A high set tail often goes with steep angle of the hind quarters.

Tail: This should flow from the croup. It should be straight and well set on, not too long, gaily carried but not much above the level of the back. Either a high-set or a low-set tail detracts from the overall balance of a dog. A Flatcoat tail must not be over-blessed with heavy feathering like a Golden Retriever's, or thin and 'flaggy' like a setter's. Working dogs shown during the shooting season must be forgiven for sporting a tail rather lacking in feathering.

The tail should be well used by the dog as this shows its character, indicating good temperament and good working style. As far as I am concerned, to see Flatcoats standing in a show ring or posed with tail hanging down is a sad picture. In my mind it relegates them to the status of any old black dog - breed unknown! A Flatcoat exhibits its happy, smiling personality so loved by us all from the tip of its nose to the end of an ever-wagging tail; often the last thing to stop as he passes away is the wagging tip of his tail.

Hindquarters: Powerful, with angulation in balance with the correct front assembly. They must be well muscled, with a moderate bend of stifle and hock. It is important that there is an optimum angulation of the hind legs to the pelvis and spine as this is the source of the power and execution with which the dog pushes its way through cover over rough ground and jumps and swims. This where the hind legs join onto the body.

Most of us have seen a hip X-ray where the pelvic girdle (acetabulum) and the head of the femur join, and have some idea of the importance of the tendons, ligaments and muscles in our own legs. We may possibly recognise the shape of the thigh bone with its shaft which ends in knee joint (stifle), which is a combination of the end of the femur - the patella (knee bone) - and the head of the tibia. This with the fibula join the metatarsal to form the point of the hock, through the rear pastern to the hind foot.

The great importance of all tendons, ligaments and muscles being well balanced can be easily understood. It is like belts and pulley wheels. If one is distorted, the whole system goes out of balance. The patella needs the correct balance and pressure to develop and work properly.

The second thigh (tibia and fibula) in a Flatcoat should be long and strong. The hock is a strong joint, well let down. When viewed from behind the hock joint and feet should turn neither in nor out. Cow Hocks (hocks turning out) and Sickle Hocks (hocks turning in) are very detrimental to the movement of a gundog.

A Flatcoat with good structure stands naturally with his weight evenly distributed at the four corners of his body.

Coat: The coat is of fine to medium texture, of good quality and as flat as possible, though a slight wave is permissible. A coat with broken areas (turns up the wrong way) is not good. Since the Flatcoat is a working retriever its coat must provide protection from all types of weather, keeping the dog warm in wet weather or when swimming and protecting it from brambles, thistles, heather and sharp objects.

The Flatcoated Retriever Breed Standard

A coat of sufficient texture, length and fullness to do this job of work is needed. The natural lanolin-like water repellent secreted from the skin gives a lustre to a coat in good condition. Protection is also given by the feathering on the back of the legs and the underside of the body and tail.

When a dog or bitch is mature and in full coat, the ears, front, chest, back of the forelegs, thighs and underside of the tail are thickly feathered, without the whole coat or feathering being silky, stringy, curly, woolly or fluffy. A mane of longer, heavier coat on the neck, extending over withers and shoulders, is characteristic of the breed and may affect the appearance of the topline and forequarters. It is important to remember that the Flatcoated Retriever is a dual-purpose dog, and that feathering which is excessive in length is incorrect. It is very unpleasant for a dog with this type of coat to work in comfort in cover, without his coat getting full of twigs, brambles, burrs and other 'foreign bodies'. In addition, a long coat is often fine and silky in texture, so the dog stays wet and absorbs more water into its coat, which on a cold winter's day can be detrimental to its health. This consideration should be taken into account when judging this dual-purpose breed: the correct quality coat, often with less length of feathering, is more typical of the breed than a long, flowing, glamorous coat.

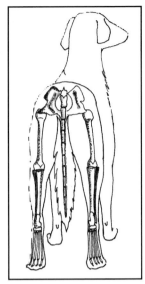

Rear view skeleton showing correct bone formation.

Although there is no mention of an undercoat in the Breed Standard, the Flatcoat does have one, although you can see its white skin when you open up a coat, even in a dog in full coat. The exposed skin is pigmented. The outer guard coat, made up of a stronger, longer hair has a definite stronger shaft and a positive colour; the softer, finer undercoat, with a weaker shaft of a less positive colour, is the coat that comes out first in a moult and blows around like a Will o' the Wisp. When it gets on your clothes it will roll off, very much like cat hair. This is not found on the head or the front of the legs, but on the rest of the body, helping to protect the vital organs from injury and the cold, especially during swimming.

Colour: Black or Liver are the only colours accepted in the breed standard. Disqualification includes yellow, cream or any colour other than black or liver.

There is no better sight than a dog or bitch in full bloom, fully furnished with a jet black or rich liver coat on a Flatcoat of good conformation.

There are many deviations within the blacks and livers, for whatever reason. I am not certain in my own mind that the poor blacks come from mating black to liver. In other breeds (for example, Cocker Spaniels) red to black produces quality blacks. In Poodles I am led to believe that mating a dark-eyed black to a chocolate produces the best blacks. However in Labradors the inclusion or introduction of the liver gene into black/yellows is considered to have had a detrimental affect. I have noticed that a true black/black breeding has a tendency to fade in some into a dull black. However, I do not claim to be an expert on this subject.

There is the possibility of yellow in some lines; some have continued with a hidden yellow gene through the century. Also, it must be remembered that it might have been present in unregistered stock used after the Second World War. Since black is dominant over all other colours the yellow gene can be dormant in the genetic make-up of a Flatcoat until it is bred to another Flatcoat carrying the same yellow gene; they will then have yellow puppies among their black or liver puppies.

The Flatcoated Retriever Society's advice is not to register these puppies at The Kennel Club, or at least to register them 'Progeny Not for Breeding '. Then the temptation to bring these yellows into the breeding pool will not be there. A Yellow Flatcoat is very like a working type Golden Retriever. The possibility of the problems of hip dysplasia, cataracts, PRA and epilepsy being transferred into our breed this way would be disastrous. I am also certain that the Golden Retriever breeders would object strongly to impurities of this type coming into their breed. The last thing either Golden Retriever or Flatcoat breeders desire is for their dogs to lose their individual identity and be known as 'Retrievers, Black, Golden or Liver'.

The problem of a dog or bitch that has produced yellows has to be tackled by you individually. If it is an ordinary family dog then my advice would be not to breed from it again. However, in the case of an outstanding dog or bitch in the field trial or show world you must weigh that individual's important qualities and good points against the possibility producing yellow puppies.

Always be open and honest about such things. Try not to mate her or him to a known producer next time. Remember that a percentage of this litter will produce yellow genes. It is something that will not go away, so must be considered as a minus when balancing up the good and bad quality of one's stock.

Trimming: The Flatcoat is shown with as natural a coat as possible and must not be penalised for lack of trimming, as long as the coat is clean and well brushed. Tidying of ears, feet, underline and tip of tail is acceptable. Whiskers serve a specific function and it is preferred that they not be trimmed. Shaving or barbering of the head, neck and body coat must be severely penalised because when this is done the dog takes on the look of a different breed. The total character and outline of a true Flatcoated Retriever is destroyed.

Movement: The Breed Standard says that sound, efficient movement is of critical importance to a working retriever. The Flatcoat viewed from the side covers the ground efficiently, and movement appears balanced, free flowing and well coordinated, never choppy, mincing or ponderous. Front and rear legs reach well forward and extend well back, achieving long clean strides. Topline appears level, strong and supple while the dog is in motion. Viewed from front or rear the legs should turn neither in nor out nor should the feet cross or interfere with one another.

This is a subject that takes a book on its own. The best book I have ever read on movement and construction is Dogsteps: Illustrated Gait at a Glance by Rachael Page Elliot, published by Howell Book House. It is a must for anyone who breeds, shows or judges dogs. This quotation is taken from Mrs Page Elliott's book:

> Good angulation facilitates a long stride - balance facilitates good foot timing - joints that control movement should flex easily and smoothly, providing strong thrust from the rear limbs and spring and resilience in the forehand to absorb constant impact with the ground - the swing and reach of the forelegs should coordinate with the action of the rear so that there will be no over-stepping or interfering. As a general rule, the feet should move rather close to the ground so as to avoid excessive bending of the joints which can be inefficient and tiring.

Poor angulation shortens the stride because bones meeting at the shoulder joint and the hip are set steeply and form joints with wide open angles. This limits the swing of the upper arm and the thigh bone, restricting reach of the forelegs and drive from the rear. Dogs so constructed must take shorter steps - and more of them - to get where they are going, and their action is bouncing rather than smooth.

There is a great deal of body weight, and much of the propulsion comes from the forehand, but when your retriever is working and hunting with his nose down, then retrieving, the power has to come from behind. This is where the well-made hindquarters take over.

When the Flatcoat does not move well in the show ring it is for the judge to decide whether this is because the dog is badly made, reasonably well made but not well muscled, or has just never been taught to move correctly in the show ring. Unfortunately it is more often than not the conformation that is at fault.

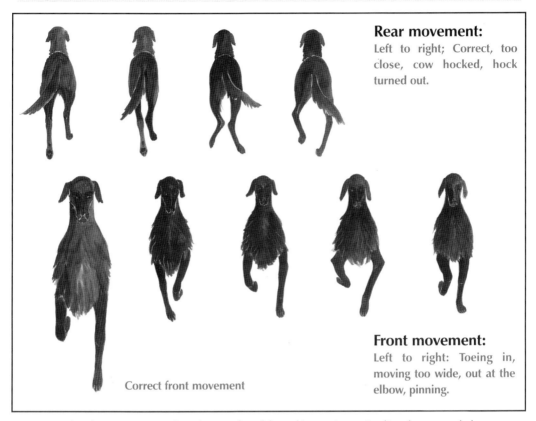

Rear movement:
Left to right; Correct, too close, cow hocked, hock turned out.

Front movement:
Left to right: Toeing in, moving too wide, out at the elbow, pinning.

Correct front movement

The Flatcoat is a strong but elegant, cheerful, working retriever. Quality of structure, balance and harmony of all parts, both standing and in motion, is essential. As a breed whose purpose is utilitarian, structure and condition should give every indication of being suited for hard work.

Temperament: Temperament is of the greatest importance. However well made a dog is as a Flatcoat, however sound, however well he works in the field, however many awards he has gained, if his temperament is not kindly and willing to please, he must not be considered a true Flatcoat. His character is a primary and outstanding asset.

Character: Character is as important to the evaluation of stock by a potential breeder as any other aspect of the breed standard. The optimum character of a Flatcoat is summed up extremely well in the American Breed Standard. From this, it can be seen that any judge who gives an award to a Flatcoat who shows aggression, total lack of confidence or over-excitability, or anyone who breeds from such a dog, is doing the breed a great disservice. Such a person is unable to understand or evaluate the unique personality that makes up a true Flatcoat.

Despite his desire to please, the Flatcoat is a confident dog in the field, with a strong opinion of his own ability and the lack of yours. Above all, as the American Breed Standard states, to reach his full potential in any field of activity the Flatcoat requires a strong personal relationship and individual attention from his owner. If you are not able to form such a relationship I would advise you not to have a Flatcoat.

Faults: The Kennel Club Breed Standard states that male animals should have two apparently normal testicles fully descended into the scrotum. In the British show ring the judge is advised that a male may be shown without testicles if there is a good veterinary reason why they have been removed.

Side Movement

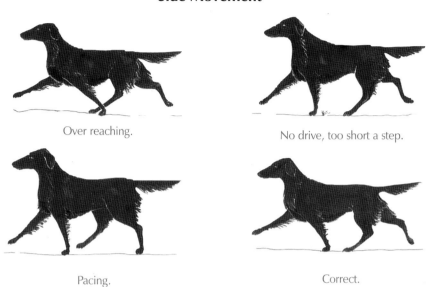

Over reaching.

No drive, too short a step.

Pacing.

Correct.

Terms used to describe the dog's outer appearance

Stop
Forehead
Foreface
Occiput
Muzzle
Neck
Flews
Withers
Back
Loin
Croup
Point of
shoulder
Shoulder
Rib cage
(Thorax)
Upper
thigh
Buttock
Breast bone
Abdomen
Upper
arm
Sternum
Stifle
Second
thigh
Point of Hock
Forearm
Hock
joint
Rear Pastern
Front Pastern
(Carpal Joint)
Paw

Forequarters   Central Body   Hindquarters

Judging

Hopefully you have been showing good Flatcoats as owner and/or breeder, you have attended breed seminars, you have stewarded, and you have a good standing within the breed. If you are invited to judge and in your heart of hearts you know it is not for you, be honest and just decline. Do what you do best; breed wonderful dogs and do other things within the breed at which you excel.

In my opinion, judges are born, not made. Yes, you can learn, and be the best at an examination, but you will still never be a judge of any note. It is the eye, perhaps what one calls the stockman's eye, that tells you at a glance why this dog is better than the next, and why that dog cannot move. A good judge's fingers talk to him the same as a surgeon's. But you must be able to see the overall dog and judge that dog as a whole; fault judging is the lowest form of judging.

If you are a breed specialist, teach yourself to look at your breed in relation to other breeds. Once you understand the mechanics and breed type of other breeds you will improve your understanding of your own. Above all, remember you are there to interpret The Kennel Club Breed Standard as written down by the originators of our breed, not according to your own personal likes and dislikes.

I have included my own notes from my Judging Workshop. I do hope they are of help:

The mechanics of judging Flatcoats (or any other breed)

After a period of time in Flatcoats, often starting with a pet, we graduate to buying or breeding our first show dog. As time goes on we learn and progress, until we feel confident enough to consider judging. Please do not be in too much hurry to start; it is a very great responsibility and should not be taken lightly. Before you start, do your homework:

* Send for The Kennel Club Gundog Breed Standards, also your breed society's Extended Standard if there is one. Read them well - get to know the construction and feel of your own dogs. Be critical of them. Close your eyes and tell yourself what you feel. Do not be like a lady in another breed on the second time of judging who asked a senior breed specialist: 'I see people put their hands down over the neck and stop. What are they looking for?'
* Ask questions of senior breeders.
* Take time and watch all the days' judging at shows; do not go home after your class.
* If you go to ringcraft classes, use your eyes to assess the dogs there, whatever the breed. If you are confident enough, ask to help. Use the time well, telling yourself what you feel and see.
* Be a ring steward for your breed regularly at open shows, and for other gundog breeds.
* Go to breed 'teach-ins'.
* Show an interest in judging matches and exemption shows. These are the best introduction you can have, especially now that limit and sanction show are becoming things of the past.

Then the day dawns when your first judging appointment comes through the letterbox. From then on keep a special book containing all your appointments. Keep all letters, schedules, catalogues and judges' books (making sure the absentees are marked up for every class). All records must be kept with great care; The Kennel Club is very strict on this matter.

As the invitations start to increase, reply to all of them, whether you are accepting or declining, within 14 days. Read them well, noting the exclusion clauses, particularly those relating to distance, or time scale. Many invitations are in an honourary capacity. If petrol costs are to be covered, write down the amount agreed.

If your answer is 'Yes', the Secretary will send you a confirmation of your judging engagement. This is now a contract and should not be broken except in unusual circumstances; for instance, your own illness, illness or death within your family, or a contagious disease within your kennel. Should such an event occur a letter will have to be written to the Secretary, who in turn will have to send it to The Kennel Club.

Never overbook in the same area. Give yourself a good space between engagements, especially at first. The Kennel Club likes well-spaced appointments covering the whole country. Get an up-to-date *Kennel Club Show Guide and Rules*. The *Kennel Club Year Book* is an excellent publication to have.

Hopefully you will have a schedule and instructions from the Secretary a week or so before your judging engagement. Check on the map how to get to the venue .

The day of judging arrives

You will have read and studied the Breed Standard. Go over your own dogs in relation to the Breed Standard for practice. Remember that, as well as judging, you will be judged! Remember also that when you judge at Championship level your judging will influence the breed for the future. You have a great responsibility; please do not take it lightly.

Dress neatly, smartly and comfortably. Comfortable shoes are a 'must'.

Arrive in good time. Go and find the Secretary and say that you have arrived. It is a good idea while you are having coffee to check your judging book. After coffee make sure you are comfortable.

Meet your Ring Steward, and discuss your ring, the placement of the dogs and where your 'new' dogs and 'old' are going to be placed.

Go round your ring and find out the problems: nails, glass, pot holes - I have found them all!

Start judging on time if possible. Find out whether another breed will follow you in your ring. Pace yourself. It is often a good idea with a large entry to discuss the timing of your classes with your stewards. We all know that there is nothing worse than a judge who is slow with the dog entry and rushes through the bitch entry.

Remember to check and sign your judge's book, making sure between classes that all absentees are noted.

Remember: you are in charge of your ring. Show kindly authority. 'Please' and 'Thank you' do not cost anything.

Do not call exhibitors you know by their names - in my opinion it lowers your credibility as judge. Mrs Sutton always impressed me with her 'Sir' and 'Madam'.

Remember to give every exhibitor a chance, and be courteous. They have all paid their entry fee.

Once you have judged all the dogs in the class, pick out at least the number for which you have prize cards, plus two more if possible. Do not fall into the trap in a large class of picking the first five from the beginning of the class and then panicking because you have too many dogs.

Pick every dog you wish to view again. In a large class I like to check the dogs I have finished with before they go out of the ring to make sure that I have not overlooked one.

Send the remaining dogs around the ring. It gives them time to settle, and you time to think; you see all the dogs that you want to consider for awards together, and you can compare them on the move.

Remember that, as well as type, quality and soundness, the character of a Flatcoat has to be there for all to see. The dog must exude the typical breed character; it must be calm but friendly, showing all the time with a wagging tail, willing to respond and show for its handler. Any Flatcoat that refuses to respond to its handler and is sullen in the ring shows a lack of true temperament; after all, it is a representative of a working gundog breed.

This is a show. Once you have established true breed type in all respects, showmanship must play a part. However good he might be, never put a dog who is not standing right, or not responding to his owner, over a dog who is equally good according to the Breed Standard but not quite the type you like. Remember: you are judging according to the national Breed Standard of the country in which you are judging, not according to your own preferences.

Be certain in your own mind before you pick out and place your final line up. It is better to warn exhibitors that this is not your final placing. When you have your line up do not start playing around with it. If you can see a mistake, put it right, then cut, and indicate that this is your final line-up: First to Fifth from Left to Right. Exhibitors will forgive your mistakes, but not your indecisions.

The decision to withhold Prize Cards or CCs is yours alone, but you must be very clear in your mind what and why you have done so. Also remember that if you excuse a dog from the ring in Great Briton for whatever reason you must give a written report to the Show Secretary. If you are uncertain about an unusual procedure or incident in your ring do ask your Steward to get the Show Manager there and then for advice.

The Kennel Club Challenge Certificate, Reserve Challenge Certificate and Best of Breed Certificate must be signed by you, the Judge, before you hand it to the exhibitor. Then, once the exhibitor has done the lap of honour with his or her dog, the first thing to be done is to add the dog's official Kennel Club name and the owner's name. Never let this certificate go out of the ring without this being done.

As I have said before, be in charge of your ring; do not let exhibitors or stewards get the better of you. Some will try. Quiet confidence and a happy atmosphere are essential in a breed ring. As you know, there are judges you enjoy showing under even when you do not do particularly well. Watch and analyse what is 'special' about these judges. As far as the other judges are concerned, note and learn by their mistakes.

If it is going to be a long day have plenty of glucose drinks with you. I find it better not to break; it destroys one's flow and concentration. But do make sure your stewards have the chance to do so. When it comes to awards, be precise and put some atmosphere into the event.

Be honest: judge the dogs on the day, not the handlers. After it is all over, thank your Stewards and the Secretary. Enjoy the social side, but do not go overboard.

Write your report for the dog papers. Remember how disappointed you are when your Fido won a CC and the Judge did not bother to write a report.

Be discreet: enjoy your judging.

Exclyst Bristol Cream of Ravenhall March 1995
Photo-Sue Keanton.

Chapter 5

Starting out with the Flatcoated Retriever

Buying a puppy of any breed is a very big commitment. Hopefully, your Flatcoated Retriever will be part of your family for the next decade or more. The ground work you do before you buy any breed pays in the long run, so when you have looked around and decided that you would like a gundog, and then for whatever reason you have narrowed this down to a Flatcoated Retriever, there are still questions to ask. Are you sure this is the breed for you? How do you find out?

All breeds have Breed Clubs, so write to The Kennel Club (see **Useful Addresses**) and ask for the Breed Club Secretary's address, or contact the Flatcoated Retriever Society Secretary (see **Useful Addresses**). We as a breed take great care to ensure that our puppies go to suitable homes, so you will be asked a lot of questions to establish whether your circumstances are suitable for you to have a Flatcoated Retriever. The Secretary will also be able to sell you the very useful *The Flatcoated Retriever Society Information Booklet* (current price £1.35). You and your family can then read about Flatcoated Retrievers and consider the breed at your leisure.

This must be a family decision, especially if this is your first dog. Remember, if any dog becomes a part of your family your house will never be the same again. If your wife is house proud, will she really cope with the extra muddy footprints, the hair loss twice a year, the scratched paint? If your husband is a keen gardener, does he really want Flatcoat 'help' with the weeding? It really is like taking on another child, but this one has **four** muddy feet! Your children will have to learn to be tidy, too; puppies do love to chew up little Tommy's best shoes and little Kate's favourite toy. Flatcoats and children will get on well, but little people can get hurt by the strong, ever-wagging tail, and puppies are particularly fascinated by little girls' lovely long hair as it swings tantalisingly just within their reach. Also, Flatcoats **do** lick. Can you cope with all this?

The children, too, will have to be trained. They must be made to understand that their new Flatcoat is a living creature, not an inanimate plaything. It must have its own bed and must be allowed to rest in it for long periods during the first few months. Until it is well-grown, it must not be allowed to play games of ball from one child to the other.

Flatcoats are very tactile dogs: they love touching you, licking and pawing you, rooting your arm and taking any member of the family for a walk by their sleeve. They love to be talked to and to be with you. To them there is no greater pleasure than to be with you all the time, around the house, in the garden or out in the car. They do not do well as kennel dogs; they tolerate kennels for short periods, but need to spend a large part of their lives with you. They are a medium to large sized dog, so will need good daily walks, even when it is raining.

Your prized flower garden will not fare well from the offices of a little puppy. Brightly coloured flowers have a fascination for puppies. Then there are the dogs' ablutions; these have to be cleared up at least twice a day, and puddles do burn your grass!

All this and more must be taken into account before you decide to go any further. On the financial side, the dog itself, dog food, vet's bills, insurance, dog equipment and the replacement of chewed articles all mount up and are very expensive. But in my opinion Flatcoats are very special dogs who are strongly addictive: once you are owned by a Flatcoat it is very difficult to give up this Peter Pan of the dog world. Many of us are living proof of this.

Starting out with the Flatcoated Retriever

When you and your family have read the booklet, if you are **all** still interested, the next thing is to meet a 'Flatcoat family'. In the booklet you should have a list of *Contact Names*. These are listed for each county; if you ring up your nearest contact and tell them you are interested in the breed and would like to meet a family who own Flatcoats they will try to help you arrange this. This is very important as it will give you an insight into the breed and their character and their suitability as your family dog. I shall deal later with a search for a show and/or working puppy as this is a more specialised area.

You have visited a family with Flatcoats, and you as a family agree that the Flatcoated Retriever is for you. What do you do next? You contact a breeder. If the breeder considers that you really have given the matter your serious consideration, they will be able to help you to find a puppy locally, or will give you the phone number of Mrs Shirley Johnson, the breed's litter recorder. Shirley will ask you many questions. Do not be put off or offended by these. They are important as we are trying to protect our breed. If she is satisfied, she will give you the name and address of a breeder with a litter, and the rest is up to you.

As we said before, most people prefer to start with a puppy. Young dogs are likely to settle more quickly in new surroundings than older individuals, although this is not always the case with Flatcoated Retrievers. Nevertheless, puppies are not without their problems. First and foremost, they will need to be house-trained. Almost inevitably carpets will be soiled at some stage during this process, so a degree of tolerance is necessary. In addition, as we have said before, puppies are likely to chew household and personal items such as table or chair legs and the children's toys and shoes, particularly during their teething phase.

Sometimes people find it less disrupting to choose a mature dog which has already been trained. Your contact for this purpose is the breed's Rescue and Rehousing Scheme Co-ordinator, Mrs Barbara Harking (see **Useful Addresses**). Barbara will ask you many questions and may even want to visit your home before agreeing to allow you to have a dog. This should not be taken personally. She simply wants to ensure that you are in a position to provide a permanent, caring home for a dog. In the case of a rescued dog, you may also have to agree not to breed from it, or possibly even have it neutered.

Dogs may find themselves homeless for a wide variety of reasons. Their former owners may have died or emigrated or the family may have split up, leaving the dog in need of another home. Obtaining a dog in this way should not be considered a cheap option; you should be prepared to give a realistic donation to the group so that they can continue their work, as they are likely to be entirely dependent on the money which they raise for this purpose.

Barbara and her helpers will try to match the individual as closely as possible with the dog to ensure that the transfer is trouble-free. For example, it is not a good idea to take an older dog which has lived with an elderly owner and suddenly introduce it to a home full of children. Similarly, a dog that has been kept for much of its life in kennels will prove more difficult to introduce into a domestic environment than one which has been used to a family life. Flatcoats, with a little help, soon find out this new life is good and has great advantages. However, it is not so common for a Flatcoat to need a new home as it is for dogs of some other breeds, so you may have to go onto a waiting list.

One point which should be clear in your mind if you are looking for a pedigree dog, male or female, is whether you want primarily a pet or are seriously considering showing, field trialling, or a working gundog, possibly with a view to breeding in the future. If you have set your heart on a potential show or field trial dog you should purchase from a specialised breeder. The word 'potential' is significant because even the most promising puppies may not turn out to be show or field trial winners.

A five-month-old puppy going through the leggy stage. He just needs time.

In Flatcoats especially, the change from puppy to immature youngster comes very quickly, and this period can last from one to two years. As long as the basics are correct, he or she is worth waiting for.

A well-grown eight-week-old.

In most litters of Flatcoats all puppies sell for the same price, but there is no fixed price per litter. Aside from the dog's show or field trial potential, the reputation of the kennels will have a bearing on its value. Big prices should not be paid for a puppy from unknown stock. If the puppy is the progeny of show or field trial winning parents its price will be correspondingly higher though this is no guarantee that you will end up with a champion of your own. Much will depend on the puppy's subsequent development and training, and your own dedication to canine exhibition and training, which is a very interesting but demanding pastime.

One word of warning: Flatcoat puppies do not stay in the pretty puppy stage for many weeks. Even by 10 or 11 weeks they start getting into the leggy stage. By four months they will remind you of a young colt: all legs, with a long tail with no feathering, looking as though there is no possibility that they will ever grow into real Flatcoats. Be patient: with time (it will take a year or even more) an adult Flatcoat will develop.

To gain some insight into the breed and knowledge of the dog show world in general it is best to start by reading the dog press, which reports Show results, advertises forthcoming events, includes individual notes on most breeds and prints regular features of particular interest.

In Britain copies of *Our Dogs* and *Dog World* may be ordered from your newsagent and are essential reading for everyone connected with the breeding and showing of dogs, whether at small, local shows or the best known of all, Crufts Dog Show, The Kennel Club's own show.

Flatcoated Retrievers

It is a good plan to visit some shows as an observer. There you will see established breeders, as well as other newcomers, and you will have the opportunity to watch dogs in the ring. You may perhaps begin to develop an eye for what the judges are seeking when they assess classes. There may also be opportunities to talk to exhibitors after the classes have been judged. Before judging, exhibitors are always very busy concentrating on the preparation of their dogs, but when the judging is finished the tension relaxes; that is the time to chat.

When you have found the person or kennel from whom you would like to buy your show puppy, go and talk to the breeder and book a puppy. All responsible breeders will put you through the 'third degree', and it is right that they should. Be patient, even if you have to wait until the next litter to get well up the list.

Even in a litter by a champion out of a champion there can be no guarantee of show quality; if you are lucky there **may** be one or two high flyers, and another two or so good quality puppies. It would be better to wait for the best possible puppy rather than accept one way down the litter or from any old litter. Showing is very expensive and your lesser quality puppy will cost you as much as the best in the litter to look after and exhibit.

There is a tendency today for people to put their names on many breeders' lists in the hope of picking the best puppy. Personally, if I knew that a prospective puppy owner had done this, I would prefer them to come off my list. I want someone who really wants to show 'my' puppy, and the rest will go to happy working/family homes.

When you are choosing an eight-week-old puppy, it is a gamble in any breed. However, the puppy must look balanced, with a good head, and it must be well made. If your puppy's front angulation is bad it will never improve, and the same goes for the hindquarters. Similarly, if the puppy is long in the loin this will not change; what you see is what you will get as far as construction is concerned. The only thing that possibly changes in a Flatcoat is the bite (teeth). A perfect bite at eight weeks can change completely by the time the adult teeth come. It is so frustrating to have a lovely puppy and at eight months to watch the mouth change completely, tooth by tooth. This happens as a result of the slow growth of the jaw as the head lengthens.

Puppies change rapidly from nine weeks onwards. They grow very fast for the first six months, then they alter considerably between six and 18 months. At 12 to 20 months (especially in the case of males) they will be well grown in front with a less developed hindquarter. Between 18 months and three years you will see the dog gradually balance up from the front to the rear. Some bitches seem to take forever to develop from the immature, gangling stage.

From about three years onwards your Flatcoat gradually comes together. If the quality is there he or she might possibly become a Champion between three and six years of age. Flatcoats stay at their best and continue to win well into veteran stage. Flatcoat bitches on the whole are difficult to show, not looking at their best for quite long periods of time, as quite a few have a full moult around or before each of their seasons. You can see from all these factors that campaigning your Flatcoat is going to take a long time. There are a few who develop very fast, mature early ... and by the wrong side of three years their show life is over. They have blossomed like an over-blown rose!

The Flatcoat can also be a working gundog, and you may have decided on the breed with this in mind. Perhaps this is your first gundog, but if you have owned another breed, a word of warning: Flatcoats, even when bred for work, are not quite the same as working Labradors or Golden Retrievers, although their characteristics are nearer in style to those of a Golden Retriever. As described in Chapter 1, they have Black Setter blood in their ancestry: in a percentage of dogs this still has some influence, so their working style is unique as far as retrievers are concerned. You must be aware of this from the start, and your training must reflect this. If you enjoy a challenge, have a good sense of humour and are an individualist, you and Flatcoats will probably get on well together. However, if you want your Flatcoat to be a working gundog, it would be wiser for you to go down a slightly different path to find your puppy, especially if you would like to develop a field trial line. Do explain your exact requirements to our litter recorder; she will still be able to help you. I have expanded this information in Chapter 8: **Flatcoated Retriever Activities**. You could also join the Breed Societies (see **Useful Addresses**).

For those of you who want to show and work your dogs there is still a high percentage of breeders who produce good looking show dogs. It would be wise to persuade a more experienced breeder friend (maybe even in another gundog breed) to accompany you when you are looking at puppies so that you can benefit from an informed opinion.

You may sometimes see advertisements in your local paper offering puppies. It is particularly important under these circumstances that you see the parents, or at least the puppy's mother. This is because puppies may be bred elsewhere, on so-called 'puppy farms', and then sold as home-bred pups to unsuspecting purchasers. Such puppies tend to suffer far more from problems such as enteritis, because of the conditions under which they have been bred and subsequently kept. It is therefore strongly recommended to buy only from a reputable source.

Very few pet shops in Britain sell pedigree puppies, or indeed dogs of any kind. The situation is very different in North America, where you may see a wide range of puppies for sale. The standards there are generally high, with the puppies usually being subject to regular veterinary inspections; you can expect to acquire a healthy puppy under those circumstances. However in no circumstances is it the place to buy a Flatcoated Retriever. As we have said before you can refer to your national kennel club for advice. In Britain the appropriate authority would be The Kennel Club.

You may have a preference for a particular colour. Flatcoats are black or liver, though the liver ones are quite rare. In addition, you will have to consider the gender of the puppy. As a general rule, bitches may be somewhat more affectionate and slightly easier to train, although their periods of heat can be troublesome times. Male dogs are reasonably easy to manage, although a few individuals may suffer from hypersexuality. These are more likely to stray, particularly if there is a bitch in season in the neighbourhood. Male dogs may also tend to urinate around the home once they mature. This does not reflect a breakdown in toilet-training, but is a natural desire on their part to mark their territory. These behavioural difficulties can be overcome by strict discipline, so that if you are simply seeking a dog as a pet the gender need not be significant.

Should the show ring be your goal it is generally better to start with a bitch puppy, though the problems with her coat described above should be borne in mind. If you are successful with her in the show ring you can breed her to a suitable dog and keep her best puppies. If you start your show career with a male dog the progress of your kennel depends on him being a consistent winner at shows so that the owners of bitches will want to use him at stud. Then the likelihood is that they would want to keep the most promising puppies themselves. Beginning with a male dog is not an impossible route to success, and some show kennels have started this way, but progress is likely to be slower. However, you do have a choice. As your kennel becomes established the significant point is that you will want to keep, or acquire, only the very best quality to complement, or improve, your own stock. At that stage an excellent stud dog can have a dramatic impact on your kennel, or on the breed in general if he is in demand by other breeders who admire him. In the case of the Flatcoat, we hope he will be a good-looking worker!

Another way of starting out, although it is not common practice in the Flatcoat breed, is to consider the possibility of a breeding terms agreement. An established breeder who has a young puppy which he or she does not wish to sell outright may be prepared to enter into an arrangement whereby you pay a reduced price, raise and train the puppy, exhibit her at shows and in due course breed a litter from her. The further arrangement may be that the original breeder has the right to choose which stud dog you use and may take one or more puppies from that litter to complete payment for the bitch.

An advantage is that as a novice exhibitor you may acquire a quality bitch you otherwise could not afford and receive good advice from the breeder. The disadvantage is that it may not save you any expense in the long run; you will have to pay for the care of the bitch, the stud fee, any

Note the development and change in length of the puppy's head between five weeks of age (above) and eight weeks of age (below).

necessary veterinary fees and the rearing of the litter. On top of this, the original breeder may request the first and third pick of litter (or some similar arrangement), with the result that your favourite puppy will not stay with you.

Breeding terms agreements, or loan of bitch arrangements, should always be set out formally in writing and signed by both parties to avoid any misunderstanding. The Kennel Club has produced a form for this purpose which can be lodged there. Such agreements vary greatly in their terms and, since they entail a great deal of trust on both sides, tend to be more common between people who know each other well than between strangers.

Sorting out the Paperwork

Do not assume that because a puppy is pure-bred it will have been registered automatically with The Kennel Club. You will need to clarify this situation when you purchase the dog. If it has been registered you will need to fill out a Transfer of Ownership form and return it to The Kennel Club, so that the official record can be altered accordingly. Should you decide to show your puppy while this transfer is still in progress, remember to put TAF (Transfer Applied For) after your puppy's name until you have received official notification that it has taken place.

It is also important to have the puppy's vaccination certificate, assuming that it has already received some inoculations. You will need to keep this in a safe place and give it to your veterinary surgeon to complete in due course. The certificate will show which vaccines have been used and when the puppy's next inoculations are due. As important is an information leaflet from the breeder, with details of the diet (how much/how many times per day), and when the puppy was wormed, what was used and when the next dose is due. The one I give out is reproduced at the end of Chapter 9.

Insurance

You should also check whether the puppy is covered by veterinary insurance at this stage. Unless the breeder has taken out cover, you will need to arrange an insurance policy yourself. It is particularly important with young puppies, who can get themselves into all sorts of mischief, and may need veterinary treatment as a result. Veterinary treatment these days is very expensive. Remember, however, that routine treatments such as vaccinations and worming are not covered by your insurance.

A Healthy Puppy

Please telephone the breeder at a convenient time when inquiring if they have any puppies available. You may find, particularly if you are seeking a puppy from a popular kennel, that you need to be patient, as there will be a waiting list. It is not uncommon to view litters from about five weeks onwards, but you will not be able to take the puppy home until it is at least two months old and properly weaned.

If you are seeking a household pet a litter which has been reared indoors rather than in kennels is to be recommended. Such puppies are likely to be much more friendly and used to domestic surroundings so they should settle quickly in a new home. But most Flatcoat breeders put a great deal of time into socialising their puppies.

Young puppies spend much of their time sleeping and then become active for short periods. When you view puppies do not be surprised if they appear quite subdued at first. The excitement of a stranger in their midst is quite likely to cause them to wake up and start to play, however. Before making any choice watch all the puppies for a few minutes. Some may appear more dominant than others, but it is hard to form an accurate impression from just a brief visit. Rely on the breeder's insight into the individual character of the puppies, as he or she will be more aware of differences between them.

Flatcoated Retrievers

The likelihood is that all the puppies in a breeding kennel will be in good health, but it can be harder to be certain of this when confronted with a single puppy in a pet shop. Try to eliminate any obvious problems. Start by watching the puppy walking or running across the floor. It should be able to do this without any difficulty, and although its ribs will be evident when you lift it, they should not be especially prominent. This can be indicative of malnutrition, or a chronic illness. Check the coat for signs of fleas (see page 207) and lice, which are likely to be encountered in puppies reared under poor conditions. A pot-bellied appearance may be suggestive of a build-up of roundworms. Experienced breeders will have wormed their puppies regularly.

Hereditary problems are obviously a matter for concern, particularly if you intend to breed. Of these, the most likely among Retrievers are Hip Dysplasia (HD) and various eye problems. The British Veterinary Association (BVA) in conjunction with The Kennel Club runs schemes for screening dogs for HD and inherited eye diseases. These schemes are voluntary, but The Kennel Club is concerned that dogs registered should be bred in a responsible manner. Further information on this, and on the law relating to the sale of registered dogs, is available from The Kennel Club. Buyers in the last few years have brought successful cases in law against breeders but the matter is too complicated to be discussed here.

In the case of HD, the breed average score published on 16 May 1995 and derived from 2090 X-rayed Flatcoats was 9.18. The hip score quoted in the BVA/Kennel Club Hip Dysplasia Scheme is the sum of the points awarded for each of nine radiographic features of both hips: the lower the score, the less the degree of hip dysplasia. The minimum score for each hip is zero, and the maximum 53, giving a total score of zero to 106. The breed mean score is calculated from all the scores recorded for a given breed and gives a representation of the overall hip status of that breed. All breeders wishing to control HD should breed only from animals with hip scores within the breed mean score.

It is a good idea therefore to ask your breeder about the scores of the sire and dam and compare them with the breed average. These scores will be on your puppy's Regulation Certificate. Veterinary advice is that sire and dam should both score below the breed average to minimise the likelihood of HD being passed on to future generations of puppies. Sires used for breeding should be those whose progeny have consistently low scores, and owners with one or more bitches should follow the same selection procedure. This lessens the risk of producing puppies with HD, which is not only disappointing but can lead to court action. For the breed hip scoring scheme to be meaningful and successful it is important that **all** X-rays should be submitted for scoring, whether or not the animal is required for breeding and whatever the state of the hips, to provide the widest possible information for use by the breed geneticist.

It is worth noting that if a dog is clinically sound and has a low hip score it is most unlikely that it will become lame as a result of HD. If it is sound but has a high score, restriction of exercise, especially during the first 18 months of life, may avoid development of lameness.

We all realise the great concern about worms and children, but with care and common sense there will be no danger to your children. A well wormed family of dogs will carry very few worms to begin with, and the puppy will be well wormed before you buy it. The list of worming dates is most important, and you must continue this with veterinary advice. The puppy will have its own bowls, with separate washing up bowl and dishcloth. The area where the puppy relieves itself must be kept clean, its messes cleared regularly, and everyone must adhere to the general hygiene code of washing hands after handling the puppy and before eating. There is a greater danger from the local cats using your garden as their toilet.

When you are handling the puppy, it is worth checking for the remains of the umbilical cord. This should be apparent as only a slight swelling under the abdomen. If it is enlarged, and there is a distinct lump under the skin, it is indicative of an umbilical hernia which will probably need surgical correction later. This can arise from the umbilical cord being severed too close to the body, or from the dam being too rough with the puppy when it was born.

You should also check whether the dew claws have been removed. These digits, equivalent to the human thumb, are positioned off the ground, on the inner side of the front legs. Their exposed location here means that the claws will grow unimpaired by wear on the ground, and they will have to be cut back regularly if they are not to curl round and penetrate the leg. There is also a likelihood that the front dew claws could be torn either in play or when the dog is being exercised. This will be painful for the dog, and inevitably means that the dew claws will then have to be removed surgically. But usually you will find Flatcoats have dew claws. Most people who work their dogs leave them on as they consider that they help a dog to get up banks; they are used as we do our thumbs. Please remember to check them regularly, however. Right from the start your puppy's nails and dew claws must be trimmed. A guillotine nail cutter is best. If a small amount is taken off regularly you will help your puppy to develop good feet.

What You Need for a Young Puppy

If you choose a puppy before it is fully independent the breeder normally expects a deposit, and you can arrange to collect it later. This gives you time to sort everything out.

In the first place, you will need suitable food and water bowls. Although plastic containers are widely available now they are not necessarily the best choice for a puppy. Some are easily over-turned and they can also be chewed around the edges. This makes them hard to clean properly and the frayed edges may harbour bacteria. Stainless steel containers are also quite light, and are largely indestructible. The best option is probably the traditional heavyweight ceramic bowl, sold in various sizes by most pet shops. These cannot be tipped over accidentally even by large dogs, and are easy to clean thoroughly.

Cleanliness and general hygiene needs some thought when you have a puppy in the house. Some people wash their dog's bowl with the family dishcloth, but it is much more hygienic to have a separate brush for this purpose. These are widely-sold by supermarkets, and can be rinsed after use, to remove any remaining food deposits. It is well worth buying from your pet shop an all-purpose disinfectant and deodoriser made with dogs specifically in mind for any 'mistakes' the puppy makes. It is a wise precaution not to use a harsh washing powder in the washing machine when washing the puppy's blankets as this can harm its skin.

When it comes to sleeping arrangements, you may prefer to opt for a temporary bed until the puppy is about six months old and has passed through its teething phase. To begin with, it may well decide to gnaw its bed. However, my preference is for a wire cage, right from the beginning. This will give your puppy a safe haven, where you can shut it out of harm's way. This is especially important if your puppy is going to live in the house; there is nothing more dangerous than a puppy under your feet when you are cooking. It will also facilitate house training, and minimise damage to the house when you are out for short periods. If you have children they must be told this is the puppy's private area. It is also a safe travelling cage for the car. Choose a cage which will be big enough for your dog when he is fully grown, and which has a dog proof closure and carrying handles. Most models also fold flat for easy storage when not in use, though they are so versatile that they are generally kept ready for use at any time. The plastic trays that come with it are also very useful and more comfortable for the dog. Put some paper on this, plus a vetbed. I am not happy with the use of ordinary blankets with Flatcoats: they are inclined to eat them! Cages are expensive, but very well worth the investment. They are available from pet shops, shows or direct from the manufacturers, who advertise in the dog papers.

Adapting a baby-gate to retain a dog in the kitchen or utility room is a good idea. A Flatcoat can also live quite happily in a well-insulated kennel with a run outside, but bear in mind that it is a dog that enjoys your company.

You will also need to obtain a suitable collar for the puppy to which he should be introduced gradually. You will need to bear in mind that as the young dog grows the collar will need to be adjusted and, to avoid causing your puppy any discomfort, replaced with a larger size as necessary. When you purchase the collar you should also buy a metal disc which should be engraved with your name, address and telephone number as required by law and attached to the collar. Should the young dog stray anyone finding it will be able to contact you easily.

Alternatively, you may prefer to obtain a capsule which attaches to the collar in a similar way. The relevant details about your dog are then written on a piece of paper, which is inserted in the capsule. Unfortunately, young dogs do seem to lose capsules more easily than discs, which generally remain legible and last for years. Whichever you choose, a regular check should be made to make sure they are still serviceable and securely attached to the collar.

If you have more than one puppy or dog, it may not be wise to leave their collars on them when they are in your house and garden. They have been known to get caught in each other's collars when playing, with tragic results. This makes it so important to have a safe, dog-proof garden.

Tattooing is a method by which you can identify a dog permanently. The tattoo can be put on the inner surface of the ear. This is often done for German Shepherd Dogs, for example, and always for Police Dogs. A special code is used for identification and registration in the scheme, which was founded by the German Shepherd Dog League in Britain. Tattooing is relatively painless and lasts for life. Dogs can be tattooed at any age but if litters of puppies are tattooed before they go to new homes their national registration number can be added to their Kennel Club registration documents as an added identification safeguard. For details of an approved tattooist in your own area in Britain and Ireland contact The Kennel Club.

A more recent method of marking a dog in a permanent fashion is by means of an implanted transponder. Your vet will be able to advise you about this method at the time of your first consultation, though some rescue centres provide implants for all dogs which pass through their kennels. Such implants can be read by a special scanner, but whereas all dogs can wear an easily read metal identification disc, or be tattooed, not all finders of lost dogs will have access to a scanner to locate a transponder. A registered tattoo number or a engraved disc securely attached to the dog's collar is at present the better option, certainly until a national transponder registration system is agreed.

A suitable lead to attach to the collar will be useful for introducing your puppy to the rudiments of training, although this will not be an essential purchase at the outset. The choice of a lead depends to some extent on the breed concerned. Nylon is now a popular, durable material used in the manufacturing of leads, but can be rather hard on the hand, so you may prefer a leather one. Either is suitable, so the choice is yours. Some leads incorporate reflective material, which is fluorescent in car headlamps. These are especially recommended for your dog in urban areas, in locations where traffic may speed along dark roads, or if you have to walk regularly along country lanes where there is no street lighting. A day glow reflected waistcoat for yourself is also advisable.

Puppies, with their playful nature, will appreciate a range of toys. Nylabone chews are ideal for this purpose. Balls are not recommended for Flatcoats, especially if you wish to consider gundog work. A puppy dummy which if thrown very occasionally will encourage your puppy to retrieve is also available, but for more details please read see Chapter 8: **Flatcoat Retriever Activities**. Any toy that you choose must be too big for the dog to swallow, as this could cause a possibly fatal obstruction to the windpipe.

It is advisable not to encourage your show puppies to carry sticks and retrieve large objects as this can chip the teeth and damage them. Once you know your puppy will retrieve it is wise to concentrate on obedience and leave retrieving until the adult teeth are well established. Damage can be done to the growing teeth and jaw and if this happens your puppy will be at a great disadvantage in the show ring.

Taking Your New Dog Home

The simplest way is undoubtedly by car, although it is advisable to have someone with you. A puppy will be unaccustomed to travel, so it may benefit from the assurance of being held for the journey. It is a good idea for the person holding the puppy to be protected by an old towel, however; the unfamiliar sensations of the car may cause the puppy to be sick.

Alternatively a carrying crate, as described above, lined with newspaper, with a towel on top should suffice for the duration of the journey. Never allow the puppy, or any dog, to travel unrestricted in the car as, apart from the risk of damage, it could distract you and lead to a serious accident. These days there are made-to-measure wire cages made to fit all estates or vans, and these are widely advertised in the dog papers. This also helps to protect your car from chewing.

Should your car have rubber mats then it will be best to place the puppy in its carrying cage on these. You will then be able to clean up easily if necessary and the puppy will not be at risk of falling off the seat if you are travelling on your own and have to brake unexpectedly.

The rear compartment of an estate car or van is also a suitable place for your carry crate, but please remember to anchor the cage. Never, never use the boot of a car for this purpose, nor the back of a hatch-back, which is also a far from a suitable place for an adult Flatcoat: there is a great danger of over heating from the direct sunlight.

If you need to break your journey home do not leave the puppy alone in the car. The temperature can rise to fatal levels within minutes on a warm summer's day. When making any journey in the car with your dog, always carry a container of drinking water for him; and his water bowl of course.

It is important that a young puppy does not come into contact with other dogs because at this stage it will not possess full immunity. This is particularly important should you need to rely on public transport when taking your puppy home. Under no circumstances should it be allowed to walk in public places. If you have bought an older dog which is adequately protected by vaccinations against the major killer diseases you will be able to walk it on a lead, but bear in mind that the dog will not yet be used to your commands, and may even be reluctant to respond as required.

Settling in at Home

If possible, arrange to collect your puppy early enough for it to have time to become familiar with its new surroundings before night fall. This should help to ensure that you have a more peaceful night's sleep! Separated from its littermates and mother, and on its own in unfamiliar surroundings, it is not unusual for a puppy to cry or howl at night until it is settled in its new home.

If you have an older family dog, it is important that you introduce the puppy correctly. This is better done on neutral ground, rather than in the house. It could be asking for trouble to come into the house and put the puppy down right in the middle of your dog's home territory. Your older dog will be pleased to see you and excited you are home, but you and the puppy will be enveloped in a new exciting smell, and to another dog the bitch/ puppy smell is very strong. It will be better, therefore, to get your dog's greetings to you over, letting him or her examine you and your new smells, and then introduce your new puppy outside, or if you have a cage for it, from inside the cage. Care taken now will be repaid with two contented friends later. Give your older dog time to accept its new family friend, and do not leave them together unattended at first; it is not fair on either of them.

Although it may seem hard, it is best to leave the puppy to sleep on its own the first night. If your resolve weakens, and you allow it to sleep in your bedroom, you are likely to be storing up future trouble, as the puppy will expect to sleep there on a permanent basis. There is then a real possibility that the carpets or even the bedclothes may be soiled, unless of course, your pup is content to sleep in its crate.

Flatcoated Retrievers

If you have a utility room, this may well be the best place to train your dog to sleep, provided that it is not too cold. It should also prove a deterrent to burglars. Alternatively, you may need to use the kitchen instead. If any accidents happen, it is less difficult to clear up here on a linoleum-type floor.

The kitchen in most family homes tends to be busy, and it can be dangerous to have a young puppy under your feet while you are cooking. The puppy pen or cage can solve this problem. It is hard to convince a young dog that it can sleep in the kitchen at night but must be elsewhere during the day, particularly as puppies need to spend much of their time asleep. The pen, or crate, is definitely a boon, but must not be used as a prison. Leave some toys in the cage or pen, and as long as the pup can see you he should be quite happy watching you when you work in the kitchen. It can be helpful to drape a cover over part of the cage as this gives the pup a sense of security.

Dogs are clean creatures by nature, in spite of the impression which puppies sometimes give to the contrary. Soiling in the home is often the result of misunderstanding on the part of the owner, who fails to appreciate the demands of a puppy. It is never too early to start house-training, and after the journey home, your puppy is likely to want to relieve itself. Place it gently at the required spot in the garden, and use whatever phrase, such as 'Clean dog' or 'Good boy', that you will continue to adopt for toilet training. It is very important to establish this procedure now. If you are intending to travel to shows with your dog there will be many strange places you will wish the dog to use. At first, the puppy is likely to scamper around, but you can obtain special preparations from pet shops which will encourage a puppy to relieve itself in the area where the product has been used. Allow the puppy to sniff around, as this is a normal prelude to this process, and then praise it when it acts in the required manner. Then carefully pick up the puppy and carry it back indoors.

If you have children, you must show them how to hold the puppy safely, right from the outset. Although young dogs, with their loose skin and fat bodies, may give the impression of being robust, they can be injured quite easily by rough handling. They are also likely to struggle if not properly restrained, and may wriggle free, falling to the ground as a result.

Puppies should be lifted with the support of the right arm along the underside of the body, their chest area lying on the palm. Your fingers can then be used to restrain the front of the body, while tucking the puppy between your elbow and chest should help to deter it from struggling. It is usually only when they feel insecure that puppies wriggle.

Try to pick up your puppy regularly, so that it becomes used to this experience. This will be useful later in life, for example when you take the dog to the vet and have to lift it on to the table for examination. A dog which is not used to being carried may actively resent this process, and will become distressed even before the vet starts to examine it. For grooming and show purposes, it is also important that a dog does not resent being handled in this way.

It is important to clean up regularly after the dog has relieved itself. You may even want to incorporate a special screened concrete area in the garden which can be used as a dog toilet, and disinfect it regularly. It is not a good idea to allow a dog to urinate on the lawn in any event; over a period of time, the acidic nature of a bitch's urine is likely to kill the grass, causing unsightly patches. However, not all owners are as concerned about the lawn as they are about the puppy being trained!

If the weather is bad, then the puppy may be reluctant to go outside. It may also want to relieve itself at night. It is useful to cover the floor with newspaper at night, just in case. It will probably take at least six months for a young dog to become fully house-trained and routinely ask to go outside when it wants to relieve itself.

Especially with a puppy, bear in mind that the act of eating and drinking is likely to trigger this urge. Always place the puppy outside after it has had a meal, and stay with it for a short time. Remember always to use your command. At first, the puppy should be supervised in the garden, but there will come a time when you want to allow your dog to roam freely. You must check the boundaries carefully beforehand so there is no risk of the young dog escaping and roaming further afield. Most puppies have no road sense and are liable to be run over if they get out into traffic. There is also the risk that they could contract diseases from other dogs, since they will not be fully protected by vaccinations in the early stages.

When checking around your garden, look closely for any gaps under fences or gates. Whereas older dogs may jump over obstacles, puppies are much more likely to squeeze under them. They will also use their heads to push their way through loose wire mesh if they are sufficiently determined. In the case of adult dogs, fences which are about 6 ft (1.8m) high will be sufficient to prevent them escaping from your garden. For a young puppy it is useful to make a temporary 'play pen' or dog run in a part of the garden near the house so you can keep an eye on him. The aforementioned mesh panels serve this purpose very well and keep your puppy safe.

There are relatively few dangers for puppies in a garden as long as there are no easy escape routes and no-one leaves the gate open. It is sensible to avoid the use of all chemicals. Metaldehyde which is present in some brands of slug pellets is harmful to your puppy. If you have a pond, be sure that the sides are not so steep that, if the puppy fell in, it would have difficulty in getting back on to firm ground. Dogs are generally good swimmers, but a puppy will need to be able to scramble up the side to safety before it becomes exhausted, and possibly weakened by hypothermia as well. The risk is perhaps greatest on a cold winter's day, when the surface of the pond has become frozen. A puppy could then find itself in serious difficulty if the ice were to collapse beneath its body weight. If you have a pond, and have not made a safe puppy pen in which a young pup can play, it would be a good plan to make a wire netting frame to cover your pond in order to avoid accidents. By the way, Flatcoats have a great love of water (especially muddy puddles!) and so, if you have goldfish in an ornamental pond, it is wise to protect them from your enthusiastic Retriever.

Living With Other Pets

Cats tend to be rather aloof by nature, and will not actively seek out the company of a new puppy. In fact, the dog is likely to make the first move, possibly chasing the cat. The resulting rebuff, in the form of hissing and even a smack from one of the cat's paws, will leave a lasting impression on the puppy. In most households, the cat is definitely the dominant individual.

You may find that at first your cat is highly suspicious of the puppy, and is withdrawn, venturing indoors through the kitchen less than usual. This is equally normal, and within a few weeks the animals will have learnt to accept each other's presence and harmony should be restored. The extent to which a dog and cat bond together depends to a large degree on the individuals themselves, although rearing a kitten and puppy together is perhaps most likely to lead to a strong sense of companionship between them.

Two litter-mates of the same sex will grow up to become close companions, but will not respond so well to you. Like twins, they will rely on each other's company before yours.

If you are out on a regular basis it may be better to choose two pups so they can keep each other company. However, if you are out very much, it could be wiser not to have a Flatcoat - or, indeed, any dog. If you do buy two dogs, you will need to consider all the additional costs, not just the purchase price. Feeding and kennelling costs will be doubled, as will routine veterinary charges for immunisations and worming medication. As I have said before, two puppies growing up together will become more reliant on each other than on you, so that training and discipline will be more difficult.

I find that having two Flatcoats of different ages works well. If there is a difference of three or four years, the puppy can learn from his elder, and there should not be any competition for 'top dog', as the pecking order will already be established. Also there will be less chance of losing both dogs at the same time; this could be very traumatic for all concerned.

Should you decide to buy two puppies, two bitches may be a good proposition, and there is no risk of future unplanned puppies. A male dog and a spayed bitch also make excellent companions and this could be the happiest combination if you simply want a couple of adorable pets.

Flatcoated Retrievers

However, you should consider that bitches are not usually spayed until after they have had their first season or 'heat', though those obtained from some rescue centres as adults are spayed or castrated before being allowed to go to new homes. If in doubt on this point, consult your own veterinary surgeon.

If you are hoping to establish a breeding kennel of your own do not purchase a male and a female puppy. Go to a reputable kennel and start with the best quality bitch you can afford, and in due course breed her to the most suitable dog available and keep her best offspring. There is no point in deliberately breeding pet puppies. You may have difficulty in selling them and it costs just as much to breed pets as it does to produce a litter which, hopefully, will contain some show quality puppies which will start you on the road to founding a successful and respected kennel.

As I have said before, an older resident dog may well accept a young puppy, but you will need to play your part to ensure a smooth transitional phase. Although the temptation will be to spend more time playing with and fussing over the puppy this is liable to lead to conflict with your established pet. It is better to reinforce its position of dominance, rather than allowing the newcomer to challenge its supremacy. Dogs, as descendants of the wolf (Canis lupus), are pack animals, and have a defined social structure when living in groups. This should be acknowledged by their owner, who must be the pack leader. You should try to avoid potential flash points. If they respect you as pack leader they will be more worried about your displeasure than their own squabbles. At meal times keep to a routine and feed in the same order and the same place. Stop any intrusion by one dog into another dog's food bowl; the offending dog must be reprimanded in a deep, gruff voice.

The newcomer should be fed elsewhere, rather than usurping the established dog's feeding position. Be sure that they are not likely to come into contact at this stage, because the established dog may well snap at the youngster if it tries to interfere with its meal. Alternatively, the puppy may lose its food to the older dog.

Bitches and neutered dogs tend to be more tolerant of a new youngster than mature entire males, but much will depend on the temperaments of the dogs themselves. Constant reinforcement of the established order will defuse potential conflict and in fact an older dog may appreciate the company of a younger individual. Over a number of years you may notice a subtle shift in dominance as the younger dog takes over the leading role from its older companion.

If there is an outbreak of aggression during the initial stages do not instinctively punish the older dog. This will simply be seen as weakening its position in the family hierarchy. It will be much better simply to remove the younger dog from the scene of the conflict. The introduction of a new puppy to the home will generate excitement, and it will become the centre of attention for a period of time. However, you must ensure that the puppy is able to sleep unmolested because even the most tolerant individual will resent being constantly disturbed. Once it has woken up it will almost certainly want to play, and then it will be ready for a meal, after which it will probably be sleepy again.

Children and adults alike must realise that if the puppy goes under the bed or chair and falls asleep in this warm, dark hole, an intrusive hand or arm pulling it out just as it falls asleep is **very frightening**. If you yourself drop into a catnap and someone wakes you up with a start, do you not jump up ready to defend yourself? Naturally the puppy will do the same. It is best to put on an a gentle, exciting voice, calling it by its name, or 'puppy, puppy' as the breeder will have done, with a tasty morsel in your hand. This way you are teaching your puppy that whenever you call it there is the possibility of fun or food.

Children will delight in having a puppy to play with but you will need to supervise them, particularly if the children are not used to dogs. You must emphasise the fact the puppies are not toys but living creatures with feelings, who can be hurt just as much as the children themselves.

In safe hands.

Children and Flatcoat puppies can grow up happily together if the child is taught care and respect for the puppies.

Play provides a means whereby a puppy can become familiar with its environment. Socialisation with people is especially vital between the ages of two and three months. Puppies kept in isolation during this period tend to be withdrawn throughout their lives. Try to give puppies as much attention as possible at this stage, as this will strengthen their relationship with you and other members of the family. This can be achieved partly by the use of toys. As mentioned earlier, well chosen toys, such as those from the Nylabone range, will help to keep the teeth in good condition as well as being of psychological benefit to your dog.

One of the earliest lessons which puppies must learn is a willingness to give up a toy on command. Remember: a Flatcoat has been bred to retrieve. Therefore, from the start (even if the object is one of your best shoes!) one gives great praise, injecting great pleasure into one's voice, even sitting on the floor with the puppy at its own level. It is better to offer the puppy another toy in exchange for the precious item, using the word 'give' or 'dead'. It is a good idea take a toy away, then to offer it back to the puppy, letting him know how pleased you are with him.

You can incorporate this as a regular feature at the end of each play routine, gently opening his mouth on the command 'Teeth!', and as you do this your puppy will get into the habit of allowing you to open its mouth without any problems. Also, if you are going to show him he will have to learn that it is normal for him to have his teeth inspected by a stranger. It is important to be able to look at your dog's teeth, as they will benefit from regular inspection and brushing to restrict the build-up of plaque, which is likely to lead to gum disease and dental decay.

His own toothbrush and toothpaste of the dog variety will serve your dog very well, and it will not matter in the least if you cannot teach him to spit after you have brushed his teeth!

In spite of having a range of toys many puppies will also gnaw items around the home, and this can be a source of considerable anger should furniture or personal items be chewed. Supervision is vital to prevent damage of this type. It is a phase that will pass once teething is completed, and the short-term answer is to prevent the young dog from being left in a room on its own for any length of time.

Dogs are creatures of routine and a puppy will soon adapt to the household environment. Try to feed the puppy at roughly the same times every day; he is likely to fret if he is hungry and you do not want to cause additional stress. Encourage it to play in the late afternoon or evening, so that it will then be ready for a sleep at night. Put the puppy outside last thing at night and encourage it to be clean, before placing it in its bed.

The dog should then settle down without problems, although at first it may be rather restless, until the routine is established. If it persists in barking at this stage, you should simply ignore it. This is a plea for attention, and the puppy will soon come to appreciate that if it barks repeatedly in this fashion you will come back to see what is wrong.

The best course of action is to do nothing, and the problem should resolve itself in a few nights. There may subsequently be times when you are awakened by your dog barking. It may be that it has been disturbed by cats or foxes in the neighbourhood, or that there are intruders around outside. Clearly, this should not be ignored, and the dog's bark will have a greater urgency than the howling notes demanding attention.

As the dog gets older, and starts going out into the garden on its own, so you may find that it tends to bark when it wants to come back inside. This can develop into a rather tiresome habit. The answer is to allow your dog out, and then call it back indoors yourself after a relatively short period of time at first. Barking tends to develop when the dog feels it is being ignored, and has been left outside for a long interval. By taking the initiative, you can show that you have not forgotten your dog.

Puppies have sharp claws and can inflict permanent damage on a door. A clear glass door seems to encourage such behaviour more than a solid barrier because the young dog can see what is going on, and wants to join in, but is unable to do so because of the glass. This is a dangerous situation as there is a risk of the glass breaking and causing serious, or even fatal, injury to the dog. Cover the panes on both sides with safety plastic as used to protect small children in the home. This is easily fitted, and ensures that even if the glass does break it will be safely retained between the sheets of plastic and will pose no threat to the dog or anyone.

Chapter 6

Feeding the Flatcoated Retriever

Dogs prove far more adaptable in their feeding habits than cats, and this difference arises from their ancestry. The wolf is the ancestor of all today's breeds, and in the wild, although wolves prefer to feed on meat, they will eat a wide variety of other foods in order to survive. The few remaining wild wolves in Italy today often scavenge around rubbish dumps for food, like feral dogs, consuming anything edible. Dogs are omnivores, that is they can eat any food; cats are obligate carnivores and must eat meat.

Under normal circumstances the main ingredients of a wolf's diet are likely to be proteins and fats derived from the carcass of its prey. Proteins are made up of constituents known as amino acid residues of which there are approximately 20 different types. Some of these are known as 'essential', because they must be present in the diet if a deficiency is not to result. They are found in animal tissues so a dog is unlikely to suffer from an amino acid deficiency if it is receiving some meat in its diet. Certain vegetable sources of protein such as soya beans are better than others in terms of their amino acid composition, and this can be significant if you want to keep your dog on a vegetarian diet, though if you insist on this option it would be advisable to use one of the commercially prepared vegetarian foods for dogs in order to ensure the correct balance of all the vital nutrients.

Protein, as the major constituent of animal tissues, is particularly important in young, growing dogs. It is also required for the healing process and can, if necessary, be broken down in the body and used as energy. This underlies the wasted appearance of starved dogs; the protein forming their muscles has been metabolised within the body to keep them alive. In time, and with proper feeding, it should be possible to restore this loss of body condition.

Protein has various specific functions in the body. In the form of lipo proteins for example, in combination with lipids (fats) protein is a vital constituent of the membranes surrounding individual cells. As proteins are comprised of amino acid residues, so fats are made up of chains of fatty acids. Some of these fatty acids, such as linoleic acid, are essential in the diet. They are used in the manufacture of prostaglandins (PGs), for example, which are required for blood-clotting and other processes in the body.

One of the major roles of fat in a dog's diet is as a source of energy. In this respect it contains double the amount of energy present in the same amount of protein. This is not surprising because fat, rather than protein, acts as a natural energy store within the body, which can be broken down readily when required. In fact, protein will only be metabolised to any extent once the body's fat stores are exhausted.

Fat also has a key role to play in transporting the so-called fat-soluble group of vitamins which are essential to the dog's well-being. The contemporary idea that fat is harmful is therefore misplaced; it is the relative quantities of the components in the diet which determine whether a dog will become obese. The key is not to cut out fat, but to achieve a balance. If you are using a canned diet this is reasonably straightforward, simply by following the feeding instructions on the label. Studies of canine nutrition reveal that the optimum protein level in the diet, expressed as a percentage of the dry matter, (which means excluding the amount of water present in the food), should be somewhere between 18 and 22 per cent. In comparison the level of fat needs to be approximately five per cent.

The third major constituent of the diet is of course carbohydrate. Yet wild dogs preying on other animals will actually consume relatively little carbohydrate. This is because it is not usually present in the body to any extent, although some will be held in the form of glycogen in the liver. As a consequence, a dog eating meat will acquire much of its energy requirement not from carbohydrate but from fat in the first instance, and protein to a lesser degree. In fact, dogs do not require carbohydrate in their diet, as it has none of the specific functions of either fat or protein there. However, as befits the descendants of a scavenging as well as a hunting species, dogs are adaptable. Vegetables and cereals contain the starches and sugars which characterise carbohydrate foods but these tend to figure more prominently in the diet of domestic dogs than in the case of their wild counterparts.

Although there is no reason why a dog cannot be kept in good health on a diet comprised of proteins and fats without carbohydrate, this is a relatively costly option. The dog's body will simply use a proportion of the meat to supply its energy requirement, whereas providing vegetables for this purpose is cheaper. There is also the likelihood that a proportion of this vegetable matter will be indigestible cellulose which serves as roughage assisting the passage of food through the intestinal tract. Dogs themselves may seek out grass for this purpose with some individuals eating it on a fairly regular basis. However, in some cases this serves primarily as a natural emetic. For example, puppies often eat grass, subsequently vomiting it back with roundworms.

Vitamins

Other ingredients must also be present in the dog's diet in small amounts if it is to remain in good health. Vitamins, whose name is actually a contraction of the words 'vital amines', are chemicals intimately involved with many of the body's metabolic processes. They can be divided into two categories on the basis of their chemical nature: the fat-soluble vitamins A, D, E and K which are stored in the liver, and the other category, the so-called water-soluble vitamins which are members of the B group and vitamin C. In contrast to those of the fat soluble group the B group vitamins and vitamin C are not stored in the body.

Each vitamin has a particular function within the body. Vitamin A, for example, helps to protect against infections and is also important to ensure healthy eyesight. The various members of the vitamin B group include chemicals which do not immediately appear to be vitamins, such as biotin and choline, but each plays a critical role in the breakdown of foodstuffs and vitamin B6 is essential for the metabolism of amino acids.

Deficiency syndromes relate to the particular function which the vitamin would perform. In the case of a B6 deficiency, anaemia and weight loss are likely to be observed, although this is a very rare condition as B6 is widely found in foodstuffs ranging from meat to cereals and, like most vitamins, it is only required in tiny quantities. In this case, just 9.9 mg/kg of this vitamin in the dog's food will be sufficient to prevent any deficiency.

Dogs require a total of 13 different vitamins in their diet. Unlike ourselves, they are able to manufacture vitamin C in their bodies in most cases, so that this does not have to be present in food. Nevertheless it is usually included in commercial dog foods and this will help to prevent any signs of deficiency. About one dog in a thousand lacks the ability to produce vitamin C, in which case you would need to supplement its diet with vitamin C regularly or your pet will develop the characteristic signs of scurvy, such as a cracked and bleeding skin.

You can provide vitamin C quite easily in tablet form, adding this to your pet's food. The usual recommendation is to calculate the amount required on the basis of 100mg of vitamin C per 25kg (55lb) body weight. Avoid purchasing a large number of tablets however, because this vitamin breaks down readily in the presence of air. Always store the tablets in a dark place with the bottle top firmly in place until they are required. There used to be a belief that increasing the vitamin C level in the diet could help in cases of hip dysplasia, and might serve to prevent the weakness developing if fed to puppies from an early age, but after scientific study this theory has now been rejected.

Flatcoated Retrievers

It is important to bear in mind that, in some cases, external factors may affect the ability of the dog to utilise vitamins, and so a deficiency can arise. Vitamin K, an essential component of the blood-clotting system, is normally produced by beneficial bacteria in the gut, and then absorbed from there into the body. Prolonged antibiotic therapy can depress these bacteria, and so lead to a potential deficiency of vitamin K, which can lead to spontaneous haemorrhaging.

The diet itself may indirectly cause a vitamin deficiency. If large amounts of fish oils containing polyunsaturated fatty acids are fed to dogs regularly it is liable to lead to a deficiency of vitamin E. This creates muscle weakness and other changes in the body, as well as causing puppies to be born dead.

Not all vitamins are necessarily present in food in their active form. Dogs are able to convert the provitamin called carotene into vitamin A; carotene itself is widely-distributed in plants as well as in vegetables such as carrots. Vitamin D is manufactured in the skin, under the influence of the ultra-violet component of sunlight. In this case, it serves to regulate the calcium and phosphorus stores in the body, controlling the amount absorbed from the intestine and lost via the kidneys, as well as acting on the stores of these minerals in bone.

A deficiency of vitamin D in young dogs causes the disease known as rickets, while the equivalent condition in older animals is described as osteomalacia. These are rare diseases even in temperate areas, since the amount of sunlight required in order to result in the synthesis of vitamin D is low. Unfortunately however the provision of additional vitamin D in the dog's diet by well-intentioned owners is more likely to be a source of problems, resulting in the condition known as hypervitaminosis D.

Minerals

These chemicals also have a vital part to play in ensuring that your dog remains healthy, and must therefore be present at the appropriate level in the diet. Some minerals interact with each other, notably calcium and phosphorus. In this case, the so-called calcium-phosphorus ratio is significant. The optimum level is 1.2:1 in favour of calcium. Body tissues generally contain an excess of phosphorus over calcium of the order of 1:30, since calcium stores are largely concentrated in the bone of the skeletal system.

Domestic dogs are particularly vulnerable to a disturbed calcium:phosphorus ratio simply because they are generally not fed the whole carcass, but just muscle meat and offal. Their wild relatives in contrast will eat bone along with flesh. In fact, a dog's dental pattern is adapted to facilitate this process, with the carnassial teeth, comprising the last premolar in the upper jaw and the first lower molar enabling them to sheer through flesh and bone. This is why a dog with a bone invariably chews it with its head tilted to one side, relying on this particular combination of teeth, which can be used for crushing purposes.

Because of their rapid rate of growth puppies are most vulnerable to an imbalance in the calcium:phosphorus ratio in their diet. Care needs to be taken over the use of supplements however, because just as with vitamins it is possible to provide a mineral excess which can be equally harmful. Dairy products such as milk and cheese are good natural sources of calcium.

A number of minerals have key roles within the blood, notably to ensure that the gaseous exchange carried out via haemoglobin, present in all red blood cells, proceeds normally. Both iron and copper have key roles for this purpose. Others are involved in ensuring the correct functioning of nerves, sodium and potassium being vital in this respect. Iodine is vital to ensure the correct functioning of the thyroid gland. This has far-reaching effects on the body's metabolic processes. Other minerals have more limited, but no less critical, areas of activity. Manganese is utilised in the metabolism of fats, while sulphur is important for the synthesis of amino acids. Cobalt is linked with vitamin B12 (also known as cyanocobalamine), with selenium being vital for the proper functioning of vitamin E.

Zinc assists the healing process, and is one of the few minerals which may be deficient in a dog's diet, even one based on commercially-available foods. This is because if there is excessive calcium supplementation this will block the absorption of zinc from the intestinal tract into the body itself.

Practical Feeding

The idea of prepared diets for dogs was introduced to Britain by an entrepreneur called James Spratt, founder of Spratt's Patent, Ltd. He had previously lived in the United States and brought back a cargo of dog biscuits for sale to the famous kennels of the period. Among his earliest recruits was one Charles Cruft, who later founded the world famous dog show which still bears his name today. Cruft did much to promote the Spratt's brand in those early days, beginning in 1866.

Today the dog food industry has grown into a multi-billion pound concern worldwide. The ready availability of prepared foods has also contributed to the popularity of dogs as pets, as feeding them on this type of diet is quite straightforward. A considerable amount of money has been invested in research to unravel the precise nutritional requirements of dog and ensure that their food is not lacking in any essential ingredients. Further refinements are still occurring, and now 'life stage' diets are starting to be more heavily promoted.

It has long been appreciated that the nutritional requirements of dogs are not constant throughout their lives. As an example, puppies are likely to need a relatively higher level of protein than adult dogs because they are growing, while at the other end of the age spectrum old dogs will require a lower energy intake as they are less active. Refined diets to take into account these particular needs are now available, although in general terms ordinary balanced foods will be suitable if such substitutes are not available.

Commercially Prepared Diets for Dogs

Prepared diets for dogs can be divided into three basic categories. The traditional canned food has the highest water content of all, typically containing around 75 to 80 per cent water. They tend to be the most palatable type of food for this reason, and are typically 'balanced' in terms of their nutritional content. This means that all the ingredients required to ensure the health of the dog are included in the food, and supplementation is therefore not only unnecessary, but is actually likely to be harmful over a period of time.

It is often recommended to feed biscuit meal with some canned foods however, simply to provide energy in the form of cheaper cereal. Otherwise, the protein in the canned food is likely to be used as a source of energy. This applies largely in the case of all-meat canned foods, which tend to be the most costly. There can be quite a wide variance in the cost of canned dog foods, and this usually reflects the relative amount of cereal present in the mixture, which is considerably cheaper than meat. Read the list of ingredients, and instructions for use, so that you are aware of the type of food and the quantity required. Do not exceed the manufacturer's recommendations or you may find that your dog starts to put on weight, particularly if it is neutered.

Canned foods have drawbacks in that they are relatively heavy to carry and bulky to store, particularly if you have a number of dogs. Nevertheless, they can be kept for as long as a year or so without deterioration, provided that the cans are kept in a cool spot and not opened. Having been exposed to the air, however, the contents of the can will deteriorate rapidly as would fresh food. Any surplus should therefore be stored in a refrigerator, and used for the next meal. Ideally, you should remove the can from the refrigerator perhaps an hour or so beforehand as dogs generally prefer food at room temperature. It is possible to buy plastic caps to fit over an open can to prevent its contents becoming tainted, or tainting other foods in the refrigerator.

When serving canned food to your dog, you may need a knife to cut the contents into a suitable-sized portion. If you are using a biscuit meal, you can simply sprinkle the required amount on top of the food, or mix it in with the meat. Dogs typically bolt their meals, with little time given to chewing. In the case of canned food however, be sure to feed your pet on a surface which can be wiped over afterwards, as spillage may occur, particularly if you have not broken up the contents of the can beforehand. Canned food is recommended particularly for convalescing dogs, not only because of its palatability, but also because the contents tend to be more readily digested. They have a higher level of fat, rather than fibre.

Semi-moist products are intended to have the appeal of canned or fresh foods, combined with the ultimate convenience of dry foods. Their water content averages around 25 to 30 per cent, and they are sold in sealed pouches, containing convenient quantities of food. The food itself is in the form of discrete chunks, often shaped to suggest meaty contents. In reality, however, semi-moist foods contain many ingredients besides meat, as examination of their packaging reveals. Soya bean meal is a common ingredient as a source of protein, with bone and poultry meal often appearing among the constituents as well. Since the processing of semi-moist food takes place at relatively low temperatures much of the original vitamin level remains; for the dog's well being, adequate supplementation is ensured in such products.

It is usual for preservatives such as fungistats and bacteriastats to be present in foods of this type, because of their moisture content. For this reason, once a sachet is opened any remaining contents generally do not require refrigeration. Even so, the packet should be kept closed as far as possible, because the food will dry out, which reduces its palatability. The texture of semi-moist foods (not unlike marzipan) reveals a high sugar content. This acts to depress bacterial growth, but also means that these foods are not to be recommended for diabetic dogs.

Semi-moist foods are highly-digestible, with sugar adding to their palatability. In terms of their energy value they possess about three times as many calories per gram as canned food. This in turn means that, compared with canned food, far less actual volume of food is required in order to meet the dog's nutritional requirements. When a semi-moist food is used there is also usually less mess at feeding time. These foods can be particularly useful for lactating bitches, since their digestibility means that food input will be converted very efficiently to meet the bitches' body requirements.

A significant difference can be seen in the preferences of dog owners in various countries when it comes to selecting a prepared diet for their pets. In Britain for example, canned foods still account for the major share of the market, but in North America dry foods predominate. They represent the ultimate convenience food, but this is achieved only by reducing their water content down to about 8 per cent, which is well below that of canned foods or fresh meat.

Dry foods are ideal for ad libitum feeding. You simply tip out a quantity into a bowl, and then the dog can feed when it wants, rather than bolting it down, although at first your pet may tend to behave in this fashion. Some dogs are more reluctant to sample dry diets, particularly if they have been used to other types of food. However, dry foods generally represent good value, because you are only purchasing food, rather than a high proportion of water. Dogs fed on a dry diet will drink more to compensate for the relative absence of water in their food. Fresh, clean drinking water should be available to your dog at all times regardless of which feeding method you use.

If your dog is reluctant to sample a dry food, then you can soak it in a little water first, but barely cover it, because otherwise the pieces may simply disintegrate into a solid porridge. Do not soak any more food than is necessary for a single meal; you will have to discard any surplus because, like fresh food, it will deteriorate rapidly.

In addition to convenience, dry food has one major advantage over canned diets: because of its crunchy nature complete dry foods provide more exercise for the teeth, and there is correspondingly less risk of the build up of tartar, which may help reduce dental problems. For dogs who do not like crunchy dry foods some dry diets are available in flake form and are served soaked. These are nutritionally sound but do not have the possible dental advantages of crunchy products.

Within the dry food sector there are also special life stage diets intended for puppies, adult and elderly dogs. It is also possible to purchase dry foods which should be soaked before feeding. These are far more concentrated in energy terms than canned food, and may be recommended particularly if you have a large kennels, as they are easier to store and handle than cans.

Sacks of dog food need to be stored in dry conditions, preferably in a metal bin. Here the contents will be out of reach of rodents, as well as being protected from damp. No foods should be stored outside. A suitable measuring scoop will also be useful, so that the dishes can be filled easily at feeding time. Be sure to check the storage date for vitamins, and do not exceed this period, otherwise the nutritional value of the food is likely to be compromised. While purchasing in bulk may be cost-effective, it will be of little value if the food is simply allowed to deteriorate before use.

Semi-moist and dry foods are generally best used within four months of purchase. Be sure to rotate your stock accordingly, emptying out feed bins and cleaning them between batches. This should eliminate the risk of fodder mites becoming established here and thus spoiling the food. Barely visible to the naked eye, their presence imparts a rather sickly, sweet smell to the food. On close examination you should be able to see them with the aid of a magnifying glass moving through the food. Keeping food stored in sealed sacks can help to deter their presence.

Quality controls on the manufacture of dog food are generally very high. In fact, pasteurised milk for human consumption frequently contains more bacteria than dry dog food, so every effort should be made to maintain the nutritional value and benefits of such food.

A less commonly-used fresh food is in the form of chubs or packs of meat. These do not necessarily offer a balanced diet however, and need to be treated like perishable food. You are likely to find them in the refrigerated section of a pet shop, and they will need to be stored under similar conditions at home if they are not to deteriorate. It is sensible to keep them away from foods intended for human consumption.

You will need to allow frozen food to thaw out before offering it to your dogs. This can usually be accomplished by allowing the required amount to stand at room temperature overnight. You can then add biscuit meal, and offer it to the dogs.

The convenience factor of prepared, balanced dog foods is achieved at a price; therefore a number of kennels prefer to supplement such foods with fresh meat items, which are usually cheaper. These typically include offals such as 'melts' (spleens), heart, and tripe, which is the stomach lining of herbivores. While melts are usually cooked and then allowed to cool tripe is fed in the so-called 'green', raw state, which gives it a most unpleasant odour, but appears to make it no less palatable to dogs.

If you decide to use fresh meat on a regular basis for your dogs bear in mind the additional time which you will need to spend on preparing it. In the first place, it should be cooked rather than being fed raw, because of parasites which could be present in the meat which may then affect the dogs. Tapeworms (see Chapter 10) are typically spread in this fashion, with the herbivore acting as an intermediate host.

The meat should be cooked for at least 20 minutes to prevent excessive loss of vitamins or drying out, and this period should also be adequate to kill any parasites. In order to save time you may prefer to cook a week's supply of food rather than carrying out this task on a daily basis; provided, of course, that you have adequate cold storage for cooked food. Allow the meat to cool, and then weigh out sufficient for each day. The required quantity should be transferred to plastic bags, and can be stored in a freezer until required. This will greatly simplify the process of feeding fresh food on a regular basis. Cutting cooked meat into small pieces before bagging and freezing it may save time, and some people find it easier to use suitable scissors for this purpose rather than a knife. When it has thawed, you will simply have to tip the contents of the freezer bag into the dog's feeding bowl.

It is also important to vary the actual meat component of the diet on a regular basis to compensate for individual variations in the nutritional value of different types of meat. For example, minced meat comprising muscle is low in vitamin A, but by adding cooked liver to the dog's diet you will be providing a valuable source of this vitamin. However, excessive vitamin A is likely to be harmful, affecting the bones and making the joints painful. Liver also contains bile salts which will have a laxative effect if consumed in large quantities.

The fresh food which comes closest to meeting the dog's protein requirement in terms of its amino-acid composition is egg. Chicken, perhaps not surprisingly, is of almost similar value, but such foods may be insufficient to fulfil the dog's need for dietary fat. This is where minced beef can be particularly valuable, as it usually contains a relatively high percentage of fat, up to 25 per cent. The need to provide a varied, mixed diet of fresh foods is essential in order to maintain your dog's health. This is obviously time consuming, and may work out to be more costly than using a prepared food, particularly when you consider the time factor in preparing fresh food.

As a means of compensating for the nutritional shortcomings of a diet based on meat alone you should also use a quality biscuit mixer which will be supplemented with essential vitamins and minerals. This helps to prevent the utilisation of dietary protein for energy purposes. The vitamins and minerals in the biscuit mixer of your choice will be shown in detail on the packaging.

The amount of meat relative to biscuit should be about 50:50 but the proportions of biscuit will need to be reduced somewhat if offal, which is lower in protein, is used. It is of course possible to substitute other sources of carbohydrate, such as cooked potatoes, for the biscuit meal, but the risk of a deficiency of vitamins and minerals is increased as a result. You may need to use a nutritional supplement to overcome this risk, sprinkling it over the food.

It is important that potatoes and any cereals are cooked in order to gelatinize their starch content and improve their digestibility. Otherwise there is a risk that the dog will suffer badly from flatulence as the starch ferments in the intestinal tract producing gas, and possibly diarrhoea too. Other vegetables, notably cabbage, can also be a cause of flatulence. They are not essential in the diet, although they will add variety and bulk. Since cabbage contains little in the way of nutritional value, consisting mainly of water, it can be helpful if you are trying to slim your dog. Try to mix vegetables thoroughly with the meat as they are then more likely to be eaten. Larger breeds generally tend to have less fussy appetites than their smaller relatives but much depends on the individual dog.

It is possible to maintain dogs in good health on a purely vegetarian diet. In the past, this meant using fresh or commercially-available ingredients from health stores and similar outlets, but now some manufacturers of pet foods produce their own formulated vegetarian dog diets. These are to be recommended, since they are carefully prepared to ensure that your pet will receive all the nutritional ingredients to remain in good health.

The main difficulty in preparing your own vegetarian diet for a dog is that plant protein is deficient in certain essential amino-acids, as mentioned previously. Protein from soya beans is best, but large amounts are likely to lead to diarrhoea. While there is no difficulty in providing carbohydrate in this form, you will also need to consider your dog's requirement for essential fatty acids. As long as linoleic acid is present however, it should be able to meet the body's needs as this can be converted to arachidonic acid.

Cheddar cheese and eggs can be useful sources of linoleic acid if no animal fat is present in the dog's diet, and you may also wish to supplement its food with corn (maize) oil which is another valuable source of this vital fatty acid. The recommended level, if no other food containing linoleic acid is offered, is just over 15 ml/kg every day. Corn (maize) oil is easily available in most supermarkets, and can simply be measured out and mixed with the dog's food.

It is much easier to persuade a dog to accept a vegetarian food from puppyhood rather than expect an older individual to alter its feeding preferences. You may be able to make it more palatable by sprinkling a yeast-based powder over the meal. Nevertheless a dog which has regularly eaten a meat-based diet will pine for such foods and may steal or become aggressive as a consequence. You can add items such as scrambled egg to the diet on a regular basis. This will of course boost the essential amino-acid component of the diet. Fish can also be offered, provided that it is properly cooked, and is free from bones. It is best to break it up with a fork to ensure that it is safe for your dog.

Some people prefer not to use white bread when it comes to feeding a dog, maintaining that it is likely to be harmful. In fact, this belief is misplaced, although in the past dogs used to suffer from eating white bread. This was due to the custom which existed in the first half of the century for bleaching flour by using nitrogen trichloride. It was discovered in 1945 that dogs were suffering convulsions after eating dog biscuits made with this treated flour. Subsequently, this bleaching process was stopped because of associated fears over human health, but the fear of using white bread still lingers on with some people.

Drinking Requirements

Dogs should always be provided with a source of fresh drinking water, though in spite of your best attempts you may often find that your dog prefers to drink from a muddy puddle when you are out for a walk together. This should not be a great cause for concern as it is unlikely to be harmful provided that it is not obviously contaminated. However, if you go to the beach, remember to take a bottle of drinking water and a bowl, so that your dog will not be tempted to drink seawater if it becomes thirsty.

You can also provide milk for your dog. This is valuable for its calcium content, but is certainly not essential if your dog is receiving a balanced diet. Indeed, not all Flatcoats are able to digest milk properly as they lack the necessary enzyme to digest the milk sugar component, lactose. This is fermented in the gut to lactic acid, and causes diarrhoea in some dogs. If you wish to give milk to your dog provide this separately after a meal. The dog should then drink straight away, allowing you to wash the feeding bowl. Avoid leaving milk out when the weather is warm as it will sour rapidly.

Always be sure to wash your dog's feeding bowl after each meaL. Use hot water and detergent for this purpose, and then rinse the bowl thoroughly. For reasons of hygiene do not wash your dog's bowl with your own plates and cutlery. If you use a brush keep it exclusively for your pet's bowl, and run it under the tap after use to ensure that no food particles are trapped in the bristles.

The Use of Supplements

A host of vitamin and mineral products can be found on the shelves of pet shops today, but under normal circumstances your dog will not need a supplement, provided you are feeding a balanced diet and the dog is eating well. In fact there are dangers to your dog's health which could result from over-supplementation, particularly of the fat soluble vitamins. These are stored in the body, as explained previously. Excessive Vitamin A is likely to result in painful, sensitive legs, and on closer examination by use of X-rays the underlying bone will be seen to be weakened. With too much vitamin D in the diet, calcium deposits may build up in the blood vessels.

The conditions caused by an abnormally high amount of vitamins in the diet vary, depending upon the vitamin concerned. Those involving A and D are most common. It is a sad fact that today an excess of vitamin (hypervitaminosis) is far more common than a deficiency (hypovitaminosis). By offering food which contains persistently high levels of such vitamins on a regular basis owners are harming their dogs out of misplaced kindness.

If you are feeding a prepared, balanced diet, then no supplementation is likely to be required. If you need to provide additional calcium to the diet, as may sometimes be recommended for puppies or lactating bitches, then sterilised bone flour can be used for this purpose. It is usually recommended to use this with cod liver oil, which provides additional Vitamin D, and so facilitates the absorption of this extra calcium into the body.

Discuss the question of vitamin/mineral supplementation with your vet to be sure that you do not overdose your dog. In the case of the water-soluble vitamins there appears to be no risk attached to using Vitamin B group supplements, in the form of yeast tablets for example. These can also prove a useful appetite stimulant if your dog is recovering from illness.

Treats

Try to avoid feeding your dog other than at meal times. Otherwise this could lead to behavioural difficulties in that the dog will expect to receive treats at regular intervals, and it could also predispose your dog to obesity. The occasional treat will do no harm, but try to avoid sweet treats such as chocolate. Instead, it is better to use the special chocolate drops for dogs that are sold at most pet shops. These contain less sugar than traditional chocolate and are supplemented with vitamins and minerals, making them more nutritious.

If you have children, it can be particularly difficult to persuade them not to feed the family dog with treats, or prevent them from slipping food from the table. Explain to them that this will be harmful; the dog will end up fat, and is likely to have bad teeth as well.

Many dogs will not need a second opportunity to steal from a box of chocolates left within reach. These are likely to be swallowed whole, even if they are wrapped in foil, and gulped down quickly. Should this happen then your dog may well be sick shortly afterwards, although alternatively the chocolates may pass through the body quite rapidly. A high intake of sugar is likely to lead to diarrhoea, and so you will need to be prepared for this eventuality if your dog consumes a lot of sweets of any type.

A healthy treat which is unlikely to cause obesity is a simple piece of carrot. This is particularly useful during the puppy's training when plenty of encouragement and material reward will help to maintain progress.

In the past dogs were often given marrow bones to gnaw, though today with the wide choice of commercially-produced dog chews this practice is less common. There is certainly no need to provide a marrow bone for your dog, and for many people the idea of a bone being dragged around the home is unpleasant. There is also the dog's safety to consider as some bones are dangerous. This applies particularly to those from poultry; they tend to split and form sharp spicules which may become stuck in the mouth or impale themselves lower down the digestive tract. Cooked bones are even more likely to splinter than fresh bones, so you will also need to be careful to ensure that your dog cannot steal a chicken carcass or chop bones from a rubbish bag or dustbin.

Always suspect that your dog may have stolen and swallowed a bone if it suddenly starts gagging and pawing at its face, trying to retch as well. Unless you can manage to dislodge the fragment of bone safely you will need to contact your vet without delay. Marrow bones (the limb bones of cattle) are relatively safe because of their thickness, but as the dog chews his marrow bone keep a watch to ensure that spicules do not start flaking off; this is the time when it must be replaced.

There is little doubt that many dogs appear to enjoy gnawing bones but, as with toys, you must persuade a puppy to give up a bone on command because it can become very possessive of such items and this would be storing up trouble for the future. Bones can help to prevent the build-up of tartar on the teeth, but so can other chews which are more hygienic around the home. Those in the Nylabone range are particularly popular and are produced in a selection of shapes and sizes. They are not primarily of nutritional value, but aside from helping to ensure dental health these chews should also serve to deter young puppies from gnawing other items around the home.

Chews of this type should not be confused with actual dog treats, which are normally highly palatable and consumed with relish by dogs of all ages. Unfortunately such treats, if fed in excessive quantities, are likely to cause your dog to become obese, so be sure to follow the feeding instructions on the packet.

Pet food companies have expended a great deal of effort in designing and packaging treats, as they now represent a substantial and profitable part of the dog food market. This is essentially for the dog's owner rather than the dog itself, so do not worry if you need to change brands at any stage. If your dog is fed largely on a canned diet it may be better to stick to treats which are dry, rather than those of the semi-moist type, as they will be of more value for your pet's health.

Dental Care

There has been considerable focus in recent years on the dental health of dogs. This is partly because more dogs are living well into old age as the result of advances in veterinary care, and therefore dental health assumes a greater significance.

Although dogs can manage with the loss of some teeth, the absence of several will clearly be a handicap when it comes to tackling certain foods. Deposits of tartar on the teeth can spread to the gums, causing inflammation and, ultimately, loss of teeth. Puppies should therefore become accustomed to having their teeth brushed regularly, so that they will not resent this handling as they become older. It is advisable to use one of the special canine toothpastes now marketed for this purpose. Cream of tartar is a traditional means of cleaning a dog's teeth, and can be used if canine toothpaste is unobtainable. Ordinary human toothpaste is less satisfactory, because it tends to foam in the mouth, but it will do in an emergency. You can also buy tooth-brushes which have been specially-designed for a dog's mouth, and these are be recommended though, as in the case of toothpaste, the human variety will serve if necessary.

If you have an older dog which is unaccustomed to having its teeth brushed you may need to try a different method. Holding the mouth open, rub the teeth with a clean piece of cotton material to which toothpaste has been applied. You will need to take care that your dog does not nip you when you are cleaning its teeth in this way.

Food Allergies and Other Feeding Problems

With an increasing emphasis on 'natural' foods there is growing concern about food additives and potential allergies. The case of nitrogen trichloride which was formerly used to bleach flour has already been discussed and, fortunately, such cases are exceedingly rare. Dog food manufacturers have gone to great lengths to ensure that their products are not only nutritionally sound, but also safe for the long-term health of your pet.

There are a number of popular misconceptions about food allergies. In the first place, the inability of a dog to digest a particular component of its diet, milk for example, is not evidence of an allergy. It simply indicates a deficiency within the dog's metabolic processes.

The effects of a true allergy take longer to become apparent. A dog which is lactose-intolerant, and in consequence suffers diarrhoea after drinking milk, will develop this problem rapidly, within hours. A small amount of milk will have not have such an adverse effect on the digestive tract as a larger volume.

In contrast a dog afflicted by an allergy will show no symptoms whatsoever for at least 10 days after consuming the food item responsible, known as the allergen. This is the length of time that it takes for the body to react to the allergen, producing antibodies to it. In the case of a genuine allergy, even a tiny amount of the food item will result in an allergic response.

A dog affected by a food allergy often develops an itchy skin which it scratches and bites at repeatedly, although obviously there are other far more common causes for such behaviour - notably an infestation by fleas or other external parasites. Breathing difficulties may also be noted in some cases, and vomiting is not unknown.

The difficulty in a suspected case of food allergy lies in actually being able to track down the source of the problem. Identifying the protein responsible can often be a time-consuming process, and calls for particular resolve on the part of the dog's owner. First it entails the use of a hypoallergenic diet, which is likely to be free of the problematical protein. This diet will be based on sources of protein not normally present in the dog's food, such as lamb and rice for example.

After a period on this diet, and assuming the signs of the allergy do not recur, it will then be a matter of adding the particular items which figured previously in the dog's diet, one at a time, in accordance with your vet's instructions. A sufficient interval must then elapse so that signs of allergy can develop before repeating the process with another food item until, hopefully, the cause of the problem can be found. Subsequently, the dog's diet will need to be adjusted so that the offending source of protein is excluded. But it is important to bear in mind that almost any food can be incriminated, and tracking it down may prove difficult. The problem may reside outside the dog's normal diet, being associated with chocolate for example, or fruit. Cases have even been traced not to the food itself, but the plastic feeding bowl, although this is exceedingly rare.

Your dog will give you no indication of the source of the allergy, since it will continue to eat the offending item, even though ultimately this makes it ill. In contrast, some dogs prove to be rather fussy eaters, and much can be done to prevent this problem early in life by introducing your dog to as wide a range of foodstuffs as possible once it is settled with you, but try not to vary the diet at first because this may lead to a digestive upset.

Feeding preferences are established relatively early in life, and a dog which has been fed entirely on canned food until middle age may prove reluctant to switch to dry food, for example, which is likely to be less appealing in terms of texture if not taste. The food should smell attractive - dogs generally rely much more heavily on their sense of smell than we do, and not just when it comes to food. You can improve the palatability in several ways. For a dog that is used to canned food, try soaking the required amount of dry food with warm water or gravy, or sprinkling a little sugar on it; this should improve its appeal.

It is important that all treats of any kind are cut out between meals because this can depress the dog's appetite. If the dog does not eat immediately when you give it its food simply leave the food and the dog together. Should food not be touched within half an hour or so, remove the bowl and only feed the dog again at the time the next meal is due.

It may be that something in the dog's immediate environment is disturbing it, and so deterring it from eating. This is most likely to arise in the case of a new pet which is unused to you and its new home. The kitchen can often prove a rather busy thoroughfare, and it may be better to choose a quieter spot where your dog can feed, even in the garden if necessary. This is not the best locality during the warmer part of the year, however, because fresh or canned food in particular will attract flies. Under normal circumstances dogs will eat a meal within a couple of minutes, but do not leave food where flies could gain access to it.

Unlike cats, dogs will rarely starve themselves for any length of time, unless they are ill. After the shock and stress of a disturbance, resulting from a thunderstorm perhaps, your dog may be reluctant to eat on the following day. Clearly, if this situation persists, or the dog appears unwell, then you will need to seek veterinary advice.

Obesity

There are certain circumstances in which you will actually want to restrict your dog's food intake. This applies after an episode of diarrhoea for example, when offering a bland diet and a reduced quantity of food will enable the dog to recover from this condition more rapidly. Rice and a little cooked chicken are often recommended for a few days following a digestive disturbance of this type.

Increasing numbers of dogs are becoming victims of obesity today. According to some surveys up to one-third of Britain's dogs are overweight. In some cases you can find the recommended weight for your dog quite easily from The Kennel Club Breed Standard but, as a rough guide, your dog will be overweight if you cannot feel its ribs easily.

As in the case of people, obese dogs are likely to encounter more health problems, in later life particularly, ranging from diabetes mellitus to heart disease. They also tend to have a shorter life expectancy and, compared with a dog of normal weight, are at greater risk when being anaesthetised for any reason.

Bitches are particularly prone to obesity, simply because they tend to have more fatty tissue in their bodies than male dogs do. Neutering worsens the situation still further, and a progressive weight gain tends to occur in many bitches and dogs from middle age onwards. Those being fed on home-cooked food are more likely to be obese, because there is less guidance on the required quantities necessary to meet the dog's nutritional needs. In comparison the recommended daily intake of food is explained on the packaging of commercial diets.

Obesity is the result of an intake of carbohydrate and fat in excess of the body's energy requirements. It can be tackled effectively on two fronts: firstly, the energy content of the diet should be reduced so the dog will then metabolise its surplus fat stores to meet its energy needs; secondly, more exercise should be given to speed up the process and ensure that the weight loss will be maintained. Often, as with human dieting, it is possible to achieve weight loss, but then the surplus pounds start to creep back. To achieve lasting success the root causes of obesity must be tackled.

You will need to note your dog's weight in the first instance, and then establish a target figure based on the Breed Standard. Discuss this with your vet, who can provide you with a special obesity diet if necessary. This is likely to contain a significantly higher amount of fibre than the dogs' regular diet, the energy value of the ration being correspondingly reduced. Your dog will therefore consume the same quantity of food as before, but a higher proportion than normal will be indigestible in the sense that it simply provides bulk, while the calorie content is significantly lower.

Flatcoated Retrievers

In most cases your vet will recommend restriction of the dog's calorific intake to 60 per cent of its former level. All other sources of food, including titbits, will need to be withdrawn - a fact that may well need to be emphasised to younger members of the family. In terms of drink, only water should be offered.

You will need to weigh your dog regularly to monitor the progress of its diet. You may be able to persuade your pet to stand on the bathroom scales, but in most cases it will be better if you lift your pet on to the scales. You can then measure your combined weights and subtract your own weight from this total to give you the weight of the dog.

A diary will be useful to keep a check on your dog's weight during its diet. Weight loss depends on the size of the breed. Smaller dogs, weighing under 20lb (9kg) can be expected to lose about half a pound every week, with this figure being tripled in the case of the larger breeds which typically exceed 40lb (18kg) in weight. It can take as long as three months for your dog to reach the target figure. In addition to the dieting, increasing the amount of exercise which your pet receives should also have a beneficial effect, provided that its overall physical health is sound.

Instead of using a special obesity diet (several of which may be available in pet shops) you can of course simply restrict your dog's usual food intake. As a starting point, if you catch the problem at an early stage, it may be sufficient simply to cut out much of the biscuit meal and slightly reduce the amount of canned food as well. This approach may however cause more behavioural difficulties, as the dog will be deprived of the quantity of food which it has become used to eating. As a consequence it is more likely to feel hungry and act accordingly, attempting to steal food or scavenging if the opportunity arises when out for a walk.

When you have managed to reduce your dog's weight by the required amount, aim to maintain it around this figure by altering its food intake on a permanent basis. You should then be offering an amount of food somewhat lower in terms of energy than was originally the case, while maintaining the level of exercise. Weigh your dog regularly every week, noting this figure, to ensure that it maintains its correct weight. Prevention of obesity is much easier than cure.

By weighing your dog regularly you can also be certain that you are providing it with sufficient food as there can also be situations when your dog is underweight, or loses weight unexpectedly. Should you find that in spite of all efforts your dog remains underweight, and is consistently below that recommended for the breed, then you should seek veterinary advice. It may be the result of a metabolic illness such as diabetes mellitus, or a renal problem. However, if you take on a rescued puppy which has been deprived of adequate food over a period of time you must expect that its growth is likely to be permanently stunted.

Special Dietary Needs

In certain situations dogs require more food than usual, particularly those which work regularly, as will probably be the case with the majority of Flatcoats. There are specially formulated diets available for such dogs, or you can simply improve the dog's regular diet by giving additional fat and a small amount of extra protein to meet the increased energy requirement. The same can apply in the case of dogs kept under freezing conditions. It is reckoned that a Siberian Husky living in Siberia requires about two and a half times the amount of food as one living indoors in Europe.

Other factors, such as a febrile illness, are also likely to raise the dog's energy requirements. It can often be difficult to persuade a sick dog to eat, and every effort must be made to encourage it. Offering a range of highly palatable foods such as liver, cooked meat or even a premium brand of canned cat food can have the required effect. Dogs respond well to individual attention when sick, and offering food by hand may rekindle a jaded appetite. Warm food is also more likely to be favoured than food kept at room temperature.

If the dog is suffering from a gastro-intestinal tract illness it should be offered small meals throughout the day rather than a larger quantity of food once or twice during this period. The food itself must also be easy for the dog to digest, soothing rather than aggravating the inflamed region. Chicken with rice or scrambled eggs are often favoured for this purpose. You may also want to use a probiotic product. These contain beneficial bacteria, which help to stabilise the bacterial population in the gut after a disturbance resulting from an infection or the prolonged use of broad-spectrum anti-biotics. While antibiotic therapy is vital in overcoming infective micro-organisms, such drugs also depress those bacteria which are naturally of benefit in the body. As a result the body's defences may be depleted, rendering the dog vulnerable to secondary infections, often by fungi. A probiotic will help to overcome this risk, enabling the gut to be repopulated by beneficial bacteria, and can be adminis-tered when the course of antibiotics is completed. (It goes without saying that it would be counter-productive to use both at once.) Many commercially-produced probiotics are now available, and simply need to be added to the dog's food. If you cannot find a probiotic in a pet shop, and provided that your dog is not intolerant to lactose, then you can use a live yoghurt instead. This will contain lac-tobacillus bacteria, which can have a protective effect in the gut.

Flatcoat puppies are particularly prone to upset stomachs at five to six weeks, when they are being weaned. They are likely to develop sudden looseness and hypersensitivity as the complete food is introduced. In this case, try other foods, and follow veterinary advice.

After an episode of diarrhoea the natural rhythm of the gut is disturbed, and the dog may then become constipated. Adequate drinking water is essential at all times, but particularly in the case of a dog suffering from diarrhoea, since fluid loss from the body will then be higher than normal. You can then add bran to the diet, as this will bulk up the faecal output, and help to prevent constipation developing.

The same applies in the case of older dogs, which can also be susceptible to constipation. You may find it helpful for your pet to switch from a dried diet to canned food at this stage, simply because of its raised water content. This should also assist in preventing constipation.

Excessive fluid loss from the body is often associated with older dogs, as their kidneys start to fail. This is considered in more detail in Chapter 10 but, aside from the medical condition itself, you will need to modify your pet's diet to stabilise the condition. Your vet can supply you with a special nephritis diet for this purpose. This will need to be used exclusively, in order to result in a noticeable improvement in your dog's condition. However, it is not just increased water consumption that is associated with nephritis; weight loss is also likely to be observed, because of loss of protein in the dilute urine.

Flatcoated Retrievers

The extent of the problem can be assessed by means of veterinary tests. Stabilisation will call for the provision of a high quality protein in order to meet the body's requirements while minimising the by-products which can accumulate in the blood. It may also be necessary to raise both the carbo-hydrate and fat content of the diet, so that this protein is not diverted towards meeting the dog's energy requirements.

Both sodium and phosphorus are excreted via the kidneys, and can therefore be lost in excessive quantities when a dog is suffering from kidney failure. These minerals must therefore be present in the diet in increased quantities. This is one of the major advantages of using a canned nephritis food as the necessary adjustments have been made in this type of product. Should you prefer to use home-cooked rations, items such as chicken will be valuable. Consult your vet so that you can formulate the appropriate diet for your dog.

It is also important to consider the vitamin B level of the diet in such cases as these vitamins are liable to be lost from the body in increased quantities when a dog is suffering from kidney failure. Signs of a deficiency, such as mouth ulceration, may then become apparent. The addition of a sup-plement to the dog's diet, yeast in tablet or powder form for example, is therefore to be recommended under such circumstances.

A dog suffering from kidney failure often has bad breath, although this can also result from a dental problem, and if the condition is not stabilised you will find that its appetite will be depressed. This results from the accumulation of the components of protein breakdown in the blood. In more severe cases vomiting is likely to occur, but provided that the condition is recognised, and the diet adjusted, your dog should be able to continue to enjoy an active life, perhaps for several years.

Progressive heart failure is another chronic illness typically associated with older dogs. This condition also responds well to dietary management and becomes stabilised in many cases, but there will be a need to encourage water loss from the body as the heart itself will not be pumping as effec-tively as normal. The use of drugs known as diuretics may be required on a regular basis for this purpose, but mild cases of heart failure can respond favourably to a reduction in the sodium level of the diet alone.

It is important in such cases to avoid prepared dog foods, as they tend to contain relatively high levels of sodium. Your vet will again be able to advise you on the best diet for your dog, with specially-formulated rations removing the worry of providing a safe diet. Many prepared household foods ranging from ordinary bread through processed snacks to canned vegetables contain additional sodium in the form of salt and need to be avoided. Additional potassium and B vitamins are also to be recommended in the diet of a dog suffering from heart failure.

There are also some metabolic disorders which can affect the way in which a dog has to be fed. Perhaps one of the most common is diabetes mellitus, which is also sometimes known as sugar diabetes. This is typically caused by a failure of the so-called beta cells of the pancreas (a gland lying in close proximity to the small intestine) to produce sufficient of the hormone insulin. Under normal circumstances insulin serves to trigger cells to take up glucose which is used for the metabolism of the cell. When there is a deficiency of insulin, glucose accumulates in the blood, and much of it is lost via the kidneys in urine which has a characteristic sickly sweet odour in such cases.

The incidence of diabetes mellitus is significantly higher in bitches than dogs and increases dramatically in middle age. Since affected individuals cannot utilise this glucose the body starts to break down fat in order to meet its energy requirements. Meanwhile an increased volume of water is lost, flushing the glucose out of the body and resulting in excessive thirst, while the dog appears ravenously hungry in spite of eating well. Subsequently, its appetite declines and it will start to vomit before entering a diabetic coma.

The treatment of diabetes mellitus is demanding, requiring daily monitoring and injections of insulin. Nevertheless, dietary adjustments can also be of value. It is particularly important that the dog's weight is held at the correct level and a fixed daily feeding routine is maintained. If the dog is overweight at the time of diagnosis you should aim to slim it down by means of a high fibre or obesity diet. This will help to stabilise the blood glucose concentration and will reduce the need for insulin. However, should your dog have lost weight, try to build up its weight using a puppy food. The frequency of feeding in the case of diabetic dogs should be increased markedly, with several smaller meals a day being provided instead of just one or two large feeds. This will help prevent rapid and wide swings in the blood glucose level following feeding.

The pancreas is also responsible for producing digestive enzymes, and if its ability to synthesise these enzymes is impaired the dog will be unable to digest and absorb its food properly. This results in weight loss, with the dog appearing extremely hungry. Although it is eating, it is also effectively starving as vital nutrients simply pass through its intestinal tract. This condition can be diagnosed from faecal samples, and treated effectively by adding the necessary enzymes to the dog's food on a regular basis. The use of 'sweetbreads' (the popular name given to the pancreas of cattle) to supplement the regular diet can also prove helpful in some cases, but inevitably long-term supplementation of pancreatic enzymes will be essential. Unfortunately, it is very difficult to build up the dog's weight even when the illness has been brought effectively under control.

Chapter 7

Care and Basic Training

There are certain basic training requirements which all dogs should be taught. A number of factors influence the ease with which these can be learned, and much depends on you, the dog's owner, and how much time you devote to training during the course of a week. The age of the dog also has a bearing, as young dogs are typically far more responsive than older individuals. The nature of the breed itself is also significant; breeds such as the Flatcoated Retriever which have been bred to work closely with people are easier to train successfully than pack hounds, for example.

First of all, a young puppy will need to become accustomed to its name. You should repeat this clearly at every opportunity when talking to your puppy. To avoid confusion it is best not to change the name of an older dog, though this can be achieved if desired.

Plenty of encouragement and praise will be of benefit, especially in the early stages with a new dog. This will help to establish a bond between you. Develop a routine by calling the puppy to you when its food is ready, encourage it to sit by applying gentle pressure to the hindquarters, then praise it and place the food bowl on the floor. As a result the puppy will soon understand the meaning of the important command 'sit'.

Right from the start, at the same time you teach your puppy to sit, teach him to stand in a well-balanced way. If he does this from puppyhood you will not have a problem when you start training him to do this should you decide to show him.

If you are going to use your puppy as a gundog it is worth getting him used to a whistle early. When you are playing with your puppy, call him back to you with short peeps and run in the opposite direction, making it a great game. Whistles can be bought in most gun shops.

From the beginning, the puppy should be encouraged to let you and your family inspect his teeth regularly, though this should not become an issue. If you are going to show him in the future, he will have to allow the judge to inspect his teeth. Attendance at Ringcraft classes will help him to become used to procedures such as this.

As puppies grow older their natural exuberance takes over, and on occasions they will inevitably try to jump up at you or other members of the family. That could be positively dangerous in the case of this breed with children or frail adults, and a dog of any size can inflict damage to clothing with its sharp claws, so this behaviour needs to be discouraged. When the puppy jumps up, grasp it gently by the shoulders and push it down to the ground, giving the firm command, 'No!', and then encourage it to sit before attempting to praise it. Your dog should soon learn that jumping up is not acceptable.

It may also be helpful to teach your dog to lie down on command. This can be achieved quite easily from the sitting position, linked with the appropriate instructions. Extend the dog's forelegs out in front of the body so that it adopts the required posture. You will probably need to repeat this procedure several times before your dog learns to adopt it of his own accord in response to your command of 'Lie down!'. Firmness and a great deal of patience pay dividends. Save the harsh tones of voice for situations which really demand strong correction.

Even within the same breed, some dogs appear to learn at a faster rate than others, and you will need to be tolerant. All the basic commands described above can be taught at an early stage, and should be given in a firm but kind voice. More elaborate lead training will follow later, when your puppy has become used to wearing a collar. To begin with this should be fitted for short periods which are then gradually extended.

When you first attach a lead to the collar do not expect too much on the part of your puppy. It may well be excited and will try to chew the lead. You will need to deal with this situation firmly, giving the command 'No!', and opening your dog's mouth to remove the lead if it will not let go voluntarily.

The tone of voice is important in the training repertoire as puppies are sensitive to harsh commands. Should you find that it persists in attempting to gnaw at the lead speak in a firmer voice. Then before you remove the lead from the puppy's mouth, hold its head gently but firmly, using the loose skin below the ears to direct its attention towards you, and say 'Dead!'. Should the puppy not respond, then you will obviously need to take the lead gently out of its mouth yourself.

It is important that the puppy learns the command 'Dead!' at an early stage because this will apply to other items, such as shoes, which it may steal as playthings. Possessiveness over objects can begin at an early age, and will store up future trouble unless you take steps to correct it. It is a very rare fault to find in a Flatcoat, but it is one that must be corrected, especially if you have children who may attempt to take toys from the dog. They too must be taught the command 'Dead!', and the dog must be trained to give up the object gently. He should then be rewarded with a kind gentle voice.

Older dogs should be approached carefully if you are uncertain whether they will surrender an object readily. This is probably the most likely situation to lead to a person being bitten in the home. In the case of a puppy, if the command 'Dead!' is ignored initially, you will need to open its jaws gently to retrieve the object, or offer a distraction in the form of a toy that is allowed or a titbit. Giving up an object should be part of the play routine of all puppies, and such actions must be greeted with profuse praise to encourage this behaviour later in life. Building a bond with your dog is something which takes place over weeks and months, even years, and cannot be established overnight. It is helpful if all members of the family take some part in the training routine as the dog must respond to their commands when you are away from home.

A young puppy will not be fully protected against the common canine diseases until it has received a full course of inoculations from your veterinary surgeon, who will advise you when it is safe to take your puppy into public places where other dogs are exercised. Until then it will be unsafe to take the puppy anywhere that other dogs have been. You can, however, take your puppy for short rides in the car to help him get used to travelling and you can begin lead training in your own garden.

Start by running through the lessons which the puppy will already be learning, such as sitting on command. The novelty of being on the lead may mean that your puppy fails to respond as required at first, so you may need to position its rear end downwards with gentle pressure on the hindquarters. Try to distract the puppy's attention from the lead at this stage by letting it hang slack as the puppy sits quite close to you. Allow the puppy to have a good view of you, so that it is less likely to stand up and turn around, pulling away on the lead. As your puppy grows into a young adult, hand signals are always useful and you can indicate that you wish the puppy to sit by accompanying this command with a downward movement of your open hand.

Although it is better to teach the puppy to walk on a conventional lead at first, an extending lead can be helpful during the training process. You can leave the puppy sitting while carefully letting out the lead and gradually backing away before calling the dog to you with the instruction 'Come!', and a backward gesture of your hand towards your body. You can also use your whistle at this time. If the puppy simply follows you, return it to the spot where it should have stayed and repeat the process. If you find that the puppy appears uncertain of what to do, and remains sitting, you can then give a gentle pull on the lead to encourage it to come to you.

Plenty of praise is important, encouraging the puppy to perform as required. Training sessions should also be kept relatively short to maintain the dog's interest as far as possible. They can be repeated two or three times a day, and need to be carried out on a regular basis if progress is to be maintained.

All this training is what one can describe as 'play learning', very much as you would do with your children. Try to make everything fun, and at this stage do not do anything that will cause your puppy to be disobedient; try to do all these things in situations where the puppy will get them right.

As soon as the puppy has shown signs of mastering the basics of coming to you when called you should repeat the process, having removed the lead but not the collar. You will not want the puppy to become used to running while on the lead, particularly in the case of a large breed. When you start training the dog to walk on the lead you are likely to find that it attempts either to pull ahead or hang back (particularly if it finds an interesting smell) rather than walking along at a convenient pace with you. However, correct lead training is an important lesson. If a dog behaves badly on the lead you may slip over and injure yourself on icy ground for example, or trip over the lead. Such accidents must be prevented if possible, and perseverance with lead training is very important.

To encourage your puppy to walk alongside you rather than pulling away in any direction you should start by walking alongside a wall or fence in the garden. The dog should always be trained to walk on your left-hand side, with you between him and the traffic. This means that when you are out together the dog will be far less likely to pull away directly into the road. Hold the lead quite tightly in your hand when training the puppy to walk with you, as this places an immediate check on it. Start walking, and when the puppy pulls ahead give a sharp tug on the lead, coupled with the command 'Heel!'. Similarly, should the puppy start lagging behind, repeat this action pulling in a forward direction. Although praise is important, do not allow this to distract the young dog when it accompanies you as required. A soft, verbal 'Good dog!' is sufficient on this occasion.

If you do not have a suitable wall or fence around the garden you can simply walk round a lawn or paved area. You may encounter the added difficulty of the dog pulling away, in which case a pull on the lead and holding it tightly should serve to communicate the message to the dog. The use of a check chain to assist in training a dog to walk correctly on the lead is favoured by some people, but you must be sure that it is correctly fitted; otherwise the dog could sustain a serious injury. A check chain is not recommended for puppies, and great care must be taken with younger dogs. It may be useful later, but if your ground work is done well there will be no need.

If you do decide to use one on an adult dog, remove the dog's collar before placing the check chain around the neck. The loop of the chain which connects to the lead should run over the top of the dog's head and, when fitted correctly, will tighten round the dog's neck when tension is applied and will slacken off immediately the pressure is released (see illustration). It will thus give the dog a constant reminder that it should not pull ahead or hang back, since it will tighten under these circumstances and cause momentary discomfort. If fitted incorrectly the check chain will not release and may hurt the dog. It is also important to choose a check chain of the correct length. This can be worked out quite easily by passing a tape measure around the dog's head and over the ears and adding an extra 5cm (2in) to this figure.

If you are uncertain regarding the use of a check chain, ask an experienced person to demonstrate its use. As I have said before, it should not be needed with your (hopefully!) well-trained Flatcoat.

Slip collars, which work on the same principle as check chains, are made in strong nylon fabric with a metal ring at each end. There are also nylon fabric slip leads available in most pet shops and at dog shows. These have a metal ring at one end and a normal lead hand loop at the other. The nylon slips work in the same way as the metal check chains, and should be used with the same care, but as they do not make the same noise, and are kinder in use, they may be better for some dogs. If you exercise sufficient patience, and do not expect instant lead training success, you may never need to resort to the use of a check chain or a slip lead.

Once the dog is walking readily on the lead you can introduce such variety to the routine as will occur when you are out together in the street. For example, tell your dog to sit, as this is to be recommended when you are at the kerb-side waiting to cross the road. Also teach him to stand still on command as this will help if you decide that you want to show your puppy. Only short training sessions of this type are required, and at the end reward your dog with your warm, soft voice and a gentle stroke of the back the head or under the chin. This must be done in a way that does not excite your dog. The use of treats is not advisable as this too is likely to distract your dog from the task in hand. Furthermore, if it has not been given a treat at each stage it will not expect them and will be content with praise as a reward.

Variations to the routine are useful as some dogs show signs of boredom if they have to repeat the same sequence of commands every day, and may start to misbehave even though they are reasonably competent at following instructions. As a change from lead-work you may want to concentrate on training your dog to follow commands off the lead. Again this should be tried initially within the confines of your garden as it is dangerous to allow your dog off the lead in public places until it is properly trained.

Start as always by instructing your dog to 'Sit'. Then walk backwards, keeping your hand pointing downwards to emphasise that the dog is expected to remain sitting. This will be repeating the lessons learnt when the dog was on the retractable lead. You should then call the dog to you, indicating this with your hand movements. Do not forget to praise the dog when it reaches you and sits down. At first, the dog will almost inevitably run towards you before being given the command. Lead it back to the spot, with no display of affection, and repeat the process. Ultimately, the dog will gather what is expected of it, and remain sitting until called to you.

There are no short cuts to achieving training success with a dog. You can seek the advice of a professional trainer but this is generally far less satisfactory and much more costly than joining a local dog training class. Although a dog may respond well to a trainer the impact of these lessons will be reduced if you are not involved because the dog will not accept your commands as readily as those of the trainer.

At a dog training class you and your dog will work together. Obedience training classes are usually run by local canine societies and the telephone number of the organiser should be available on request from The Kennel Club (see **Useful Addresses**). Alternatively this information may be available at your local library or at your vet's surgery. Although you may not be able to take your puppy for some weeks it is a good idea to enquire about joining a course at an early stage as such classes are very popular and there may be a waiting list. In addition to obedience training, another benefit of attending such classes is that it gives your pet an opportunity to socialise with other dogs. This can help prevent excitable behaviour when your dog meets strange dogs when you are out for walks.

Having mastered the basics at a training class you may decide to progress to one of the more advanced obedience courses, or perhaps you would like to try training your dog for competition in agility classes which are great fun for all involved. These are sometimes held at major dog shows where dogs are being assessed for type, but the interest in agility competition has become so great that many agility shows are now a separate entity. Even if your dog is never likely to be a breed champion it can still participate in obedience competitions and agility stakes where a close bond between dog and owner will be vital for success. However, the most usual activities for the Flatcoated Retriever are detailed in Chapter 8.

It is important for your dog to be obedient in the home as well as outside. It is essential that you provide proper guidance from the outset to prevent any confusion in the mind of your puppy. If you do not want your dog to sleep on chairs or sofas when he is an adult do not allow him to do so when he is a puppy. Above all, be consistent in your approach. Remember to praise his good efforts and correct him firmly, but never too harshly, when necessary. He will want to please you, so let him see that you are pleased with good behaviour. But do remember what we have said before: all this education must be fun for you and your puppy.

House-training is a critical phase in the puppy's development. In general terms dogs are clean animals and will not readily soil their environment. A newly-acquired puppy will need to relieve itself more frequently than an adult dog however, and this needs to be borne in mind to avoid accidents around the home. You need to be alert to this fact and should place the puppy outdoors in the garden for this purpose whenever it wakes up - particularly first thing in the morning and always just before you go to bed at night. The puppy will almost certainly want to relieve itself soon after eating, and on awaking from a nap. Careful supervision will help to prevent accidents at other times. Dogs do not simply relieve themselves, but sniff around for a likely spot beforehand. All puppies, male and female alike, squat when they urinate; males only cock their legs on reaching maturity, which is likely to be from the age of six months onwards. Right from the start it is a good idea, every time you take your puppy out to the designated area, to say 'Good boy/girl, hurry up!' or some such words as the puppy starts, and praise him profusely as he finishes, so that he knows that he has pleased you. Then, when you are away from home, for example going to a dog show in a strange place, your dog will relieve himself on command, overcoming his initial reluctance to do this away from home.

If you suspect that the puppy wants to relieve itself you should allow it to go out to the garden without delay. By the age of four or five months old, your puppy will be indicating a desire to go outdoors when it feels the need to relieve itself. Some dogs are more easily house-trained than others but most dogs should be adequately house-trained so that they will not soil indoors well before they are six months old. There are, of course, exceptions.

Should you actually catch a puppy relieving itself indoors you should scold it in a harsh voice and move it immediately outdoors. There is simply no point in rubbing its nose in the spot; this has no value as a deterrent and the puppy will not be able to understand your action. It is simply an unpleasant old wives' tale. It is also not effective to punish a puppy if you discover the carpet soiled at a later stage. Dogs do not possess a long-term memory with regard to their actions, and scolding a puppy after the event is likely to confuse it and weaken the bond between you.

It is important to clear up thoroughly after an accident indoors or the puppy is likely to return to this spot and repeatedly soil the area. You will need to remove all trace of the scent that attracts the puppy here, and it is possible to buy special products for this purpose from many pet shops. Blotting up moisture with paper kitchen towels is a good start and disinfecting the area is to be recommended, especially if you have young children. Choose your disinfectant carefully as those containing ammonia will simply reinforce the scent, and select one which will not damage your furnishings. Diluted sodium hypochloride (household bleach) may be fine on kitchen floors, but would not be good for your carpets! Some excellent disinfectant/deodorisers are available in most big pet shops.

You should train your dog to relieve itself in a particular part of the garden where its faeces can be cleaned up easily. This also applies when you start to take the dog out for walks in public places, such as parks. Much of the criticism directed at dog owners in recent years has stemmed from irresponsible owners who allow their pets to soil indiscriminately on pavements, in parks and other similar sites. Apart from the unpleasant aspect of dog faeces littering public areas there is also a risk of Toxocara infections becoming established there (see Chapter 10), and these can pose a direct threat to human health.

In many areas dog owners are legally obliged to clear up after dogs which deposit faeces in public places. You can obtain special scoops and bags for this purpose from most pet shops, but the ordinary plastic bags which accumulate in most homes are just as good. Never go 'walkies' without them. For many people, this task is more easily carried out at home, but you cannot guarantee that a puppy will only need to defecate when in its own garden!

On occasions there can be lapses in toilet training but if you encounter serious difficulty in persuading your dog to be clean seek veterinary advice as there may be an underlying medical problem. The ureter, which normally carries urine from the kidney to the bladder, may for example connect directly to the urethra and cause incontinence. This defect, which typically becomes apparent between 12 weeks and six months of age, may be corrected by surgery.

Older male dogs may start urinating persistently around the home. This is likely to be caused by a desire to mark their territory, a practice carried out by wild dogs. In my opinion, this is the time to remind your dog that you are the pack leader and will not tolerate such behaviour. It can also sometimes happen as a young dog realises that he is fully mature. In the older dog, neutering can lead to a spectacular cessation of such behaviour where training has proved to be ineffective. Lapses of toilet training later in life are likely to be the result of illness, such as kidney failure, and although in some cases it may be possible to stabilise the condition, this may only be feasible on a temporary basis.

The Big Outdoors

Although you should not take your puppy for walks outside your garden before his immunisations are complete it is a good idea to take him for short rides in the car. This will allow him to have a look at the outside world and also give him a chance to get used to the motion of the car. Many puppies are car sick at first, so be prepared for that, but persevere with short trips and do not take him in the car immediately after his meal. If you do not use a travel crate for your dog then you need a passenger to hold him comfortably and reassure him while you drive. If the dog's travel sickness persists consult your vet for a suitable remedy.

When your puppy is three months old he should have completed his course of immunisations and then you can start to take him for very short walks beyond the confines of your garden. Even so, it is not a good idea to let a young dog run off the lead at this stage. Take things a stage at a time, especially if you live in an urban area where there are likely to be other dogs and passing traffic.

Follow the lead training routine, ensuring that the dog is kept on your left-hand side. At first, it may prove to be less obedient than when being trained in home surroundings. This is to be expected because of the numerous distractions, strange scents and new sights which he will encounter for the first time.

Some puppies may prove to be rather nervous at first, and you will need to make encouraging sounds. One of the major problems is likely to be that the dog will pause at almost every fence and lamp post, sniffing at the scents left by other dogs. This is a natural reaction on the part of the dog, and a firm 'Leave!', spoken in your sternest voice, should suffice as you continue on your way. Having scolded him verbally for sniffing remember to praise him for obeying your command.

As your dog becomes used to the world outside your home, and its behaviour improves, you can take it into busier areas. Do not plan on taking your dog with you on shopping trips at this stage, as most shops will not admit dogs. Use this training phase to introduce your dog to traffic and people so that he is not nervous of them.

It may also be a good idea to familiarise your pet with public transport, but before boarding make sure that your dog will be accepted. In the case of buses, if dogs are allowed, be prepared to lift him on and off the platform, and ensure that inside he does not prove a nuisance to other passengers or block the gangway.

On the underground, or wherever there are moving escalators, it is essential to carry your pet; dogs can suffer horrendous injuries if they become trapped in the moving mechanism by their claws or toes. If you are going on a longer journey by train, then be sure that your dog will not want to relieve itself during the course of the journey. It is not a good idea to take a young dog by train over any distance before it is fully house-trained. Never embark on a journey by public transport with your dog unless you are certain that your dog will be accepted.

Travelling

Most of your travelling with your dog is likely to be by car. You can accustom a puppy to this unfamiliar sensation at an early age by taking it with you for car rides, and as long as you do not take the pup for 'walkies' out of the car you can begin before its course of vaccinations is complete. Short trips are best just in case the puppy feels sick at first, and do be prepared for this to happen. A 'puppy pack' containing a roll of paper kitchen towels and a plastic disposal bag, a bottle of water and a bowl will take care of little upsets en route.

Do not take your puppy out in the car just after his meal. If you do not use a travel crate you will need a passenger to hold the pup and give him a feeling of security. If a puppy's car sickness is persistent consult your vet regarding a suitable remedy. Sometimes a travel sickness pill is recommended shortly before the journey, but such medication may work better if given several hours before travelling, perhaps last thing the night before if you are making a very early start. In such cases trial and error may provide the right answer, but patience on your part may be needed too; it is no use scolding a puppy for being car sick. A puppy will get over his car sickness if, when he is allowed to go out, you take him for a short car ride, then for an exciting walk

Of course you should never leave the puppy alone in the car, particularly if the weather is warm. The temperature in the interior of a locked car can rise to a fatal level literally within minutes under these circumstances. Furthermore, there is a real risk that a puppy will soil or chew the interior of the vehicle while on its own here. Larger dogs can totally wreck the upholstery in a comparatively short time.

Puppies cannot travel by air until they are 12 weeks old. Their travelling boxes are purpose-made and must be to airline standards.

In the longer term, you will need to decide on the best means of travelling with your dog in the car. It is inadvisable to allow it to roam around freely, even when you are in the vehicle. A momentary distraction caused by your pet could easily result in a possibly fatal accident. If you have a hatchback or estate car mesh dog guards are available on a made-to-measure basis to fit all makes of vehicle. Mesh guards are safer than those comprised simply of bars, and are sold easily when advertised in the Dog publications, should you change your car. In my opinion, if you are having a dog guard behind the seats another one at the back is a must; this will give you peace of mind when you lift up the back door. There are also fitted, made-to-measure cages for most estate cars. My personal preference is for a van with two dog guards if you have more than one or two dogs, especially if you are showing or working your dogs; certainly there will be less dirt and dust damage. I am amazed how far a wet dog can shake its mud!

It is also possible to acquire purpose-made seat covers to protect the car upholstery from mud and dogs' hairs. Alternatively, you may prefer to have a mesh travel crate for your dog. Collapsible designs which are easy to store when not required are available. The best selection can be seen at championship dog shows or the larger pet shops. They are also regularly advertised in the weekly canine press, *Our Dogs* and *Dog World*. Crates can be used in the home as well as the car, but make sure the model you choose will fit easily into your car. They are a most useful and versatile piece of equipment, long lasting and worth the initial expense.

Crates or cages are also useful when transporting dogs to shows, and a carrier of this type may fit inside an ordinary car, depending on its size and the possible permutations of the car seating arrangements. Your dog will be more comfortable resting in the crate on an old blanket or a piece of vetbed, washable fabrics of course. If, however, you intend to travel often with your dog in the car please remember that estate cars are cooler than hatchback models as the sloping rear windows on the latter make the rear compartment a veritable sun-trap. If you need a guideline, ask yourself if you would want a baby in a carrycot to travel in the spot where you intend to put your dog's crate.

Some dogs become excited when travelling in a car, particularly at first, once they recognise that this will mean a walk. If your dog starts to become a nuisance as a result, then the answer will be to simply take it out for a drive, so that it does not automatically associate the car with a walk. Older dogs which have not been used to car travel will have to become accustomed to it gradually in the same way as a puppy would.

Insurance

One important aspect of dog ownership which assumes greater significance once you are taking your pet out regularly is the matter of insurance. If your dog causes an accident or injury you could be held legally liable for its actions and ordered to pay financial compensation to people who have suffered loss or injury as a result. You may be covered on your household insurance policy for third party liability in the event of your dog causing an accident, but you should check this carefully, and speak with either your broker or company concerned if in doubt.

Today most pet health insurance policies provide third party liability cover as a matter of course. It is a good idea to take out one of these policies as soon as you acquire your dog, so that you will have adequate cover if the unthinkable happens. You may want to discuss this matter with your vet at your first visit with your dog or contact a pet health insurance company direct. Pet health insurance policies may not cover routine vaccinations, but could save you a really heavy bill in case of accidents or illness.

Out and About

Once your dog is reasonably well-trained and will sit or return to you on command you can think of letting it run free off the lead. In the first instance, choose somewhere well away from roads. It is also important to ensure that your pet cannot gain access to farmstock. If a farmer considers it to be worrying his animals, then he is within his rights to shoot your dog.

A quiet spot where you are unlikely to meet other dogs is preferable as they could cause your dog to run off and disappear. Simply slip the lead from the collar, and walk along normally. Call your dog if it disappears from sight or starts to lag behind.

At first you may find that it dashes off, but after this initial burst of freedom your dog is likely to return to you, hopefully without problems. This is where your whistle training will come into its own, and even if you are never going to do gundog work you will find it a godsend. Dogs have much more sensitive hearing than our own and are able to hear sounds of higher frequency. Although a blast on the whistle will be almost inaudible to us at a distance, your dog will be able to hear it from far away, and hopefully should remember its lesson and return when called in this fashion. As I have said before it is a good idea to practise this in a controlled area before experimenting in open country.

There may be occasions when a dog misbehaves when taken out for a walk. After a bath, which removes their natural odour, some dogs feel socially disadvantaged and will then head off in search of a suitable substitute, cow pats being favoured for this purpose. You should therefore take particular care when exercising your dog for a few days after bathing it. Some dogs, especially Flatcoats, cannot resist such delights, and they are often even more strongly perfumed than cow pats.

A bitch in heat will attract a male dog from a considerable distance, her scent wafting on the wind, and he will head off in search of her. A neutered male is unlikely to respond in this fashion. It is foolhardy to think of exercising a bitch while she is in season and likely to be looking for a mate herself. She will need to be supervised closely through this period to prevent any accidental matings.

It is useful to take an old towel with you in the car when taking your dog out for a walk. You can then dry it off if it gets wet or muddy. Wipe off the worst of the mud and leave the rest to dry on the way home. If your dog is very wet and cold the towelling coats are ideal to put on; often by the time you get home you have a dry dog, and you can then simply brush or comb the mud out of the coat.

On a hot summer's day, a drinking bowl and a bottle of water are essential, so that your dog can have a drink after its period of exercise. Try to avoid walking the dog when the sun is at its warmest as dogs can succumb to heat stroke, and will not enjoy being out at this time of day. Flatcoats are always dark, usually black, and black absorbs the heat, so please be careful. The same towelling coat soaked in cold water will help to keep your dog comfortable in very hot weather.

Flatcoats enjoy swimming but, before you let your dog swim, find out more about the river, lake or canal you are walking alongside. Make sure you are allowed to let your dogs swim (it might be a designated fishing area). Make sure the water is safe to swim in. Nowadays rivers and lakes are often polluted, so your dog could be very sick after swimming. Clear water is not always safe, and rivers with quantities of green algae could be dangerous, especially if it comes through farm land. Find out the source of the water; your local water authority (NRA) should be able to advise you. In winter, bear in mind that dogs can succumb to exposure very rapidly if they fall through ice, and under such circumstances it can be almost impossible to save them.

At times when you are out together your dog is likely to come into contact with other dogs of different sizes. The vast majority of these encounters pass off uneventfully and should be allowed to follow their natural progression. The dogs are likely to approach each other somewhat warily, sniffing rear ends, and walking round together for a few moments. If the encounter is likely to be aggressive there will be some noticeable warning signs, the aggressor baring its teeth to drive off the other dog.

Its tail will be kept upright and the hackles (the hair at the back of the neck) will be raised. Should this display of ferocity not be adequate the teeth will be fully exposed, accompanied by snarling. The ears are directed slightly forwards, in a further gesture of aggression.

By this stage, if the other dog is not withdrawing, conflict will be almost inevitable. Nevertheless, most encounters of this type do not result in physical injury. The dominant individual simply drives off the subordinate dog, chasing it some distance away before returning to the spot and often urinating in this vicinity to reinforce its territorial claim.

The risk of serious fighting is greatest when both dogs respond in identical fashion and neither will back down in this battle of wills. Care needs to be taken if you decide to separate them at this stage because, as you remove your dog, you may be pursued by the other dog, and there is a real risk of being bitten. Try to prise your dog away, using the lead as a noose for this purpose. Clearly, the aim should be to prevent an encounter of this type, calling your dog back if there are signs of trouble. This is most likely between two entire males, although bitches may sometimes become involved in disputes.

Another problem which can arise when a dog is out walking is a close encounter with a jogger or cyclist. Most young dogs are naturally playful and their instinct is to chase after people in such circumstances. Clearly, such behaviour is not to be recommended, and needs to be corrected before it becomes habitual. This situation worsens as your dog sees the cyclist disappearing into the distance, as it takes this as a sign that it has achieved its aim of driving away a weaker individual.

If your dog shows any tendency to behave in the above manner call it dog back to you immediately. Should it persist try walking the dog on the lead along roads or paths where you are likely to encounter cyclists and joggers. Only when the dog has learned that chasing people is not acceptable behaviour should you let it off its lead here. However, with careful training right from the start, your dog should respond to your verbal commands.

However annoying disobedience may be (and all dogs will attempt it at some time) try not to lose your patience, and always remember to praise your dog when it does obey, even if it is sometimes a case of being grateful for small mercies!

There will be times when you have to go out and cannot take your dog with you. On such occasions it is necessary to ensure that it will not wreck the home in your absence, or bark unnecessarily over a long period, disturbing your neighbours. With a young puppy, short absences on your part will enable the dog to come to terms with being left on its own for a while. You should be sure to provide suitable distractions in the form of chews, and it is a good idea to play with or walk the dog beforehand. Then, almost certainly, it will curl up and go to sleep rather than fret for any length of time while you are away. Often a radio left on can give the dog the sense of people being present. When you return, praise your dog, and give it plenty of attention, having allowed it to go outside to relieve itself first. There is little point in criticising a young dog which soils inside the house when you are out as this is simply likely to increase its anxiety while you are away from home. Clearly you should encourage the dog to relieve itself before you go out.

Initially, particularly in the case of a young dog which is likely to be teething, you should keep it confined in the kitchen or elsewhere in the home where it can cause only minimal damage while unsupervised. Even with an older individual which is fully house-trained it is probably safer to restrict its movements around the home in your absence. In all cases you can spread newspapers on the kitchen floor in case of toilet accidents. Do not scold your pup for using such facilities; just be grateful that he has, clear them up and let him out into the garden, praising him if he relieves himself there.

The barking instincts of domestic dogs varies somewhat between individual breeds. Under some circumstances it is desirable for dogs to bark. Again, consistency in training from an early age should help to prevent problems in later life. While you should praise your dog when it barks to alert you to the presence of someone at the door, you should deter it from continuing to bark, or from barking in situations where this is not desirable, by scolding in a firm tone of voice.

Provided that the dog is ready to sleep when you go out it is most unlikely to start barking at this stage, and hopefully will not fall into the habit. Should you find that it does bark repeatedly, keep it confined in another room, and pretend to go out. You can then scold it if you catch it misbehaving. Encouraging your dog to stay peaceably in another room for certain periods while you remain in the house is a useful part of its training as there are sure to be times when you have visitors who do not share your interest in dogs, or are afraid of them.

Hitting a dog which misbehaves is not really effective, especially in the case of a newcomer, as this is likely to weaken the developing bond between you. The dog will probably become nervous of having your hand raised near it for fear that it will be hit, and this may even cause it to strike out and bite. A more effective means of punishment is to get hold of the dog and roll it over on to its back, scolding it at the same time. In this way you are effectively placing the dog in a subordinate position, leaving it in no doubt that it has offended you.

Should you ever feel that a smack is necessary it is better to do this by means of a sharp tap on the nose with a rolled-up newspaper. Using your hand will simply confuse matters as the dog will have difficulty in distinguishing whether you are punishing it, or offering it a treat. Clear distinctions should be drawn and maintained from the outset of the training process.

Holiday Time

Going away can present particular problems when you have a dog. Under certain circumstances it may be possible to take your dog with you. Some guide books list hotels which are prepared to take dogs, but check in advance as hotel policies may have changed since the guide was printed. If you are going abroad then you must make suitable arrangements for the care of your dog well in advance of your holiday dates. Under no circumstances should a dog be left on its own while you are on holiday, with someone just popping in to feed it at night. Apart the fact that it is cruel, your dog will inevitably become bored and frustrated under such circumstances.

Having booked your own holiday, make arrangements for your dog as soon as possible, and budget for the expense. Depending on a friend or neighbour to care for your dog during your holiday is not a good plan. Should you not wish to move your dog, you can contact a special pet-sitting agency, who will provide a resident 'dog sitter' for your pet. In this way your dog will be exercised and cared for, and so will your home. Provided you select a reputable agency, and take up references, this option can give you great peace of mind. Of course, if you have a friend or relative who will house-sit for you in this fashion it could be an even better alternative. Check your household insurance policy though, just in case any accidents happen in your absence.

For most people it will be a matter of finding a good boarding establishment in their area to care for their dog while they are away. This is likely to be less expensive than employing a home-sitter, unless you have a number of dogs. The best means of finding a good kennels of this type is by recommendation. Ask your vet, or dog-owning friends, and then telephone the kennels to arrange a visit. You can then assure yourself of the care that your dog will receive, and sort out details such as whether you need to supply any food. Generally, this is provided by the kennels, but there may be circumstances where you will need to supply special food, such as a prescription diet for nephritis for example.

If your dog has a particular medical problem you should advise the kennels beforehand to ensure that they can accommodate its needs. In any case you should leave the name and telephone number of your vet, as well as a contact number in case of an emergency. Most dogs settle well in boarding kennels and enjoy the change of lifestyle, but do not worry - your dog will be delighted to greet you on your return.

If you have a bitch and expect that she may come into season while you are away tell the boarding kennel owner. You may also wish speak to your vet about the advisability of deferring this, usually by means of an injection. Boarding kennels need to know whether a bitch is due in season as they will not wish to kennel her next to a male dog as this would be too disturbing. Most kennels are used to caring for bitches in season, but definitely prefer to have advance warning of the possibility. Taking a blanket and perhaps a favoured toy will help your pet to settle down more quickly once you have left.

Choose a boarding kennel where your dog has its own individual kennel with an attached run. Both kennel and run should be of a size suited to your dog's needs. If you have two dogs it is usual to kennel them together, in which case check that the accommodation is large enough for the pair. This type of kennel plan is strongly recommended.

Your dog will suffer no ill-effects from a stay in a recommended, reputable boarding kennel, but even in the best-run institutions there is a slight risk that your dog could contact the respiratory infection known as kennel cough. Although this is rarely life-threatening, it can cause considerable discomfort for your pet (see Chapter 10), so immunisation against this illness is recommended. Advice on this should be sought from your vet in advance of our holiday. Do not leave this till the last minute! Reputable kennels will check that your dog is fully immunised against the major canine diseases before accepting your booking.

Satisfied customers tend to patronise the same kennels every year, so vacancies during peak holiday times such as August and Christmas can be hard to find at short notice. Arrange your booking as early as possible to ensure the greatest likelihood of obtaining a place for your pet.

Should you decide instead to tour with your dog you will need to plan your journey carefully. Under no circumstances should the dog be left alone in the car when the weather is hot, as mentioned previously. Hopefully your dog will already be thoroughly used to travelling in the car, but in any case be prepared for his needs as well as your own. Almost certainly your dog will encounter things on holiday which it has not seen before, and you will need to ensure that its behaviour or health do not suffer as a result. Not everyone appreciates the company of a dog and, largely as the result of the vocal nature of the campaign waged by the anti-dog lobby, dogs are banned from many beaches, parks and gardens. Whether dogs are acceptable varies greatly around the country, and if you want to find out the situation at a particular resort call the local Environmental Health Officer for advice. These by-laws are made by local authorities, and while in some areas there may be a total ban, in other cases this will only apply for certain months of the year.

Your dog must not make a nuisance of itself on a beach in any event. If you intend to spend most of the day there, remember to take a bottle of drinking water and a bowl for your pet, because it is likely to get thirsty at some point, and drinking seawater with its high salt content will be harmful. Shade is also important when the weather is hot, and a large umbrella where you can both shelter from the sun is advisable. Most dogs enjoy splashing around at the water's edge, but knowing Flatcoats they will enjoy the new challenge of swimming in the sea. Watch your dog carefully to ensure that it is not swept out to sea by a strong current. This can also be a particular risk if you are walking down a breakwater, and your dog decides to plunge into the sea.

You must ensure that your dog does not interfere with the enjoyment of other beach users. If the area is crowded, then it may be better to keep your dog with you on its lead. Dogs running around in groups can soon become a problem, particularly if people are picnicking. Windsurfers often appear to attract dogs as well, and if any equipment is damaged by your dog, you could end up with a hefty bill.

When you head back to the car be sure to put your dog on a lead. Dogs should always be kept on a lead when walking along a street, as there is a possibility that your pet could be distracted by a cat for example, and may run off in pursuit creating a trail of havoc in its wake.

Festive Periods

Although Flatcoats are gundogs, some still dislike loud noises, and will react badly to fireworks, either by barking persistently or cowering away and refusing to go outdoors even when they are over. Prepare for this eventuality by encouraging your dog to relieve itself before dusk when fireworks are imminent, and stay with your pet, offering reassurance. Even some happy, working gundogs are very disturbed by thunderstorms.

Should you have a barbecue take care that no scraps of food are left where your dog could steal them and be burnt as a consequence. Broken glasses are another hazard associated with parties as dogs may slice their paws badly on a sharp sliver. If in doubt keep your dog indoors until you can check around in daylight, exercising it last thing on a lead away from the party area.

In most homes, Christmas can be a chaotic period, and an unsupervised dog may well create havoc. You will need to ensure as far as possible that all food is kept well out of the dog's reach. Otherwise cakes, sweets, and even the Christmas turkey may be seized and consumed with relish, causing great heartache and annoyance after all the careful preparations for the festivities, and inevitable sickness for the dog! Children must also be reminded to keep new toys which might be chewed in a place away from the dog.

It is definitely not a good idea to introduce a new puppy to the household at this stage, unless you are having a very quiet Christmas on your own. Dog ownership is not something which should be undertaken lightly in any event, and dogs should never be given as Christmas presents unless the recipient is ready and willing to make the necessary commitment.

There are various hazards which your dog is likely to encounter around the home at Christmas time. Puppies often find the decorations on a Christmas tree fascinating, and will frequently attempt to take them off the branches if they are within reach. In doing so they may pull down the entire tree wreaking havoc in the room, and may cut themselves badly if the tree is decorated with glass baubles.

You must keep chocolate gifts and other presents away from the base of the tree until the last minute, because these may be ripped apart by an inquisitive puppy. It is also important to clear up any tree needles as they fall, because these can penetrate into your dog's feet, and may then actually track up the leg like grass seeds causing intense irritation.

Festive periods, like holidays, are meant to be enjoyed but when making your preparations remember your dog as well as the human family, particularly children who become forgetful in the excitement. Advance planning and keeping a watchful eye on potential hazards should ensure happy occasions for all concerned.

Flatcoats in their Winter Wonderland.

Chapter 8

Flatcoated Retriever Activities

Flatcoated Retrievers are enthusiastic dogs and there are many activities in which they can participate with their owners, but all these have to be researched well beforehand. It is also important to remember that, however many training classes you attend, there is always homework. To take your dog to any of these activities without teaching him or her step by step at home is unfair to the dog and to the breed it represents.

OBEDIENCE

This is a very useful starting point for any owner with a new puppy. Even if you have no intention of competing, you and your pet Flatcoat can take part and enjoy it. In the end you will have a more responsive dog who is a pleasure to live with and you will have made some new friends, two- and four-legged.

Please do remember that you must practise every day for a few minutes between classes. Even if you have very little time during the day other than for a good walk with your dog, most houses now have outside lights, so a 10 minute practice is possible, even in the winter. Please do not be disappointed if you do not progress as quickly as you would like in any of these activities; it is no disgrace to go through the classes for a second time. It is far better for you and your dog to understand the lessons well before progressing.

If you go to your local Advice on Activities Office they should be able to tell you your nearest local obedience class. Your local pet shop can often help too, also your Flatcoat County Representative or The Kennel Club (see **Useful Addresses**).

You may enjoy going to the local Good Citizens Dog Scheme Classes. Here you will receive help in training your dog to be well behaved and will be given advice on grooming, exercise, diet and general health care. The scheme is open to all dogs, young and old. At the end of each course a certificate is awarded to those passing a short test. You will meet new people and, as you and your Flatcoat progress, come home proudly with your first certificate.

Considering the bad publicity that dogs get in the press these days, the more manners a dog has within the home and outside the better. So do go with your dog; you and your family will enjoy it. Details can be obtained from The Kennel Club (see **Useful Addresses**).

My personal opinion is that Flatcoats are not the ideal material for going right through the obedience competitions, especially if you are very competitive. However, if you have a sense of humour and are willing to enjoy yourself and take on a challenge, you will enjoy obedience work with your Flatcoat. If you and your dog like this work but want to get out and enjoy a wider activity, gundog and working trials are the obvious ones.

Competitive Obedience

I have had no experience of competitive obedience nor of the preparation of a puppy for this purpose so I enlisted the expertise of Mrs Alison Wood, who has been in competitive obedience for 17 years. She competed at Crufts from 1987 to 1995, coming fourth in 1994 with her Border Collie Obedience (Ob) Ch Teika of Kathrow, a bitch from working sheepdog lines and a grand-daughter of Thomas Longston's Bess, International Supreme Champion in 1986. Alison has kindly given us the following advice.

Flatcoats in Obedience

Flatcoats are becoming more popular in competitive obedience and seem to be achieving a reasonable level of success. The Flatcoat's basic love of life and people, if channelled correctly in a young puppy, can build a productive working relationship. Even if you have no interest in competitive obedience, the adult Flatcoat is a large, boisterous dog, and as such needs to understand and obey basic commands to be able to enjoy life as a rewarding companion.

Your New Puppy

The first night home with your new puppy is very important. Alison has found it advantageous to pick up a puppy late in the day, so that he is tired and should sleep on the journey home. Make sure that the puppy has not been fed before you set out. Before you bring your puppy home you should have decided already where it is going to sleep, preferably away from other pets, in a warm, dry place. A cage or a box with a blanket in it will be best; it will probably be the first time the puppy has slept without its litter-mates and it will feel the cold without some sort of blanket. The main thing to remember on the first night is that if the puppy cries you must not give in to it. A sharp, corrective 'No!' should get a good response from your puppy.

If the puppy is put to bed late at night and you get up early, immediately put the puppy outside to relieve itself. Always praise the puppy for being clean and introduce a word to encourage him. 'Hurry up!' is one of the usual ones. House training is easy when you use a cage, provided you remember that a puppy will always want to relieve itself after a sleep or a meal.

First Training

Flatcoats are slow-maturing dogs compared to Border Collies, for instance, who can be trained to a high standard at 12 months. A 12-month-old Flatcoat is still very much a baby. Having said that, it should know the basic commands 'Sit!' and 'Down!' and walk in a controlled manner when on a lead.

When teaching any dog you should always, always show it exactly what you want of it. Only give one command, for example 'Sit!', and as you say the command put the puppy into the Sit position and immediately praise it. With all dog training you have to find a way of praising the dog which the dog enjoys, and, most importantly, which shows you are pleased with him. Alison finds it helps to use the lead (a soft rope lead) as a play aid. The puppy is encouraged to play tugging at the lead, but even with this the trainer shoud remain in control. If you can develop an effective method of praise with either a lead or the use of a toy you can start to introduce different exercises to stretch the puppy's attention and learning periods.

You must never train the puppy for too long nor allow him to become bored. Always finish the lesson while the puppy is still keen to learn. Ten minutes, three or four times a day if possible, is about right.

Flatcoats can find Dog Training Classes either boring or happy places depending on the type of Training Club. I would advise you to try to find a dog trainer who can give one-to-one attention to you and your dog.

Picture 1

Picture 2

Picture 3

Sit

(Picture 1)

With the dog on your left hand side, bring the lead up (holding the lead in your right hand). As you bring the lead up, push the dog's rear down with your left hand at the same time as you give the command 'Sit!' Only give the command once. As soon as the dog is steady in the sit position, release it and praise.

(Picture 2)

When you have got your dog to sit still, progress to moving around - a single step at first. If the dog attempts to move tighten the lead by holding it up, repeating the command 'Sit!' When the dog is steady again, loosen the lead. Release and praise.

(Picture 3)

When stages 1 and 2 are mastered, progress to pulling the lead while standing in front of the dog. The dog will pull back against the lead to remain in the Sit position. Release with praise.

Down

(Picture 1)
Tell the dog to sit. Kneel next to the dog and pick up its left front leg with your right hand. Place your left hand on the dog's right shoulder as you give the command 'Down!' Gently pull the left front leg forward and towards you. Apply pressure to the shoulder, easing the dog into the Down position.

(Picture 2)
Keeping your left hand on the dog's right shoulder, apply pressure, repeating the command 'Down!' as you gently pull the lead to emphasise the command as you did with the Sit.

(Picture 3)
Progress to moving around and pulling on the lead as you did when teaching your dog to sit. Release and praise.

Picture 1

Picture 3

Picture 2

Picture 1

Stand

(Picture 1)
At this stage your dog should be responsive and stable in the commands you have previously taught. The teaching of the Stand should now be the easiest exercise to teach. Have the dog on your left side and, without manhandling, gently encourage it to stand. Pull the lead upwards with your right hand and apply pressure with your left hand to the dog's shoulder as you give the command 'Stand!' Move your left hand along to the hips and again push downwards saying 'Stand!' The dog should be stable in this position. Release and praise.

(Picture 2)
As with the previous commands, progress to standing in front of the dog and pulling on the lead. The dog should pull back to maintain its standing position. Release and praise.

(Picture 3)
Practise until your dog will stand on a loose lead. At any sign of the dog moving, tighten the lead and repeat the command. Release and praise.

Picture 2

Picture 3

Novice Recall

To teach a fast, happy and precise Novice Recall the exercise should be split into 3 sections: Sit, Recall, and Present. We have covered the Sit.

Recall: with the dog on a lead, sitting in front of you, begin to run backwards, encouraging the dog to follow you, using its name and giving it lots of praise (see Picture 1). Come to a halt. Do not tell it to sit. Release and praise. Continue to practise this until the dog responds readily to you when you begin to run backwards.

Present: Have the dog in the Sit in front of you, with your hands in the dog's collar (see Picture 2). Maintaining your dog's head position, on the command 'Come!', pull the dog into Present position (Picture 3). Be firm if the dog objects. When the dog is stable in this position, release and praise. With practice the dog will anticipate the pull and will react correctly to the command 'Come!' When both stages are mastered leave the dog in the Sit position. Call it by name and when it is a yard away from you give the command 'Come!' Praise.

Picture 1

Picture 2

Picture 3

Picture 1

Finish

The Finish should always be taught separately from the Novice Recall.
(Picture 1)
Put the dog in the Present position. Pass the lead behind you so that you are holding its end in your left hand.
(Pictures 2 and 3)
On your command 'Finish', encourage the dog to pass around behind you into the Watch position, remaining as close to you as possible. Release and praise.
Only put the Recall and Finish together when your dog is well advanced and ready to compete in the ring. This will help to maintain enthusiasm and stop the dog anticipating the Finish.

Picture 2

Picture 3

Heel-work

Heel-work consists of two main factors. Firstly, attention: your dog's attention must focus on you and you alone. Secondly, position: where the dog is in relation to your left leg. To teach these two thoroughly do not rush; be prepared to spend a considerable amount of time getting things right. Position should not be taught until you are able to get and keep your dog's complete attention.

Attention can be split into two stages: Watch and Close.

(Picture 1)

Watch: Have the dog in the Sit position on your left-hand side with your feet together and the lead gathered short in your right hand. Hold the dog's head as shown in the picture. Be gentle but firm if the dog resists. When you have eye contact with the dog give the command 'Watch!' Release with praise. Continue to practise this until your dog readily assumes the Watch position while sitting next to you in response to your command. Release and praise. Praise should be liberal to maintain the dog's enthusiasm.

Picture 1

(Picture 2)

Close: Do not progress to this stage until the Watch is 110 per cent certain. Have the dog in the Stand position on your left-hand side. Stand with your feet apart, the left foot forward. The dog's front feet should be slightly behind your left heel. Tell the dog to 'Watch!' but maintain the Stand position by applying pressure to the shoulders or hips with your left hand while saying 'Close!' This can be rather confusing for the dog as he will associate the Watch command with sitting. Be patient and use plenty of praise to keep the dog in the Close position while maintaining the Watch. Release and praise.

Continue to practise Watch and Close until the dog readily assumes either position when given the appropriate command. This could take weeks or even months. Use a generous amount of praise because you must keep the dog's enthusiasm.

Depending on the progress of the individual dog, go on to moving forward with the dog, keeping its Close position. If the dog loses its position, stop and return the dog to the Close position and, with lots of praise, move forward again. Always start and finish each session of heel-work with the dog in the Watch position. Progress to a figure-of-eight with the dog in the Close position.

Picture 2

Retrieve

To end up with a happy, confident and precise Retrieve in the adult dog, start teaching your puppy as soon as possible. Play with your puppy with a toy which he likes (Picture 1). When he readily chases it when you throw it, build up to catching hold of his collar gently when you have thrown the toy (Picture 2). This teaches him to Mark it. As you release the collar, give your chosen retrieve command ('Fetch', 'Hold' or whatever). Encourage him to bring it back (Picture 3) but do not snatch it from him. Pat him and encourage him to bring and to hold onto it, telling him how clever he is. Very slowly build up to gently putting the dog into the Sit while you hold the collar, and over a still longer time teach the dog to Sit before taking the toy from his mouth (Picture 4). As your Novice Recall teaching progresses and the puppy understands the command 'Come!', introduce this into your retriever training.

If the Retrieve is taught in this manner over a period of time you should end up with a good retriever. Do not expect to achieve it in a week. Take your time and remember to praise.

Picture 1

Picture 2

Picture 3

Picture 4

Further Obedience Training

If after reading and possibly using these introductory notes you are interested in taking obedience training further I would strongly suggest that you find a trainer who can help you. Do not take your puppy to your local dog club until you have checked to see if they train dogs to obedience competition standard: companion dog training is a totally different thing. Contact Ann Devizio at The Federation of Dog Trainers and Canine Behaviourists (FDTCB) (see **Useful Addresses**).

FLATCOATS AS COMPANIONS AND HELPERS

It must have become clear by now that Flatcoats are dogs who love people. There are various ways in which this love and dedication can be put to good use which have little or nothing to do with their gundog function.

The Family Dog

The majority of Flatcoats become family dogs. I remember Patience Lock saying what good nannies Flatcoat dogs made. In my mind this conjured up the picture that it could have been a Flatcoat who was Nana in Peter Pan! I also remember that, when she was getting old and not so good on her feet, Patience Lock's Daniel was never far away. If she fell down he was always there to help her up. However most of us also remember him as a very exuberant, active dog.

Flatcoats are very adaptable dogs, fitting well into family life and then making delightful companions when the children have left home. Flatcoats enjoy all country pursuits. There is an old picture of Mr Cook fishing, with a Flatcoat acting as his gillie. Recently there was a fishing programme with two Flatcoats enjoying their master's pursuit. When I had a horse my Flatcoats always enjoyed exercising with her. (This is not something for young dogs!)

Flatcoats, however, are not everyone's ideal dog. You have to be a certain type of person to tolerate being owned by a Flatcoat. They are not town dogs and living in flats does not suit them, though they can live happy lives in suburbia. As I have said before, they must take part in family activities. An unexercised, bored Flatcoat is a total disaster. They are not for you if you go out to work all day. They have some disadvantages in families with small children: those ever-wagging tails can catch little people across the face and, together with the ever-licking tongue, can add up to a mother's nightmare.

Village or country life suits Flatcoats admirably. They enjoy the occasional (or more than occasional) shooting or fishing day. Even those funny, mock-shooting days on a sunny summer day with the family are to be enjoyed, especially if that wonderful thing called water is involved. ('Well, I did forget myself when I rolled on that rather smelly pigeon, my dear - it smelt like Chanel No 5 to me!')

Exercising the ponies and picking up are also enjoyable. Also gardening, always with the caveat that, although they consider themselves very good landscapers, the family gardener does not always agree! A trip to the village shop to pick up the children, with one's own personal chauffeur, is another aspect of The Good Life in your Flatcoat's opinion.

David Taylor and his Flatcoat bitch Misty have an excellent relationship. David spends most of his time in a wheelchair. Misty has been with him since she was a puppy, and they have built up a very special rapport, although she has had no special training. David writes:

David Taylor with his friend and companion Misty.

Misty is always with me; she even sleeps in my room at night! She carries things downstairs for me, like books and papers. She is always very pleased to see me, especially when I come home from work. She always has something to show me, like a cushion or a shoe, and there are always lots of licks and tail-wagging. I have shown her on a couple of occasions and can walk her on my own, on flat ground.

Minstrel demonstrates 'Alert', the way in which a Hearing Dog indicates that it has heard a sound.

A Flatcoat Retriever Hearing Dog for the Deaf.

Guide Dogs for the Blind

A few Flatcoats have been used as guide dogs for the blind, but on the whole they are considered too active for this work. I have heard over the years of Flatcoats being trained with their owners when their owners are partly sighted.

Hearing Dogs for the Deaf

Flatcoated Retrievers have played an important part in the early work of the Hearing Dogs charity. There are two Flatcoats working as demonstration dogs. These demonstrate the work of the trained hearing dog to the public at talks, shows and open days. The extrovert, happy nature of this breed makes them ideal for this work.

'Minstrel' (Warresmere Quill), featured in the photographs, is a liver Flatcoat owned by Claire Guest, National Training Manager of Hearing Dogs for the Deaf (HDFD), and has demonstrated for the Charity for the last six years. Minstrel has done numerous demonstrations, including television work, appearing on BBC Prime Time and the children's programme Motormouth. 'Emma' (Earlsworth Gail), a black eight-year-old bitch belonging to Wendy Stratford, a Placement Officer, has been demonstrating for the past four years. Both Minstrel and Emma have appeared in demonstrations at Crufts during this time.

The first Flatcoat to be placed with a deaf recipient was Rebel, a black male Flatcoat found abandoned at Wood Green Animal Shelter. 'Rebel' was renamed 'Revel', and has worked tirelessly for his recipient for six years. He is greatly loved and helps the charity by collecting with a box attached to a harness at fund-raising functions. A new recruit kindly donated by a breeder is now in training at the Southern Centre and was placed with a deaf recipient in 1995.

Hearing Dogs for the Deaf is a registered charity which carefully selects and trains dogs to respond to specific sounds within the home or a public building. Most dogs are chosen from Rescue Centres, which effectively gives unwanted dogs useful lives to the benefit of deaf people.

In the photograph Minstrel demonstrates the Alert, the way in which a Hearing Dog indicates that it has heard a sound. Instead of barking the dogs are taught to alert the deaf person by touch, using a paw to gain attention and then to identify each sound source by leading to it. However if the smoke or fire alarm should ring the dog will Alert and then immediately lie down on the floor to indicate the potential danger. Training takes place in purpose-built training houses designed to simulate the environment in which the dog will eventually work after placement with the recipient.

The practical value of a hearing dog is immediately obvious, but the therapeutic value should not be underestimated. Among the reported benefits, many find their increased confidence and independence encourages them to go out more and participate in activities which were previously avoided, particularly situations which involve conversation. Hearing dogs are free to deaf people because each dog is sponsored by a group, company or individual happy to raise the £2500 needed for training it.

Deaf people now have a choice. They no longer have to rely on mechanical equipment such as flashing lights or vibro-tactile devices for awareness to sounds because a hearing dog can provide not only awareness to sound but also the additional blessing of companionship, mobility, increased independence and feeling of security. The success of the scheme can be measured by the increase in the demand for trained dogs, The organisation has placed over 290 dogs since its inception in 1982 and opened a second centre in Cliffe, North Yorkshire in July 1994.

For the information in this section I am indebted to Claire Guest, the National Training Manager for Hearing Dogs for the Deaf (see **Useful Addresses**).

The PAT Dog

Many Flatcoats and their owners enjoy becoming members of Pets As Therapy (PAT), but you must have the time and commitment to do this because of the eagerness with which the elderly folk look forward to your and your dog's visits. Mrs Anne Brooks of the Culmquill affix has kindly given us an insight into the enjoyment that she, the dogs and their elderly friends get out of their visits:

My dogs have been PAT Dogs for nearly 10 years, visiting a home for the elderly and The Day Hospital for the Elderly at Watford. Poncho (now five) has been a PAT Dog since he was six months old. He is a natural, walking quietly around off the lead, wandering from person to person, receiving such comments as 'Oh what a lovely kiss, the first kiss I have had for ages!' One deaf and dumb lady who is really very withdrawn loves to stroke him; then her face really lights up. Conversations start up when he arrives in the lounge, stimulating memories of dogs owned or known. He has a cup of tea in a disposable bed-pan (causing much amusement!). He knows where the biscuits are kept, and has been known to help himself to a biscuit absentmindedly held in a hand, causing the hand's owner to wake up with a start! These are just some of the things that make PAT Dog visiting so enjoyable. We have both made many friends and been invited to many parties - Poncho's favourite, because every one wants to give him a sausage or a crisp ...

SHOWING YOUR FLATCOAT

This is an activity in which all the family can take part. Your children can enter child handling classes as soon as they are old enough and join The Kennel Club Junior Organisation (KCJO), getting a great deal of fun and education within the dog world.

Flatcoats enjoy the show ring in moderation but, as with everything else, you must keep a control on your enthusiasm. I feel so sorry for the dog who, from six months of age, has been dragged from one end of the country to the other, sometimes attending three shows in a weekend. This is not fair to your dog or your family. You and your dog will get a lot of pleasure from showing, provided you keep it in perspective.

Shows exist primarily for dogs of the same breed to compete against each other, for the judge's opinion and grading and for the future improvement of the breed. Hopefully the winner will be the dog who is closest to the Breed Standard, so that correct quality specimens can be used for breeding in the future. Breed type, temperament and health are all of equal importance.

So you have a Flatcoated Retriever whom you have decided you would like to show! It is a good idea to go to shows first to find out about the breed. Go to a big open show or a Gundog Group show where there are breed classes, or better still to a championship show. Give yourself all day; go and sit down at the ringside and watch. Do this several times. You will start to get the feel of the breed, and you will also start to pick out breeders and dogs you like. They will start to stand out from the rest. Find out from the catalogue the dogs' names and follow their fortunes. Order one of the weekly dog papers, *Dog World* or *Our Dogs*, as these will give you an insight into the world of dogs. Get to know the exhibitors and ask questions but, do remember, not just as they are going into the ring! Top winning Flatcoat exhibitors are generally very helpful if approached at the right time.

Once you have decided that your puppy really does have show potential, please, please do not rush off and enter him or her for a championship show. It will be far too stressful and tiring for both of you. Your local ringcraft class will have schedules for open, limit or exemption shows. Please start off for the first few months with these types of show. You and your puppy will learn a considerable amount and you will both gain confidence. Then, when your puppy is about nine or 10 months old and if you have done well at open shows, it might be time try a championship show.

The entry form for any show is important. At present, exemption shows are the only ones you can enter on the day. You will see in your dog paper the advertisements for all kinds of shows at the back. Send a stamped, addressed envelope to the secretary and you will receive your schedule. It is difficult to get used to the entry dates; they close at least four weeks before an open show and about six weeks before a championship. Your entry must be with the secretary by the day advertised. I advise you when sending your entry to get a Certificate of Posting (a form available free of charge from the Post Office), and ensure that it is completed correctly and countersigned by the Post Office counter staff, as this is the only proof of posting that the Kennel Club will accept if your entry is lost.

You will have to put together a 'show bag'. Almost all championship shows will be benched, so you must buy a regulation benching chain which you will attach to a strong collar. Please remember that it is wise to have your name and address on a disk on the collar, and also that your puppy should wear it all the time when travelling. Never, under any circumstances, leave your puppy on a slip lead tied to the bench, nor on a long chain; you could come back to a tragedy. The end of the benching chain has a spring loaded clip which can be quickly undone in an emergency. It is nice for the puppy to have some sort of bedding on the bench.

Remember that you or your family must stay with your puppy until it settles, especially the first few times on a bench. Remember also that your dog is your responsibility, and that there have been cases where dogs are tampered with on their benches.

Do take some water or milk and water with you, and add some glucose to it. It is important that your puppy has plenty to drink and does not dehydrate, especially at summer shows. It is a good idea to put a litre bottle three-quarters full of water into your deep freeze the day before the show, so that your dog will have a refreshing drink available all day. A bottle of fruit squash prepared in the same way is refreshing for you, too.

You will also need show leads (a black nylon slip lead suits a Flatcoat) and your grooming equipment. A small first-aid box is useful as well, containing plasters, panadol, piriton tablets for stings, some stomach-settling tablets, and a bottle of Bach Flower Rescue Remedy. In summer a towelling coat that can be soaked in water and put on the puppy helps when we have hot days. Remember that black dogs absorb the heat and benching tents get very hot and humid.

If you are going to an unbenched show do not leave any dog in a car for any length of time without outstanding ventilation. Even a shaded car or van with the back open and a special dog cage or dog gate is only safe for a short period. Never leave your dog in a car with windows open a few inches: it is a death trap for your dog. Most Dog Show Committees will refuse to accept entries at their future shows from exhibitors who, in the opinion of the Committee, have left their dogs in cars in a distressed condition. This will be reported to The Kennel Club, and they could discipline you.

Always get to the show in plenty of time especially with a puppy. It is your responsibility to be there for your class. You will also throw your puppy's chances away by rushing him into the ring before you and he are settled. Remember there are hundreds of other people with the same idea often going through one gate to the car park.

A Few Hints on Showing

You have been to ringcraft classes, so hopefully you have been taught the mechanics of showing your puppy. At your first few classes, do not go to the front, but get well into the body of the class and watch the ring procedure. Try to relax, as the tension will go down the lead and, knowing Flatcoats, they will take advantage of you! You will have practised the best pace for your puppy (remember this will change as he grows). Do not worry: all Flatcoat judges, especially breed specialists, started in the same way, so they all know how naughty Flatcoats can be and how they can take advantage of their handler for fun.

Never go in the ring with your shoulders down, your body language apologising for yourself and your dog. Go in with relaxed shoulders, knowing that your dog is very special to you and that, win or lose, you will go home with the best dog in the show as far as you are concerned.

Learn to show your dog to its best advantage. Do not push or be pushed around in the ring. Watch out for other dogs lunging at your dog. Just be one step ahead of everything.

As far as baiting is concerned, a small titbit discreetly used can be an advantage to your dog. Your dog will not starve in the ring, so please do not stuff him with food. It is discourteous to feed a dog when the judge is trying to go over it as the judge could land up with slime and food all over his or her hands. You could possibly lose the class because of the greedy, foreign expression on your dog's face as he tries to pull away from the judge to get at the food. I would certainly mark down a dog for this, as I am looking for the soft, smiling expression of a Flatcoat. However, a small titbit to keep your dog's attention when all the dogs are standing could work to your advantage.

Grooming preparation for a show starts at least 10 days before. In the course of your normal grooming you will have kept his coat in good condition, his toe nails trimmed (the guillotine type of cutter is one of the best), and regularly checked his ears (your vet will give you advice on what to use, but please be very gentle or you will do damage).

A Flatcoat does not need very much trimming. His ears will need tidying with thinning scissors; if you are clever this will come out better with hand stripping. The thinning scissors can be used down the neck, just around the ear and downwards, just to tidy; get another Flatcoat owner to show you how. The feet also need trimming, up the pasterns and the hocks, and the long hair at the end of the tail and underneath the tail needs tidying. All this should be done well before you bath your puppy. In no circumstances should you use clippers on your Flatcoat. In most countries the Breed Standard states that shaving or noticeable barbering of neck, body coat or feathering to change the natural appearance of the dog must be heavily penalised.

Flatcoated Retrievers

If you are going to bath your dog, this should be done two to five days before a show, depending on the individual dog's coat. I suggest you experiment and note the time his coat takes to settle. A dog out of coat will look better for a bath two days before, but for a dog in full coat five to seven days may be needed. In fact, a dog in full, gleaming coat may not need a bath at all. If you have a liver coloured Flatcoat, take advice on what shampoo to use, as the one used on your blacks will often not suit your liver.

When entering your puppy, enter by his age in the first place:

6 to 9 months	Minor Puppy
6 to 12 months	Puppy
12 to 18 months	Junior
12 to 24 Special	Yearling

Adult classes are Maiden, Novice, Undergraduate, Graduate, Postgraduate, Mid-limit, Limit, and Open. The class you enter will be determined by your dog's previous successes in shows, Open being for all champions and dogs that have won their way out of Limit. All the definitions of classes will be listed in each show schedule, so please read carefully. If you enter your dog in the wrong class (for instance, in Minor Puppy when he is over nine months of age) you must go to the Secretary of the show before your class and take the Secretary's advice. If you win the class with an over-aged dog, your win will be taken away by The Kennel Club. It is a good idea to buy a special Show Awards book, or write all the puppy's wins in a notebook. As well as being useful it will be interesting to look back on later.

I think it is a good idea to work your way right through the classes. By doing this you will not be over facing your dog. A youngster who looks good in Junior will often look like a baby in Graduate or Postgraduate. All Class winners, as long as they are not beaten in any following classes, compete for Best of Breed (BOB) if it is an Open Show with mixed classes. If it is an Open Show with the sexes split, Best Dog and Best Bitch will be decided, then Best of Breed.

At a Championship Show the Dog Challenge Certificate (CC) and the Dog Reserve Challenge Certificate (RCC) are judged, and then the same procedure is followed for the bitches. Then the Dog and Bitch CC winners compete for Best of Breed (BOB). The Best Puppy is selected from the winners of the Minor Puppy and Puppy Classes, with some technical exceptions.

This is a very generalised explanation. There is much more to learn, and I am sure that, if you ask, many people will be willing to help.

If you have been lucky enough to buy a Flatcoated Retriever who competes and wins well, and you win three CCs under three different judges, you will have a Show Champion, and will be entitled to put the letters 'Sh Ch' before his name. (You will never forget your first CC.) You then have three ways of qualifying your dog as a full champion:

* An award at a field trial.
* Running your dog in a special qualifier at a field trial once you have a CC.
* Once you have a first at a championship show you may run your dog in a 'Special Show Dog Qualifier' for your breed or one of the other retriever breeds. The Field Trial Secretary (see **Useful Addresses**) will give you details of when it will be taking place. He will also tell you what your dog must do to pass.

You will learn many other things as time goes by. One of the most important of these is Good Sportsmanship. Whatever today's judge has decided, there will be another day and another judge. You made the choice to enter your dog under a specific judge: nobody forced you to do so. However much an honest judge likes your dog, if on the day the dog is out of coat, too fat or too thin, or if another dog is simply better or has blossomed, it is to the best dog on that day that the award must go.

Be honest with yourself. Know your dog and do not be 'kennel blind'. Remember that it is a sport, and be a sport! The dog you take home with you is still your best friend who sits by your fireside and goes on walks with you each day as your loyal companion.

WORKING TRIALS

I have no experience of working trials competition, although I did some training with one of my male Flatcoats some years ago and found it very good fun; the dog enjoyed it as well. I have therefore taken the following information from an article written for me by Shena Wells of the Gilduffe affix, owner of Lakemere Classic Reflection at Gilduffe CD EX UD Open, and I am very grateful to her for her help with this section.

It is certainly worth considering working trials if you enjoy the close contact of working your dog out in the countryside, but gundog work does not appeal to you.

Any Flatcoated Retriever who is biddable and obedient and who retrieves and enjoys life is capable of competing in working trials. A working trial is the dog equivalent of the horse world's Three Day Event. Your dog should be fit, over 18 months old and have good hips. There are many clubs around the country that will be happy to give advice and training for working trials. Working trials are fun and a great chance to use your Flatcoat's natural abilities, such as soft mouth, good nose and agility, as well as making new friends. You will be competing against a standard and if you are successful you will be entitled to a Certificate recording your success.

Any Flatcoat who has obtained a Kennel Club Good Citizen Award is already on the first rung of the ladder. The heel-work required in working trials need not be as precise as in competitive obedience, but it still needs to be neat. There have been, and still are, gundogs competing in working trials who have been worked in working test and field trials. However, it is easier for the beginner to teach a dog to track and search for human scent before he has worked on cold or fresh game and then, if desired, to do the training to the gun. Competing in working trials will not stop your Flatcoat from doing agility, obedience or any other disciplines.

Working trials consist of five stakes at both open and championship levels. The stakes are:

Companion Dog (CD):	No Track
Utility Dog (UD):	30 minute old track
Working Dog (WD):	90 minute old track
Tracking Dog (TD):	180 minute old track
Patrol Dog:	(This involves teaching manwork, which I would not recommend for a Flatcoat.)

In working trials you compete against a standard and if you reach the qualifying mark you obtain a certificate. Exercises are divided into groups, and to qualify at least 70 per cent must be achieved in each group. The groups in CD are Control, Stay, Agility, and Retrieve and Nosework, which is a Search. In UD, WD, and TD there are only three Groups: Control, Agility and Nosework. If a dog's total marks are more than 80 per cent then he will gain a Certificate of Merit (COM) at an open level or a Qualifying Certificate at championship level. The latter will entitle him to the letters CD.Ex, WD.Ex or TD.Ex after his registered name and this will go on record with The Kennel Club.

To date the only Flatcoat to qualify TD.Ex was Mrs R Aubrey's Blakeholme Jet. This dog was shown up to Postgraduate level and was used as a picking-up dog. Mrs J Shore's famous dog Ch Puhfuh Phineas Finn qualified up to WD and was a complete all-rounder. His is an example for all to try to emulate.

Details of the groups in working trials and what they involve follow:

A training day for agility.

Wanton Warrior approaching the long jump.

Six foot vertical scale.

Control

This involves having a biddable and obedient dog and includes Heel-work on and off the lead, a Recall and a Sendaway in CD. In the higher stakes it includes steadiness to gunshot and there is no heel-work on lead.

Stays

The stays in CD have a two-minute Sit stay and a 10 minute Down stay, both of which are done with the handler out of the dog's sight. In the higher stakes there is no Sit stay. Stays are usually done on the Control field in groups.

Agility

There are three jumps: the Six-foot Vertical Scale, the Three-foot Clear Jump and the Nine-foot Long Jump.

The scale consists of a vertical wall of planks and the dog is asked to go over and then wait on the far side (out of sight of the handler) until the steward or judge asks the handler to recall the dog. The dog then returns over the scale.

The clear jump is a simple hurdle which has a removable top bar. The dog is required to jump over and remain on the far side under control until the handler is asked to join his dog.

The long jump is a series of angled planks which the dog has to clear. Again, he has to remain at the far end until his handler rejoins him.

These jumps are well within the capabilities of a Flatcoat.

Search

In CD there are three (well-scented) articles in a 15-yard square and the dog is allowed four minutes to locate and retrieve them. In all other stakes the time allowed is five minutes and there are four articles. Two articles must be recovered to qualify. The square will be marked by four poles, one at each corner, and the handler must not enter the square. Marks will be given for each article found and for the style and handling. A fresh piece of ground will be used for each dog.

Track

There is no track in CD. The track is approximately half a mile long and will have been laid half an hour before in UD, one and a half hours before in WD and three hours before in TD.

In UD two articles are left on the track, one in the first half of the track and one at the end. A pole will mark the start of the track and 25' yards out a second pole will mark the direction of the first leg of the track. An article must be found to qualify. Marks will be allotted for each leg completed.

In WD there are two articles but only one pole at the start of the track, and in TD there are three articles on the track. In WD one article must be found while in TD two articles must be recovered to qualify.

The track will consist of a number of legs and turns and fresh ground will be used for each dog. The dog will be worked on a harness and tracking line. The competitor will not have seen the track laid, nor will he have seen the pattern, which is the same for all competitors in that stake.

Steadiness to Gunshot

The gun used will usually be a handgun and will not be discharged without prior warning. The dog is not to show fear or aggression when the gun is fired.

Recall

The dog will be left in the Sit or Down position and recalled on command. It should return smartly in front then go round to heel. The handler waits for the judge's or steward's command.

Stays

The handler is out of sight of the dog and the dog must remain in either the Sit or Down position (whichever is being tested) until the Judge or Steward signals that the test is over.

No marks will be awarded to a dog who changes position from Sit to Down or vice versa, or stands or crawls more than its own length. Re-testing will be allowed if there is interference from another dog.

Retrieve

The dog should not move until the order is given by the judge or steward and there should be no mouthing or playing with the dumbbell. The dog goes forward and collects the dumbbell, sits in front of the handler, and then goes to heel.

Speak on Command

Your dog has to bark when asked and cease on your command as directed by the judge. This exercise is only in the TD stake.

Sendaway

The minimum distance is 20 yards for CD and 50 yards for all other stakes. In TD there will be a redirect to either right or left. In practice the distance is usually nearer 50 than 20 in CD but will be something fairly obvious to handler and dog, such as a white pole, bush or tree, but may be just towards those objects. This is a bit like doing an unseen except that there is nothing to retrieve.

Flatcoated Retrievers

Allocation of Marks

The exact allocation of marks in each of the stakes is given in the Tables below.

Companion Dog Exercises

Group 1: Control

Heel on Lead	5
Heel Free	10
Recall to Handler	5
Sendaway	10
Group Total	30 (Minimum Qualifying mark 21)

Group 2: Stays

Sit (2 minute)	10
Down (10 minute)	10
Group Total	20 (Minimum Qualifying mark 14)

Group 3: Agility

Scale		10
Scale	(5)	
Stay	(2)	
Recall	(3)	
Clear Jump		5
Long Jump		5
Group Total		20 (Minimum Qualifying mark 14)

Group 4: Retrieve and Nosework

Retrieve a dumbbell	10
Search (15 yd sq)	20
Group Total	30 (Minimum Qualifying mark 21)

Stake Total	**100 (Minimum Qualifying mark 70)**

Utility Dog Exercises

Group 1: Control

Heel Free	5
Sendaway	10
Retrieve	5
Down	10
Gun	5
Group Total	35 (Minimum Qualifying mark 25)

Group 2: Agility

Scale	10
Clear	5
Long	5
Group Total	20 (Minimum Qualifying mark 14)

Group 3: Nosework

Search (25 yd sq)	35 (4 articles)
Track (90)	
Articles (10+10)	110
Group Total	145 (Minimum Qualifying mark 102)

Stake Total	**200 (Minimum Qualifying mark 141)**

Working Dog Exercises

Group 1: Heel free   5

Sendaway	10
Retrieve	5
Down	10
Gun	5
Group Total	35 (Minimum Qualifying mark 25)

Group 2: Scale   10

Clear	5
Long	5
Group Total	20 (Minimum Qualifying mark 14)

Group 3: Search (25 yd sq)   35

Track (90)	
Articles (10+10)	110
Group Total	145 (Minimum Qualifying mark 102)

Stake Total	**200 (Qualifying mark 141)**

Tracking Dog Exercises

Group 1

Heel free	5
Sendaway and re-direct	10
Speak on command	5
Down	10
Gun	5
Group Total	35 (Minimum Qualifying mark 25)

Group 2

Scale	10
Clear	5
Long	5
Group Total	20 (Minimum Qualifying mark 14)

Group 3

Search (25 yd sq)	35
Track (100)	
Articles (+10+10+10)	130
Group Total	165 (Minimum Qualifying mark 116)

Stake total	**220 (Minimum Qualifying mark 155)**

Further Information

Further and more detailed information can be obtained from books and videos on the subject, some of which are listed in the Bibliography at the end of this book. Lists of books on training can also be found in *Dog World*, *Our Dogs* and *Working Trial Monthly*. Many of these books will be available at your local public library.

Equipment

Initially you will not need much equipment: a collar and lead, dumbbell, some poles or bamboos, assorted small articles for Search and some basic items to train your Flatcoat to jump on command. Later you will need access to jumps or you will have to make some. You will also need a tracking harness and line if you wish to compete in the higher stakes in which there is a track.

Useful Organisations

The main periodical for working trials is *Working Trials Monthly*, and the main association is the Associated Sheep, Police, Army Dogs Society (ASPADS). Addresses for both of these can be found in the **Useful Addresses** section.

AGILITY ACTIVITIES

These are great fun, but as with working trials you will have to wait until your puppy has done its growing, or young limbs can be damaged. You should be able to find a training club in your area, or your obedience club may have an Agility class you can join. All these activities are run by experienced trainers, whose advice must be followed. One of the newest activities is Flyball.

THE KENNEL CLUB JUNIOR ORGANISATION

If your Flatcoat is a family dog, and your children also have an interest in dogs, there is a well-developed organisation for them to join which gives juniors a good insight into every aspect of world of dogs, and is also great fun. The Kennel Club Junior Organisation (KCJO) covers the age group of 8-18 years. For the purposes of the KCJO the British Isles are split into eight regions, each with its own Regional Organiser answerable to The Kennel Club. Many facets of the dog world are covered, including showing, handling, obedience, agility and the Junior of the Year award. Showing involves KCJO Classes at either championship or open show level. Winners of the former are invited to compete in a final at Crufts, and winners of the latter compete at regional level. It is the dog who is judged in this selection. The handling is judged in each region in three age groups: 8-11 years, 12-15 years and 16-18 years. The judging here is based purely on handling. Again the winners of each age group at regional level go forward to Crufts. Heat winners play off against each other for the overall winner's inclusion in the International Junior Handler of the Year Competition.

In the obedience section, after taking a test each junior gets a chance to qualify for their regional team of four who compete at Crufts.

The agility section have their own classes at agility shows with a final at Crufts.

The Junior of the Year competition entails a written project and a diary to do with dogs. This is submitted and judged in the usual three age groups, the winners being presented with their awards at Crufts.

The juniors or their immediate family have to own the dog they handle in the showing classes. In the handling section, however, juniors may handle any dog. In the past a few Flatcoat juniors have been well represented at Crufts in all the disciplines.

This information was supplied by the KCJO, and is used with their permission. For further information, contact the KCJO Manager at The Kennel Club (see **Useful Addresses**).

TRACKING

In this country tracking activities fall mainly within working trials. Flatcoats love tracking, the only problem being that they often have such good noses that they wind the final object and take a short cut across to the end of the track. Very little equipment is needed other than warm country clothing, good boots, a tracking harness for your dog and rope or webbing lunging reins.

In Switzerland I know of Flatcoats who take part in this activity regularly; one young Flatcoat bitch there became the country's youngest Tracking Champion at 15 months of age.

However, both here and in Scandinavia, tracking does come up in a different context. In this country the use of trained dogs for finding

Wanton Warrior CDEx UDEx WDEx tracking.

wounded deer has come to the fore. The British Deer Society run courses for this. A friend of mine who is a professional stalker uses his Flatcoat for this purpose and finds her very good. Further information can be obtained from The British Deer Society (see **Useful Addresses**).

In Scandinavia there are courses and diplomas for tracking elk, and many Flatcoat owners in Sweden do this with their dogs. The dogs are then on a register in their area and are on call to track elk known to have been injured in road accidents. Flatcoats have a good reputation for this.

SEARCH AND RESCUE DOGS

In some countries, Norway among them, Flatcoats have been trained to search and rescue people. This involves a long and expensive training course, but some Flatcoats have followed it through and work as qualified Search and Rescue dogs. This is difficult and exacting work for any dog, but the reward of finding a lost person or someone caught in an avalanche must be so great. Remember, this work is often done in freezing conditions, so the dogs and handlers can only work for short periods of time. I have watched Charley (Norwegian Ch Exclyst Kestrel) in Norway demonstrate his ability in this field and his intense concentration and memory as he worked will always stay with me.

Search and Rescue training in Norway.

In April 1995 another Flatcoat, Raven, helped search the ruins of the Federal Building in Oklahoma City for survivors after the bombing. More details about her can be found in the section on the United States of America in Chapter 3.

SNIFFER DOGS FOR DRUGS

This is another task for which Flatcoats are used in some countries. The ability of these dogs is outstanding, and it is extremely exciting to watch the partnership of handler and dog as they work so closely together. They certainly take their job of work seriously, and I have seen the same dog become a show dog, and even a gundog, even though a rather unconventional one. More details about this can be found in the section on Norway in Chapter 3.

GUNDOG WORK

You have done all your basic gundog training and maybe you have made the decision that field trialling is not for you or your dog, but you both enjoy the work and you would love to learn more. You are a member of a Gundog Working Club, and have been to Gundog Training Classes, read the books and studied the videos. Maybe you have taken part in a summer working test in your area.

Experienced handlers will often help a novice owner and dog who are willing to learn. They might be willing to take you out to help you understand the work involved, or perhaps they will invite you to accompany them to a small local shoot.

Please remember to condition your dog as you would a horse you are going to hunt. Improve the quality of the food and increase road work and free exercise. It is just the same as for a horse or a person: the unfit dog breaks down and injures itself. You too will be in a better condition for a hard day's work.

You must equip yourself with the usual uniform. The first item is a wax or waterproof coat. A good, reasonably-priced quality wax jacket is best for picking up. It will soon get dirty, covered in feathers and blood, and the brambles and barbed wire will catch you. They do not stay new for very long! Waterproof leggings and a good rain hat are also essentials. Do not forget your dog whistles and leads, and you will also need a double headed game carrier, which can be bought at most gun shops. Another important item is a priest (a short length of weighted wood, metal or horn that can be used to dispatch game humanely). Do get someone to show you the right way to do this as it is very important. Do handle a live bird firmly after you have taken it from your dog. It is best to hold it where the wings meet the body with its legs away from you. Take care that it does not dig its feet into you, as that can be very painful.

It is best to take a flask and sandwiches unless you are told otherwise, and also a snack for your dog. I always carry a Mars bar for mine in my jacket, as it is a fast replenisher of energy. Water is also important, as it can get very warm in September and October and some areas do not have any natural water. A dog needs a drink, especially when it is working hard. A towelling jacket to put on your dog when the day is over is important. This is not me being over-protective of my dogs - it is a very practical thing, especially if it is wet. Most of us travel some distance to and from a shoot, so your dog will drying off on the way home. A towelling jacket will keep your car cleaner, and, most importantly, it will help to keep your dog in good condition. Over the years I have found that this way my dogs keep in better condition, as they do not have to use that extra energy keeping themselves warm in a cold car. It also helps offset arthritis. 'Warm joints ease, cold joints seize', so in the long run you have a dog who goes to the vet less and has a longer active working life. I also find that a small handful of dog biscuits is much appreciated when the dogs get into the car. It is like when you have a cup of tea and a biscuit before you start for home; you warm up that much quicker. I leave the coats on the dogs for an hour or two after I return home. This reminds me after supper to check them over for thorns, cuts and other minor injuries. This is very important, as they can easily be overlooked and Flatcoats do not let you know.

Picking Up

This what most Flatcoats call 'Heaven'. In my experience, this is where they excel. They are usually tenacious game finders. If you go about it in the right way, you and your dog or dogs will have every spare day from October to the end of January booked. However, there is a great deal of training and hard work to do on the way.

To be a good picker-up takes time. You must be willing to learn and to do as you are told, never overstepping the mark. In essence you are taking payment to do a job of work with your dogs: you are not out to teach your dogs to be gundogs or train them for field trials. You are a member of a team working under the gamekeeper, who delegates to a senior picker-up the responsibility for ensuring that all areas behind the guns are covered and that all game is quickly, efficiently and humanely retrieved and dispatched.

Preparing the dog to be
sent for the retrieve.

The send.

The first cold game retrieve must
be done with care.
Photos - Liz Phillips.

You and your dog will be given an area from which to clear the birds. Please remember to ask how far back you can go. You must be reasonably quiet at all times. Pheasants can hear voices at a great distance. So can the gamekeeper, and if the drive does not go as he has planned, you will be blamed.

Do not stand close to the guns unless you are particularly told to do so. Many guns have their own dogs and will be upset if all birds are cleared by the end of the drive so that there is no work for their own dogs. Remember, they are paying for their day's sport. However, it is a good idea to go back after they have gone and do a quick check of the surrounding area.

A happy working Flatcoat picking up.   Photo - Liz Phillips.

It is your responsibility that the ground within your area is cleared. You are usually told where to stand, but make sure it is safe. If you are near a gun make sure he or she is aware of you, especially on hilly ground. My personal preference is for 'back picking', which means being 200 yards or more back from the guns. The further back the better, as pheasants can glide on a long way after being shot, especially if they are high birds.

This is no place for a novice dog: it is too full of temptation! It is fascinating to watch an old, well-campaigned dog sitting quietly while many birds go over him. All at once you can see him watch a bird (I think it is the sound of the bird that is different). Then, off he goes, coming back moments later with the bird. It fascinates me how much the dogs learn about the ground they work, especially if they work it on a regular basis, and how quickly they learn the horn or whistle blast at the end of the drive. One moment they are sitting beside me, the next the horn goes - and they are off sweeping. This is a very important part of the exercise, as birds can glide in behind you from any direction and in the heat of a heavy drive one does not always see everything. I teach my dogs to work on different sides of the cover rather than together, and I usually walk with the dog back through the cover in the direction most birds have flown past me, working out any area thoroughly if it looks as though a bird could hide there and encouraging the dog to look everywhere. An experienced dog seldom has to be told. My own dogs have a tendency to point or set, but time being the essence I usually verbally encourage them to flush. I have known several birds be in the same clump of bramble. I remember one crisp winter's day at Lowton Manor with snow on the ground when Bernard went on point and moved slowly round a clump of brash, pushing out 12 hen birds, one at a time. Of such stuff are the memories of dog work.

All this has to be done as quickly as possible as there is a set period of time before it is time to go off to the next drive. However it is those wounded or dead birds far back that fill the bag. Three or four of these difficult birds and a picker-up and his dogs pay for themselves. That is why we are there, as the dead birds around the guns can be picked up by hand by any person.

Having said that, never put your dog in danger. No bird is worth your dog being swept away in a strong river or going over a dangerous steep drop. Do be careful trying for a bird near a road. It is better to work from the road into a field, because if the bird runs it will then probably run into the field, not across the road into the path of an oncoming car. The worse part of picking up is carrying the birds out to the game-cart. Each bird seems to increase in weight every step of the way.

You and your dog will arrive home tired but satisfied. It certainly makes the winter fly by. For me, winter starts in the first week of February. You will work hard, meet some great people, have good memories of your dogs working and see a great variety of wild life and fascinating changes in the countryside - all things which you would miss otherwise. Each day your work will be different and challenging. An outstanding picking-up dog may not have field trial or show awards, but memories of that dog will live on.

Rough Shooting and Wildfowling

This is another place where Flatcoats come into their own. It is much more of a one-to-one sport, the owner hunting and shooting birds on his own. Wildfowling is mainly done on marshes, foreshores or ponds. Flatcoats on the whole are good strong swimmers and, because of their thick coats, they can stand the cold wet winter conditions. They are also good all-round gundogs who enjoy working ground, finding game, flushing it, then retrieving it.

I have great pleasure in going out rough shooting with my husband, working my dogs as spaniels through the covers and hedgerows. One dog suddenly freezes and the second dog comes round and honours the first. It is fascinating to watch, to see the the dogs fix their eyes on the bird, waiting till its nerve goes and it flushes. These dogs certainly know the difference between game that is fit and injured. There is something very exciting about this, though maybe it is not the purest of gundog work, and not all Flatcoats will do it. It is an aspect of Flatcoat behaviour that one discourages when training a dog for field trials.

Many gamekeepers still regularly work their Flatcoats and find that they do a good job. As many Flatcoats are still being worked in diverse activities, provided they are properly trained, they will have a place as utility gundogs in the future. The important factor with any breed is the continuing use of the trainability within a dog, and our Flatcoats are bred for trainability.

The Shooting Dog Certificate

The Shooting Dog Certificate was the brain child of The Hon Mrs Jessel (see Chapter 1). It was outstanding in its concept, but it is not utilised to gain the maximum advantage. Once a dog is found to have the ugly label 'show breeding' it is often totally stone-walled by the field establishment, even after gaining an 'A' certificate. Even field trial winning dogs not in the right hands are lost by the lack of use at stud. The breed suffers greatly from this blinkered approach.

During the last 15 years, however, a nucleus of hardworking 'field trial' people have been working their dogs in Any Variety Field Trials. Mrs Joan Marsden in particular has been outstanding in her efforts to establish the reputation of Flatcoats in Variety Trials, using Tarncourt Byron, Tarncourt Crofter, Tarncourt Charm and Tarncourt Noteable to name but a few. Mr Clive Harrison of the Blackrake affix also has run his dogs in Variety Trials for many years.

Mrs Sheila Neary of the Collarm affix has kindly contributed an article to this book entitled *Training the family companion dog to the gun.* This is printed in its entirety in Appendix B.

A Working Test water retrieve.

FIELD TRIALS

The heyday of the Flatcoated Retriever was before the First World War and between the Wars, but even then their popularity was declining. They were owned mainly by men who had large estates, where the sporting side of life had priority. Their owners kept large kennels of all breeds of gundogs and employed many trainers.

All this changed with the Second World War. Post-war life took time to settle back to normal. The first Field Trial was held in 1947 but it took time to establish lines again and it was also a while before there was the time, money or petrol to do them justice. In 1953 the only Flatcoat to distinguish himself in Any Variety trials was Ch Waterboy, and it was not until 1959 that Flatcoats started again to be recognised in Variety Stakes.

Field trials are judged by Kennel Club approved field trial judges on the A or B list, although sometimes one probationary judge (a judge approved and supported by his or her own field trial society or breed club prior to being invited onto the B list) may be included. Each dog has its own unique retrieves and is marked on a grading system A+, A, B+, B, C+ and C on each retrieve. The object is to assess the dog's ability and the quality of its work against the difficulty of each individual retrieve. The dog with, say, A+ under all three judges would win the trial against a dog with an A, B+ and B. (This is a simplistic explanation.)

The early 1960s saw the emergence of names such as Ch Claverdon Jorrocks of Lilling, Claverdon Skipper, Claverdon Corker, Hartshorn Midnight, Ch Collyers Blakeholme Brewster, and Hartshorn Moonshine, to name a few. In 1965 Hartshorn Sorrel won her first awards.

In 1967 most field trials were cancelled because of foot and mouth disease. Major Wilson's bitch Hartshorn Sorrel became a Field Trial Champion when she won the 24-dog Open Stake of the Ulster Retriever Club. His dog Nesfield Michael won the Any Variety Non-winners Stake of the Golden Retriever Club of Scotland. (All post-war winners in field trials are listed in Appendix A.)

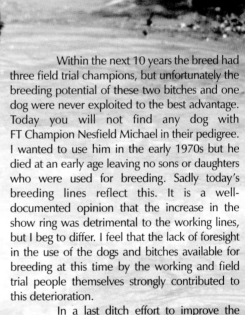

Within the next 10 years the breed had three field trial champions, but unfortunately the breeding potential of these two bitches and one dog were never exploited to the best advantage. Today you will not find any dog with FT Champion Nesfield Michael in their pedigree. I wanted to use him in the early 1970s but he died at an early age leaving no sons or daughters who were used for breeding. Sadly today's breeding lines reflect this. It is a well-documented opinion that the increase in the show ring was detrimental to the working lines, but I beg to differ. I feel that the lack of foresight in the use of the dogs and bitches available for breeding at this time by the working and field trial people themselves strongly contributed to this deterioration.

In a last ditch effort to improve the working lines a Working Group was formed. This failed to some extent because one must not be too insular in a breed with such a small gene bank as Flatcoats; one must exploit every potential. In the course of my research I found it very interesting to note that it is possible to win with show/working lines over specialised working lines. Perhaps the key to this is to have good trainers who can understand and utilise able Flatcoats, whatever their breeding.

For further tips about training dogs for field trials, see Sheila Neary's article in Appendix B.

WORKING TEST

The working test became popular after the war as gundogs became more numerous and the concept of a family pet became a reality. People had more money and more spare time, so they wanted to get out into the countryside and enjoy their dogs in the company of like-minded friends.

Many friends met together, helping each other to train their gundogs. Working gundog clubs were formed during the late 1950s and all through the 1960s. Field Trial clubs that had been running trials nearly as long as there had been gundogs as we know them today expanded their activities during summer to include a working test and gundog training section.

Working tests were developed to help improve the quality of gundog work. They are a totally different concept to a field trial. Working tests are now run under the umbrella of The Kennel Club, and the judges are often field trial judges, but they are just as often well-respected gundog owners and competitors. Wins at working test are not registered with your dog's awards at The Kennel Club as are field trial and championship show awards.

All the individual tests are set before the working test, and all 12 or 24 dogs run the same test. They are marked from 10 to 0, and the dog with most points at the end of the day is the winner.

The working test today has a place in the preparation of working gundogs and dogs for field trials, but you must understand the different concepts. There is an increasing band of enthusiasts who only do working tests. Great care has to be taken that these tests, in which live game is not used, do not become a vehicle for handlers' circus tricks. It is vital to support the concept of encouraging and enhancing the natural abilities of the gundog to be biddable and quiet, able to work its ground whether cover or water, use its nose, find wounded game quickly without disturbance, and retrieve it without damage.

If you decide that you would enjoy working test activities with your Flatcoat, you can follow the training programme that we have put together for field trial training. This will give you a sound base upon which to build. You could be nearly ready to enter a Puppy/Novice working test. However, I would strongly advise you to join a local working gundog training class, or contact The Flatcoated Retriever Society's County Representative to see if there are special Flatcoat gundog training classes. These training classes are usually held during the summer months, and will give your young Flatcoat confidence and invaluable experience in the company of other dogs. Please do not push him on too fast: make it fun!

FLATCOATED RETRIEVER BREED CLUBS AND SOCIETIES IN GREAT BRITAIN

Over the years, various Flatcoated Retriever breed clubs and societies have come into being in Great Britain, to establish and maintain the breed standard and to co-ordinate the many activities in which Flatcoat enthusiasts are involved. It seems a good idea to end this chapter on Flatcoated Retriever activities by listing thoese societies, past and present, which have had such influence on the evolution of today's Flatcoat in Great Britain.

Past Breed Clubs and Societies

The Flat-coated Retriever Association was founded by a number of sportsmen in 1923 to promote the breed in field trials. Its main object was to encourage the breeding of working Flatcoated Retrievers. The first field trials were arranged in 1924. The Association also approved judges and drew up the Breed Standard. This was accepted by The Kennel Club and is still recognised today, with only the mandatory Kennel Club changes of all breed standards in the 1980s.

The Flat-coated Retriever Club was established in 1937. There had been a split within the Association, as some members felt that not enough energy was directed towards the show promotion of the breed. (Show entries in fact had fallen.) A number of members formed the Flat-coated Retriever Club to encourage the breeding of a type of Flatcoat suitable for the show bench and also possessing good working qualities: in other words, a dual-purpose dog. This club was established and did much to promote the showing of Flatcoats until the outbreak of the war stopped the activities of both clubs.

The Flat-coated Retriever Society In 1947 the Flat-coated Retriever Association started field trials again, and at the same time its President, Mr R E Birch, realised the need to strengthen Flatcoat ranks. He approached the Flat-coated Retriever Club in 1948: after preliminary talks, the executives of the two bodies met at Chester and agreed to amalgamate, forming The Flat-coated Retriever Society under the presidency of Mr W J Phizacklea. The new executive undertook that the promotion of field trials should have high priority and that funds would always remain available for that purpose. It was on this condition that all the field trial cups and trophies (formerly the property of the Association) came into the possession of the Flat-coated Retriever Society.

The Gamekeepers Flat-coat Club At about the time the Flat-coated Retriever Society was formed certain Flatcoat supporters, many of whom were gamekeepers, disapproved of the mating of black to liver-coloured dogs. They argued that the black progeny of these matings were genetically impure, and that when subsequently mated, whether to genetically pure (black) or impure (liver) dogs, they could impair the blackness of coat and the depth of eye colour of their progeny.

For this reason, to show their condemnation of liver Flatcoats, they opted out of the new Society and formed yet another club, The Gamekeepers Flat-coat Club. One of the policies of this club was to bar liver Flatcoats. The new club made representation to The Kennel Club to remove the colour from the Flatcoated Retriever Breed Standard, but this was unsuccessful. The club carried on for a number of years but never gained very much support and gradually went out of existence.

My source for this information was Dr Nancy Laughton's book *The Review of the Flatcoated Retriever.*

Flatcoated Retrievers

Present Breed Clubs and Societies

The Flat-coated Retriever Society continued to develop and increase in size as the breed expanded and is known today as **The Flatcoated Retriever Society**.

The Society has a membership of more than 2000. It still runs field trials: at least two Novice; one All-Aged; and one 12-dog Open. Grounds are generously lent by landowners and syndicates interested in the Flatcoat as a working retriever.

In the summer several Working Test Novice and Open are run in different areas of the country under the Field Trial Secretary's wing.

The Society's Secretary in 1995 is Mrs Joan Maude, and her address is given in **Useful Addresses**. Joan is very approachable and very willing to help genuine Flatcoat enthusiasts.

There is also a Show Secretary who organises and runs a championship show, usually in the spring, with an entry in the early 1990s in the region of 400 to 500 Flatcoats. Two open shows are also organised in different areas of the country. Breed seminars on health and breed type are organised, plus smaller 'Judges' Workshops'.

You will have seen before the mention of County Representatives. These are members who represent their breed within their counties. They can be approached for help and local information on the breed and activities. They will be able to point you in the right direction for information and advice. If you are thinking about going into the breed they are ideal people to visit to get an unbiased opinion. Some County Representatives also organise fun events. These are the troops on the ground, but they are all under Mrs Maude's umbrella. They make no policy decisions for the Society.

Within the Society we have the Rescue, Rehousing and Welfare Scheme. The Secretary/Co-ordinator is Mrs Barbara Harkin and again her address is given in **Useful Addresses**.

The Illness/Accident/Death Scheme is also there to support Flatcoat owners. When you have dogs proper arrangements should be made for them should anything happen to you. There is a leaflet with further information and a card to complete with the details of the person you wish to take care of your dogs. Alternatively if you have no one, you might wish the Rescue, Rehousing and Welfare Scheme to be entrusted with them.

I should like to remind you that the best introduction to the breed is to send to Joan Maude for *The Flatcoated Retriever Society Information Booklet*. The current price is £1.35.

The Flatcoated Retriever Club of Scotland was founded in 1985 by a group of breed enthusiasts headed by Miss Jean Lackie of Longforgan by Dundee. Miss Lackie was appointed Secretary/Treasurer at the inaugural meeting and held this position until 1990 when she stood down because of business commitments.

Two shows are held each year: a championship show in April and an open show the last Sunday in October. The club also holds breed seminars and has hosted scurries and working tests open to all Gundog breeds. An annual Newsletter keeps members up-to-date with what is going on.

The Club has its own code of ethics and criteria for selecting judges for the Kennel Club lists. It has recently set up a Breeders' Register. The Register is for members use at a fee of £5 per annum and forms are available from the Secretary. Judges' Questionnaires are also available from the Secretary, who welcomes enquiries from breed specialists and all-rounders.

The Club hopes for a continued genuine interest in the breed and will endeavour to encourage the existing membership and any new members to show and train their dogs, always remembering that the Flatcoat is a dual-purpose gundog. Hopefully, with sustained effort in that direction, the Breed will survive as a dual-purpose gundog in spite of the working instinct in so many other gundog breeds today.

Mrs M Scougal is the Secretary/Treasurer, and she is listed in **Useful Addresses**.

The Northern England Flatcoated Retriever Association is a proposed society, currently seeking recognition from The Kennel Club. The Secretary is Mrs S Kitching. She too can be found in **Useful Addresses**.

Chapter 9

Breeding Flatcoated Retrievers

Each year brings many unwanted puppies of both pure-bred and cross-bred origins, so you should not consider breeding without giving a thought to the subsequent welfare of your bitch's offspring. You must ensure as far as possible that you have homes for any puppies which are surplus to your requirements before planning to mate your bitch, or alternatively be prepared to keep surplus puppies until responsible homes can be found for them. The latter entails having sufficient accommodation for growing youngsters and being prepared for a great deal of work and expense. Breeding a litter is not a get-rich-quick proposition. It starts with a bill well over £100 to have your bitch's hips X-rayed and her eyes tested under the BVA scheme, and it is a good idea too to ask your veterinary surgeon to check her heart while he is X-raying her, as he will be able hear better without the wagging tail.

It is a common but erroneous belief that because a dog or bitch has a pedigree it must be worth breeding. In fact, the majority of dogs in the popular breeds would not be considered of sufficiently high quality to be used for breeding purposes, and owners should understand that it is not necessary to breed a bitch simply for the sake of her health. Serious breeders and exhibitors aim to improve the quality of their stock with each generation and therefore concentrate on breeding the best to the best both in physical type and mental soundness.

An irresistable liver pup. However, each year brings many pups that are difficult to place, especially males.

If you have a well-bred Flatcoat bitch, breeding successfully from her still entails careful selection of a mate. If you have attended some dog shows or field trials, particularly if your bitch has been shown or worked and is a prize-winner, you may already have some idea of a possible stud dog for her. If she is simply a lovable pet, ask yourself if you really want her to have puppies, and give yourself an honest answer.

If you have decided to go ahead, and are about to select her mate, bear in mind that the perfect dog has never yet been born! Then, giving due consideration to The Kennel Club's official Breed Standard and your bitch's faults and virtues (be honest!), choose a mate who excels in the points in which she is weak. For example, if your bitch has a rather poor head you must choose a stud dog who has an excellent head himself and, even more important, one who is known to sire puppies with excellent heads.

Of course a good head is only one feature for consideration. As with many other features, heredity (nature) plays its part, but proper rearing and general care (nurture) also have a part to play; this applies to all breeding matters. It is not sensible to breed from a bitch of extremely poor quality as even the most glamorous stud dog cannot work miracles and it would take several generations to eliminate the faults. Similarly, a male dog of indifferent quality has nothing to offer as a stud dog. This in no way affects the worth of such animals as faithful and loving pets, but it is best to let them enjoy life in that way.

Presuming your bitch has no outstanding faults, how would you choose the most suitable mate for her? If you are already an exhibitor you may have noticed a male dog you would like to use and, as it is far better to consider breeding plans in advance, you should approach the owner for information concerning the dog's availability at stud, and with regard to his fee. Be prepared for this to be quite substantial! You may also find that the stud dog owner will be able to advise you further on your choice if necessary.

The example given above of choosing a stud dog with an excellent head if your bitch does not have a very good head was used because this is an obvious feature. There are, of course, other features upon which you may wish to improve, and some which are not visible which you should try to avoid. Hereditary diseases come into this category, and information is available from the Breed Club Secretary, from your veterinary surgeon, from The Kennel Club and also from the stud dog's owner, who should be prepared to discuss these matters frankly with you before any mating takes place.

You may have seen occasional references to such diseases as hip dysplasia, luxating patella (sometimes referred to as slipping kneecaps or stifles) which may cause lameness, heart problems, and eye problems such as hereditary cataracts (HC), progressive retinal atrophy (PRA), or glaucoma, which may lead to blindness. These are but a few of the problems which face conscientious dog breeders. In Great Britain The British Veterinary Association and The Kennel Club have set up a joint examination arrangement, known as the BVA/KC Scheme for the Control of Hereditary Diseases, under which a panel of veterinary surgeons conducts regular examinations of breeding stock in susceptible breeds and certifies those which show no clinical evidence of the disease concerned.

In breeds which have known hereditary problems it is essential to breed only from stock which has been tested and cleared of these diseases and which holds currently issued BVA/KC Certificates of Clearance. However, the problem is that in some cases a dog, or bitch which is not itself affected by a hereditary disease may carry a recessive gene allowing it to pass on that disease if its mate also carries the unseen recessive. While it is essential that only tested and cleared stock is used in breeding programmes, it is also evident that some misfortunes will occur despite the most careful preparations. For this reason, if none other, the breeding of pedigree stock must be planned very carefully and only undertaken when all the factors have been considered.

Flatcoated Retrievers

It is estimated that there is a failure rate of five per cent among Flatcoated Retrievers tested officially in countries which, like Great Britain, have set up a procedure for checking hip X-rays. In a period of three years in Great Britain, 2783 Flatcoats were bred and 395 were X-rayed. Dr M B Willis, Senior Lecturer in Animal Breeding and Genetics at the University of Newcastle-upon-Tyne, reported to the Flatcoated Retriever Society (1 April 1993) that in his opinion 'most breeders could set a maximum level of 15 without much difficulty and there is certainly little excuse for using dogs over 20 except in exceptional circumstances'. He goes on to say that 'five per cent of the breed are over 20 which is about twice the breed average score.' Out of 728 Flatcoats X-rayed up to 1995, 73 dogs have scores over 16; of those 43 have scored 16 to 19. Thirty Flatcoats have scored 20 and over. There are also a few known cases of clinically diagnosed puppies too young to be scored.

Breeders X-ray their stock to ascertain which dogs register high scores and avoid breeding from them; one does not X-ray and then continue to breed from these affected dogs. Remember that buyers of puppies from such unions are entitled to take the breeder to court and claim damages, as the breeder has knowingly bred from affected stock. More importantly, the pain and discomfort of those poor dogs affected and the stress and worry to the owners of dysplastic puppies is so great it cannot be contemplated by any responsible breeder.

The temperament of your Flatcoat must also be considered if you are planning to breed from your bitch. Temperament is given a brief description in the official Breed Standard and you must ask yourself whether your bitch is typical of this description. Every dog is equipped with the means to defend itself when necessary: a good set of sharp teeth! However, no dog should be deliberately vicious. Most Flatcoats are friendly and outgoing. Your Flatcoat must not be hyperactive or excitable, and should not be so shy that he or she either backs away from strangers or displays aggression toward them: this is not Flatcoat behaviour. When planning to breed from your bitch, choose a stud dog with a normal temperament who is not shy, aggressive or over-excitable. It is the responsibility of the stud dog owner to make sure that he fits the breed's temperament standard.

When you are thinking of breeding from your bitch you will probably start to look carefully at pedigrees. You may hear comments about 'inbreeding' or 'line-breeding' or 'outcrossing'. Inbreeding is the mating together of close relatives; line-breeding is the mating of animals less closely related; and outcrossing is the use of unrelated animals of the same breed. These three terms are discussed in more detail below. There is a tendency among newcomers to dog breeding to consider inbreeding totally undesirable, but this is not necessarily so. However, it needs a great deal of experience of the breed concerned before decisions on any particular breeding formula can be made. Many may consider that line-breeding is a safer bet, but again it depends on many factors, most of which may be unknown to a novice breeder.

The one definite point regarding outcrossing is that the result will be unpredictable, unless you have used a prepotent stud dog (one which passes on its own good type regardless of its mate). However, outcrosses are sometimes made for a special purpose: to improve a specific feature in your stock. Again, just imagine that the need is to improve upon the head, as this is something reasonably easy to see from an early age. Having chosen a sire with a superb head, the pups you keep from this union should be the ones with better heads. These outcross pups, however, should themselves in due course be line-bred, or even inbred; otherwise in the next generation you may lose type altogether. If you become interested in pedigrees and study those of various well-known dogs and bitches in your breed you will see how people have made successful breeding plans in the past. Pedigrees are extremely fascinating documents.

Breeding Methods to Establish a Strain

The term 'strain' as applied to dog breeding denotes that these animals come from one family with varying relationships. This does not always mean that all dogs under, say, the Exclyst affix will be from the same family. Some might have been bought in by the breeder and be totally unrelated. These, however, will be 'of Exclyst'.

As has already been mentioned, there are three methods of establishing a strain:

Outcrossing: As I have said before, it would be very difficult to produce consistently good stock generation after generation this way. Although you might have good results in the first generation if the dogs were outstanding, it is unlikely they would continue to breed true to type unless they were mated back to their close relations. So if your puppies from this mating have the right type, quality and temperament, the only method of fixing these outstanding qualities for the future generations is by mating them to their relations, who are likely to carry similar genes.

Line-breeding: This term refers to the mating of dogs related, in varying degrees, to one outstanding dog or bitch. The aim is to keep the relationship as near as possible to that dog and to perpetuate his or her qualities. The best results here occur when the related dog and bitch are themselves good specimens, closely resembling their famous ancestor. It is useless to use this method on mediocre dogs as the whole object of line-breeding is to reproduce greatness. Typical examples of this line-breeding relationship is mating uncle to niece or cousin to cousin. To line-breed successfully you must recognise the faults which could be transmitted as well as the good points which you hope to establish, and with this in mind select the individuals from which to breed carefully.

Example of Line-Breeding

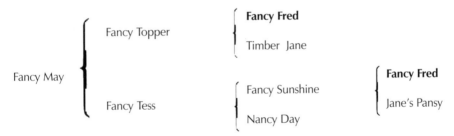

(In this pedigree Fancy Fred is the common ancestor, appearing as Grandfather on the male line and Great-grandfather on the female line.)

Inbreeding: This can be the quickest way to fix type. It is the mating of very closely related dogs, such as father to daughter or brother to sister. These dogs would have to conform as nearly as possible to the Breed Standard. The resulting puppies would then be expected to carry in duplicate the genes for the outstanding characteristics of the parents. However, you could as well duplicate the genes for outstanding faults or health problems. This method is not advocated for the novice. To create a successful strain in this way you need to have a full and intimate knowledge of their forbears. Like line-breeding, inbreeding can fix virtues and also stamp in faults. It will not introduce anything new to a strain; it merely brings out what is latent, both good and bad. Because of this the dogs used for inbreeding must themselves be outstanding in type and temperament, and have no physical defects or weaknesses. When this method fails it is not the fault of the system of inbreeding; it is most often the result

Flatcoated Retrievers

A black bitch with her liver puppy.

Photo - Y Jaussi.

of faulty judgment on the part of the breeder concerning the dogs used. If one is a realist there are very few kennels with the depth of quality to support an inbreeding project.

Are there any breeding plans which you should shun? Yes. Firstly, if your breed has hereditary problems, never use untested stock, or stock without a good family hip status. Secondly, if your bitch has not already had a litter, do not consider mating her to a dog which has never sired puppies. If such a mating proved unfruitful you would not know whether the dog was infertile or the bitch barren, and if it produced puppies you would have no idea what to expect from them with regard to future development. Experienced breeders sometimes mate two unproven animals within their own kennel because they have considerable knowledge of their antecedents, but an unproven dog would not normally be offered at stud to a maiden bitch. Most importantly, you should never breed your Black or Liver Flatcoat to a Yellow Flatcoat.

Examples of inbreeding

(Mating of full brother and sister.)

(Mating of father to daughter.)

Planning Future Matings

If you intend to develop your own strain of Flatcoats, much time and thought must be given to planning future matings. Pedigrees should be worked out: *The Flatcoated Retriever Directory*, compiled by Sue Kearton and myself, and Rona Dixon's computer pedigree service are useful for this purpose. It is helpful to put different pedigrees together to see how they 'tie up', at the same time taking into consideration how the individual animals are likely to suit one another physically and mentally. This research will broaden your overall knowledge of the breed. It is useful to plan several unborn generations out on paper. This is not often possible, however, and the first or second mating results may not turn out as you had hoped; the dogs may not come up to the desired standard.

As I have said, the dog and bitch must both be of a high quality; the good points that you want to reproduce must be seen in both partners. Conversely, it is not wise to mate two dogs with similar faults, so if your bitch could have better forequarters, you mate her to a dog that is as perfect as you can find in his forequarters. It is useless, for example, to mate a weak-headed bitch to a coarse-headed dog hoping to produce a middle-of-the-road head. The chances are that you will have some puppies resembling the bitch and others the dog. The best thing would be to mate your weak-headed bitch to a dog with a head of the correct strength, hoping thus to improve the general type of heads in your litter.

The Breeding Cycle

The bitch is likely to have two periods of heat each year, although this can vary somewhat. During this time she will be responsive to a male and likely to conceive after mating. The first period of heat is likely to occur when she is somewhere between six months and a year old, but it could be later.

You will notice that her vulva becomes swollen, and you may also observe spots of blood there or on her bedding. The bitch will lick herself repeatedly, and may appear rather fretful, as well as urinating more often than usual. She will play with male dogs, who are likely to be attracted to her, but she will not permit mating at this stage of her oestrus cycle, which is described as pro-oestrus. However, it is unfair to all concerned to let a bitch in any stage of oestrus run with male dogs. She needs to be under your control at all times to avoid the possibility of an accidental mating with a wandering canine opportunist.

After a period of nine to thirteen days, the bloody discharge from her vulva will be replaced by a paler or clear discharge. This signals the start of the oestrus phase when mating must occur if puppies are to be conceived. At this stage, if approached by a male dog, the bitch will probably switch her tail to the side and allow mating to occur. It is important to detect the start of the oestrus period accurately, because this is when mating is most likely to be successful.

It is not a good idea to mate a Flatcoat bitch until she is over two and preferably three years old: she is still relatively immature until this age. During any season you will need to supervise her carefully. Check that the garden fences and gates are secure so that there is no risk that she will slip out and find her own mate, nor that a hopeful male wanderer can get into your garden as her scent wafts on the air. An undesired mating can be annulled with an injection given by your vet, but prevention is always better than cure.

Assuming mating does not occur, the oestrus period subsides and is followed by the anoestrus phase of the cycle. The bitch's vulva returns to its more usual appearance and the accompanying behavioural changes cease.

Male dogs attain puberty at a similar age to that of their female counterparts, although there can be some marked breed differences in this respect. They are not usually used for breeding purposes until they are about a year old (they will not have BVA hip scores or certificates that their eyes have been tested before then). The stud dog will be approaching two years of age before his progeny are in the show ring and may be available to 'approved bitches only' during this time. This proviso allows his owner to refuse bitches not considered suitable, or to offer the use of another dog instead.

Unlike a bitch, the male dog does not undergo a seasonal cycle, but can mate effectively at any stage through the year. A young dog may have his first mating experience with an older bitch who is less likely to resent him. Conversely an inexperienced young bitch is usually better mated to an experienced older dog. Apart from the first mating for either sex, the choice does not usually rest on the age and experience of the two concerned. In fact the dog-breeding experience of the stud's owner is a major factor, as all matings need to be supervised. If you have a male dog as a pet it is not necessary for him to mate at all. Celibacy will not adversely affect his health.

Simply allowing a mating pair to run together is unsatisfactory as there may be outbreaks of aggression resulting in no union at all. The owner of the bitch will usually be asked to hold her head, and she should be wearing a leather collar. Slipping the thumbs inside her collar allows the owner to take a firm but gentle hold if the bitch starts to fuss. The owner of the stud dog will assist him, if necessary, and the dog and bitch must be gently restrained during the 'tie'. They cannot separate during this period, which may last only a few minutes, but could last more than half an hour. Fortunately they are generally content and quiescent at this stage, though their owners may suffer from cramp!

It is important to telephone the owner of your chosen stud as soon as your bitch comes into season, verify the possible date of mating and check the amount of the stud fee, which is normally payable at the time of service. If you enter into any form of stud agreement instead of paying the stud fee outright, this should be organised at the time of booking, and a written agreement stating the exact terms of the arrangement must be kept by both parties. If a stud fee is not paid the owner of the dog may request the first choice from the litter, or perhaps the first and third choice. Sometimes this is a satisfactory arrangement, but it may mean that you lose your best puppy! If you purchased your bitch on a breeding terms agreement you will have to honour that, but there is no hard and fast formula for such things; it is really a matter of individual agreement in each case. Consider such plans with due care before agreeing.

It is not always certain that a bitch will be ready for mating on a particular day. You may not have noticed the first day or two of her season, or her pro-oestrus period may have been a day or two longer, or shorter, than usual. You will need to check her regularly and watch for that colour change and the switching of her tail when her vulva is touched. If you have to make a long journey to the stud dog, make the preparations in advance so that you are ready to go when the time is right.

It is more usual in Britain to take the bitch to the stud dog when she is ready for mating rather than send her to stay at the kennels for an extended visit during her season, though the latter plan may be necessary in certain circumstances. One satisfactory mating is usually sufficient but two stud services are sometimes preferred, or advised. That may mean a second journey to the stud dog, or the bitch staying over for a few days. Discuss all these possibilities with the stud dog owner when making the initial arrangements.

In large countries such as the United States of America, Canada, Australia or on the continent of Europe, breeders may wish to use a stud dog belonging to a kennel situated thousands of miles away. In such cases it would be necessary to send the bitch to the stud dog's home kennel well in advance of her probable mating date, and air travel may be the most sensible method. Find out the facts about such travel arrangements well ahead of time.

The Stud Dog

Because you have a male Flatcoat, it does not follow necessarily that he must be used at stud. He must have something genuine to offer the breed, he must be truly typical of the breed in type and temperament, and he must be reliable and have a stable mentality. He must also have the ability to use his brain and be biddable and able to do his job of work (gundog) or any other reasonable job (obedience, working trials, tracking or whatever). If your dog is a family pet it may be wise not to use him at stud; if he is used occasionally this could be storing up trouble for yourself later, as he may start to wander when his thoughts turn to love! This in turn could put him in danger of being run over on our busy roads.

If you have a dog of such high quality that you decide to place him at public stud it is your duty as owner to have him tested for all hereditary faults that are known to exist in the breed. He must have his hips X-rayed under the BVA/KC scheme and his eyes tested for PRA, cataract and glaucoma. He should also have his heart checked; it is a good idea to ask your vet to do this while your dog is being X-rayed. It is also your responsibility to make sure he is in good condition and virile, and that he is physically and mentally sound. A full veterinary health check is advisable.

It is usually taken for granted a dog at public stud is a proven sire. No stud fee must ever be taken until a stud dog has sired puppies. The best procedure is to agree on a stud fee (half to two-thirds of a full stud fee) to be paid when there are live puppies in the nest. The stud dog owner does not sign the green Kennel Club Registration Form until the stud fee arrives, but it is wise that all these agreements are in writing and signed by both parties.

As has already been stated, it is advisable that the first mating for your maiden dog is to a proven producer because:

* if a maiden dog and bitch are put together one will never really know why if no puppies arrive.

* a good-tempered matron will help your young dog; it is very easy to dent a young dog's confidence if he is frightened or hurt.

It is advisable that your young dog serves at least one bitch between his first and second year, but that he is restricted to a few bitches until well matured. Think twice if asked to mate your dog to poor quality bitches; your dog's reputation as a stud will stand or fall on his first crop of youngsters. You must always remember the responsibility that you as a stud dog owner have to the breed; your stud dog could have a greater influence on the breed than most bitches. All breeding should be for the improvement of the breed.

Take great care when signing the green form; never sign it before you have been paid the stud fee, make sure that the details of the bitch that has been mated to your dog are correct and that the bitch's owner has signed his or her side in your presence. You will have no redress afterwards if you do not receive your stud fee; this is your responsibility.

A stud fee is for the mating of Dog A to Bitch B. It is best to keep a stud book, fill it out with the bitch's owner, and then sign the counterfoil and give it as your receipt for the mating. Most stud dog owners give a free return to the stud dog if there are no puppies.

It is important to look after your stud dog. He must be well-housed, well-nourished, well-exercised, and neither too thin nor too fat. He should also be kept, like all your Flatcoats, as part of your family, and his function as stud dog should only be a very small part of his life style: a low key affair. If you have more than one stud dog it is important that, once the used stud dog is back to normal and they are back together, no misbehaviour is tolerated. You must show your dominance as pack leader, so that your 'boys' are more concerned about your displeasure than their rivalry. Personally I find that it is best to have two to three years' age difference in a family pack, be they males or females.

The Mating

When you take or send the bitch to the stud dog it is as well to ensure that her vaccinations are current. This will in turn help to ensure that the resulting puppies receive protection from their dam before their own immune systems are fully functional, and will also protect her from infection. Once a bitch is pregnant no live vaccine must be administered to her because this may harm the puppies.

The presence of a bitch in heat will encourage the dog to perform, and most stud dogs are very well aware why a strange bitch has arrived on the scene. At this stage, her body secretions contain sex pheromones. These are chemical messengers whose scent is often wafted some distance in the air, attracting males to her. At close quarters her scent is a particularly potent stimulant for mating purposes.

The bitch will indicate her readiness to mate by standing with her tail to one side, but it is usual for her to be held by the collar so that she cannot turn round and snap at her intended partner. The male then climbs on to her back, using his front feet to hold on to her in front of the hips, and penetration occurs. His penis will have become engorged by an increase in blood flow, resulting in the tip becoming swollen. Within the penis itself, there is a bone called the *os penis*, which provides additional support during the mating process.

Once penetration occurs, the muscles at the entrance of the female's vagina then tighten around the penis. This results in what is known as the 'tie', and the pair are effectively locked together. The thrusting movements of the male soon result in ejaculation of the sperm, but the two do not usually separate immediately. Instead, the dog drops down off the bitch's back, and swivels round, by lifting a hind leg over her back so that their heads face in opposite directions.

They will remain in this position for 20 minutes on average, although this time interval can be either longer, up to 75 minutes, or significantly shorter. In fact a tie does not have to be formed for the mating to be fertile because the actual ejaculation of the spermatozoa occurs early in the mating process. Seminal fluid is then transferred during the remainder of the union, and this serves to facilitate the passage of the sperm through the bitch's reproductive tract into the uterus where the ova are fertilised.

The ova are released from the ovaries and, assuming fertilisation occurs, the number will determine the maximum size of the litter. Most bitches will give birth to between five and nine puppies, although much larger litters consisting of a dozen or more offspring are not unknown, and sometimes there may be only one or two pups. It is common practice to repeat the mating a day or two later in case ovulation has not occurred on the first occasion, but this is not always necessary. Experienced dog breeders can usually determine whether a second mating is advisable.

It can be difficult in the case of some bitches to determine when they started pro-oestrus. Aside from direct observation it is also possible to assess this by means of cytological study. A swab placed in the vagina will yield cells, and these can then be viewed under a microscope by your vet to assess the bitch's state of readiness to mate. This procedure is generally not necessary unless a bitch has failed to conceive at previous matings and a litter from her is particularly desired.

When your bitch has been mated to the chosen stud and is back in your own home again she will still be sexually attractive. You must be careful to keep her away from male dogs until her period of oestrus is completely finished, as she could mate successfully with more than one partner. This is clearly undesirable as part of a planned breeding programme.

Should you have the misfortune to discover her mating with a dog of her own choosing, do not try to separate them. It is unlikely to be of any benefit because ejaculation of the sperm will probably already have occurred. The traditional remedy of throwing a bucket of water over them is likely to be equally ineffective. Bitches can give birth to puppies of two different male dogs in one litter. While in the past it may have been impossible to distinguish between such pups, this is now possible with DNA studies. This is a costly procedure, but by matching and comparing the genetic profiles of the dogs concerned an effective paternity test can be carried out.

The length of a bitch's season may vary with the individual, but a span of three weeks altogether is a reasonable estimate. If she has been mated, hopefully she will have conceived a litter. If not, she will revert to a period of anoestrus, her vulva will return to its more usual appearance and her behavioural changes cease.

Generally it is more satisfactory to pay the required stud fee outright. Remember, you are paying for the service, not the result. However, occasionally the stud dog owner may accept a puppy in lieu of a stud fee, or perhaps you may have purchased your bitch on a breeding terms agreement which will have to be honoured. Some such agreements work amicably but just as it is more satisfactory to buy your original puppy outright so it is better to pay the required stud fee at the time of the mating. You then have full control over your own litter, can keep your best puppy, or puppies, and may sell the rest on whatever terms you choose. You should let the owner of the stud dog know when the litter arrives as he or she may wish to see the puppies. If so, his or her experience may guide you in the choice of the best puppies.

Pregnancy

At first it may be difficult to tell if the mating has been successful, simply because there will be few external signs. Inside the uterus, the fertilised eggs will start to divide, but they are unlikely to implant into the wall until almost three weeks after mating. Subsequently, differentiation continues, and a placental connection to the dam is established at this point.

The major growth phase of the puppies takes place during the final part of the pregnancy. This will become manifest by a swelling of the bitch's abdomen about five weeks after mating. It is likely to be most pronounced in the case of bitches who have not bred before or those carrying large litters. The teats will also start to swell up at this stage, becoming softer as the pregnancy proceeds.

Unfortunately, there is a condition, described as pseudo, or false, pregnancy, which mimics the effects of true pregnancy, even to the production of milk. It is possible for pregnancy to be confirmed by your vet about a month after mating when a careful examination will reveal the presence of foetuses before the fluid in their surrounding amniotic sacs makes them indistinguishable from abdominal organs. However, most owners have a very good idea whether or not their bitch is in whelp and, provided the bitch is not distressed in any way, allow nature to take its course with no interference.

Even your vet would not be able to give you a definite guide to the number of puppies present; this could only be confirmed at a later stage, when the bitch is about seven weeks pregnant and the puppies' skeletons contain sufficient calcium to show up on an X-ray. This would not normally be undertaken because of the risk of harming the puppies by exposing them to radiation. Never mind: guessing the possible number of puppies is quite exciting!

It is not possible to use blood or urine tests to reveal a pregnancy in the case of the bitch because the hormonal changes associated with this condition are indistinguishable from those which result in false pregnancy. After an ovum has been released from the ovary a structure called a *corpus luteum* forms. It produces the hormone progesterone, which prepares the uterus to receive the ovum. Under normal circumstances, if none of the ova were fertilised, the corpora lutea soon cease functioning and no obvious signs of pregnancy develop. In a few cases however, for reasons that are unclear, the *corpora lutea* persist in the absence of a pregnancy. The resulting physical changes mimic those of pregnancy with the uterus enlarging and external changes such as swollen nipples and even the production of milk becomes apparent. A bitch suffering from a false pregnancy will undergo behavioural changes as well. She is likely to adopt a favoured toy, perceiving it to be a puppy, and will become very protective towards it. If you have children, it is important to impress upon them the need not to attempt to take this toy away from her as even the most docile bitch may actively resent such interference at this stage.

False pregnancies can arise whether or not the bitch was mated, and they can recur after each period of heat. Breeding is not the answer because the signs may become even more pronounced at subsequent heats after a real pregnancy. The phase will pass, although you may need to obtain hormonal treatment from your vet for the bitch, or tranquillisers if she appears very upset. In the long term the only real solution to this problem will be to have her spayed.

Whelping

Pregnancy in the bitch typically lasts between 58 and 63 days, but puppies may be a few days early or late. In the early days of pregnancy there is no need to vary the bitch's routine; encourage her to take exercise as usual in order to maintain her muscle tone. Consult your veterinary surgeon with regard to worming your bitch during pregnancy to prevent the infection of her puppies. Worming is usually carried out about a month after mating.

Only in the latter third of pregnancy, when the foetuses will be growing in size, will you need to increase the bitch's food intake markedly. Up to this point, you can increase the amount of food slightly, but in the latter stages, it should be raised by up to 50 per cent, depending on her appetite. Be sure to use high protein items if you are relying on fresh foods and maintain the overall balance of the diet. Discuss diet supplements with your vet so that you do not inadvertently provide a potentially harmful excess of any mineral or vitamin. If you are using a commercially prepared complete dry food which needs no extra supplements, follow the given directions for feeding a bitch in whelp, and in any case make sure that fresh drinking water is always available.

It is important to make early preparations for the birth to settle the bitch in advance. You will need a deep-sided whelping box which is large enough for her to lay out comfortably on her side. My own preference is for a 120cm x 120cm x 120cm (4ft x 4ft x 4ft) box. With large breeds it is usual to place poles around the sides so that there is no risk of the bitch accidentally laying on top of her newborn puppies and crushing them. The front of the box must be lower than the sides to enable the bitch to move in and out easily while keeping the puppies securely confined in this area.

The floor of the whelping box should be covered with several layers of newspaper which can be changed easily when it becomes soiled. Place your bitch's blanket here, and encourage her to sleep in the whelping box during the latter stages of her pregnancy. Then hopefully when the time to give birth is imminent she will return to this bed. Professionally made whelping boxes with hygienic, easily washable surfaces can be purchased at dog shows, or by way of advertisements in the weekly canine press, or you can construct your own.

In the latter stages, you are likely to find that the bitch becomes restless. Keep an eye on her outdoors to ensure that she does not suffer from constipation. If she does you will need to provide her with a laxative such as medicinal liquid paraffin (not heating oil!) or corn oil added to her food.

It is important to place the whelping box in a quiet location in the house where the bitch can feel secure; otherwise she is likely to seek out another spot, and if this happens there is little that you can do. One of the signs that the birth is imminent will be when she starts to make a nest, ripping up the paper for this purpose. Her hip bones may become more prominent along the back in the last day or so as her ligaments here relax prior to the birth.

It is quite normal for droplets of milk to appear at the teats before birth occurs. Similarly, the bitch is likely to lose her appetite at this stage. A discharge from the vulva will often be seen immediately prior to the birth, and the vulva itself may appear more distended at this stage.

In the vast majority of cases, there is no need to interfere in the birth process. You should keep a discreet watch on events, however, and notify your veterinary surgeon when you are sure that the process has started in case you need professional help later on. Flatcoat bitches in the main want their owners with them; I have never left a bitch to whelp by herself. Internal contractions will cause the bitch some discomfort, and she may pant and shiver. These may last for perhaps 12 hours, but it may start more or less immediately before the puppies are born. Once true contractions of the abdominal wall are seen the first puppy should be born within the hour. If this does not happen, and the bitch is straining without result, call your veterinary surgeon without delay.

Each puppy will be wrapped in its 'water-bag', the amniotic sac which enveloped it in the bitch's uterus. This may break just before the birth; otherwise the mother will tear it apart to free the new-born puppy. She will lick the puppy vigorously, stimulating it to start breathing. If your bitch has not given birth before she may appreciate your reassurance. Do not worry if she cries out as the puppy is born as this is unlikely to cause her physical injury, but if she then ignores the pup you will need to break open the amniotic covering in the vicinity of its mouth or there is a risk that it will drown in the fluid when it starts breathing.

Dry off any mucus around its nose and mouth with a piece of clean paper towelling, and gently put your finger in its mouth, to encourage it to breathe. If you have a puppy that appears dead, do not give up hope. Hold it gently upside down, so that fluid will drain out of its lungs and swing it back and forth. Then place it on its side, and rub it vigorously with a towel on the side of its body. Once the puppy has revived, place it back with its mother, where it can snuggle down with its litter-mates. If the puppy turns blue, blowing up its nose may encourage it to start breathing; if all else fails, placing it in a bowl of cold and then of warm water may have the required effect. You will then need to dry the young puppy in a towel, so have ready plenty of soft old towelling, or rolls of absorbent soft paper towels, just in case.

In the excitement of the puppy's arrival you may overlook the placenta which provided the vital connection between mother and offspring. It is important that all the placentae are passed out of her body, because any which remain attached in the uterus are likely to give rise to an infection later. The placenta of each puppy usually emerges within five minutes or so of the puppy being born. It will resemble a piece of liver and may be accompanied by green fluid which should give no cause for concern. Do make sure that each pup's placenta is accounted for.

It is not uncommon for the bitch to consume the placenta, or afterbirth as it is often called. This is quite normal behaviour, and not indicative of impending cannibalism of the litter. The placenta will be attached to the umbilical cord. If this is not torn by the bitch, you will need to free the puppy from this encumbrance. It is vital not to break this too close to the body because in doing so you could cause an umbilical hernia which may well require surgical correction when the puppy is older. Instead, sever it at least 2.5cm (an inch) from the body, preferably using your fingers rather than cutting it. This sends the tissue into spasm, sealing off the blood vessels more effectively, and so restricting blood loss to a minimum. However, have sterilised scissors handy if you prefer that method. Take particular care not to pull on the cord as this is likely to injure the puppy.

Most puppies are born head first, but you may well encounter breech presentations, when their rear ends emerge first, to be followed by their hind legs. The bitch will often manage to pass the puppy in this position, but if it is clear that it is stuck at this point you will need to act within five minutes to free it.

Provided that the legs are outside the bitch's body you should wrap the puppy's body in a clean towel and attempt to release it by pulling in a downward direction, without compressing its body. If you work with the bitch's contractions it will hopefully be possible to overcome the blockage, and then you may need to carry out the steps recommended previously to start the puppy breathing properly.

If you suspect that your bitch is having a problem contact your vet without delay. This applies particularly if no puppies appear after one hour of obvious straining. A number of problems can occur internally which may require a caesarean section.

Puppies are normally born in fairly rapid succession. Once the litter is complete the bitch will appear more restful, sitting or lying down in close proximity to her litter, and the puppies will receive further cleaning as they start to suckle. I like to get each puppy sucking as soon as it is born; you are then aware that the puppy has sucked and will suck. I also feel that the act of suckling often stimulates the bitch to produce another puppy. Early suckling is vital for their subsequent welfare: protective anti-bodies which help to guard them from infection until their own immune systems are fully functional are contained in this 'first milk' or colostrum. This is produced for the first 48 hours or so.

If all is going well, I find my bitches appreciate a drink of milk with Glucose added through-out the whelping, and I continue this (as much as the bitch wants) for the next five days. I am always concerned to ensure that the bitch is passing plenty of urine. I continue to give her plenty of milk or milk and water until she stops feeding her puppies. I find that at this time Flatcoat bitches are able to tolerate milk, although at other times this is not so.

Contented babies a day or so old.

Photo - Y Jaussi.

New-born puppies are totally helpless, and quite incapable even of regulating their body temperature, which will fall dramatically at birth. Their surroundings should therefore be kept warm, above usual room temperature, at a minimum of 21 degrees C (70 degrees F), or probably a degree or two higher at first, but check that the bitch is not too warm. Most breeders use an overhead dull emitter infra-red heat lamp and reflector suspended over the whelping box to provide gentle extra warmth for mother and babies. Infra-red lamps are advertised in the canine press, or may be obtained from an agricultural supplier under the name of a 'pig lamp'. Other young creatures need warmth too!

Make arrangements for proper warmth for your litter well before they are due to be born. Chilled puppies do not thrive; check the temperature in the whelping box with a thermometer. While the pups need warmth, the bitch will not want to be too hot. Adjusting the height of the lamp should sort things out as far as temperature is concerned. I buy new 'green-back' veterinary bedding for each litter; this is non-allergic bedding which allows free drainage, so that your puppies stay warm and dry.

The posture adopted by the puppies will give a clear insight into their degree of warmth. They huddle together to conserve body heat, and then tend to separate once they are warm. Immediately after birth, they will stay together in close proximity to their mother. Any which are pushed to the side, and appear neglected, are likely to be weak so guide them back to their mother and the milk bar and see that they start sucking. Bigger pups sometimes push the smaller ones away from the source of food and the weaker ones will cry piteously. Similarly the larger, healthy pups are quiet as they have full tummies. Pups may cry persistently if they are either cold or hungry. It is wise to make sure the small puppies are put on to the milk bar first each time. It is also a wise precaution to have a low light on in the room where the bitch and puppies are, and I find I am happier sleeping close to them.

Most bitches prove excellent mothers, but there can be occasions when problems arise in the immediate period after giving birth. A retained placenta is a common reason underlying metritis, or infection of the uterus. The bitch will be generally off-colour with a temperature, and is unlikely to show much interest either in her puppies or food. Rapid veterinary attention and antibiotic treatment is required under these circumstances. I think it is a wise precaution to ask your vet to pay a home visit to mother and puppies the day after they are born. This gives you peace of mind.

A local infection of the nipples underlies the condition known as mastitis. The bitch will resent the puppies suckling on the affected teats, which swell up, and are clearly more sensitive than usual. This may occur later in the suckling phase, as the puppies' teeth start to emerge when they are about three weeks old. Alternatively, they may be scratching her with their claws. Puppies' claws can be quite long and sharp, so you should cut just the tips off the claws with your sterilised scissors or a guillotine nail cutter; this should be done regularly during the time you have the puppies. Keep a close watch for signs of mastitis as, provided it is detected early, it generally responds quite rapidly to appropriate antibiotic treatment. It is a wise precaution to just run your hands over the bitch's udder each night and morning.

The puppies will suckle frequently, at least once every two hours, during the first week of life, establishing no order of dominance, though they tend to prefer the rear teats. Avoid disturbing the bitch during these early days more than necessary, and do not allow any visitors. Your own family members should also be encouraged not to disturb her unnecessarily. You will need to increase the amount of food which you offer her as the litter grows older; more frequent meals as well as increased quantities will be the answer.

By the second week she should be having twice her normal ration, and three times more than usual over the next fortnight. This can then be reduced back down to a double quantity in the fifth week, by which stage the puppies will be starting to feed themselves. Provide her with as many as four meals spaced at roughly even intervals through the day.

Careful management should help to prevent the disturbing condition known as 'milk fever' or eclampsia which can strike some bitches, particularly those with large litters. An affected individual may at first seem very distressed and may then ignore her litter, start staggering and appear unsteady on her feet before ultimately collapsing. This is a metabolic illness resulting from a severe drain on the bitch's calcium stores as she feeds her litter. This does not mean you should give calcium above the recommended amount to your bitch; this will do as much damage as too little. Rapid veterinary attention is required, but recovery can then be equally spectacular, although you may need to make alternative arrangements for feeding at least some of the puppies. If necessary your vet may be able to give you some help in finding a suitable foster mother, such as a bitch suffering from a false pregnancy. If you are adding to an existing litter, be sure to disguise the newcomers as far as possible by rubbing the scent of the existing puppies over them. This will greatly enhance the chances of the bitch accepting them as her own.

Fostering is generally a more effective, and certainly easier, method of dealing with orphaned puppies compared with attempting to rear them yourself. If the latter is necessary they will need to be fed almost around the clock at first, depending on their age. You should use one of the specialist milk substitute diets rather than ordinary cows' milk, because of significant differences in the nutritional values between them.

The milk produced by a bitch is more concentrated in terms of its levels of fat and protein, as well as with regard to its calcium and phosphorus content, than cows' milk. If you have to use a commercial brand of puppy milk follow the instructions for making up the milk substitute implicitly, cleanliness being essential at all stages of the feeding process.

You can purchase special feeders for puppies which will make the task easier, and so lessen the risk of choking. It is a very wise plan to purchase a special puppy feeder just in case. If you have to resort to artificial feeding always allow yourself adequate time so that you do not have to rush the feed. The puppy must be allowed to consume the milk at its own pace; if too much is forced upon it there is a real possibility that it will choke, or fluid entering the lungs could develop into inhalation pneumonia.

You will need to wipe the puppy's mouth gently to remove any traces of milk, and then rub its body in a similar fashion with damp cotton wool, mimicking the way in which the bitch cleans her puppies. This will encourage pups to relieve themselves. In order to keep the puppies warm between feeds you can buy special incubator-type units suitable for them in which the temperature can be precisely controlled and varied. Alternatively the infra-red lamp can be used, leaving an area to which the puppy can move if it becomes too hot.

Wash the feeding equipment thoroughly with detergent after each feed to remove all trace of grease, and then sterilise it in a solution intended for babies' bottles. You will then need to rinse it off before the next feed. It can be helpful to add a probiotic to the food of a young, orphaned puppy; it will not be receiving the benefit of protective bacteria from its dam, as would normally be the case, and this could leave it more exposed to infection. A probiotic will help to correct this deficiency.

I find that, right from the start, the bitch needs to be taken out regularly to relieve herself. This period of separation can be lengthened as the days go by. It is not long before my bitches start to go for walks with the other dogs, and I find this has a beneficial effect on them, the exercise taking the cramp out of their muscles and helping their wombs to contract. They then come back to their puppies mentally refreshed. This is possible for mine as they are country dogs, but I realise that if one lives in a town it is not so easy. Even a short car trip to a safe field will be beneficial if your bitch is happy to do it. Having other dogs, I have found that having to leave a bitch at home causes far more problems than taking her. I always make sure the puppies have had a feed just before I take the bitch, and it is a wise precaution to wash and dry her udder before she returns to the puppies.

Weaning

By the age of three weeks puppies are more mobile and they are likely to begin to express interest in solid food. The weaning phase, which is completed when the puppies are feeding entirely on their own rather than suckling, lasts until they are about two months old under normal circumstances.

Do not worry if the bitch vomits her food near the pups at this stage, as this is how wolves and other wild dogs wean their offspring. A more acceptable method is to offer a special puppy food made up into a fairly thick liquid consistency. At first the puppies may only sniff at this or wade in it, but soon they will start to eat it. Try to introduce them to solid food when they are on their own, because otherwise the bitch is likely to eat their food. Using one of the complete commercial puppy foods is a great help at this stage as it will contain all the necessary nutrients. Serve it as directed on the package.

As the puppies grow older their dam's milk will decline naturally, and she is likely to dissuade them from suckling as much as possible by standing up and walking away. Then you will need to increase the amount of food given to the puppies in accordance with the recommended feeding instructions. At this stage the puppies become really interesting, playing and running around on their own, and you can see individual characteristics developing as well as differences in type. This is often when you pick your favourite, though it has been known for experienced breeders to spot a future champion at the time of birth.

This is also the time when it can be difficult to keep a check on them in the home. It is therefore a good idea to have a collapsible pen, just as human babies have play pens, which you can use to restrain them, particularly when people are going back and forth through your home. This is essential for their safety and your peace of mind. Try to spend as much time as possible with each of the puppies individually. At about one month old they start to absorb much about the world around them and this becomes a vital learning period in their lives.

Health matters must also be attended to. Worming medicine is a necessity, so buy some from your veterinary surgeon. You may need to trim the puppies' nails again as the points can become rather sharp. This is best accomplished with special guillotine-type nail clippers. You must ensure that you do not cut the nail too short because if you cut the quick it will bleed. If you are in doubt, seek advice from your vet beforehand. You will need to locate the blood supply, which appears as a pinkish-red streak running down each claw. Cut a short distance away from where this disappears to avoid causing bleeding. It is best to examine the claws in a good light when attempting to clip them, although it can be difficult to spot the blood supply if the claws are dark in colour. The dew claws are not removed in Flatcoats.

At this stage you must be careful that your puppies do not pick up any little friends. Before you spray your puppies, do seek the advice of your vet: some flea sprays can have a detrimental effect on young puppies.

Transferring Ownership

You will have received your Application for Registration Certificate from the stud dog owner after you have paid your stud fee. The stud owner must sign this, adding the stud dog's name and Kennel Club Registration Number or Stud Book Number. You fill in the rest of the form, sending it with the correct fee to register the puppies with The Kennel Club. If this is your first litter and you are going to continue breeding, you may decide that you would like your own registered affix. This should have been done several months before the puppies are born as it is a process that takes time. You write to The Kennel Club asking for a Registration of Affix Form. At this time it will cost you £45.00 to register your affix plus a yearly maintenance fee of £15.00. Your affix will be your own individual kennel name: it cannot be used by anyone else as long as you are paying for it. Your application will be published in the monthly *Kennel Gazette*, which can be purchased from The Kennel Club on a yearly subscription and is well worth reading. When you have been granted your affix, this may be added for a fee to the end

of your bitch's name. For example, Kennel Jane would become Kennel Jane of Hourglass. However the puppies you have bred as registered owner of the bitch would now all have 'Hourglass' at the beginning of their official names (for example, Hourglass Harry).

You will wish to keep control of your litter. In your Application for Registration you will find after the Alternative Name section the Endorsements. It is a wise precaution at this stage to mark all your puppies:

    (a)   Progeny not eligible for Registration
    (b)   Not eligible for the issue of an Export Pedigree.

This gives you more control over your puppies: puppy farms and unscrupulous dealers might be all too happy to acquire them. I am sure you want to do the best for these little people that you have loved and nurtured, so you must tell every potential puppy buyer that your puppies are endorsed with these clauses, telling them that when they come back to you in two or more years with a good hip score and a clear eye certificate you, as breeder, will write to The Kennel Club and ask for the endorsements to be removed. Only the breeder has this authority. You will have the support of The Flatcoated Retriever Society on this matter. If for any reason your puppies' registrations have not arrived before they leave you, do give the buyers a written statement, signed by both parties, that the registrations are endorsed.

You may also want to take advantage of puppy insurance. I consider it a wise precaution to sell the puppy with at least one month's insurance, as a personal safeguard.

I do not advise advertising your puppies in the local paper. The Flatcoated Retriever Society has a Puppy Register available to members and non-members (see Chapter 5). You must always remember that it is your personal responsibility to question all potential puppy buyers. It is better to contact this register at a relatively early stage, soon after they are born, before they are weaned and ready to go to new homes, as you will then have a longer period to attract potential purchasers.

When a puppy is going to a new home, be sure to provide information about its food, in terms of a detailed diet sheet, which should help to minimise the risk of any digestive upset. I have given an example of this at the end of this chapter. You should also provide the new owner with a copy of the puppy's pedigree and the necessary documents, so the new owners can notify The Kennel Club and have ownership of the puppy transferred into their names. I have enclosed a basic useful information and diet sheet. There is also a very useful information booklet on the Flatcoat available from the Litter Recorder or The Flatcoated Retriever Society Secretary (see **Useful Addresses**) for a small price.

The bitch will usually not miss her puppies for any length of time, although at first she may appear rather distressed. In any event, you should not be in a hurry to send them off to their new homes. Keep them until they are at least two months old, even if they are fully weaned before then, and remember that it may take much longer than expected to find suitable homes for them. A puppy pen with a kennel will be necessary before they can be put into the garden with safety. Puppies over five weeks of age will need plenty of fresh air and a warm bed sheltered from the elements. All this is common sense, as you want good healthy puppies going at eight weeks to their happy owners.

Artificial Insemination

This procedure can be carried out quite successfully in the case of dogs, but is not widespread at the present time. In fact, it is not generally encouraged for dogs in Great Britain. Information on the subject is updated regularly and should be obtained from The Kennel Club. As it stands at present, you would need a valid reason and written permission from The Kennel Club before carrying out artificial insemination (AI) on your bitch.

Outside Great Britain, there is an increasing interest in AI. Semen from Flatcoat dogs is preserved by various procedures such as 'chilling' and 'freezing' and then sent to other parts of the world, successfully producing puppies. AI is an expensive process, however, and it is vital to adhere to all the regulations of the country of importation. New Zealand, for example, has used AI with success, but the collection point for the sperm in Great Britain is nominated and specific blood test results and health certificates must be produced for the stud dog. This applies in other countries, too.

Find out about charges and procedures. Remember: it takes time and organisation. Consider: do you know and trust the owner of the brood bitch? Will he or she care responsibly for the puppies? You too must be responsible and honest if there is any possibility of problems being passed on by your stud dog.

The Reproductive Life of the Bitch

After your bitch has reared her litter she should be allowed to rest. At this stage she may have lost some body condition, but this will soon be made good provided that she receives a nutritious diet. She should now be having the quantity offered before becoming pregnant.

If you wish to have a further litter from her, it is better to wait for 18 months to two years, though if her first litter was small in number this is not an absolute necessity. It is important to see how the first litter develops before taking a second. However, be sure to keep her away from male dogs when she is next on heat to prevent an accidental mating if you do not want a second litter too soon. It is possible to give the bitch hormonal treatment to prevent her coming into season, but this may have undesirable side-effects, and so is best avoided if possible.

A bitch will continue to have periods of heat throughout her life (there is no menopause) so, once she has produced the requisite number of litters, it is much better to have her neutered. This not only avoids the complications associated with a period of heat, but also means that she will not fall victim to pyometra later in life. It should be remembered that The Kennel Club will not register a litter if the bitch has passed her eighth birthday.

The hormonal changes accompanying the ovulation result in an increased level of progesterone in the bitch's circulation. This acts on the lining of the uterus, as mentioned previously, stimulating its growth to receive the fertilised eggs. In turn, the uterine secretions provide a fertile breeding ground for bacteria, which may gain access here from the vagina.

A bitch suffering from pyometra will go off her food, and start to drink more, as her uterus fills with fluid. She will then start to vomit, and ultimately is likely to collapse. In the case of an 'open' pyometra, you are likely to see a discharge from the vulva which may contain traces of blood, pus or both. The more serious form is the closed-cervix pyometra where there is no discharge and the fluid builds up in the uterus, which may even rupture, with dire consequences.

A pyometra is likely to occur between one and two months after a period of heat. If you suspect this condition, seek veterinary advice without delay as urgent treatment will be required. The most appropriate method of dealing with this situation is by spaying, removing the ovaries and uterus together, although this also ends the bitch's reproductive life.

In the case of a particularly valuable individual, depending upon her condition, medical treatment may be attempted first. There is still an approximately one in ten risk, however, that the infection may have resulted in the bitch becoming infertile. The risk of a recurring pyometra after the next and subsequent periods of heat is high in any event, and so a bitch should be mated on the next occasion without fail, and then spayed after she has had her puppies.

A particular problem facing the keen exhibitor and breeder is being able to manage their kennel and at the same time not to be overrun with dogs. There is likely to be a time when you wish to keep a young promising bitch, for example, rather more than an older dog which has served you well. This can pose a very difficult dilemma. You may be fortunate, however, in discovering someone, perhaps an older person who does not wish to go through the rigours of integrating a puppy into their household, who would welcome the company of a dog in their life. This may well be the answer, and you may be able to keep in touch with your dog by this means, especially if you can find a new owner locally. In my opinion it is better to rehome a youngster who perhaps is not quite up to standard, or a middle aged bitch who has had breeding problems and been spayed, than an older dog who has given you the best years of its life. There is something special with the elder statesman that is missing in the youngsters.

It is important not to 'over-dog' yourself: you and your dogs will all lose out if you do. Try to keep a good age difference in your dogs. If you have too many dogs of the same age they will all get old at the same time. There is nothing more soul-destroying then having several older dogs come to the end of their lives together. That last visit to the vet can be so heart-breaking!

These two-week-old puppies are just starting to show an interest in solid food.

A group of happy seven-week-old puppies.

SAMPLE DIET SHEET
EXCLYST FLATCOATED RETRIEVERS

DIET AND INFORMATION SHEET: for an eight-week-old **Flatcoated Retriever Puppy**

This puppy has been having: [Name of Puppy Food]

BREAKFAST: ..... oz of [name of puppy food] soaked in warm water for a good period of time, then served with some warm water. (Most complete puppy foods contain milk. I do not give any milk at all at this age.)

DINNER : the same as breakfast.

TEA TIME: the same as breakfast.

SUPPER TIME: the same as breakfast.

Puppy diet is especially formulated for growing puppies; no other food is needed.

No mineral or vitamin supplement is needed while your puppy is on one of these special puppy foods.

Your puppy weighed...... today, so is having [so many oz] of Puppy Food per day divided into four meals. This is 0.05oz per pound body weight per day. I weigh my puppies every **week** and feed according to weight, increasing the amount of food as the puppies gain weight.

Please **do not** change your puppy's diet until it has finished its course of **vaccinations** at approximately 14 weeks of age. I would prefer you to continue it throughout Puppyhood to at least five or six months of age. If your puppy goes off its food when you get it home, do not push food but give it plenty of fluids, taking several days to get back to the full diet. Always have fresh water available for the puppy, it will drink quite a lot of water, especially if it is on a complete diet.

Your puppy was wormed at three weeks and seven weeks, so should be wormed again at ten weeks. It was wormed with Panacure [or named wormer]. I suggest you buy the wormer from your vet.

Important: Your Puppy was vaccinated at six weeks of age; the next vaccination is due at 12 weeks of age. **It is not safe to take your puppy out from your home except to the vet until after 14 weeks.**

At 12 weeks of age cut the number of feeds **(not the overall amount)** down to three, then at five months of age to two meals per day.

Do not over-exercise your puppy. No long walks until after the age of six to seven months. **No exhausting games with the children** either.

If you consider breeding do not breed a litter from your bitch before she is three years old. Dogs and bitches must always have their **hips X-rayed** and their **eyes tested** before you consider breeding from them, as their father and mother did.

If you want any help **please telephone me.**

If there is any reason you **cannot keep your Flatcoat** at any time (things do go wrong through no-one's fault) **please contact me first and I will help.**

Useful Address: **Flatcoated Retriever Society**
Secretary: Mrs J Maude, The Homestead, The Causeway, Mark, Highbridge, Somerset (Tel: 01278-641343)

Breeder: **Mrs Brenda Phillips** 'Exclyst' 12605

Chapter 10

Health Care and Old Age

CHOOSING A VETERINARY SURGEON

There are various ways of choosing a veterinary surgeon and perhaps the best is by recommendation. However, even if you simply select a practice from a telephone directory, you can be certain that all vets undergo the same rigorous training and will be able to help you. It is better to pick a small animal practice rather than one which concentrates mainly on farm animals, as the former is likely to be better equipped for your purposes.

You could telephone several practices in your neighbourhood and choose the one which sounds most friendly. If you intend to breed and show your dogs regularly you are likely to require more in the way of veterinary services than is a pet owner so it is obviously best to pick a practice which makes you feel welcome and suits your needs.

Should you be interested in homeopathy as a means of veterinary treatment, then you should enquire whether the practice concerned uses complementary (or 'alternative') as well as allo-pathic veterinary medicine. You can also find out from the homeopathic associations which vets are sympathetic to such treatments. This topic is dealt with in more detail in Chapter 11: Environmental Awareness and Natural Remedies.

It is a good idea to decide which veterinary practice you wish to patronise before you collect your new puppy and to introduce yourself to them. This does not commit you if you change your mind.

If you are starting out with a young puppy you should arrange a check-up as soon as possible as well as an appointment for the first or second set of inoculations. These are usually given when the puppy is about 12 weeks old, but if you are worried about the dog's health before that be sure to contact a vet without delay. The stress associated with a change in a puppy's environment, and probably an alteration in its diet, sometimes triggers illness. Diarrhoea is frequently associated with puppies when they move to new surroundings. This is particularly dangerous in young dogs as they can become dehydrated rapidly, so seek veterinary advice promptly.

HEALTH INSURANCE FOR YOUR DOG

This type of insurance policy generally will not cover routine costs for things like immunisations or neutering, but can provide considerable reassurance against unexpected veterinary costs. If, for example, your dog has the misfortune to be involved in an accident, skilled orthopaedic work can result in a very substantial bill.

As with all insurance policies you should read the small print carefully. A range of policies are currently marketed, and there can be some significant differences between them. All should offer sub-stantial cover against veterinary costs and third party liability. Some will allow you to pay the premium in monthly instalments, which can be particularly helpful if you own a number of dogs, and offer a discount when insuring more than one animal.

It is possible to have routine cover for advertising (up to a prescribed sum) should your dog stray. You should be able to find a selection of such policies either at your veterinary surgery, or track down companies in this field by studying the specialist canine press.

IMMUNISATION AGAINST SPECIFIC DISEASES

Assuming everything proceeds normally your puppy can be taken to the surgery in due course for his immunisations. You should have received a certificate showing the date and type of any vaccines given to the puppy before it came to you. Take this along to your vet. Your puppy will be given a general health check before the immunisations are given, and this may reveal possible problems such as an umbilical hernia or heart murmurs.

If you are worried by the sight of needles do not hesitate to ask to wait outside. This will be infinitely preferable for all concerned to your passing out in the surgery! The injection is typically administered under the skin at the back of the neck, and causes the puppy very little if any obvious discomfort; in fact most Flatcoats do not notice the injection because they are too busy wagging their tails! Serious after-effects are uncommon.

Immunisations have helped to revolutionise dog care by effectively eliminating all the major canine diseases such as distemper (hardpad), leptospirosis, infectious canine hepatitis and parvovirus. If your dog is not protected it can still be at risk from these potentially deadly diseases, so pay particular attention to when a booster shot will be required. This is usually given annually. An up-to-date vaccination certificate is vital if you want to board your dog at any time or if you plan to attend dog shows.

Distemper

Distemper is a viral illness, typically spread by contact with the infected urine of another dog or its saliva. The virus initially localises in the tonsils, causing the dog to be off-colour for a few days, and it may be overcome at this stage. In other cases it spreads around the body causing serious signs of illness including a high temperature, vomiting and, fairly characteristically, a runny nose and eyes. The virus is also likely to attack the nervous system and the resulting effects, such as fits, are often seen years after the original illness, assuming the dog survived the initial period of the infection. No treatment is possible at this stage and the symptoms can only be alleviated.

Infectious Canine Hepatitis

Another serious disease which can be prevented by vaccination is infectious canine hepatitis. As its name suggests, this affects the liver and is likely produce the symptoms of jaundice, yellowing of the mucous membranes inside the mouth being a conspicuous sign. This illness is sometimes also known as 'blue eye' because of the characteristic opacity which develops over the eyes in about 25 per cent of cases approximately a week after clinical signs of the illness develop, but this usually disappears gradually.

Puppies are especially vulnerable to infectious canine hepatitis and their temperature may rise in excess of 40 degrees C (104 degrees F). The blood-clotting mechanism is also affected to the extent that haemorrhages may develop within the body. Assuming the dog survives, it will only regain its lost weight slowly and it will be infectious to others for a long period. The virus is present in body secretions and is excreted in the urine for up to six months after infection. Vaccination will, however, provide good protection against this illness for which no direct treatment is available.

Leptospirosis

This also represents a serious threat to a dog's health, and vaccination is strongly recommended. This is given in a dose combined with the other vaccines. Dogs who are likely to come into contact with rats at any stage are particularly at risk from this bacterial illness. If your dog is going to be a gundog he will often have to work ditches and river banks where there could be rats, especially near to farm buildings. This disease can also be transmitted to humans.

The effects depend upon the bacterium involved. *Leptospira canicola* is 'dog-to-dog' transmission (for example, by sniffing lamp-posts in urban areas) and strikes primarily at the kidneys, causing damage which is likely to be permanent. *Leptospira icterohaemorrhagica* is 'rat-to-dog' and can affect the liver in humans, in which case it is known as Weil's disease. Infection is spread easily by contact with urine and through contaminated water.

If you are handling a dog suspected of suffering from leptospirosis it is important to wear gloves to prevent any risk of the bacteria entering through your skin. Antibiotics in this case can help to overcome the infection, but it will almost certainly cause long-term harm, possibly resulting in renal failure later in life. High doses of dihydrostreptomycin can be used to treat dogs which are excreting the bacteria and which represent a hazard to others.

Parvovirus

Parvovirus is a more recent addition to the list of diseases against which dogs should be vaccinated. It came into prominence in about April 1980 and epidemics occurred in some areas. The effects of the virus appear to depend upon the age at which the dog is infected. In young puppies, typically around five weeks old, the heart muscle is most likely to be damaged. This can lead to sudden death later in life, assuming the puppies survive the initial infection.

In the early days of parvovirus outbreaks the only vaccine available was that given to cats to protect against feline panleucopaenia. Parvovirus infection occurs in many species of animals and in humans, but each species has its own specific virus, which does not transfer to other species. We therefore used one of the cat vaccines only until a dog-specific vaccine had been produced and licensed. Today, dog-specific vaccines are widely available, and strongly recommended, as there are no effective means of treating parvovirus. It is a very resistant virus which survives well in the environment. You can walk it into the kennels on your shoes and then transfer it to food bowls. Disinfectants specifically against parvovirus are available.

Rabies

Rabies is undoubtedly the most serious viral disease associated with dogs. The relaxation of border controls across Europe means that the likelihood of this disease reaching Britain (currently free from the virus) is now increased. This is why quarantine controls are considered essential to maintain our rabies-free state. In mainland Europe, dogs have long been protected against rabies by vaccination, but this is not permitted in Britain except for dogs which are being exported and those arriving in quarantine.

The rabies virus is transmitted in saliva, and it is not necessary to be bitten in order to become infected. If you have an open cut on your hand you could be at risk. Should you have the misfortune to be exposed to a rabid animal in this way, or bitten, wash out the wound with alcohol as an emergency procedure and seek medical assistance immediately.

The length of time for clinical signs of rabies to develop depends partly where the virus was introduced into the body. If the dog was bitten close to the foot, then the virus will need to track up through the peripheral nervous system into the central nervous system; its effects will then become obvious. A bite close to the neck is likely to result in the more rapid emergence of symptoms, possibly within three weeks rather than two months later.

Kennel Cough

For show dogs in particular, or those being kennelled, it is worthwhile considering protection against kennel cough, although its effects on your pet's health are less serious than those of the diseases already described. Nevertheless, kennel cough is a troublesome complaint, most likely to be acquired where dogs are in close proximity to each other in kennels or at shows.

Though no single organism is responsible for kennel cough a vaccine has been developed which gives good protection against the most common causes of this illness. Unlike other vaccines the kennel cough product is given intra-nasally, simply being squirted up the dog's nostrils. Two doses are usually recommended, spaced about a month apart, to be followed by an annual booster. The viral components may be covered in the full annual booster, canine adenovirus and para-influenza virus.

The most characteristic sign of the illness is a dry, rasping cough, which can be elicited simply by touching the throat region. In most cases the cough abates after about five days, although it may persist for nearly three weeks. Complications can include a nasal discharge and even broncho-pneumonia, although this is only really likely to occur in either very young or old dogs, whose immune systems are not fully functional.

TESTING FOR HEREDITARY PROBLEMS
Eye Problems: PRA, Cataract and Glaucoma

Testing for PRA, cataract and glaucoma is considered a wise practice. Your Flatcoats' eyes should be checked by a specialist on the British Veterinary Association/Kennel Club/International Sheep Dog Society panel. Your vet will refer you to your nearest regional panellists.

When he is tested after 12 months of age your dog will have an official certificate stating whether or not he is free of any problem. At the same time the specialist will check the whole eye and will comment on whether any scars, cysts, distichiasis, entropion or ectropion are present. This information will be lodged with his registration certificate at The Kennel Club and from then on will appear on all transferred registration for himself, and for his puppies the sire's and dam's eye status and date of testing will be recorded. The certificates are valid for 12 months.

Your bitch must always have a current valid certificate to cover the period of whelping. It is important that all stud dogs have a yearly test throughout the period of their stud work. Photocopies of the current eye certificates and hip score certificates of both father and mother must be available to all puppy buyers.

It should be noted that at this time there are no known cases of hereditary PRA or cataract among Flatcoats in Great Britain.

Progressive Retinal Atrophy (PRA): This is an inherited, irreversible blindness in dogs resulting from retinal degeneration. The retina is at the back of the eye. Fortunately the mode of inheritance is known. PRA has been determined to be due to simple recessive genes, so although it is at this time not seen in Flatcoats, it is very important that your breeding stock is tested regularly. The records are kept by the BVA/KC, so if PRA should appear in the breed, they can be consulted and your stock cleared..

Hereditary Cataract: A cataract is the clouding of the lens of the eye, and in some cases can be hereditary. Hereditary cataract is not seen in this breed, but there have been proven cases of non-hereditary cataract.

Primary Glaucoma: This is an inherited condition. The term glaucoma does not refer to a single disease, but is applied to a large group of ocular disorders in which the common feature is an abnormal rise in the internal fluid pressure on the eye, resulting in damage to and destruction of the retina and optic nerve, and hence sight. It can present as an acute onset, painful and immediately blinding condition, or an insidious, non-painful, slowly blinding problem. Emergency treatment to reduce the fluid pressure is essential if the blindness is to be reversed, and it can be, providing that fluid pressure is brought to within normal limits within hours of the pressure rise occurring.

Flatcoated Retrievers

A suddenly painful eye which may appear milky (the cornea) and red (the conjunctiva/sclera) indicates a glaucoma attack. Veterinary attention must be found immediately; otherwise the damage to the optic nerve becomes irreversible.

A few Flatcoats have been found with this condition over the years, so it has become a wise precaution to have all breeding stock tested. This can be done at the time of your dog's first eye test by your regional panellist, if you specify that you want a 'gonioscopy' or a glaucoma examination. There is a separate fee for this, but it only needs to be done once in the dog's life.

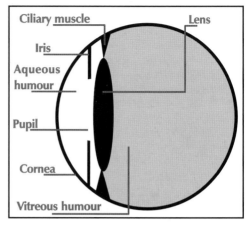

Cross section of an eye.
Vitreous humour is a jelly-like substance supporting the posterior chamber of the eye. Aqueous humour is a fluid, derived from blood, but without cells in it. It provides nutrients for the cornea.

Distichiasis and Ectopic Cilia: These terms both relate to supernumerary lashes in the eyelids, and upper and lower eyelids can be affected. In distichiasis there is a second inner row of eyelashes on the rim which should not be present. They grow out of little glands along the edge of the lid, so that the lashes lie on the cornea surface. In ectopic cilia there are single or multiple extra eyelashes growing in the conjunctiva in the inside lining of the eyelid, usually about centre but not invariably so, causing a lot of irritation and rubbing on the front part of the eye. The dog may squint or screw up the eyelid or there may be an overflow of tears or even a corneal ulcer. They are painful and always cause irritation and a lot of discomfort.

These two problems are considered to be the same condition, and the condition is hereditary. At this time the exact mode of inheritance is not known, so precise advice on breeding cannot be given. However, the degree of severity must be taken into account and veterinary advice taken.

If only a few extra lashes are present, the owner may be able to pluck them using eyebrow tweezers. If they are causing a severe problem, however, an operation to remove lashes and roots should be considered.

Entropion and ectropion: A disparity between the skin of the head and the skull shape can result in either an in-turning of the eyelids, resulting in the hair on the outer surface of the lid resting on the corneal surface (entropion) or the turning out of the lower lid with the exposure of the inner conjunctiva and recurrent conjunctivitis (ectropion, also known as 'red eye').

Severe cases may be obvious early in the dogs's life. Some may be apparent or become worse during the growing phase, improving once the dog has matured; these are generally mild cases and may need no surgical intervention. However, in severe cases, especially when a young animal is in distress, surgical correction of the deformity will be required. In some cases the dog may need a series of operations as he grows.

The condition is considered congenital and the factors relating to its development are hereditary as far as head shape, rate of growth and skin elasticity are concerned, so an affected individual should not be bred from.

Secondary ectropion may result from other causes of eye disease. When the dog screws up its eye in pain arising from the primary condition, the eyelids turn inwards. The entropion generally disappears once the primary condition is treated, and this form of entropion is not as worrying as primary congenital entropion.

Hip Dysplasia (HD)

For the following information I am indebted to Dr M B Willis' *Hip dysplasia in the Flatcoated Retriever: a report on hip scoring* (1 April 1993).

Scientific data suggest quite clearly that hip dysplasia is an inherited trait controlled by several genes. It is probable that the Flatcoat heritability will be similar to other retriever breeds at 25 to 30 per cent (Willis 1998, 1991, 1992).

Hip scoring is a system whereby hip X-rays are assessed on nine different aspects, and scored out of six for each aspect, each hip being scored separately and a high score being indicative of a deformed hip. A score of 54 for one side, or 108 for both, would therefore indicate bad problems. Dr Willis considers that most breeders could set a maximum total level of 15 for breeding purposes without much difficulty; there is certainly little excuse for using dogs who score over 20 except in exceptional circumstances, and the prospective mate should have a correspondingly low score. One must remember that any dog scoring 20 or over is showing more than twice the breed average of just under 10.

It must be remembered that a 0/0 dog is of little value to the breed if all the dog possesses is a good hip status. In contrast, a moderate-hipped dog of excellent type and character may be of value to the breed if used with care. The problem comes when breeders do not know what hip scores their dogs have because they have not had them tested. A breeder relying solely on movement without X-ray could unwittingly use a potentially high-scoring dog, which could cause serious problems for the kennel and the breed.

Each breeder must set his own upper limits within the known criteria and try to stick to them. If the breed is to progress, however, the aim must be to use the lower scoring dogs, all other things being equal. It should be remembered that the considered opinion of the Orthopaedic Specialist is: 'When you breed a dysplastic dog to a clear dog, that offspring still carries recessive, polygenic gene(s) for dysplasia, and is four times more likely to pass on dysplasia whether the entire litter is clear or not'.

According to the figures published by The Kennel Club in May 1995, the average score of the 2090 Flatcoats tested by the British Veterinary Association (BVA) was 9.18, the scores ranging from zero to 85. The advice given by the BVA and The Kennel Club is that sire and dam should both score below the breed average. Although the screening is voluntary it should be noted that successful law suits have been brought by owners of registered dogs against breeders where it has been claimed that breeding has not been carried out in a responsible manner.

One of the most important aspects of selection for hip scoring is progeny testing. The test results of five progeny are about as reliable as the dog's own score, but results of tests conducted on 20 progeny are much more reliable than the dog's own result, to the point that the dog's own score becomes almost irrelevant. If tests on more than 20 of his progeny produce bad hip scores then he should be regarded as suspect even if he scores 0/0 himself!

It is very important that you ask the hip status of the mother and father of your puppy before you buy it. Get photocopies of their certificates and, if you are still not sure, ask your vet's opinion. It follows that it is also important have your breeding stock X-rayed before you have a litter and investigate the family hip status of the prospective sire and dam. The important data can be found in

Flatcoated Retrievers

The Progeny Tests for Hip Scores: Flatcoated Retriever by Dr M B Willis, and this information is available from the Breed Society.

At present Flatcoated Retrievers do have a better breed average than either Golden or Labrador Retrievers, but it would be detrimental to our lovely breed if we let our standards slip. Do not be fooled: there are Flatcoated Retrievers with hip dysplasia. I had a bitch with dysplasia many years ago, and she was the saddest Flatcoat I have ever owned. Because of the pain and trauma she went through, and the pain and trauma a few Flatcoats are still going through today, it is inexcusable, in my opinion, knowingly to consider breeding together two Flatcoats who have the slightest chance of producing dysplastic puppies.

ROUTINE MAINTENANCE

I have called this section 'routine maintenance' because it deals with common problems which can sometimes be treated by the owner, often during grooming.

Anal Gland Impaction

Dogs rely on their anal glands to deposit their individual scent on their faeces, which act as a scent marker. Sometimes these glands do not function properly, becoming blocked and causing discomfort. The dog will then attempt to relieve this irritation by dragging its rear end along the ground, a behaviour pattern sometimes described as 'scooting'. Contrary to popular thought, this does not indicate worm infestation.

It is not difficult to empty these glands and many breeders and professional dog groomers attend to this matter themselves, but your vet will be able to empty them for you. In severe cases the dog may need to be anaesthetised so that the sacs can be washed out with saline, but this is quite rare and hopefully should help to prevent further recurrences. Adding more fibre to the dog's diet in the form of bran may also help.

Ear Problems

These can be a source of great discomfort to dogs, causing them to paw repeatedly at the affected ear. If allowed to continue without attention ear problems can soon result in serious complications or even deafness, but curing them effectively can also be difficult. Ailments of this type often represent a combination of fungal and bacterial infections, exacerbated by microscopic ear mites which add to the complications.

Never poke down the ear canal with a cotton wool bud. Instead, arrange an early appointment with your vet, who can inspect the interior carefully with an auroscope and provide you with the most appropriate treatment. Massaging behind the ears after giving the medication will help to distribute it more effectively.

It is important even if your Flatcoat is not a show dog that his ears are kept trimmed, especially around the opening. This will help prevent the possibility of grass seeds working their way into the ear. If you do find a grass seed in your dog's ear, do not try to remove it; it is a job for your vet.

Eye Infections

It is not uncommon for discharges from the eye to occur and, although this tear staining is not indicative of a serious health problem, it will need to be wiped off. The simplest means of doing this is with a cotton wool bud and tepid water. Should you need to apply eye ointment or drops be sure to repeat this as frequently as advised because the medication tends to be washed out rapidly in tear fluids. Try to hold or otherwise distract your pet for a few moments afterwards if you are using ointment or he may attempt to rub this away before it can dissolve.

Warning: in the case of an acute eye infection, go to your vet as soon as possible.

Foot Problems

The maintenance of the nails and the feet of your Flatcoat is important. Right from the first few days of life the puppies' nails must be trimmed. At first you must remove the little clear tips and from then on it is important to keep them trimmed, especially for your bitch's sake; if the puppies scratch her she will probably become sore, and there is even a possibility that infection might get into the tissue of the mammary gland this way.

I have never removed dew claws (the thumb-like nail higher up on the inside of your puppies front legs); a Flatcoat is a working dog, and the dew claws will help him to grip as he goes up and down steep banks. It is important that the nail is kept as short as possible, however.

All nails must be trimmed regularly, but dogs with good feet who are given plenty of road work rarely need very much trimming. It is the dog with poor feet that can be improved upon with trimming. I prefer a guillotine cutter, and it is also wise to get a small jar of potassium potash crystals. If you do cut a little too much, take a pinch of dry crystals, make a pile and dip the bleeding toe into it; the bleeding will soon stop.

Foot inspection should be a regular part of grooming. Look carefully around each toe, especially the nail bed; infection easily gets in here, and, if not caught in time, could cost your dog a toe.

I find the Vetzyme tube of green cream most useful for feet.

Parasites, External

Ticks: Ticks represent a problem, particularly in sheep farming areas or areas where there is a resident population of deer. Ticks can transfer themselves to dogs. They anchor onto the skin by means of their mouthparts, and then suck the dog's body fluids, swelling noticeably in size as a result. Although you can treat ticks with chemical sprays the most effective means of dislodging them is simply to smear their body with petroleum jelly. This will block the breathing pore, causing them to drop off intact. Otherwise, they will simply break if pulled, leaving their mouthparts still buried in the dog's skin, and this can result in a localised infection. In some areas, notably where there are deer, ticks can be associated with Lyme Disease, transmitting this infection both to dogs and humans. It results in fever, and also arthritic changes in the joints.

Lice: Lice will probably be apparent, at least to your vet, when you take the puppy for its check-up. These parasites are most likely to reveal their presence in the form of their egg cases, called nits, which are attached to the dog's hairs. Lice themselves are very small and hard to observe, being translucent in appearance. They spend their entire lives on a dog, and are spread by direct contact.

As puppies spend the early part of their lives in close proximity to each other and their mother it is easy for these parasites to spread under such conditions. They often indicate ill-thrift, and can cause the young dog to scratch more than normal.

Lice are broadly divided into two categories, both of which can sometimes be found on dogs. There are those which suck body fluids through the skin, remaining anchored in place, and members of the more mobile Mallophaga group, which bite intermittently. It takes about a month for their life cycle to be completed, and suitable treatment in the form of a powder or medicated shampoo will overcome the infection easily.

Fleas: Fleas present more of a problem. They breed and can live part of their life-cycle off the dog's body, infesting its bedding or even your carpets. The warmer environment of centrally-heated homes today means that they can prove a problem throughout the year rather than just in summer.

A dog can be afflicted with fleas at any age. Repeated scratching is a common sign, and in cases where the irritation is especially severe the dog will actually bite itself to the extent of breaking the skin if left untreated. It is always useful to have a flea comb handy, because this provides the most reliable means of detecting these parasites. Be sure to groom your pet outdoors when searching for fleas; if any jump off outside they will create less of a problem.

As you run the flea comb through the coat with the lie of the fur concentrate on the area close to the base of the tail. This is where fleas tend to lurk, although in most cases you are more likely to find evidence of their presence in the form of flea dirt rather than fleas themselves. The tiny black specks actually contain remnants of the dog's blood which the fleas suck through the skin. You can confirm that it is flea dirt rather than ordinary dirt by tipping the hair and dirt on to a piece of white paper and pouring a few drops of water over it. If there are then red marks on the paper you can safely assume that they are caused by the flea dirt dissolving in the water and that your dog has fleas.

Powder and sprays are available to treat this condition, but read carefully the instructions for their application, taking particular care to avoid contaminating ponds or fish tanks: the chemicals in such products are usually toxic to fish. Similarly they may be harmful to cats, but be sure to treat any cats in your household with the appropriate feline preparation as well; dogs and cats can spread fleas to each other. You should also wash or replace your dog's bedding, as well as the bed itself, and vacuum very thoroughly in this vicinity to remove any immature fleas which may be lurking.

It is now possible to obtain special tablets to add to the dog's food, or drops to apply to the back of the neck, which will act systematically, preventing it from becoming badly bitten in the first place. There is also a flea treatment which can be given once per month to your dog in pill form. This renders infertile any fleas your dog may pick up, thereby decimating the flea population! Treatment at an early stage is important, not only to minimise the risk of tapeworm infestation (see **Internal Parasites** below), but also to prevent your dog developing an allergy to the fleas' saliva. This allergy can cause really severe irritation as the result of just one flea bite.

Mites: Mites represent another aggravating problem, particularly the cheyletiella mange mite. As their name suggests, mites are too tiny to be seen by the naked eye, and often the presence of the cheyletiella mite is only apparent when one, or some, of the human family develop a rash for which no usual cause can be found. Occasionally an affected person may be told he or she is 'allergic to the dog'. This is particularly sad when a child who has been given a new puppy develops the intensely itchy rash and the doctor's orders are to get rid of the pup.

The presence of cheyletiella mange mites should be suspected if your dog has what appears to be scurf or dandruff, and is scratching frequently. If you stand your dog on a sheet of brown wrapping paper with the shiny side up, or a black plastic bin liner, and comb out some of the 'scurf', note whether it moves. If it does, remember that another name for cheyletiella is 'walking dandruff'!

Not everyone in your family may be allergic to the cheyletiella mite, and for this reason those who are may be mis-diagnosed by their doctor, who will recognise an allergy but probably not this particular allergen. If the dog is suspected, you may be advised to get rid of it - totally unnecessary, of course. Ask your vet for the appropriate shampoo to kill off the mites, but be warned, you will have to repeat the shampoo on the affected dog, and other dogs if you have them, and wash all the dog bedding too. It is unfortunate that the cheyletiella mange mite can also survive away from the dog, which means that your carpets and soft furnishings can become infested. In addition to shampooing the dogs the remedy is to confine them to an area which has washable floors (the utility room, kitchen, or kennel if you have one) until the infestation is conquered.

Scabies: Sarcoptic mange (scabies) has been a particular problem in several areas, especially where foxes are prevalent. Skin lesions on legs, face and ears are very itchy. Scrapings taken by your vet may reveal mites, but not always. Treatment is by using a sponge-on preparation.

Demodectic mange: This is caused by the mange mite (*Domedox folliculorum*). The main symptom is hair loss on the legs or head, especially around the eyes, and it is less likely to be itchy. Scrapings show mites. The lesions may be pustular and a secondary infection can occur. The disease is more usually seen in young dogs where the immune system is compromised, but it can develop at any age from dog to dog. Most dogs carry a few mites and show no signs, but bitch to puppies is the usual method by which it spreads.

Ringworm: In spite of its name, ringworm is not a parasitic ailment but results from infection by a skin fungus. Although ringworm is not especially common in dogs it is serious in that it can be spread to people, typically causing red circular patches on the forearms where the dog is picked up. Cats are more likely to be affected and a vaccine is being developed for them. Specific antibiotic treatment from your vet will be required in the event of this disease being confirmed. Suspect it if your dog shows any unexplained thinning of hair in a circular pattern.

Parasites, Internal

Roundworms: In addition to arranging for vaccinations you will also need to obtain advice from your vet concerning de-worming treatment. The eggs of the roundworm *Toxocara canis* are of greatest concern, because these can ultimately result in human infection, with children being particularly at risk. These eggs will survive for at least two years in the environment, and are remarkably resistant to disinfectants.

If a person ingests Toxocara eggs which have matured after a period of several days outside the dog's body, the larvae hatch in the human body and move to organs such as the liver and kidneys. This process is called visceral larval migrans. If the larvae reach the eyes blindness may result. Fortunately such cases are very rare, but it is strongly recommended that children do not play where dogs or cats defecate: not all dogs or cats are regularly de-wormed. Similarly, children should always be taught to wash their hands after playing with a dog or cat and before eating food.

Puppies can acquire the infection before birth, as the larvae can move across the placental barrier, and then directly from their mother. De-worming the bitch about a month into her pregnancy will help to prevent infection in their environment. Panacur used from half-way through the pregnancy to the start of the post-partum stage dramatically reduces transplacental spread and environmental risk. The dose is low and well tolerated. Always ask your vet for advice, however.

The puppies are treated from about three weeks of age onwards and this will help to ensure that the parasites do not build up in their bodies. Treatment should be repeated every fortnight or so, depending upon your vet's instructions, until weaning.

Further treatment at three and six months is usually recommended, regular de-worming then being carried out about twice a year throughout the dog's life. The incidence of Toxocara infections is higher in dogs kept in urban areas, because they are in closer contact with each other. While cleaning up after your dog will help to reduce faecal contamination there is no doubt that this is not adequate to remove all the potential microscopic eggs from the environment, and not all dog owners can be persuaded to clean up after their dogs have defecated.

Tapeworms: Roundworms such as *Toxocara canis* can be distinguished quite easily from tapeworms because of a difference in their basic shape. Whereas roundworms are similar in appearance to small earthworms, or thin spaghetti, and are white in colour, tapeworms are flat, like a piece of ribbon, and segmented. One of the most common tapeworms found in dogs has a life cycle involving the flea. In this case control of fleas should help to lessen the risk of a tapeworm problem. *Dipylidum caninum* eggs are consumed by fleas, and begin their development in the flea's body. Only if the flea is actually swallowed by the dog as it grooms itself will the tapeworm then establish itself in the dog's gut.

Tapeworm eggs do not represent a direct threat to a dog's health; they have to pass through another species, which is often described as an intermediate host. In some sheep-farming areas another tapeworm called *Echinococcus granulosus* can represent a threat to human health. Its eggs will undergo development in the body's organs, forming structures called hydatid cysts which can grow to 15cm (6in) in diameter before rupturing. This illness is called hydatidosis.

It is important to note that drugs such as piperazine sold to combat roundworms will be ineffective against tapeworms. In most cases dosing dogs once or twice a year should be sufficient, but in sheep-farming regions regular treatment every two months or so is advisable to combat the risk of hydatidosis. Dogs must not be fed on raw sheep meat either, because this is the natural source of infection for them. The infection would normally be recycled via the dog's faeces, contaminating the ground where the sheep are grazing; fortunately the spread to humans is not part of the usual life cycle of this parasite.

Tooth Care

It is important these days, especially now that most Flatcoats are fed on complete food, that care is taken of your dog's teeth. There are some things for which you should watch out as your puppy changes from its milk teeth to its permanent adult teeth between 14 weeks and six months. It is best to inspect gently every week, especially as the last of the adult teeth come through; this is often the time the mouth gets crowded and teeth start to go in the wrong direction. A good hard daily rusk or one of the special Nylabone toys or cones especially developed to help clean teeth will also dislodge stubborn milk teeth. It is better to take veterinary advice and have them removed if they are solid and causing problems with the adult teeth. Once you have established your puppy will retrieve, leave it during this time; then there is no possibility of damage, especially if you are hoping to show.

There are many different tooth pastes and gels on the market which, if used regularly, will prevent the build-up of tartar, which can cause infection of the gums. This is the most common cause of tooth loss in dogs. If there is a build-up of tartar, it is best removed by your vet: your dog will thank you!

OTHER CONDITIONS AND EMERGENCIES
Arthritis

Each joint surface is covered by a layer of cartilage which protects the bone from the concussion caused by movement and provides a smooth surface upon which it can move. Lubrication is provided by a viscous substance know as synovial fluid, which is produced by the synovial membrane which lines the joint capsule and ligaments. This also provided nutrients to the cartilage.

The term 'joint problems' covers a wide variety of conditions. Arthritis is the most common final outcome, often arising through injury to the bone, ligaments or tendons. Aging also affects structures such as ligaments or cartilage, which gradually wear out, leading to secondary degenerative changes such as we see in our hard-working picking-up dogs.

Arthritis can also arise from bacterial or viral infection or from auto-immune conditions leading to inflammatory arthritis. The joint problems may be forms of hip dysplasia or OCD: the dog may have shown signs of joint disease when a young dog, but some do not, and the first symptoms that the patient exhibits are due to the secondary degenerative disease, arthritis.

Symptoms will vary from dog to dog, depending on the severity of the problem and the dog's pain threshold. The most common sign is stiffness, particularly evident after a period of rest. This is often aggravated by cold, damp weather, but often eases up quickly with a Flatcoat: even in old age, they will not let discomfort interfere with their enjoyment of life! You may notice that they have more difficulty in climbing stairs and jumping and that they slow up on walks after the first excitement has passed. If you know your Flatcoat well you will also notice a certain look that replaces that happy, smiling expression.

You should consult your vet if you think your Flatcoat has a problem. Although a thorough clinical examination may well give your vet the answers, he might decide to X-ray and do further investigations. If your dog is overweight, put it on a diet; extra weight puts undue stress on tendons, ligaments and joints. There are many other long-term ways to treat your Flatcoat, involving conventional treatment, herbal homeopathic methods and acupuncture, provided your vet agrees.

There is one important thing to remember: if, as a youngster, your Flatcoat injures itself, sustaining a blow to its shoulder or any other limb injury, please, please do follow your vet's instructions on rest and restricted exercise. This is one way in which your vet hopes he can prevent your dog from getting arthritis in that injured joint. It may be difficult in the short term, but it will pay dividends in the long term.

Bites

Bites from other dogs ('they never clean their teeth properly') must be watched with care, as they can swell up very fast. Serious bites are a veterinary emergency. Small bites or a small tear in the ear will bleed profusely. If the wound is dirty, clean it with a mild antiseptic solution of Savlon, Dettol or TCP. If it is bleeding well and clean, dust it with wound powder and apply a gentle, firm pressure. An ear will usually go on bleeding for quite a while and make quite a mess.

Fresh wounds may be suitable for suturing, but old wounds have to heal by secondary intention, because of infection.

Burns and Scalds

Apply cold water as a first-aid measure, depending where the injury is. If it is a foot or a leg, put it in a bucket of cold water, continuing this treatment for at least 15 minutes; if it is on the back or head, run constant cold water from a hose-pipe for the same amount of time. Ring your vet for advice and then take your dog to the vet. Cover it in cold, wet towels.

Cancer

As in humans, the incidence of cancer in dogs in general is quite high. It is a very sad situation to lose one's beloved Flatcoat at a young age from cancer. However, there is a possibility that this might be how you will lose your friend.

Breeders have been very aware of the loss of Flatcoats with cancer for many years. It was decided within The Flatcoated Retriever Society to support a Tumour Survey by the Oncology Pathologist, Dr Jane Dobson (Department of Clinical Veterinary Medicine, Madingley Road, Cambridge CB3 OES). Dr Dobson reports that sarcomas feature strongly, and that through this survey they are beginning to understand the pattern of cancer within the breed bases on over 250 tumours that have so far been examined up to 1995. Research is also been carried out in the USA, supported by the American Flatcoated Retriever Society. Hopefully research will give us some answers which will be able to help all.

It is important to be aware of any unusual lumps or bumps on your dogs, and to ask your vet to check them. If they are removed, remember that your vet can send biopsies, excisional or post mortem specimens to Dr Dobson at the address above. The Flatcoated Retriever Society will pay for their examination. It is an excellent service and the result will be sent back to your vet in just a few days. If there is no form available at your veterinary surgery, you as owner need to send your name and address, the kennel name of your dog, its age or date of birth, sex, colour and site of tumour. Your veterinary surgeon will need to send his name and address and the clinical history of your dog with the site and type of tumour.

On the positive side, the treatment for cancer improves every year. There is therefore a strong possibility of help, especially to improve the quality of life for your dog.

Constipation

This sometimes occurs in older dogs or dogs fed on bones. Add fibre such as wheat-bran and brown rice to the diet. A little raw liver or a dessert-spoonful of liquid paraffin will act as a laxative. If the condition continues ask your vet for advice.

Coughing

There are many possible reasons for your dog's coughing. If the cough persists for more than a day seek veterinary advice. Benelyn Linctus is very soothing.

Kennel cough due to *Bordetella bronchiseptica*, a bacterium combination plus an assortment of viruses, is very infectious and you must not take any of your dogs out to a public place or to a Kennel Club event if they might be suffering from this condition (read the declaration you sign on your Show Entry Form).

If the dog suddenly starts coughing violently and is retching at the same time, there is a strong possibility that it is an emergency. Look down the dog's throat, and also above to the roof of the mouth, especially between the back teeth; a stick or bone may be stuck or a splinter of bone gone down further. This is an emergency.

If there is discolouration to the mouth and a strange smell, this also could be an emergency (possible poisoning). Contact your vet and get advice. A hot dog coming home from a walk will drink from a bucket without thinking, even if it is full of disinfectant.

Coughing can also be a sign of heart disease, lungworms and other conditions, so a check-up by your vet is advisable.

Cystitis

Inflammation of the bladder, generally caused by an infection, stones or a growth. Urine is passed very frequently with a sense of urgency, but there may be straining, and the dog will often go into the urinating position without passing urine. There can also be blood in the urine. This condition needs veterinary treatment. Take a fresh sample with you, so that the vet can do a simple dip stick test.

Diabetes

This condition is caused by a failure on the part of the pancreas to produce insulin, bringing about a rise in sugar levels in the blood. The dog will have an excessive thirst, will urinate more frequently and have a voracious appetite. Make an appointment with your vet and take a urine specimen with you. This condition is controllable with diet modifications and with injections of insulin, daily in severe cases.

Diabetes is more common in unspayed, middle-aged or elderly bitches. The hormonal cycle makes the diabetes unstable and treatment can therefore be unreliable until the bitch is spayed.

Diarrhoea

Diarrhoea is a clinical sign that all is not well in the dog's intestine. The cause can be located in the small or large bowel, and the nature of the material passed will give you and your vet some clue as to the cause. The faeces may have the appearance of semi-digested food, it could be black (old, digested blood) or red (fresh blood, generally from the lower bowel); it may be completely fluid or semi-solid, and may have mucus on it. A careful description will help in the diagnosis of the cause.

Severe diarrhoea, especially accompanied by vomiting, can result in profuse dehydration, which may necessitate intravenous fluids.

Less severe cases may respond adequately to restriction of food for some hours or days and the provision of electolyle solution (Lectade) in place of water.

Mild cases may only require starvation for a day or so.

In all cases, when feeding can be resumed it is generally advised to feed a low-residue, easily-digested, light diet several times a day while the damage to the intestinal lining is repaired.

The causes of diarrhoea are many and varied. The Flatcoat, like the Labrador, is an inveterate dustbin raider; rubbish in the hedgerows, old dead rats and other, similar delicacies are all acceptable as far as they are concerned.

Food poisoning (ie *Salmonella,* and other bacteria) causes severe diarrhoea, as do certain viral infections such as parvovirus. Dietary allergies may lead to chronic diarrhoea. Colitis and inflammatory condition of the large bowel (indicated by bulky, pale faeces, mucous and fresh blood) is another cause. Lack of enzyme production by the pancreas or bouts of pancreatitis also result in a dog which does not thrive and has a tendency to have diarrhoea.

Drowning

Hold the dog up by its hind legs to drain out the water.

You can give artificial respiration to your dog in an emergency of this type. Check that the airway is not blocked by the tongue. Pull the tongue forward to make a clear airway. Put the dog on its side. Push down rhythmically over the rib cage every five seconds or so; hopefully this will induce breathing.

If this fails, then mouth-to-nose resuscitation can be tried. Do check heart-beat as well. Dogs tend to be able to survive longer without oxygen than people and, hopefully, it will be possible to revive your dog.

Electrocution

Live electrical flexes can represent a hazard if gnawed by the teething puppy who is quite oblivious to such dangers. Do not forget Flatcoats remain puppies for a long time!

Do consider a trip switch in the fuse box to isolate any damaged circuit. You should keep plugs disconnected as far as possible when the equipment is not in use, and if your puppy does chew a cable it is vital that you switch the plug off at the mains before attempting to remove the flex from the puppy's mouth. If it is not possible to turn off the power do not move the dog with your hands; get a wooden broom and move the dog away from the flex with this.

When you have removed your dog from the source of the electricity, follow the procedure for artificial respiration described above in **Drowning**.

Eclampsia

Eclampsia (milk fever) is caused by a sudden drop in calcium associated with whelping and lactation. It often happens in the first few days after whelping, but it can happen later in lactation.

In the early stages the bitch appears restless and apprehensive, there is a strange expression on her face and in many cases her eyes will look wild. The puppies are often restless too. If left, your bitch will often collapse and have convulsions.

Prompt veterinary attention is needed. Never wait and see: the progress of milk fever is rapid. Treatment is the an injection of calcium and, provided it is given in time, your bitch will make a rapid recovery.

Care must be taken of this bitch now and in the future. Do not think that large doses of calcium before whelping will solve the problem; it could make the problem worse. Take your vet's advice on the amount of calcium to give your bitch; it will depend on the quality of the food and amount of calcium in it. Post whelping calcium is of more benefit, but it must be in correct balance with dietary phosphorous.

Fits

Fits are the result of a variety of causes, which your vet will investigate for you. The dog will suddenly collapse, the jaws will clamp shut, the limbs will be extended and rigid, there could be frothing at the mouth and its bladder and bowels may involuntarily empty. As the fit progresses the dog may cry out and paddle its feet.

Recovery will take from a few minutes to half an hour from the onset. The dog may appear dazed when consciousness returns and may take time to regain full vision.

Keep the dog warm and quiet in a darkened room during and after a fit. Do not attempt to administer any medicine until the dog is completely conscious and do not try to handle the dog; you might get bitten.

Heart Attacks

These are more likely to happen in middle-aged or old dogs. The dog will suddenly collapse, and may appear to be dead. It usually recovers in about five minutes. There may be an involuntary evacuation of the bowl and bladder and the eyes may rotate upwards.

Keep the dog quiet and warm and let him recover from the attack. Contact your vet for advice and get expert treatment. The dog may be given an ECG examination to assess the extent of the problem.

Hiccoughs and Wind

Puppies sometimes suffer from this. It can be helped by giving one teaspoonful of babies' gripe water in a dessert-spoonful of milk (yes, it works very well!).

Wind can occur in older dogs. This might come up, it might go down, it might give the dog a bloated look, or all three could happen together. Gripe water often helps to relieve this too. It is worth discussing with your vet.

It might be wise to look at the food your dog is eating. There may be vegetable matter in it that does not suit your dog. If he is having complete food the day's amount divided into two or three small meals may be better. I find a spoonful of Forgastrin (bismuth and charcoal) helps.

WARNING: If your dog looks bloated, especially soon after food, and is in distress, it is an emergency; ring your vet and get to the surgery fast. There is a strong possibility he is in need of emergency treatment for gastric dilation torsion.

Hypo-glycaemia

This sometimes happens to a dog who is working hard, especially on a strenuous picking-up day. There may be several underlying reasons why this is happening to your dog that your vet can investigate.

The dog has an exhausted demeanour. He will stagger and give the impression of not quite knowing where he is.

The best thing is to carry a Mars bar or glucose tablets, and give them to your dog, or bread or sweet cakes will work just as well. It will work instantly. Make sure your dog is having a high energy quality dog food during this working period. If your dog has this tendency it is better to give him small frequent meals through the day.

Some dogs never know when to stop. Put them on a lead and make them rest. Carry a bottle of glucose and water in the picking-up vehicle so that you can give him a small drink between drives.

Mastitis

This is an inflammation of the milk glands in a bitch, caused by a bacterial infection. It often takes the form of an abscess, often only in one gland. It can also be related to an old injury, especially in a working bitch.

The main symptom is the reddening and hardening of the milk glands, which is very painful. The bitch will often also have a temperature.

You should treat as your vet advises. Antibiotics are frequently given, and some vets advise hot fomentation, though great care should be taken not to burn the bitch. I have found that you can often break down the swelling by applying some vegetable oil to your fingers and gently massaging the swollen gland. I have never taken the puppies off the bitch and have had no bad effects from this. In fact it is best for the pups to suckle and express the milk to help to remove the infection.

Metritis/Pyometra

This is an accumulation of material, fluid and debris in the uterus, occurring four to six weeks after a bitch has been in season. This condition can be seen in any unspayed bitches, but is more common in elderly ones.

The most obvious sign is the increase in thirst and frequent urination. She is in a depressed state, often with a raised temperature, and she may be vomiting. In the case of open pyometra there may be a vaginal discharge, either creamy white or brown red. In this case, your bitch probably will not be as sick as if there were no discharge (closed pyometra). Milder cases may be termed Endometritis and may respond to antibiotics, but in general it is vital to perform an ovarian hysterectomy to save the bitch's life. This is a serious condition: contact your veterinary surgeon immediately.

Poisoning

This is a veterinary emergency. Take as much evidence as possible to the surgery: vomit and packets, tins or plants that your dog has been chewing.

Poisoning is a potential hazard for all dogs, and sometimes it can be hard to isolate the cause. Always seek veterinary advice should your dog start to act strangely, or collapse. Bear in mind that some poisons such as the rodenticide Warfarin are long-acting in their effects.

Take great care that your dog cannot gain access to anti-freeze as this is actually attractive to dogs in spite of its possibly lethal effects. The same applies in the case of metaldehyde, used as a slug and snail killer around the garden.

Banish all poisonous substances from your property if you can. Remember also that human tablets must be kept in the medicine chest; dogs love 'Smarties' as much as children do.

Road Traffic Accident

Sadly more dogs are being injured on the roads as the amount of traffic increases. If you encounter this situation remember above everything else that the dog will be distressed and may bite. Approach it with care, and be careful also that you do not end up being hit by a car when attempting to catch a loose dog in the street. The simplest method is to use a belt or leash as a noose, and then you can lead it to safety.

If the dog is lying flat in the road, move it carefully to the verge or pavement by placing your arms under its body. Try to avoid tipping it as this may simply worsen its injuries. Moving an injured dog on a car rug or blanket is better, if one is available. Clearly, the dog will need veterinary attention, but if you move it in a car, be sure to line the rear area with paper or plastic, because the shock may well result in the dog relieving itself or vomiting.

By law, all collisions involving a dog must be reported to the police. If the accident occurs in a strange area at night the police should be able to direct you to their duty vet, although all practices are obliged to provide round-the-clock care for emergency situations.

Snake Bites

The only poisonous snake native to Great Britain is the adder, which can be found on sandy heathland and downland areas throughout the UK. Should your dog be bitten, carry him back to the car as quickly as possible, rather than allowing him to walk. Give him a dose of antihistamine (piriton) and cool the limb with ice cubes. (It is wise to carry piriton with you if you regularly exercise in these areas, as you never know when this could help your dog or someone else.)

Vomiting

Like diarrhoea, this is a symptom which may have a variety of causes, often dietary in origin, but possibly due to viral or bacterial infection.

Starve the dog for 12 to 24 hours, only allowing small sips of water or lactate, and then keep it on a light diet for a few days. Persistent vomiting, especially in young dogs and not-so-young Flatcoats, may indicate a blockage caused by a foreign body or, in tiny pups, an intusseception.

Wasp and Bee Stings

Stings are another hazard which a young dog may encounter through snapping at a sluggish wasp or bee. Stings may occur to feet, face or within the mouth. The swelling is often of minor irritation and no consequence, but inside the mouth, on the tongue or at the back of the throat the resultant swelling can block the airway, sometimes swelling up dramatically. In such cases veterinary help may well be needed.

There is also a small risk that your dog could be allergic to the sting, but in most cases dogs recover uneventfully and soon learn to leave such insects alone. Piriton from the medicine cabinet is a very good first aid measure, but please check with your vet.

This information has been compiled with the help and support of Jane Alexandra, B Vet Med, Cert VA, MRCVS, owner of the Rehyrb affix of Flatcoated Retrievers.

SIGNS OF OLD AGE

As a result of advances in veterinary care dogs are now living longer, but it is impossible to prevent signs of ageing. The most conspicuous is likely to be loss of pigmentation in the coat. This will be most apparent in dark-coated dogs like Flatcoats, the area around the muzzle becoming greyish.

The teeth are likely to need attention in old age, although regular brushing and de-scaling at intervals should mean that dental problems here are kept to a minimum. Other typical symptoms of old age include cardiac failure, the symptoms depending on what part of the heart is affected. Stabilisation of such conditions by use of appropriate drugs and alterations to the dog's diet and life-style should help to ensure that it has several more years of a relatively active life ahead. The same applies in the case of kidney problems and emphasises the value of regular veterinary check-ups for older animals.

Any unexplained lumps which appear on the dog's body must clearly be viewed with suspicion, particularly in the region of the mammary glands of bitches. These tend to be the most common tumours in dogs and early diagnosis will often prove vital in ensuring successful treatment. Aside from surgery, both cryosurgery, which entails freezing the tumorous area with liquid nitrogen to kill off the unhealthy cells, and radiotherapy are being utilised increasingly, the costs being recoverable in most cases against a health insurance plan.

Unfortunately Flatcoats do get cancer, sometimes at an early age. The Flatcoated Retriever Society do support The Department of Clinical Veterinary Medicine at Cambridge, who are looking into the occurrence of all types of tumour in Flatcoats. Samples from any growth found in Flatcoats (whether alive or put to sleep) can be sent by your Veterinary Surgeon to Cambridge. Forms are available from the Hon Secretary or Mrs Johnson (see **Useful Addresses**)

Eventually the time will come when your dog's quality of life has deteriorated to the extent that you need to consider euthanasia. This is always a very difficult decision, but you can be sure of the help and support of your vet when considering whether this is the best course of action to take. When the end comes you can stay with your dog or say your farewells at the surgery door. No-one will think badly of you for leaving your pet at this point. The vet will give an injection in exactly the same way as for an anaesthetic, but in this case the drug used will be correspondingly more potent. The dog gently falls asleep and stops breathing almost immediately. It is a very peaceful end.

Your vet will subsequently be able to arrange the dignified disposal of your Flatcoat's body. Alternatively, you can arrange a burial at a special animal cemetery, and return to visit at intervals if you wish, or have a private cremation with ashes returned in a casket if requested.

It is not unnatural in any way to grieve for your Flatcoat. This is vital if you are to come to terms with your loss. After a few weeks, however, you will hopefully feel strong enough to think of introducing another dog to your home, not as a substitute, but as an individual in its own right.

Ch Exclyst Bernard at 14 years of age.

Chapter 11

Environmental Awareness and Natural Remedies

ENVIRONMENTAL AWARENESS

I consider environmental awareness to be a major consideration in keeping your Flatcoat and your human family healthy today. Whatever the breed, your dog will be more susceptible to health problems resulting from the environment than you will, because of its faster metabolic rate and shorter life span. A simple explanation of the immune system from a lay person might help you to understand.

What is Immunity?

Immunity is the body's effort to recognise and destroy any intruder that might be a source of harm. This includes just about everything: bacteria, viruses, the wrong type of blood, fungi, cancer cells, or anything else you care to name.

The thymus is of total importance to a new born puppy, who has only the immune factor passed on from the bitch's blood. The puppy has in its bone marrow a host of microscopic, immature white cells, called lymphocytes, and these are passed to the thymus via the bloodstream. It is the thymus' task to hurry them towards maturity and pass them to the spleen, lymphatic system and other organs for final maturing. The thymus also gives these organs hormonal stimulus to prod them into activity. Within days it has the puppy's immunity in hand and continues to run the system afterwards.

Sometimes these lymphocytes over-estimate the danger and respond too aggressively, producing an array of annoying symptoms. The over-response to an invader is termed an allergy.

The puppy has two immune systems. One has its headquarters in the bone marrow and, containing B lymphocytes, is mainly concerned with bacterial invasions, and the other, based in the thymus and containing T lymphocytes, is active against a wide variety of fungus infection and foreign tissue.

T lymphocytes come in a number of varieties: T suppressors, T killers, and T helpers. Each has a specialised task and complex function in the protecting the dog's body from all kinds of invaders. The thymus secretes within itself and injects into the bloodstream certain hormones which are essential to the normal growth and efficacy of the T cells.

Nothing as complex as the immune system can be expected always to function perfectly and modern life subjects it to ever-increasing stress. This does not only relate to our dogs; it also relates to our families. This is why we must have a heightened awareness of our environment and our food.

Things Worth Thinking About

I list below points which should be taken into account when you consider your Flatcoat's welfare.

* Take time to allow your puppy to grow up. Think about what is going on inside him, how fast he is growing and how all these systems are developing. Stress at this time of rapid development has the potential to cut off several years at the other end of his life or trigger a crisis in his immune system. Fun training is essential; stress training is a no-no.

* Do not send him off for gundog training when he is less than one year old. This applies especially to a Flatcoat, who will be slow to mature. Think of the stress on his system. Neither should you put him on a hard show circuit until he is well over 18 months of age. Flatcoats do not mature and look like Flatcoats until they are at least two or three years of age, and will probably be at their best at four or five, or even more. It is well known for a Flatcoat to win a CC out of Veteran (seven years and over). They have even won them at over 10 years of age. The original breeders bred Flatcoats that way: as a very slow-maturing breed. If you

develop them into a fast-maturing dog you will lose the essential growing balance of the Flatcoat and put all the natural body clocks that have been developed over the last century out of rhythm.

* Take great care where you exercise your dogs, and plan the walks beforehand. Observe the area carefully: the countryside today is very dangerous for us all, especially highly-developed farming areas. Even 'set-aside' areas have possibly been sprayed with growth retardants. Country dogs have a high incidence of liver damage as I have found out to my cost. Remember, dogs absorb through their feet: they eat grass as they walk along the country lanes, they walk through puddles and drink from puddles which could contain chemicals from sprays. (The last point applies to town dogs as well, and it is too late when you see the tell-tale yellow borders along the footpaths.) Get to know your farmers; they will tell you when they are going to spray the fields close to your house and kennels. At such times, keep the dogs in, throw away all water, clean the water bowls and wash down the yard and the kennels. My dogs have a daily dose of B+ to help their livers counteract the toxins that they might pick up. Go to walk in places such as National Trust Public Areas that welcome dogs. It is better to make an effort and travel by car to a safe area.

* Over the years I have seen dogs swimming in polluted water, and have often wondered if it has had a detrimental effect on them in the long run. Even water that is apparently perfectly clear could be less innocuous than it looks. It is worth checking on a map to see if there is a possible source of pollutants upstream. Ring up your local River Authority and enquire. Great care should be taken in still ponds where wildfowl have been; the bacteria content could be very high. In the summer, streams in farming areas with a high incidence of dark green algae should be avoided.

* Your own garden holds dangers if family members are keen gardeners. Do not use a herbicide to spray lawns: there is known to be an increase in malignant lymphoma in dogs related to the use of such chemicals. Slug pellets also are a known poison to pets. Think before you use anything, especially if you have pets and children.

* We must be aware of our environment not only for our dogs' sake, but also for our families'. We should be aware of the possibility of petrol fumes when we are filling up our cars; our dogs and children are usually in the back, near the fuel tank, and there is documented evidence of the detrimental effects. In America I hear there are special filler caps that absorb a proportion of the fumes. After all, we know the detrimental effect of smoking on our dogs and children.

* We must question what goes into our food and our dogs' food.

* We must question the reliability and side effects of drugs and vaccinations. However, I do remember life without vaccination for our dogs, and none of us today would wish to return to the great losses that were then the norm in a kennel, especially among the young stock.

The list is long, and does not add up to a good scenario. It is our responsibility to try and change it. Remember: complacency will kill our beloved Flatcoats and, even worse, our beloved families!

ALTERNATIVE MEDICINE

All drugs, whether natural or synthetic, have beneficial effects and side effects. In some drugs the thera-peutic level and toxic level are very critical; other drugs are relatively safe. So-called 'natural' products can be dangerous, as there may be non-therapeutic, toxic components in the formulation (for instance, dried foxglove leaves); a purified, or artificial/synthetic form of the therapeutic compound may be far safer. The other problem with natural, or herbal, forms is that the percentage of active ingredient in one gram of dried herbs will vary according to such factors as weather and growing conditions and season of harvest.

Doses of herbal medicines that you have given to your dog should be mentioned when you go to your vet, as they may affect and interact with your vet's choice of medication for your dog.

Remember: all the remedies listed are first-aid treatments and do not take the place of vet-erinary advice and treatment, unless prescribed by a homeopathic veterinary surgeon. Many of these substances are complementary to prescribed treatment.

Natural Remedies

The healing power of plants has been known throughout history, though not always understood as it is today. Their healing qualities in the past led them to be regarded as sacred or even magic. For this very reason, 'scientific' man poured scorn on the use of herbs as he became more sophisticated. Now that their function can be analysed by biological science and their powers re-interpreted, they are once again acceptable; after all, modern orthodox or allopathic medicine has its roots in the use of plants.

Until the 1940s, nearly all drugs in common use had a herbal origin, and many still do today. Aspirin, probably the best-known and most used of all drugs, is extracted from the Black Willow. Amphetamines are based on an alkaloid, ephedrine, extracted from a Chinese herb, *Ephedra sinica*. Steroids, once hailed as 'wonder drugs' but now known to have worrying side effects, are made from a chemical extract from an African yam (genus: *Dioscorea*). The foxglove produces a well-known heart drug called digitalis. Morphine also is a plant derivative, as are many others.

The scientific approach tends to view a person or animal as a biochemical laboratory where specific chemicals have specific effects. When the animal dies all these chemicals are still present in the body but the integral life force is missing. Alternative medicine, especially homeopathy, aims to stimulate this life force by treating the body as a whole and encouraging it to heal naturally without artificially masking symptoms which may well recur later.

Many people today, worried about possible unknown side-effects of drugs, are turning to natural cures, which are gentler and safer and have been found to work just as well for animals as for human beings. They are not new or 'trendy'; they have been known about and used for centuries.

Homeopathy

Homeopathy is an exceptionally safe form of medicine which treats the whole being. It was developed 200 years ago and is based on the principle of treating like with like. The remedies are prepared from plants and minerals in a way which makes them safe and without harmful side-effects.

Homeopathy can be used to treat all kinds of conditions, either on its own or in conjunction with conventional medicine, although some drugs, such as steroids, can hinder the effectiveness of homeopathic treatments. When an animal has reached the stage of needing surgery it should not be delayed but, when used before and after surgery, homeopathic remedies are especially valuable in counteracting anxiety, shock and adverse reaction to anaesthetic as well as speeding the process of recovery. In cases of chronic disease, homeopathy has been known to achieve results where orthodox medicine has failed.

Environmental Awareness and Natural Remedies

Samuel Hahnemann, born in 1755 in Meissen, Saxony, was the founding father of homeopathy. He discovered that, if a substance normally used as a cure for a certain disease was given to a healthy person, it caused symptoms similar to the disease in that person. He experimented first with Quinine which was used to treat malaria. Over the years he went on to investigate the symptoms produced in a healthy individual by other substances, many of them poisons. From this he developed his theory of curing like with like. He went on to find that the more a substance was diluted using a method of shaking or 'succussion', the more powerful it became in overcoming the symptoms that it caused in its undiluted form. Hahnemann never used above the 6c (1:1,000,000,000) potency, but his followers went on to use much higher ones. So diluted are the substances used in homeopathic remedies that the amounts occurring in the pills that you are given are minute in the extreme; so do not be worried when a homeopathic vet prescribes arsenic or belladonna for your dog. Homeopathy differs from herbalism both in the preparation of remedies and because the remedies contain only a minimal dose which aims at stimulating self-healing; the two forms of medicine are not, as often thought, the same.

The above is a very simplified account of a very complex subject, and finding the correct cure for an individual involves analysing such factors as past illnesses, temperament and likes and dislikes to produce a general picture. It is always best to seek the advice of an experienced homeopath, but there are remedies which can be used safely in low potencies as first-aid treatment. These are usually available from your chemist or health shop.

When administering homeopathic remedies, handle them as little as possible. Most dogs will readily eat the pills or powders, which should not be given with food or water but put into the mouth with a clean spoon. Keep the remedies in a cool, dark place and, if you are giving more than one remedy at the same time, leave a gap of at least 5 minutes between them. If the symptoms do not start to clear up quickly, call your vet.

When treating an acute condition give 2-3 tablets daily (only low potency, say 6c); for chronic conditions give one dose a week or even less.

Wait and see what happens. If the symptoms become less pronounced, continue treatment; if they clear up, stop. If the animal improves in itself but still has some symptoms, you probably need a different potency.

Rough Guide to Homeopathic Remedies

CONDITION	DESCRIPTION	REMEDY
Abscess	Red hot and painful but no pus	Belladonna
	When pus is present	Hepar Sulph
Accident	To help shock	Aconite & Arnica
Appetite	(Loss of)	Lycopodium
Birth	To help contractions	Caulophyllum
	Afterwards	Arnica
Bleeding	From small wounds	Arnica
Bruising & Stings		Pyrethrum Tincture & Arnica & Apis
Burns & Scalds	For shock	Aconite
	then	Cantharis
Collapse	Crush tablet & place in mouth	Carbo Veg or Bach Flower Rescue Remedy
Constipation		Nux Vom
Cystitis		Cantharis
Diarrhoea	With sickness and drinking often	Arsenicum Album
	Loose stools and Excessive drinking	Mercurius Corrosivus
Ears (Itching)	Clean ear flap with	Calendula lotion (dilute)
	then give	Hepar sulph
Eyes	Watery - sore	Euphrasia
	Suddenly red	Belladonna
False Pregnancy	Many Flatcoat bitches respond well to	Pulsatilla
Fever	Early stages	Aconite
Flatulance	Obvious discomfort	Carbo veg

Environmental Awareness and Natural Remedies

Fractures	For shock & bruising	Arnica
	For pain	Hypericum
	For swelling	Ledum
	To aid mending of bone	Symphytum
Lactation	To increase milk	Urtica Urens (high potency)
	To get rid of milk	Urtica Urens (low potency)
Nervous	(at shows)	Aconite or Gelsemium
Pining	(or new puppy)	Ignatia
Sprains	Torn ligaments	Ruta Grav
	Swelling	Ledum
	Better for movement	Rhus Tox
	Worse for movement	Bryonia
Stroke		Aconite, Arnica, Rescue Remedy
Travel Sickness		Petroleum or Cocculus
Small Wounds	Bath with diluted	Calendula lotion
	Small, deep puncture wounds	Hypericum
	Thorn in pad (For about 5 days. Check daily, bath in Calendula. Will often come out with gentle pressure after a few days.)	Hypericum & Hepar Sulph

Biochemic Tissue Salts, produced by New Era and available at your chemist or health shop, are combined homeopathic remedies which again work well for dogs. There are about 12 of these and they are useful for such problems as skin and coat disorders, rheumatism and nervous problems.

Bach Flower remedies are similar in many ways to classical homeopathic remedies, but are prepared differently. They come in liquid form, brandy being used to preserve the energy of each plant. They are good for treating such problems as behavioural disorders and states of anxiety. Rescue Remedy has already been mentioned and is most valuable; it has a calming and soothing effect in almost any emergency, for dog and owner! The dosage is one to two drops twice daily of the chosen remedy diluted in water or even dropped onto the tongue. This should be continued for two weeks or until the condition improves.

Helpful Bach Flower Remedies

For trauma, shock, etc	Rescue remedy
For extreme shyness or timidity	Mimulus
For aggression	Chicory
For the animal which gives up when unwell	Elm
Jealousy , distrust	Holly
Exhaustion	Hornbeam
Impatient, hyperactive	Impatiens
Highly strung, never relaxes	Vervain
Moody, resentful	Willow

If this section has interested you and you want to know more, you can join The Homeopathic Society for Animal Welfare (HSAW). The Co-ordinator is Mrs N J Brook (see **Useful Addresses**). You will receive good advice when you need it and an interesting quarterly newsletter. Current subscription is £7.00 a year.

If you cannot find the address of a local homeopathic vet (of whom there is an ever-increasing number) in your Yellow Pages, send a stamped, addressed envelope to Christopher Day, the Hon Secretary of the British Association of Homeopathic Veterinary Surgeons (BAHVCS) (see **Useful Addresses**), who will send you a list of them.

You will find a free information leaflet about the New Era Salts at your chemist or health shop. Free factsheets are also available from Denes Natural Pet Care Ltd, who also run Denes Advisory Service (Tel: 01273-325364).

Again, I am indebted to Mrs Jane Alexander, BVet Med, Cert VA MRCUS for her kind help and support in the writing of this chapter.

Flatcoated Retrievers: Statistics and Champions

The following abbreviations are used in Appendix A:

Ch	Champion
Sh Ch	Show Champion
A/A	All-Aged Stake
FTW	Field Trial Winner
CC	Challenge Certificate
RCC	Reserve Challenge Certificate
BIS	Best In Show
BOB	Best Of Breed
N/W	Non-Winners Stake
F/C	Flatcoated Retriever
AV	Any Variety Retriever
COM	Certificate of Merit

Appendix A1
Post-War Registrations

1946	1947	1948	1949	1950	1951	1952	1953	1954	1955	1956	1957	1958
91	74	142	107	110	68	82	86	75	64	89	127	95

1959	1960	1961	1962	1963	1964	1965	1966	1967	1968	1969	1970	1971
132	127	119	218	117	153	N/K	N/K	N/K	N/K	N/K	N/K	N/K

1972	1973	1974	1975	1976	1977	1978	1979	1980	1981	1982	1983	1984
306	427	421	239	109	124	317	519	701	667	715	818	860

1985	1986	1987	1988	1989	1990	1991	1992	1993	1994
992	940	971	914	1409	1266	1265	1358	1427	1244

Post-War Champions in the Show Ring

Flatcoats gathered together for the first time after the war in 1946.

1946

The first Post-war Challenge Certificates (CCs) were won by: Atherbram Nobbie (dog) and Claverdon Jet (bitch).

The Flat-coated Retriever Club Show was held at Wolverhampton and the judge was Mr W Simms:

Dog CC:	Atherbram Nobbie (winner in a non-qualifying class)
Open Dog:	**1st:** Waterman **2nd:** Peddars Fraction **3rd:** Revival of Ettington
Bitch CC:	Claverdon Jet
Open Bitch:	**1st:** Claverdon Jet **2nd:** Scylla of Peddars **3rd:** Dilys of Adlington

Dogs and Bitches in Stud Book 1946 were:

Dogs	**Sire**	**Dam**
Atherbram Nobbie	Atherbram Gunner	Cemlyn
Monkslane Toby	Specialist	Speck
Peddars Fraction	Atherbram Prince	Peddars Lass
Revival of Ettington	Technician	Miss Celeste
Waterman	Atherbram Simon	Atherbram Prince

Bitches		
Claverdon Jet	Atherbram Gunner	Cemlyn
Dilys of Adlington	Rastus of Adlington	Gwyneth of Adlington
Scylla of Peddars	Dusk of Riverside	Lassie

1947

Challenge Certificates were won by:
Dogs: Ch Waterman; Burghpark Nigger (Atherbram Simon ex Atherbram Nellie)
Bitches: Ch Claverdon Jet; Ch Oathill Sheila (Atherbram Monty ex Atherbram Bridget)

1948

At **Crufts** the judge was Mr E Turner:
Dog CC: Ch Atherbram Nobbie
Bitch CC: Ch Claverdon Jet

Challenge Certificates were won by:
Dogs: Ch Atherbram Nobbie; Ch Waterman
Bitches: Ch Claverdon Jet; Oathill Sheila; Atherbram Brenda; Atherbram Breezey; Corner Lady; Dilys of Adlington

1949

Challenge Certificates were won by:

Dogs: Ch Atherbram Nobbie; Duke of Glascote; Ch Waterman; Burghpark Nigger; Shot of Forestholm.

Bitches: Ch Claverdon Black Satin; Atherbram Rosebud; Ch Oathill Sheila; Dilys of Adlington; Dorfield Judith; Towerwood Gift.

1950

At **Crufts** the Judge was Mr W Skerry

Dog CC:	Ch Waterman	**Dog RCC:**	Ch Atherbram Nobbie
Bitch CC:	Lilly Marlene	**Bitch RCC:**	Atherbram Rosebud

Challenge Certificates were won by:

Dogs: Ch Atherbram Nobbie; Ch Waterman; Ch Shot of Forestholm; Bryn of Adlington; Ch Patricia's Bruce; Claxton Cadet.

Bitches: Ch Lily Marlene; Ch Dorfield Judith; Ch Atherbram Rosebud; Dilys of Adlington; Forestholm Black Magic.

1951

At **Crufts** the Judge was Brigadier General F Lance.

Dog CC:	Ch Waterman	**Dog RCC:**	Waterboy
Bitch CC:	Flash of Ibaden	**Bitch RCC:**	Wrothampark Rettendon Wigeon

Challenge Certificates were won by:

Dogs: Ch Black Lion Rex of Ibaden; Ch Waterman; Ch Waterboy; Burghpark Nigger; Dairyman Mike; Patricia's Bruce; Pewcroft Plug; Forestholm Blackcock; Claxton Cadet.

Bitches: Ch Flash of Ibaden; Claverdon Firefly; Ch Pewcroft Pitch; Dairymaid Steller; Sequin of the Sherrards; Cover Girl; Wrothampark Rettendon Wigeon.

1952

At **Crufts** the Judge was Mr E Turner.

Dog CC:	Ch Waterman	**Dog RCC:**	Denmere Prince
Bitch CC:	Wrothampark Rettendon Wigeon	**Bitch RCC:**	Sequin of Sherrards

Challenge Certificates were won by:

Dogs: Ch Pewcroft Plug; Waterman; Forestholm Blarney; Ch Atherbram Nobbie; Black Lion Rex of Ibaden.

Bitches: Ch Watchful; Forestholm Jill of Homeland; Sh Ch Sequin of the Sherrards; Dairymaid Steller; Wrothampark Rettendon Wigeon; Pewcroft Pitch.

1953

At **Crufts** the judge was Mr R Kelland.

Dog CC:	Ch Waterman	**Dog RCC:**	Ponsbourne Black Knight
Bitch CC:	Lilly Marlene	**Bitch RCC:**	Wrothampark Rettendon Wigeon

Challenge Certificates were won by:

Dogs: Ch Roland Tann; Daleland Dastur; Ch Waterboy; Forestholm Blackcock; Ch Pewcroft Plug.

Bitches: Ch Lily Marlene; Dilys of Adlington; Ch Claverdon Powderbox; Ch Watchful; Ch Claverdon Waternymph; Towerwood Marie; Ch Pewcroft Pitch

1954

Challenge Certificates were won by:

Dogs: Ch Roland Tann; Ch Workman; Ch Forestholm Blackcock; Ch Waterboy; Atherbram Pedro; Shiner of Fredwell.

Bitches: Ch Pewcroft Picture: Claverdon Waternymph; Ch Lily Marlene; Claverdon Miss Tinker; Claverdon Powderbox.

1955

At **Crufts** the judge was Mrs Wentworth-Smith.

Dog CC:	Ch Workman	**Dog RCC:**	Ch Atherbram Pedro
Bitch CC:	Ch Watchful	**Bitch RCC:**	Grange Jane

Challenge Certificates were won by:

Dogs: Ch Workman; Sh Ch Forestholm Blackcock; Ch Atherbram Pedro; Claverdon Pegasus; Ch Roland Tann.

Bitches: Ch Claverdon Powderbox; Ch Claverdon Miss Tinker; Pewcroft Peep; Ch Pewcroft Proper; Pewcroft Prim; Ch Lily Marlene.

1956

At **Crufts** the judge was Mr F Parsons.

Dog CC:	Ch Workman	**Dog RCC:**	Forestholm Hawk
Bitch CC:	Ch Watchful	**Bitch RCC:**	Grange Jane

Challenge Certificates were won by:

Dogs: Ch Workman; Ch Atherbram Pedro; Sh Ch Forestholm Blackcock; Kim of Castlespie.

Bitches: Ch Pewcroft Proper; Ch Watchful; Mounthilly Bess; Woodland Picture; Ch Claverdon Miss Tinker; Atherbram Sarah.

1957

At **Crufts** the judge was Lt Col J Downer Powell.

Dog CC:	Ch Workman	**Dog RCC:**	Ch Atherbram Pedro
Bitch CC:	Ch Watchful	**Bitch RCC:**	Ponsbourne Beauty

Challenge Certificates were won by:

Dogs: Ch Pewcroft Prospector; Moorland Monarch; Ch Workman.

Bitches: Ch Watchful; Ch Pewcroft Proper; Ch Pewcroft Pitch; Biddy of Adlington; Mounthilly Bess; Atherbram Sarah.

1958

At **Crufts** the judge was Mrs L Bilton.

Dog CC:	Ch Workman	**Dog RCC:**	Adonis
Bitch CC:	Claverdon Tawney Pippet	**Bitch RCC:**	Happy Wanderer

Challenge Certificates were won by:

Dogs: Sh Ch Adonis; Ch Workman; Moorland Monarch; Waterboy of Springon; Sh Ch Lydisdale Lancer of Ardagh.

Bitches: Ch Asperula; Ch Claverdon Tawney Pippet; Alyssum; Ch Happy Wanderer; Ch Ryshot Misty Dawn.

Appendix A

1959

At **Crufts** the Judge was Mr A MacNab Chassels.

Dog CC: CH Workman   **Dog RCC:** Ryshot Dare
Bitch CC: Claverdon Tawney Pippet   **Bitch RCC:** Happy Wanderer.

Challenge Certificates were won by:

> **Dogs:** Ch Workman; Lydisdale Lancer of Ardagh; Pewcroft Pitcher: Ch Adonis; Claverdon Jorrocks of Lilling; Forestholm Donard.
>
> **Bitches:** Ch Claverdon Tawney Pippet; Ch Asperula; Pewcroft Prop of Yarlan; Ch Happy Wanderer; Ch Ryshot Misty Dawn.

1960

At **Crufts** the judge was Dr Nancy Laughton.

Dog CC: Sh Ch Pewcroft Pitcher   **Dog RCC:** Ch Adonis
Bitch CC: Ch Claverdon Tawney Pippet   **Bitch RCC:** Fenrivers Daffodil

Challenge Certificates were won by:

> **Dogs:** Sh Ch Pewcroft Pitcher; Sh Ch Lydisdale Lancer of Ardagh; Ch Claverdon Jorrocks of Lilling; Ch Adonis; Ryshot Copper Beau; Ryshot Incentive; Pewcroft Perch.
>
> **Bitches:** Ch Claverdon Tawney Pippet; Atherbram Bracken; Ch Asperula; Ch Pewcroft Prop of Yarlaw; Sandylands Rungles Witch; Halstock Dinah

1961

At **Crufts** the judge was Mr Colin Wells.

Dog CC: Ch Claverdon Jorrocks of Lilling   **Dog RCC:** Sh Ch Pewcroft Pitcher
Bitch CC: Ch Asperula   **Bitch RCC:** Halstock Dinah

Challenge Certificated were won by:

> **Dogs:** Ch Claverdon Jorrocks of Lilling; Ch Strathendrick Shadow; Ch Woodlark; Sh Ch Rungles Wag; Sh Ch Shadyoak Defender.
>
> **Bitches:** Ch Asperula; Sh Ch Sandylands Rungles Witch; Blakeholme Joke; Sh Ch Rungles Lady Barbara.

1962

At **Crufts** the Judge was Mr E Rowlands.

Dog CC: Ch Woodlark   **Dog RCC:** Pewcroft Perch
Bitch CC: Ch Pewcroft Prop of Yarlaw   **Bitch RCC:** Wave

Challenge Certificates were won by:

> **Dogs:** Ch Woodlark; Ch Forestholm Donard; Claverdon Skipper; Ch Strathendrick Shadow; Sh Ch Rungles Wag; Claverdon Comet.
>
> **Bitches:** Ch Pewcroft Prop of Yarlaw; Fredwell Rungles Happy Wendy; Sh Ch Sandylands Rungles Witch; Sh Ch Halstock Black Jewel; Blakeholme Jinny; Seira Buzz.

1963

At **Crufts** the Judge was Mr Warner Hill.

Dog CC and BOB:	Ch Woodlark	**Dog RCC:**	Sh Ch Rungles Wagg
Bitch CC:	Fredwell Rungles Happy Wendy	**Bitch RCC:**	Wave

Challenge Certificates were won by:

Dogs: Ch Woodlark; Ch Strathendrick Shadow; Ch Rungles Wag; Strathendrick Haze; Pewcroft Priam.

Bitches: Fredwell Rungles Happy Wendy; Wave; Sh Ch Hollowdale Wendy of Birchcott; Black Beauty of Luda; Sh Ch Halstock Black Jewel; Claverdon Seashanty.

1964

At **Crufts** the Judge was Mrs G Broadley.

Dog CC:	Sh Ch Rungles Wag	**Dog RCC:**	Skelddyke Blakeholme Jentyl.
Bitch CC and BOB:	Sh Ch Rungles Lady Barbara	**Bitch RCC:**	Halstock Black Donna.

Challenge Certificates were won by:

Dogs: Sh Ch Rungles Wag; Sh Ch Strathendrick Haze; Ch Claverdon Comet; Sh Ch Sandylands Challenge; Daleland Diplomat; Collyers Blakeholme Brewster.

Bitches: Sh Ch Rungles Lady Barbara; Sh Ch Ryshot Copper Bracken; Sh Ch Hollowdale Wendy of Birchott; Black Bird of Yarlaw; Stolford Hartshorn Memory; Seira Blackie; Dewmist Lullaby; Sh Ch Sandylands Rungles Witch.

1965

At **Crufts** the judge was Mrs A M Bilton.

Dog CC and BOB:	Sh Ch Sandylands Challenge	**Dog RCC:**	Fenrivers Golden Rod.
Bitch CC:	Hartshorn Mudlark	**Bitch RCC:**	Black Bird of Yarlaw

Challenge Certificates were won by:

Dogs: Collyers Blakholme Brewster; Hartshorn Mudlark; Sh Ch Sandylands Challenge; Jack of the Hill; Stolford Black Knight; Stolford Whinchat.

Bitches: Black Bird of Yarlaw; Hartshorn Mudlark; Ryshot Minx; Sh Ch Hollowdale Wendy of Birchcot; Sandylands Cloud; Ch Wave; Sh Ch Hartshorn Memory.

1966

At **Crufts** the judge was Mr J Braddon.

Dog CC:	Ch Fenrivers Golden Rod	**Dog RCC:**	Sh Ch Sandylands Challenge
Bitch CC and BOB:	Sh Ch Leighfoss Rungles Breeze	**Bitch RCC:**	Sandylands Cloud

Challenge Certificates were won by:

Dogs: Ch Fenrivers Golden Rod; Jack of the Hill; Downstream Hercules; Ch Stolford Whinchat; Waveman.

Bitches: Ch Black Bird of Yarlaw; Black Lass of Yarlaw; Halstock Jingle; Halstock Joanna; Halstock Juliette; Ryshot Velvet; Rungles Bryony; Sh Ch Leighfoss Rungles Breeze; Rungles Lady Barbara.

1967

At **Crufts** the judge was Mrs I Parsons.

Dog CC and BOB:	Ch Fenrivers Golden Rod	**Dog RCC:**	Ch Waveman
Bitch CC:	CH Ryshot Velvet	**Bitch RCC:**	Sh Ch Leighfoss Rungles Breeze

Challenge Certificates were won by:

Dogs: Ch Fenrivers Golden Rod; Donovan; Downstream Hercules; Longforgan Black Shadow; Ryshot Copper Ablaze; Ch Stolford Whinchat; Ch Waveman.

Bitches: Ch Ryshot Velvet; Heronsflight Black Bell of Yarlaw; Ryshot Hartshorn Snowdrop; Ch Woodpoppy.

1968

At **Crufts** the judge was Mr W Bradshaw.

Dog CC and BOB:	Ch Fenrivers Golden Rod	**Dog RCC:**	Tonggreen Sparrowboy.
Bitch CC:	Ch Stolford Wychmere Blackseal	**Bitch RCC:**	Lindenhall Blakeholme Justice.

Challenge Certificates were won by :

Dogs: Ch Fenrivers Golden Rod; Ch Donovan; Ryshot Conquest; Rungles Trewinnard Cornish Miner; Ryshot Copper Ablaze; Ch Stolford Whinchat; Tonggreen Sparrowboy.

Bitches: Ch Stolford Wychmere Blackseal; Ch Ryshot Velvet; Ch Woodpoppy; Ch Heronsflight Black Bell of Yarlaw.

1969

At **Crufts** the judge was Mrs D Whitwell.

Dog CC:	Ch Fenrivers Golden Rod	**Dog RCC:**	Ch Donovan
Bitch CC and BOB:	Ch Woodpoppy	**Bitch RCC:**	Ch Heronsflight Black Bell of Yarlaw

Challenge Certificates were won by:
> **Dogs:** Ch Fenrivers Golden Rod; Ryshot Copper Ablaze; Belsud Fellmist; Ch Tonggreen Sparrowboy; Cleve Trademark; Pegasus of Luda; Courtbeck Taurus; Ryshot Immaculate; Ch Downstream Hercules; Ch Stolford Wynchat; Walford Black Diamond.
> **Bitches:** Ch Woodpoppy; Ch Ryshot Velvet; Blakeholme Just So; Ch Stolford Wychmere Blackseal; Ryshot Minx.

1970

At **Crufts** the Judge was Mr M Gilliat.

Dog CC and BOB: Pegasus of Luda   **Dog RCC:** Ryshot Immaculate
Bitch CC: Sh Ch Halstock Joanna   **Bitch RCC:** Ch Stolford Wychmere Blackseal

Challenge Certificates were won by:
> **Dogs:** Pegasus of Luda; Fenrivers Kalmia; Courtbeck Mercury; Sh Ch Hallbent Gipsy Lad; Ch Tonggreen Sparrowboy; Parkburn Brandy Boy.
> **Bitches:** Blakeholme Heronsflight Try; Blakeholme Just So; Sh Ch Halstock Joanna; Ch Ryshot Velvet; Ch Stolford Wychmere Blackseal; Claverdon Flapper; Jane of Windgather; Stolford Missis Mopp.

1971

At **Crufts** the Judge was Mrs J Wells.

Dog CC: Ch Fenrivers Golden Rod   **Dog RCC:** Belsud Felmist
Bitch CC and BOB: Ch Woodpoppy   **Bitch RCC:** Ryshot Copper Ring O' Fire

Challenge Certificates were won by:
> **Dogs:** Ch Fenrivers Golden Rod; Woodway; Walford Black Diamond; Fenrivers Kalmia; Ch Oakmoss Ambassador; Longforgan Black Shadow; Ch Hallbent Gipsy Lad; Ch Courtbeck Mercury; Yarlaw Black Streak; Woodman; Parkburn Brandy Boy.
> **Bitches:** Ch Woodpoppy; Claverdon Flapper; Sh Ch Halstock Joanna; Ryshot Idyll; Blakeholme Just So; Hallbent Teal; Claverdon Fidelity; Downstream Calliope; Halstock Jemima of Wizardwood.

1972

Junior Warrant winners:
Andromeda of Kempton (Owner: Mrs D Ormsby)
Wizardwood Sandpiper (Owners: Mr and Mrs P Forster)

At **Crufts** the Judge was Mr R Flowers.

Dog CC and BOB: Ch Hallbent Gipsy Lad   **Dog RCC:** Claverdon Gaff
Bitch CC: Ch Blakeholme Just So   **Bitch RCC:** Black Fritta of Yarlaw

Challenge Certificates were won by:
Dogs: Bordercot Stolford Doonigan; Ch Courtbeck Mercury; Ch Fenrivers Kalmia; Ch Hallbent Gipsy Lad; Stolford Indelible; Wizardwood Sandpiper; Ch Woodman.
Bitches: Black Fritter of Yarlaw; Blakeholme Jumilla; Ch Blakeholme Just So; Braidwynn Halstock Titania; Collyers Skeets; Downstream Lamia; Heronsflight Sedge; Ch Ryshot Velvet; Tonggreen Courtbeck Venus.

1973

Junior Warrant winner:
Belsud Magpie (owner: Mrs M Grimes)

At **Crufts** the Judge was Mr W Cass.
   Dog CC and BOB: Ch Tonggreen Sparrowboy **Dog RCC:** Ch Woodman
     Bitch CC: Hallbent New Novel   **Bitch RCC:** Ch Tonggreen Courtbeck Venus

Challenge Certificates were won by:
    Dogs: Belsud Courtbeck Taurus; Ch Bordercot Stolford Doonigan; Hallbent Woodcock;
           Ch Oakmoss Ambassador; Sh Ch Parkburn Brandy Boy; Ch Tonggreen Sparrowboy;
           Ch Wizardwood Sandpiper; Ch Hallbent Gipsy Lad.
 Bitches: Andromeda of Kempton; Ch Black Fritta of Yarlaw; Ch Claverdon Fidelity;
           Ch Downstream Calliope; Hallbent New Novel; Halstock Alica of Wizardwood;
           Rase Rumaigne; Vbos Velma; Ch Tonggreen Courtbeck Venus.

1974

Junior Warrant winner:
Exclyst Bernard (Owner: Mrs Brenda Phillips)

At **Crufts** the judge was Mr J K Hart.
          Dog CC: Kenstaff Whipster   **Dog RCC:** Ch Wizardwood Sandpiper
  Bitch CC and BOB: Ch Black Fritta of Yarlaw **Bitch RCC:** Belsud Magpie

Challenge Certificate were won by:
    Dogs: Ch Belsud Courtbeck Taurus; Ch Bordercot Stolford Doonigan; Kenstaff Whipster;
           Torwood Trader; Ch Wizardwood Sandpiper.
 Bitches: Ch Black Fritta of Yarlaw; Braidwynn Beau Blue; Ch Claverdon Fidelity; Damases Tara;
           Hallbent New Novel; Halstock Alica of Wizardwood; Heronsflight Sedge; Ryshot
           Copper Ring of Fire; Stonemeade Gipsy Bell; Sh Ch Vbos Velma; Yonday Merry Maid.

1975

Junior Warrant winners:
Branchalwood Tummel (Owner: Mr D Bell)
Puhfuh Francesca (Owner: Mrs J Shore)
Puhfuh Phineas Finn (Owner: Mrs J Shore)

At **Crufts** the judge was Dr N Laughton.

Dog CC and BOB:	Ch Wizardwood Sandpiper	**Dog RCC:**	Monarch of Leurbost
Bitch CC:	Ch Claverdon Fidelity	**Bitch RCC:**	Black Fritta of Yarlaw

Challenge Certificates were won by:

Dogs: Ch Wizardwood Sandpiper; Glidesdown Teal; Rase Sambo; Ch Damases Tarquol of Ryshot; Ch Bordercot Stolford Doonigan; Monarch of Leurbost; Branchalwood Tummel; Exclyst Bernard; Leahador Wanderer of Tonggreen.

Bitches: Ch Claverdon Fidelity; Sh Ch Damases Tara; Ch Andromeda of Kempton; Ch Ryshot Copper Ring of Fire; Ch Black Fritter of Yarlaw; Kilbucho Honeybee; Ch Rase Rumaigne; Ch Stolford Missis Mopp; Flowerdown Ebony Sonata.

1976

Junior Warrant winners:

Elizabeth of Exclyst (Owner: Mrs Brenda Phillips)
Wizardwood Hawfinch (Owner: Mrs F Thomas)

At **Crufts** the Judge was The Hon Mrs A Jessel

Dog CC and BOB:	Ch Wizardwood Sandpiper	**Dog RCC:**	Ch Bordercot Stolford Doonigan
Bitch CC:	Ch Belsud Magpie	**Bitch RCC:**	Sh Ch Damases Tara

Challenge Certificates were won by:

Dogs: Ch Damases Tarquol of Ryshot; Ch Bordercot Stolford Doonigan; Exclyst Bernard; Ch Monarch Of Leurbost; Rase Romulus; Wizardwood Teal; Fenrivers Ling; Ch Puhfuh Phineas Finn; Ch Belsud Courtbeck Taurus.

Bitches: Ch Belsud Magpie; Sh Ch Damases Tara; Halstock Leonora; Belsud Blackcap; Belsud Reedling; Yonday Merry Maid; Puhfuh Francesca; Ch Stolford Missis Mopp; Ch Flowerdown Ebony Sonata; Elizabeth of Exclyst; Rase Pipistrelle; Sh Ch Vbos Velma; Ch Wizardwood Wigeon; Leahador Dusk of Tonggreen; Hallbent Teal

1977

Junior Warrant winner:

Belsud Black Kestrel of Waverton (Owner: Mr and Mrs Hutchinson)

At **Crufts** the judge was Mrs G Broadley.

Dog CC and BOB:	Fusilier of Ryshot	**Dog RCC:**	Ch Puhfuh Phineas Finn
Bitch CC:	Ch Elizabeth of Exclyst	**Bitch RCC:**	Ch Belsud Magpie

At the first **Flatcoated Retriever Society Championship Show** the judge was Mr Reed Flowers.

Best In Show and Bitch CC:	Barnway Springles
Best Opposit Sex and Dog CC:	Rase Romulus
Dog RCC:	Can and Am Ch Parkburn Deextenzing of Casuarina
Bitch RCC:	Tonggreen Song Linnet
Best Puppy:	Downstream Little Locket

Challenge Certificates were won by:
- **Dogs:** Fusilier of Ryshot; Ch Exclyst Bernard; Ch Rase Romulus; Fenrivers Ling; Black Wave of Halstock; Ch Wizardwood Hawfinch; Can/Am Ch Parkburn Deextenzing of Casuarina; Tonggreen Stream; Downstream Fiddler; Ch Bordercot Stolford Doonigan; Ch Monarch of Leurbost; Wizardwood Teal.
- **Bitches:** Ch Elizabeth of Exclyst; Ch Wizardwood Wigeon; Barnway Springles; Ch Leahador Dusk of Tonggreen; Ch Andromeda of Kempton; Sh Ch Kilbucho Honeybee; Braidwynn Halstock Titania; Kempton Antigone of Wolfhill; Ch Belsud Magpie; Downstream Little Locket; Sh Ch Yonday Merry Maid.

1978

Junior Warrant winners:
Branchalwood Frisa (Owner: Mr and Mrs Scott)
Shargleam Blackcap (Owner: Miss P Chapman)
Torwood Poppet (Owner: Mrs Griffiths)

At **Crufts** the Judge was Mrs P Robertson.

Dog CC and BOB:	Ch Puhfuh Phineas Finn	**Dog RCC:**	Ch Bordercot Stolford Doonigan
Bitch CC:	Ch Elizabeth of Exclyst	**Bitch RCC:**	Vbos Vogue

At **The Flatcoated Retriever Championship Show** the judge was Dr N Laughton.

Best in Show and Dog CC:	Woodland Whipcord
Dog RCC:	Ch Puhfuh Phineas Finn
Reserve BIS and Bitch CC:	Ch Leahador Dusk of Tonggreen
Bitch RCC:	Barnway Springles.

Challenge Certificates were won by :
- **Dogs:** Ch Puhfuh Phineas Finn; Ch Monarch of Leurbost; Sh Ch Wizardwood Hawfinch; Woodland Whipcord; Can Am Eng Ch Parkburn Deextenzing of Casuarina; Nortonwood Black Bart; Ch Belsud Black Buzzard; Ch Wizardwood Teal; Ch Rase Romulus.
- **Bitches:** Ch Wizardwood Wigeon; Ch Wizardwood Brown Owl; Ch Leahador Dusk of Tonggreen; Sh Ch Vbos Vogue; Ch Stolford Missis Mopp; Ch Rase Rumaigne; Yonday Willow Warbler of Shargleam; Nicks Jade; Halstock Primula of Ravenscrest.

1979

Junior Warrant winners:
Nashville Dawn of Segedunum (Owner: Mr and Mrs MacCallum)
Palnure Pride (Owner Mr and Mrs Dalziel)

At **Crufts** the Judge was Mrs V Yates.

Dog CC and BOB:	Ch Puhfuh Phineas Finn	**Dog RCC:**	Shargleam Blackcap
Bitch CC:	Ch Wizardwood Brown Owl	**Bitch RCC:**	Ch Yonday Willow Warbler of Shargleam

At **The Flatcoated Retriever Society Championship Show** the judges were Mrs J Mason (Dogs) and Mr P Johnson (Bitches).

BIS and Dog CC: Ch Puhfuh Phineas Finn **Dog RCC:** Shargleam Blackcap
Reserve BIS and Bitch CC: Ch Leahador Dusk of Tonggreen **Bitch RCC:** Woodland Wakeful

Challenge Certificates were won by:

Dogs: Ch Puhfuh Phineas Finn; Sh Ch Wizardwood Hawfinch; Sh Ch Nortonwood Black Bart; Ch Shargleam Blackcap; Ch Greinton Dugald; Bruderkern Rainbeau; Ch Belsud Black Buzzard; Ch Monarch of Leurbost; Kenjo Black Knight.

Bitches: Ch Wizardwood Brown Owl; Sh Ch Rase Pipistrelle; Ch Leahador Dusk of Tonggreen; Ch Midnight Star of Exclyst; Ch Yonday Willow Warbler of Shargleam; Ch Torwood Poppet; Branchalwood Maree; Skeldyke Arla of Bruderkern; Larg Linnet of Pendlewych.

1980

Junior Warrant winners:
Belsud Brown Guilimot; Bordercot Guy; Falswift Apparition;
Black Velvet of Candidicasa at Waverton; Larg Linnet of Pendlewych; Shargleam Sparrow Hawk; Tonggreen Swift Lark of Shargleam.

At **Crufts** the Judge was Mrs M Grimes.

Dog CC, BOB and BIS: Ch Shargleam Blackcap **Dog RCC:** Ch Puhfuh Phineas Finn
Bitch CC: Tormik Ash **Bitch RCC:** Sh Ch Rase Pipestrelle

At **The Flatcoated Retriever Society Championship Show** the judges were Mr C Wells and F/Lt G Snape.

Dog CC: Ch Shargleam Blackcap **Dog RCC:** Exclyst Imperial Mint
Bitch CC and BIS: Ch Shargleam Willow Warbler **Bitch RCC:** Tormik Ash

Challenge Certificates were won by:

Dogs: Ch Shargleam Blackcap; Ch Puhfuh Phineas Finn; Rase Orpheus; Ch Greinton Dugald; Tonggreen Squall; Tonggreen Stream; Bordercot Guy.

Bitches: Fabiennes Katoomba; Ch Shargleam Willow Warbler; Tormik Ash; Stantilaine Garnet of Glendaruel; Sh Ch Rase Pipestrelle; Wizardwood Little Owl; Skeldyke Arla of Bruderkern; Midnight Star of Exclyst; Halstock Primula of Ravenscrest; Maybrian Ballerina; Belsud Am I Wong of Rondix; Nashville Dawn of Segedunum; Shargleam Black Orchid; Tonggreen Swift Lark of Shargleam.

1981

Junior Warrant winners:
Branchalwood Kindar; Falswift Auriga; Shargleam Water Pipit;
Waddicombe Bulrush; Waverton Drambuie of Earlsworth; Withybed Country Maid of Shargleam.

At **Crufts** the judge was Mrs V Foss.

Dog CC and BOB: Ch Shargleam Blackcap **Dog RCC:** Ch Puhfuh Phineas Finn
Bitch CC: Ch Leahador Dusk of Tonggreen **Bitch RCC:** Nashville Dawn of Segedunum

At **The Flatcoated Retriever Society Championship Show** the judges were Miss Chester Perks and Mrs M Grimes.

Dog CC and BIS:	Ch Puhfuh Phineas Finn	**Dog RCC:**	Ch Shargleam Blackcap
Bitch CC:	Stantilaine Garnet of Glendaruel	**Bitch RCC:**	Halstock Bridget

Challenge Certificates were won by:
- **Dogs:** Ch Shargleam Blackcap; Ch Puhfuh Phineas Finn; Ch Bordercot Guy; Falswift Apparition; Ch Greinton Dugald; Wolfhill Box Car Willie; Tonggreen Sweet Pea.
- **Bitches:** Ch Leahador Dusk of Tonggreen; Halstock Bridget; Stantilaine Garnet of Glendaruel; Tonggreen Swift Lark of Shargleam; Ch Midnight Star of Exclyst; Ch Halstock Primula of Ravenscrest; Shargleam Black Abby of Withybed; Belsud Brown Guillemot; Sh Ch Nashville Dawn of Segedunum; Palnure Pride of Branchalwood; Branchalwood Maree; Torwood Poppet.

1982

Junior Warrant winners:
Blue Boy of Braidwynn; Brackernwood Talysman; Branchalwood Whinyeon; Darillens Super Trouper; Eskmill Boonwood; Nantiderri Playboy; Riversflight Twill; Shargleam Corncrake.

At **Crufts** the judge was Mrs Joan Mason.

Dog CC and BOB:	Ch Shargleam Blackcap	**Dog RCC:**	Tonggreen Sweet Pea
Bitch CC:	Withybed Country Maid of Shargleam	**Bitch RCC:**	Shargleam Water Pipit

At **The Flatcoated Retriever Society Championship Show** the judges were The Hon Mrs A Jessel and Mr G Lancaster.

Dog CC and BIS:	Ch Shargleam Blackcap	**Dog RCC:**	Downstream Nimble
Bitch CC:	Sh Ch Belsud Brown Guillemot	**Bitch RCC:**	Downstream Kittiwake

Challenge Certificates were won by :
- **Dogs:** Ch Shargleam Blackcap; Ch Puhfuh Phineas Finn; Ch Bordercot Guy; Ch Falswift Apparition; Ch Exclyst Imperial Mint; Ch Monarch of Leurbost; Withybed Country Lad; Shargleam Sparrow Hawk; Llecan Ambassador of Clowbeck.
- **Bitches:** Stantilaine Garnet of Glendaruel; Ch Tonggreen Swift Lark of Shargleam; Withybed Country Maid of Shargleam; Shargleam Black Abby of Withybed; Sh Ch Belsud Brown Guillemot; Exclyst Indian Mist of Clowbeck; Falswift Auriga; Branchalwood Whinyeon; Wolfhill Dolly Parton; Branchalwood Frisa; Ch Torwood Poppet; Ch Shargleam Water Pipit.

1983

Junior Warrant winners:
Falswith Black Storm; Heronsflight Pan's Promise; Pendlewych Plover; Pendlewych Puffin; Shargleam Fieldfare; Shargleam Willow Wren.

At **Crufts** the Judge was Mrs Audrey Forster.

Dog CC and BOB:	Ch Shargleam Sparrow Hawk	**Dog RCC:**	Ch Shargleam Blackcap
Bitch CC:	Ch Belsud Brown Guillemot	**Bitch RCC:**	Ch Shargleam Water Pipit

At **The Flatcoated Retriever Society Championship Show** the judges were Mr Reed Flowers amd Mrs S Johnson.

Dog CC and BIS:	Ch Shargleam Blackcap	**Dog RCC:**	Ch Bordercot Guy
Bitch CC:	Ch Shargleam Water Pipit	**Bitch RCC:**	Ch Branchalwood Whinyeon

Challenge Certificates were won by:

Dogs: Ch Shargleam Blackcap; Ch Bordercot Guy; Ch Falswift Apparition; Ch Exclyst Imperial Mint; Ch Monarch of Leurbost; Shargleam Sparrow Hawk; Wizardwood Tawny Owl; Tonggreen Squall; Emanon Parkgate Boy; Hallbent Kim; Heronsflight Pan's Promise.

Bitches: Glendaruel Gumboots; Ch Tonggreen Swift Lark of Shargleam; Withybed Country Maid of Shargleam; Ch Belsud Brown Guillemot; Falswift Auriga; Ch Branchalwood Whinyeon; Black Velvet of Candidacasa at Waverton; Ch Shargleam Water Pipit.

1984

Junior Warrant winners:

Branchalwood Mennock; Branchalwood Skye of Cleovine; Royal Merrymaker; Cliffordine Solo of Riversflight; Exclyst Quentin; Pendlewych Petrel; Withybed Holly Berry, Glidesdown Kingfisher.

At **Crufts** the judge was Dr Nancy Laughton.

Dog CC:	Ch Falswift Apparition	**Dog CC:**	Falswift Black Storm
Bitch CC and BOB:	Ch Belsud Brown Guilimot	**Bitch RCC:**	Amellia Astral

At **The Flatcoated Retriever Society Championship Show** the judges were Mr Dennis Izzard and Mrs Peggy Miller.

Dog CC:	Ch Bordercot Guy	**Dog RCC:**	Riversflight Arun
Bitch CC and BIS:	Exclyst Moonshine	**Bitch RCC:**	Paddiswood Affection

Challenge Certificates were won by:

Dogs: Ch Shargleam Blackcap; Ch Bordercot Guy; Ch Falswift Apparition; Ch Exclyst Imperial Mint; Torwood Blue; Ch Shargleam Sparrow Hawk; Waverdon Drambuie of Earlsworth; Torwood Puzzle at Lakemere; Ch Puhfuh Phineas Finn; Darillens Super Trouper; Rase Lysander; Maybrian Trail Blazer; Withybed Country Lad; Stantilaine Rory of Branchalwood; Shargleam Fieldfare; Branchalwood Kindar.

Bitches: Ch Withybed Country Maid of Shargleam; Ch Belsud Brown Guillemot; Ch Falswift Auriga; Ch Branchalwood Whinyeon; Exclyst Moonshine; Ch Larg Linnet of Pendlewych; Ch Shargleam Water Pipit; Wolfhill Dolly Parton; Exclyst Bernadette; Braemist Storm Lady of Riversflight.

1985

Junior Warrant Winners:

Branchalwood Iona; Clowbeck Fine Feathers; Eskmill Explorer; Kenjo Krackerjack; Pendlewych Piper; Pendlewych Pipit at Cleovine; Rase Gladiator; Riversflight Bobbin.

At **Crufts** the judge was Mrs Wells Meacham.

Dog CC and BOB:	Ch Bordercot Guy	**Dog RCC:**	Ch Shargleam Blackcap.
Bitch CC:	Ch Shargleam Water Pipit	**Bitch RCC:**	Withybed Country Lass

Appendix A

At **The Flatcoated Retriever Society Championship Show** the judges were Mr Bill Garrod and Mrs Brenda Phillips.

Dog CC and BOB:	Ch Shargleam Blackcap	**Dog RCC:**	Ch Bordercot Guy
Bitch CC:	Watchingwell Blackbottom	**Bitch RCC:**	Ch Halstock Bridget

Challenge Certificates were won by:

Dogs: Ch Shargleam Blackcap; Ch Bordercot Guy; Ch Falswift Apparition; Langfell Bright Star of Linfern; Ch Torwood Blue; Ch Heronsflight Pan's Promise; Sh Ch Hallbent Kim; Courtbeck Willow Wren; Bruderkern Consul; Sh Ch Emanon Parkgate Boy; Vbos Video; Shargleam Kingfisher; Tonggreen Storm Petrel; Ch Withybed Country Lad; Brackernwood Talysman; Ch Shargleam Fieldfare; Belsud Capercaille.

Bitches: Ch Belsud Brown Guillemot; Ch Falswift Auriga; Ch Branchalwood Whinyeon; Ch Shargleam Water Pipit; Ch Wolfhill Dolly Parton; Branchalwood Shira of Linfern; Watchingwell Black Bottom; Shargleam Willow Wren; Shargleam Turtledove of Fossdyke; Riversflight Aire; Branchalwood Iona; Black Velvet of Candidacasa; Falswift Black Lace; Pythingdean Black Cherry; Pendlewych Puffin; Pendlewych Plover; Wolfhill George Elliott; Glencooley Water Girl; Paulnure Pride of Branchalwood; Roglans Lady Arabella.

1986

Junior Warrant winners:

Black Squire; Wizardwood Black Magic of Shiredale; Shargleam Linnet; Hallbent Spring Lad by Withybed.

At **Crufts** the Judge was Mr Keith Hart.

Dog CC:	Ch Bordercot Guy	**Dog RCC:**	Ch Shargleam Blackcap.
Bitch CC and BOB:	Ch Halstock Bridget	**Bitch RCC:**	Riversflight Bobbin

At **The Flatcoated Retriever Society Championship Show** the judges were Miss Ogilvy Shepherd and Mrs R Brady.

Dog CC and BIS:	Ch Falswift Apparition	**Dog RCC:**	Hallbent Spring Lad
Bitch CC:	Withybed Country Lass	**Bitch RCC:**	Sh Ch Tormik Ash

Challenge Certificates were won by:

Dogs: Ch Shargleam Blackcap; Ch Bordercot Guy; Ch Falswift Apparition; Ch Heronsflight Pan's Promise; Sh Ch Emanon Parkgate Boy; Sh Ch Shargleam Kingfisher; Ch Withybed Country Lad; Brackernwood Talysman; Ch Shargleam Fieldfare; Sh Ch Maybrian Trail Blazer; Blue Boy of Braidwynn; Kenjo Woodpecker; Ch Exclyst Imperial Mint; Eskmill Boonwood; Ch Shargleam Sparrow Hawk; Russlare Zorro; Darillens Super Trouper; Glidesdown Kingfisher; Hallbent April Storm.

Bitches: Withybed Country Lass; Ch Branchalwood Whinyeon; Exclyst Moonshine; Ch Shargleam Water Pipit; Wolfhill Dolly Parton; Ch Halstock Bridget; Torwood Laughing Girl; Rase Iona of Fossdyke; Riversflight Bobbin; Maybrian Swanley Gem; Wolfhill George Elliott; Darillens Morning Dew; Palnure Pride of Branchalwood; Bruderkern Oliver; Sh Ch Shargleam Turtledove of Fossdyke; Yonday Pandora; Moelswood Belle of Lacetrom; Sh Ch Amelia Astral; Pendlewych Puffin; Ch Belsud Brown Guillemot.

1987

Junior Warrant winners:
Astral Avenger; Black Pearl of Falswift; Exclyst Vandyke;
Exclyst Viking; Exclyst Victoria; Falswift Ceasars Comet;
Llecan Gambit; Riversflight Bobbin; Riversflight Dulas; Riversflight Gwili; Riversflight Lady Dee;
Shargleam Kestrel; Viking Hendrick; Waverton Jullip.

At **Crufts** the judge was Mr Tony Pascoe.

Dog CC and BOB:	Ch Bordercot Guy	**Dog RCC:**	Belsud Black Jackdaw
Bitch CC:	Sh Ch Shargleam Willow Wren	**Bitch RCC:**	Wizardwood Black Magic.

At **The Flatcoated Retriever Society Championship show** the judges were Mrs A Forster and Mr Peter Johnson.

Dog CC:	Ch Heronsflight Pan's Promise	**Dog RCC:**	Puhfuh Gollywog
Bitch CC and BIS:	Wizardwood Black Magic of Shiredale	**Bitch RCC:**	Ch Branchalwood Whinyeon.

Challenge Certificates were won by:

Dogs: Ch Bordercot Guy; Ch Falswift Apparition; Ch Heronsflight Pan's Promise; Sh Ch Emanon Parkgate Boy; Sh Ch Shargleam Kingfisher; Ch Shargleam Fieldfare; Blue Boy of Braidwynn; Ch Exclyst Imperial Mint; Eskmill Explorer; Russlare Zorro; Darillens Super Trouper; Hallbent April Storm; Vbos Video; Rase Gladiator; Belsud Capercaillie; Wizardwood Tawny Pheasant; Withybed Silent Knight; Clowbeck Cock Robin; Agra of Newbury for Casuarina.

Bitches: Ch Branchalwood Whinyeon; Ch Exclyst Moonshine; Ch Riversflight Bobbin; Sh Ch Amellia Astral; Pendlewych Puffin; Everace Tender Seeker; Rase Iona of Fossdyke; Eskmill Gambit; Llecan Dove; Bright Star Brandysnap; Withybed Meadow Falcon of Gunmaker; Riversflight Weaver; Belsud Amber Owl; Waverton Julip; Ch Falswift Auriga; Pendlewych Puffin; Glendaruel Hilarity; Trisham Alice of Venazale; Sh Ch Shargleam Willow Wren; Wizardwood Black Magic of Shiredale.

1988

Junior Warrant winners:
Branchalwood Benvane; Branchalwood Stroan; Cleovine Meadow Foxtail; Cleovine Woodland Ringlet; Crystal Echo of Brigadell; Gayplume Pirouette; Hazelmere Hosta; Larksdown Fire Opal; Rodgwood Tobison; Ryliper Elm; Shargleam Gyr Falcon; Waverton Katinka; Venazale Charlock at Russlare.

At **Crufts** the judge was Mr L Page.

Dog CC:	Ch Withybed Country Lad	**Dog RCC:**	Ch Bordercot Guy
Bitch CC and BOB:	Ch Falswith Auriga	**Bitch RCC:**	Wizardwood Black Magic of Shiredale

At **The Flatcoated Retriever Society Championship Show** the judges were Mrs Joan Mason & Miss Pat Chapman.

Dog CC:	Sh Ch Darillens Super Trouper	**Dog RCC:**	Black Squire.
Bitch CC and BIS:	Herringstone's Little Gem	**Bitch RCC:**	Ch Branchalwood Whinyeon

Challenge Certificates were won by:
Dogs: Ch Bordercot Guy; Sh Ch Shargleam Kingfisher; Ch Shargleam Fieldfare; Exclyst Viking; Sh Ch Eskmill Explorer; Sh Ch Russlare Zorro; Sh Ch Darillens Super Trouper; Hallbent April Storm; Vbos Video; Belsud Black Jackdaw; Ch Wizardwood Tawny Pheasant; Ch Withybed Country Lad; Visam Gimlet; Grangehurst Brambly Hedge; Withybed Silent Knight; Shargleam Kestrel; Wizardwood Tawny Quail; Starmoss El Dorado.

Bitches: Ch Exclyst Moonshine; Riversflight Aire; Ch Amelia Astral; Sh Ch Llecan Dove; Bright Star Brandysnap; Sh Ch Riversflight Weaver; Belsud Amber Owl; Waverton Katinka; Ch Falswift Auriga; Glendaruel Hilarity; Ch Wolfhill Dolly Parton; Sh Ch Wolfhill George Elliot; Herringstone's Little Gem; Saucy Susie of Gayplume; Wizardwood Black Magic of Shiredale; Clowbeck Fine Feathers; Gelhamson Huastec; Sh Ch Bruderkern Olivia; Sh Ch Shargleam Skylark of Shardik; Sh Ch Wizardwood Water Witch; Falswift Black Lace; Shargleam Lapwing; Riversflight Lady Dee; Pythingdean Country Girl.

1989

Junior Warrant winners:
Black Pearl of Ajays; Clowbeck Polystickle; Enchanters Nightshadow; Exclyst Watchman; Fenstorm Indi; Larksdown Coral; Rase Brigantine; Ravenhall Aperitif; Riversflight Shuttle; Shargleam Meadow Lark; Shargleam Sedge Warbler; Uskelf Dillon; Websters Choice.

At **Crufts** the judge was Mr Arnold Hall.

Dog CC and BOB:	Emanon Water Starwort	**Dog RCC:**	Ch Heronsflight Pan's Promise
Bitch CC:	Sh Ch Herringstone's Little Gem	**Bitch RCC:**	Shargleam Willet of Elvelege

At **The Flatcoated Retriever Society Championship Show** the judges were Mr Read Flowers and Mrs Rosemerry Talbot.

Dog CC:	Ch Shargleam Kestrel	**Dog RCC:**	Belsud Black Jackdaw
Bitch CC and BIS:	Sh Ch Visam Margarita at Madison	**Bitch RCC:**	Ch Wizardwood Water Witch

Challenge Certificates were won by:
Dogs: Sh Ch Shargleam Kingfisher; Falswift Black Storm; Sh Ch Vbos Video; Ch Belsud Capercaille; Sh Ch Visam Gimlet; Ch Shargleam Kestrel; Emanon Water Starwort; Watchingwell Foxtrot; Candease A Hard Day's Night; Venazale Charlock at Russlare; Sh Ch Vbos Vervine; Belsud Little Black Hen Harrier; Roscoe Bowdart; Riverbank Swift; Sh Ch Clowbeck Cock Robin; Heronsflight Magic.

Bitches: Exclyst Victoria; Sh Ch Bright Star Brandysnap; Sh Ch Waverton Katinka; Sh Ch Glendaruel Hilarity; Sh Ch Herringstone's Little Gem; Sh Ch Clowbeck Fine Feathers; Sh Ch Bruderkern Olivia; Ch Wizardwood Water Witch; Riversflight Lady Dee; Sh Ch Visam Margarita at Madison; Glidesdown Wendy; Alderby Shimmering Beck; Shargleam Willet of Elvelege; Branchalwood Penwhrin; Pendlewych Puffin; Heronsfleet Sugar'n'Spice; Branchalwood Benvane; Waverton Julip; Pendlewych Plover; Paddiswood Burnt Lobelia.

1990

Junior Warrant winners:
Larksdown Quartz at Fenstorm; Shargleam Black Thorn; Cleespring Chiroubles of Marlcot; Cleespring Chambertin; Tribryn Canna Queen of Rainscourt.

At **Crufts** the Judge was Mr George Lancaster.

Dog CC:	Brown Keston of Varingo	**Dog RCC:**	Candease A Hard Day's Night
Bitch CC:	Wizardwood Silver Fox	**Bitch RCC:**	Sh Ch Glidesdown Wendy

At **The Flatcoated Retriever Society Championship Show** the judges were Mrs P Westrop and Mrs M Grimes.

Dog CC and BIS:	Llecan Gambit	**Dog RCC:**	Withybed Quartermaster of Huntersdale.
Bitch CC:	Gadfly Cinnamon Sedge	**Bitch RCC:**	Shargleam Sedge Warbler

Challenge Certificates were won by:

Dogs: Llecan Gambit; Candease A Hard Day's Night; Heathland Gamekeeper; Sh Ch Ebony Kingsman; Ch Belsud Black Jackdaw; Sh Ch Falswith Black Storm; Ch Belsud Capercaille; Sh Ch Vbos Vervine; Sh Ch Exclyst Viking; Ch Shargleam Kestrel; Happy Harry; Ch Heronsflight Pan's Promise; Heronsflight Magic; Exclyst Watchman; Larksdown Fire Opal; Exclyst Vandyke; Astral Avenger; Branchalwood Stroan; Ch Shargleam Kingfisher; Brown Keston of Varingo.

Bitches: Gadfly Cinnamon Sedge; Sh Ch Bright Star Brandysnap; Ch Wizardwood Water Witch; Belsud Brown Quail; Sh Ch Glendaruel Hilarity; Saucy Suzie of Gayplume; Shargleam Linnet; Colona Black Satin; Shargleam Wood Sorrel; Sh Ch Riversflight Lady Dee; Cleovine Feathered Thorn; Ch Waverton Julip; Ch Heronsflight Moss; Sh Ch Glidesdown Wendy; Colona Moonlight; Sh Ch Exclyst Victoria; Shargleam Sedge Warbler; Sh Ch Branchalwood Benvane.

1991

Junior Warrant winners:
Gayplume Dixie; Waverton Maderia; Ambercroft Blackthorn of Belsud; Gayplume Domino; Paravan Hazel; Hartshead Victoria Black.

At **Crufts** the judges were The Hon Mrs A Jessel and Mr Read Flowers.

Dog CC and BOB:	Ch Shargleam Kingfisher	**Dog RCC:**	Clandrift Black Admiral
Bitch CC:	Sh Ch Bright Star Brandysnap	**Bitch RCC:**	Sh Ch Glidesdown Wendy

At **The Flatcoated Retriever Society Championship Show** the judges were Mrs C Dugdale and Mr G Lancaster.

Dog CC and BIS:	Ch Branchalwood Stroan	**Dog RCC:**	Llecan Gambit
Bitch CC:	Sh Ch Riversflight Lady Dee	**Bitch RCC:**	Exclyst Sequin

At **The Flatcoated Retriever Club of Scotland Championship Show** the judge was Mr P Johnson.

Dog CC:	Branchalwood Stroan	**Dog RCC:**	Wizardwood Tawny Quail
Bitch CC and BIS:	Wizardwood Water Witch	**Bitch RCC:**	Ch Waverton Katinka

Appendix A

Challenge Certificates were won by:
Dogs: Ch Shargleam Kngfisher; Ch Branchalwood Stroan; Sh Ch Visam Gimlet; Ch Exclyst Watchman; Heronsflight Magic; Taranbeck Mossberg; Sh Ch Ebony Kingsman; Sh Ch Heathland Gamekeeper; Sh Ch Larksdown Fire Opal; Ch Happy Harry; Sh Ch Llecan Gambit; Shargleam Black Thorn; Venazale Charlock at Russlare; Lacetrom Cardow of Bordercot; Clowbeck Bourach.

Bitches: Wizardwood Water Witch; Colona Black Satin; Waverton Katinka; Paddiswood Burnt Lobelia; Sh Ch Glidesdown Wendy; Withybed Meadow Falcon of Gunmakers; Shargleam Wood Sorrel; Sh Ch Saucy Susie of Gayplume; Shargleam Wood Fern of Goldingale; Braemist Dusky Queen; Exclyst Sequin; Gayplume Dixie; Shargleam Willet of Elvelege; Ravenhall Aperitif; Sh Ch Exclyst Victoria; Ebony Gleam of Darillens.

1992

Junior Warrant winners:
Riversflight Juba; Tom Thumb; Shargleam Song Swift; Exclyst Bristol Cream of Ravenhall; Shargleam Heather Warbler; Windyhollows Phantom.

At **Crufts** the Judge was Miss Pat Chapman.

Dog CC:	Shirdale Magic Moments	**Dog RCC:**	Ch Branchalwood Stroan
Bitch CC and BOB:	Sh Ch Gayplume Dixie	**Bitch RCC:**	Ch Wizardwood Water Witch

At **The Flatcoated Retriever Society Championship Show** the judges were Mr Peter Forster and The Hon Mrs A Jessel.

Dog CC and BIS:	Ch Branchalwood Stroan	**Dog RCC:**	Bumblyn Joshua Jopp
Bitch CC:	Ch Riversflight Bobbin	**Bitch RCC:**	Braemist Dusky Queen.

At **The Flatcoated Retriever Club of Scotland Championship Show** the judge was Mrs R Furness.

Dog CC:	Ch Branchalwood Stroan	**Dog RCC:**	Kintore of Rosenberg
Bitch CC:	Ch Waverton Maderia	**Bitch RCC:**	Cleovine Thyme of Pendlewych.

Challenge Certificates were won by:
Dogs: Shirdale Magic Moments; Ch Branchalwood Stroan; Sh Ch Taranbeck Mossberg; Sh Ch Kenjo Black Mark; Ch Pendlewych Puma; Ch Shargleam Black Thorn; Ch Brown Keston of Varingo; Ch Happy Harry; Sh Ch Heathland Gamekeeper; Kintore of Rosenberg; Sh Ch Lacetrom Cardow of Bordercot; Ebony Saxon Prince; Sh Ch Clowbeck Bourach; Rhapsody the Dark Knight; Kulawand Wood Nymph of Windyhollows; Cleovine Derrynane; Ch Candease A Hard Day's Night; Sh Ch Llecan Gambit; Sh Ch Larksdown Fire Opal.

Bitches: Sh Ch Gayplume Dixie; Ch Riversflight Bobbin; Sh Ch Shargleam Sedge Warbler; Ch Waverton Maderia; Sh Ch Braemist Dusky Queen; Ch Waverton Katinka; Sh Ch Riversflight Inny; Hallbent Winter Berry; Black Pearl of Ajays; Trisham Alice of Venazale; Sh Ch Glidesdown Wendy; Eskmil Intrigue; Larksdown Coral; Colona Sunwheel.

1993

Junior Warrant winners:
Wizardwood Rough Water; Hartshead Conquering Hero; Cannimore Vagabond; Rainscourt Baron; Rainscourt Beck; Stranfaer Trooper.

At **Crufts** the Judge was Mrs R Brady.

Dog CC and BOB:	Ch Happy Harry	**Dog RCC:**	Ch Exclyst Watchman
Bitch CC:	Ch Paddiswood Burnt Lobelia	**Bitch RCC:**	Sh Ch Shargleam Willet of Elveledge

At **The Flatcoated Retriever Society Championship Show** the judges were Mrs P Miller and Mrs S Johnson.

Dog CC and BIS:	Sh Ch Kenjo Black Mark	**Dog RCC:**	Kysheemy Countryman of Pythingdean
Bitch CC:	Ch Wizardwood Water Witch	**Bitch RCC:**	Everace Tender Seeker

At **The Flatcoated Retriever Club of Scotland Championship Show** the judge was Mrs S McCombe.

Dog CC:	Sh Ch Llecan Gambit	**Dog RCC:**	Pendlewych Puma
Bitch CC and BIS:	Ch Wizardwood Water Witch	**Bitch RCC:**	Laxton Felltrina

Challenge Certificated were won by:

Dogs: Ch Branchalwood Stroan; Sh Ch Kenjo Black Mark; Ch Pendlewych Puma; Ch Brown Keston of Varingo; Ch Happy Harry; Sh Ch Heatherland Gamekeeper; Kintore of Rosenberg; Sh Ch Lacetrom Cardow of Bordercot; Sh Ch Clowbeck Bourach; Kulawand Wood Nymph of Windyhollows; Sh Ch Llecan Gambit; Sh Ch Larksdown Fire Opal; Ch Exclyst Watchman; Gilduffe Fiach; Braemist Fire Falcon; Tom Thumb.

Bitches: Sh Ch Gayplume Dixie; Sh Ch Braemist Dusky Queen; Ch Waverton Katinka; Sh Ch Glidesdown Wendy; Ch Wizardwood Water Witch; Ch Paddiswood Burnt Lobelia; Braidwynn Briony; Sh Ch Bright Star Brandysnap; Daisy May at Dunctonwood; Wizardwood Firefly of Heronsfleet; Branchalwood Penwhirn; Branchalwood Fionnlighe;Grangehurst Total Eclipse; Bitcon Castaspell; Ravenhall Aperitif; Foxoaks Peewit at Wizardwood; Coalport Coral Sky; Shiredale Magic Touch.

1994

Junior Warrant winners:
Riversflight Kelsa; Riversflight Leader; Alkhamurst First Edition; Braidwynn Bonnie Lad; Waverton Renaissance; Websters Choice.

At **Crufts** the judges were Mrs Brenda Phillips and Mrs Mari McCallum.

Dog CC and BOB:	Ch Branchalwood Stroan	**Dog RCC:**	Sh Ch Kenjo Black Mark
Bitch CC:	Gayplume Pirouette	**Bitch RCC:**	Hartshead Misty Swansong

At **The Flatcoated Retriever Society Championship Show** the judges were The Hon Mrs A Jessel and Mrs P Miller.

Dog CC and BIS:	Exclyst Bristol Cream	**Dog RCC:**	Ch Exclyst Watchman
Bitch CC:	Paraven Hazel	**Bitch RCC:**	Riversflight Kelsa

Appendix A

At **The Flatcoated Retriever Club of Scotland Championship Show** the judge was Mrs Joan Mason.

Dog CC:	Kintore of Rosenberg	**DogRCC:**	Ch Lacetrom Cardow of Bordercot
Bitch CC and BIS:	Ch Wizardwood Water Witch	**Bitch RCC:**	Hartshead Misty Swansong

Challenge Certificates were won by:

Dogs: Exclyst Bristol Cream of Ravenhall; Sh Ch Kintore of Rosenberg; Ch Branchalwood Stroan; Ch Exclyst Watchman; Ambercroft Black Thorn of Belsud; Sh Ch Braemist Fire Falcon; Sh Ch Clowbeck Bourach; Hartshead Conquering Hero; Sh Ch Kenjo Black Mark; Sh Ch Larksdown Fire Opal; Ch Tom Thumb; Sh Ch Withybed Quartermaster of Huntersdale; Donascimento Black Pearl; Stranfaer Trooper; Candease Eight Days A Week.

Bitches: Gayplume Pirouette; Paraven Hazel; Sh Ch Coalport Coral Sky; Ch Wizardwood Water Witch; Branchalwood Fionnlighe; Ch Shargleam Wood Fern of Goldingale; Sh Ch Shiredale Magic Touch; Ch Spira Moonlit Sapphire; Sh Ch Bitcon Cast A Spell; Gadfly Cinnamon Sedge; Sh Ch Gayplume Dixie; Exclyst Bewitched; Ravenhall Barley Wine; Alkhamhurst First Edition; Orambourn Liquorice Fizz at Lakemere; Colona Moonlight; Wizardwood Zephyr.

Post War Winners in Field Trials

1947

The first post-war Field Trial was held by **The Flatcoated Retriever Association**. This was an **All-Aged (A/A) Stake**.

- 1st: Greenfield June
- 2nd: Patch of Sauch
- 3rd: Maesmynan Patricia

1948

The Flatcoated Retriever Society held its first **All-Aged Stake**.

- 1st: Maesmynan Patricia
- 2nd: Nobby of Riverside
- 3rd: Greenfield June
- 4th: Oathill Sheila

Gamekeepers Flatcoat Club

- 1st: Maesmynan Patricia
- 2nd: Oaklady
- 3rd: Oathill Sheila

1949

A/A Stake

- 1st: Joy of Riverside
- 2nd: Ch Claverdon Jet
- 3rd: Nobby of Riverside
- 4th: Ch Waterman

Open Stake

- 4th: Nobby of Riverside

1950

A/A Stake

- 1st: Joy of Riverside
- 2nd: Ch Claverdon Jet
- 3rd: Maesmynan Patricia
- 4th: Ponsbourne Black Sue

1951

A/A Stake

- 1st: Ch Claverdon Jet
- 2nd: Joy of Riverside
- 3rd: Overash Ben
- 4th: Claverdon Rettendon Whistler

1952

A/A Stake

- 1st: Overash Ben
- 2nd: Ch Waterboy
- 3rd: Claverdon Rye Whiskey
- 4th: Claverdon Powderbox

1953

A/A Stake

- 1st: Ch Waterboy
- 2nd: Ch Claverdon Waternymph
- 3rd: Towerwood Marie
- 4th: Bob of Riverglade

Any Variety (AV) Gundog Open Stake

- 2nd: Ch Waterboy

1954

A/A Stake

- 1st: Ch Claverdon Powderbox
- 2nd: Ch Waterboy
- 3rd: Ch Workman

Any Variety Gundog Trials

- 3rd: Non-winner (N/W): Bob of Riverglade
  Minor Awards (N/W): Overash Ben

1955

A/A Stake

- 3rd : Ch Flash of Ibaden

Reserve: Ch Waterboy

1956

A/A Stake

- 1st: Ch Waterboy
- 2nd: Pewcroft Page
- 3rd: Shinner of Fredwell
- 4th: Claverdon Tawney Pippet

1957

A/A Stake

- 1st: Alyssum
- 2nd: Pewcroft Page
- 3rd: Ch Waterboy
- 4th: Claverdon Turtledove

AV Gundog Trials

3rd N/W: Pewcroft Page

1958

A/A Stake
  2nd: Claverdon Beaujolais;
  3rd: Ch Waterboy;
  Res: Pewcroft Page
AV Gundog Trials
  3rd Novice: Claverdon Beaujolais

1959

Claverdon Jorrocks of Lilling: 1st F/C Open,
                               1st A/A
Claverdon Sailor: 3rd Novice
Claverdon Skipper: 4th and COM
                    Puppy
Pewcroft Page: 1st Open
Claverdon Beaujolais: 2nd F/C Open,
                      2nd A/A
Claverdon Tawney Pippet: 4th F/C
Pewcroft Pageant: COM F/C Open
Pewcroft Prop of Yarlaw: 3rd N/W, 3rd
                         Novice
Wave: 3rd F/C Open,
      3rd A/A

1960

Claverdon Clipper: 4th F/C Open
Claverdon Comet: 4th F/C Novice
Claverdon Jorrocks of Lilling: 4th and COM
                               Open
Claverdon Skipper: 1st F/C Open
Claverdon Turtledove: 3rd Open, 3rd
                      Novice
Pewcroft Pagent: 4th Open
Pewcroft Prop of Yarlaw: 2nd Novice,
                         2ndA/A,
                         4th N/W
Wave: 1st F/C Novice

1961

Claverdon Corker: 3rd Open
Claverdon Jorrocks of Lilling: 4th A/A, 3rd A/A
Claverdon Skipper: 3rd A/A
Woodlark: 2nd F/C N/W
Claverdon Cindy: COM F/C Open
                 and Novice
Claverdon Turtledove: 1st F/C N/W,
                      1st F/C Open
Pewcroft Prop of Yarlaw: 2nd Open
Wave: 4th Open

1962

Claverdon Jorrocks of Lilling: 3rd and 4th Open
Claverdon Skipper: 2nd Open, COM A/A
Claverdon Vivacious: 3rd Amateur
Collyers Patch: 1st Puppy
Hartshorn Moonshine: 2nd F/C N/W,
                     4th Novice
Pewcroft Prop of Yarlaw: 1st F/C Open

1963

Collyers Blakeholme Brewster: COM Puppy
Albifrons: COM
           N/W 62, 63
           and 64
Fenrivers Fern: 2nd N/W
Claverdon Cindy: 3rd N/W
Hartshorn Midnight: 3rd Open
Hartshorn Moonshine: COM A/A and
                     COM Open in 63
                     and 64
Hartshorn Sou'wester: COM Puppy and
                      Novice
                      2 x COMs 64

1964

Black Prince of Yarlaw: 1st N/W
Ch Claverdon Comet: 2nd F/C Open,
                    COM N/W
Claverdon Jorrocks Junior: 2nd COM Open
Collyers Blakeholme Brewster: 4th N/W
Claverdon Cindy: 2nd F/C N/W,
                 3rd F/C Open,
                 COM Open
Claverdon Patch: COM Open
Fenrivers Evergreen: 4th Open
Hartshorn Midnight: 2nd Open
Hartshorn Sorrel: 3rd F/C N/W,
                  1st F/C Open,
                  COM Open

1965

Ch Claverdon Comet: COM A/A
Ch Collyers Blakeholme
Brewster: 2 x COMs Puppy N/W
          1st N/W AV
Blakeholme Jenet: COM N/W
Claverdon Cindy: COM A/A , COM Open F,
Hartshorn Moonshine: 2nd Open F/C
Hartshorn Sorrel: 1st Open F/C
Albifrons: 3rd Open F/C,
           COM Open A/V

1966

Black Prince of Yarlaw:	1st F/C A/A
Collyers Blakeholme Brewster:	3rd F/C A/A
Woodlark:	4th A/A
Beechshaw Riversedge Jess:	1st Puppy N/W
Blakeholme Jenet:	3rd F/C N/W
Claverdon Rhapsody:	2nd N/W,
	2nd F/C N/W
Collyers Patch:	COM
Waveman:	COM
Hartshorn Moonshine:	COM
Dewmist Lullaby:	4th F/C Novice
Downstream Manto:	4th F/C N/W
	1st F/C Novice
Hartshorn Bluebell:	2nd F/C Novice
Hartshorn Sorrel:	2nd F/C A/A,
	1st, 4th and
	COM Open
Hartshorn Sou'wester:	3rd F/C Novice
Miss Suzie:	1st F/C N/W

1967

Hartshorn Sorrel became a Field Trial Champion.

Collyers Blakeholme Brewster:	COM A/A
Nesfield Michael:	COM N/W,
	COM Open
Claverdon Rhapsody:	2nd Open and
	other awards
Int FT Ch Hartshorn Sorrel:	1st Open

1968

Black Prince of Yarlaw:	1st F/C A/A
Claverdon Nesfield Gunner:	COM A/A
Collyers Blakeholme Brewster:	COM A/A,
	3rd A/A
Donovan:	COM
Downstream Manto:	COM
Nesfield Helmar of Maar:	COM
Hartshorn Nesfield Maggie:	3rd F/C A/A
Miss Suzie:	2nd F/C A/A
Woodpoppy:	4th F/C A/A

1969

Ch Collyers Blakeholme Brewster:	COM A/A,
	1st F/C A/A
Nesfield Michael:	1st Open
Walford Black Diamond:	4th F/C A/A
Downstream Charm of Roysia:	2nd F/C A/A
Downstream Manto:	3rd F/C A/A
Hartshorn Nesfield Maggie:	COM A/A
Int FT Ch Hartshorn Sorrel:	2nd Open
Nesfield Halmar of Maar:	3rd Novice.

1970

Nesfield Michael became a Field Trial Champion

FT Ch Nesfield Michael:	1st Open
Ch Tonggreen Sparrowboy:	4th F/C A/A
Black Fritter of Yarlaw:	COM
Hartshorn Peg:	COM
Claverdon Fantasia:	1st F/C A/A
Downstream Manto:	2nd F/C A/A
Int FT Ch Hartshorn Sorrel:	3rd F/C A/A,
	2 COMs Open

1971

Rondix Tsai-Chin:	1st F/C Open
Collyers Skeets:	2nd F/C Open,
	3rd F/C N/W
Downstream Charm of Roysia:	4th F/C Open

1972

Int FT Ch Hartshorn Sorrel:	3rd F/C A/A,
	COM Open
Halstock Exclyst Lucinda:	4th F/C A/A,
	2nd F/C N/W
Penmayne Woodwave:	COM A/A
Claverdon Gaff:	4th Open,
	1st N/W
Woodsprite:	3rd F/C N/W
Courtbeck Mercury:	4th F/C N/W
Lingwood Collyers Brinkman:	COM
Collyers Skeets:	COM
Downstream Robina:	COM
Whipling:	COM

1973

Claverdon Gaff:	3rd F/C A/A, COM
Biddy of Claverdon:	COM, 2nd Open
Penmayne Woodwave:	3rd N/W, 2nd N /W
Claverdon Little Jem:	3rd N/W
Halstock Exclyst Lucinda:	3rd Novice, 1st N/W, 2nd N/W
Linda of Puhfuh:	2nd F/C N/W
Wizardwood Whimbrel:	3rd Novice, 2nd A/A

1974

Briston Otter:	4th N/W
Claverdon Lionheart:	4th F/C A/A, 2 x COMs
Kenstaff Whipster:	2nd F/C A/A
Magic Dive:	1st F/C A/A, 2 x COMs
Rum Punch of Warresmere:	2nd F/C N/W
Downstream Robina:	1st N/W
Halstock Exclyst Lucinda:	3rd Open
Wizardwood Whimbrel:	1st F/C A/A, COM A/A
Rondix Tsai Chin:	3rd F/C A/A
Werrion Redwing of Collyers:	3rd F/C N/W, 3rd N/W

1975

Fenrivers Ling:	1st Open
Magic Dive:	2nd F/C Open
Rondix Tsai Chin:	3rd F/C Open
Rum Punch of Warresmere:	4th F/C Open, 1st F/C N/W
Claverdon Kiss:	2nd F/C N/W
Blakeholme Joy:	4th F/C N/W
Wizardwood Whimbrel:	4th Open
Kenstaff Whipster:	COM
Wizardwood Wigeon:	COM
Woodland Waxwing:	COM
Torwood Trader:	COM
Downstream Fiddler:	4th N/W

1976

Werrion Redwing of Collyers:	1st F/C N/W, 3rd N/W
Blakeholme Joy:	2nd F/C N/W, 4th Open, 3rd Open
Claverdon Kiss:	3rd F/C N/W
Rum Punch of Warresmere:	1st F/C Open
Torwood Trader:	2nd F/C Open
Wizardwood Whimbrel:	4th Open
Bruderkern Witch Hazel of Tarncourt:	2nd Novice
Rondix Tsai Chin:	COM
Woodland Waxwing:	COM

1977

Werrion Redwing of Collyers:	1st F/C Open
Bruderkern Witch Hazel of Tarncourt:	2nd A/A
Woodland Waxwing:	3rd F/C Open
Downstream Kittiwake:	3rd F/C N/W
Penmayne Pepper:	2nd F/C N/W
Venazale Prunella:	3rd F/C N/W
Rum Punch of Warresmere:	2nd Open, 3rd Open, COM N/W

1978

Werrion Redwing of Collyers became a Field Trial Champion

Marlcot Nicks Otter:	2nd F/C N/W
Harecroft Samba:	3rd F/C N/W
FT Ch Werrion Redwing of Collyers:	1st F/C Open, 1st A/A, 3rd A/A
Wizardwood Whimbrel:	2nd F/C Open
Penmayne Pepper:	3rd F/C Open
Magic Dive:	4th F/C Open, COM Open
Rum Punch of Warresmere:	COM Open

1979

Woodland Whipcord: 2nd F/C N/W
Moatwood Maytime: 3rd F/C N/W
Tarncourt Byron: 2nd F/C Open
Bracken of Warresmere: 3rd F/C Open
Puhfuh Ferdinand: 4th F/C Open
FT Ch Werrion Redwing of
Collyers:
Wizardwood Whimbrel: COM F/C Open
Rase Ocelot: 4th N/W
Kenstaff Damson
of Glenwherry: 1st N/W
Fenrivers Myosotis: COM
Heronsflight Toss of Casuarina: COM
Tarncourt Bronte: COM
Torwood Delinquent: COM

1980

Tarncourt Byron: 1st A/A,
2nd Puppy N/W,
4th N/W,
2nd F/C A/A

Collyers Rose Mallow of
Palgrave: 1st A/A
Penmayne Pepper: 4th F/C A/A
Woodland Whipcord: 3rd F/C A/A
Torwood Delinquent: COM F/C A/A
Warresmere Cedar: 4th F/C N/W

1981

Collyers Mannered: F/C N/W
Tarncroft Crofter: 2nd Novice
Claverdon Ladybird: 2nd N/W AV
COM A/A
Torwood Potty: 3rd N/W AV
Exclyst Kittywake: 2nd F/C N/W
FT Ch Werrion Redwing of
Collyers: 3rd F/C A/A
Warresmere Cedar: 4th F/C A/A
Warresmere Woodruff: 3rd Novice AV
Windmill Rob Roy: COM N/W F/C
Black Velvet of Candidacasa
at Waverton: COM Puppy
N/W AV
Pebble Picker: COM N/W F/C

1982

FT Ch Werrion Redwing of
Collyers: 4th F/C A/A
Claverdon Lysander: COM F/C A/A
Torwood Percel: 3rd F/C N/W
Waddicombe Bulrush: 4th F/C N/W,
2nd Novice AV,
COM F/C N/W
Collyers Mannered: COM F/C N/W
Tarncourt Crofter: 1st F/C N/W,
COM N/W AV
2nd Novice AV
Warresmere Woodruff: 2nd F/C N/W,
COM N/W AV
Ansoncha Greenwell Glory: COM F/C N/W
Creekside Dinas of Leeglen: 3rd N/W AV
Gunstock Collyers Mustered: COM Novice AV
Tarncourt Charm: 1st F/C N/W
Windmill Ellarene: 3rd F/C A/A
Claverdon Ladybird: 2nd F/C A/A,
2 x 2nd A/A AV
Warresmere Cedar: 2nd F/C N/W,
1st F/C A/A
Torwood Dazzler: 4th N/W
Black Velvet of Candidacassa
at Waverton: COM F/C N/W,
N/W AV

1983

Werrion Junket: 4th F/C A/A,
COM
Claverdon Lysander: 4th F/C N/W,
COM
Torwood Vignette: COM F/C N/W
Tarncourt Crofter: 2nd F/C A/A AV,
COM A/A AV
24-dog
Warresmere Woodruff: 1st F/C N/W AV,
COM F/C A/A
Creekside Dinas of Leeglen: 2nd F/C N/W,
2nd Novice AV
Gunstock Collyers Mustered: 2 COMs N/W,
COM A/A F/C,
COM Novice AV

1983 (continued)

Tarncourt Charm:	1st F/C A/A
Claverdon Ladybird:	2nd F/C A/A,
	COM A/A,
	COM AV
Warresmere Ceder:	2nd F/C N/W,
	1st F/C A/A
Black Velvet of Candidacassa	
at Waverton:	COM F/C N/W
Tarncourt Clover:	COM F/C N/W,
	2nd F/C A/A
Riversflight Twill:	3rd Novice AV,
	3rd F/C N/W
Jane of Ortolan:	3rd Novice AV
Laurentia Moonfly:	4th F/C N/W
Westering Salute:	2nd F/C N/W,
	2nd Novice AV
Glenwherry Hazel:	3rd F/C A/A,
	1st F/C N/W
Fenrivers Pheasant Eye:	3rd F/C N/W

1984

Burnet of Kentene at	
Casuarina:	4th Puppy N/W AV,
	2 COMs N/W
Eskmill Boonwood:	3rd F/C N/W
Marlcot Nicks Dolphin:	4th F/C N/W
Torwood Blue:	4th N/W AV,
	COM F/C N/W
Creekside Dinas of Leeglen:	1st F/C N/W
Fenrivers Pheasant Eye:	3rd F/C A/A
Tarncourt Charm:	1st F/C A/A,
	3rd Open AV
	24-dog
Claverdon Ladybird:	4th F/C A/A AV
Warresmere Wishful:	2nd F/C N/W
Warresmere Sandstone:	COM F/C N/W
Tarncourt Nimbus:	2nd F/C N/W
Westering Salute:	2nd F/C A/A

1985

Glenwherry Cinammon:	3rd F/C N/W
Glenwherry Saffron:	1st F/C N/W
Casuarina Kwacha:	2nd F/C N/W
Paddiswood Affection:	4th F/C N/W,
	3rd Novice AV
Tarncourt Plover:	2nd Open AV
Tarncourt Charm:	COM Open AV
Burnet of Kentene at	
Casuarina:	COM Open AV
Creekside Dinas of Leeglen:	COM A/A AV
Gunstock Collyers Mustered:	COM A/A F/C
Torwood Blue:	1st A/A F/C
Warresmere Wishfull:	2nd N/W AV,
	COM A/A F/C
Tarncourt Noteable:	1st N/W AV,
	2nd A/A AV
	24-Dog
Downlands Jessica:	1st N/W AV
Glenwherry Tansy:	3rd N/W AV
Kernewekcum Pigeon:	COM N/W AV
Casuarina Merveille du Jour	
of Collyers:	COM N/W AV

1986

Midnight Lad of Leeglen:	2nd N/W F/C
Belsud Black Jackdaw:	COM N/W F/C
Tinebrook Donna:	COM N/W F/C
Falswift Black Jewel of	
Larksdown:	3rd N/W F/C
Zephyr of Ditchingham:	2nd N/W AV
Prince Henry of Hasweth:	COM A/A F/C
Tarncourt Noteable:	1st A/A F/C,
	COM Open AV
Tarncourt Naiad:	2nd A/A F/C
Gelhamson Quechua:	3rd A/A F/C,
	1st Novice AV
Ch Torwood Blue:	3rd Open AV
Glenwherry Tansy:	1st N/W F/C
Waverton Grenadine at	
Peckers:	COM N/W F/C,
	COM Novice AV

1986 (continued)

Glenwherry Saffron:	4th and COM A/A F/C
Fraginpani of Casuarina:	COM N/W F/C
Jane of Ortolan:	COM Novice AV
Tarncourt Charm:	COM Nominated Stake AV
Paddiswood Affection:	1st N/W F/C

1987

Gelhamson Quechua:	1st A/A AV
Tarncourt Noteable:	2nd A/A F/C, 4th Open AV
Bold Bokhara:	COM F/C N/W, 4th A/A F/C
Jane of Ortolan:	1st F/C N/W
Mandinka Hullabaloo:	2nd F/C N/W, 1st F/C N/W
Risalda of Casuarina:	3rd F/C N/W
Gunstock Dark Ranger:	4th and COM F/C N/W
Falcons Spectre:	COM F/C N/W
Glenwherry Cinnamon:	4th and COM F/C N/W
Buckleberry Bell of Wavendon:	COM F/C N/W
Prince Henry of Hasweth:	3rd A/A F/C
Ch Torwood Blue:	4th A/A AV
Shargleam Reed Warbler:	3rd Novice AV
Tarncourt Naiad:	COM N/W AV, 1st Novice AV

1988

Brown Keston of Varingo:	COM F/C Novice
Cliffordine Solo of Riversflight:	1st Novice F/C
Hermitage Hector:	4th and COM Novice, 1st F/C Open
Wemdon Bright Bond of Tarncourt:	1st Novice AV
Wemdon Mears Wader:	COM F/C Novice

1988 (continued)

Belsud Black Jackdaw:	2nd F/C Novice, COM N/W AV
Gunstock Dark Ranger:	COM F/C Novice
Leeglen Midnight Lady:	2nd F/C Novice, 2nd Novice AV
Riversflight Bobbin:	3rd Novice
Jane of Ortolan:	3rd F/C Open
Gelhamson Quechua:	4th and COM F/C Open, COM Open AV
Bold Bokhara:	3rd Novice, 1st Novice AV
Tarncourt Noteable:	3rd Open AV, 2nd Open, 4th Open AV
Smiler of Claverdon:	COM N/W AV, 1st Novice AV
Tarncourt Rejoice:	2nd Novice AV, 1st Open AV
Claverdon Defender:	3rd Novice AV

1989

Apollo of Arts:	1st Novice AV
Bryshot August Sun:	COM Novice AV
Darrells Crocodillo:	3rd Novice AV
Heathland Juniper:	2nd F/C Novice
Mister Pip of Taurgo:	COM F/C Novice
Riversflight Genil:	COM Novice AV
Tarncourt Ranger of Collyers:	COM F/C Novice
Warresmere Pedlar:	4th Novice
Brown Keston of Varingo:	3rd F/C Novice
Claverdon Defender:	2nd F/C Novice, 2nd F/C Open
Wemdon Bright Bond of Tarncourt:	1st A/A AV, COM A/A AV, 1st F/C Open.

1989 (continued)

Artemis The Huntress:	1st Novice AV
Claverdon Dime:	3rd Novice AV
Buckleberry Bell of Wavendon:	4th Novice AV
Tarncourt Rejoice:	COM Open AV
Belsud Black Jackdaw:	COM F/C Novice

1990

Hipsley Henry:	1st Novice, 4th Open F/C
Jet of Staverton:	2nd Novice, COM N/W AV, 1st Open F/C
Claverdon Dime:	COM Novice, 4th Novice AV, 1st A/A F/C
Mister Pip of Taurgo:	COM Novice
Hazelmere Hosta:	COM Novice
Riversflight Genil:	1st Novice
Brown Keston of Varingo:	2nd Novice F/C, 3rd and COM Novice AV
Valeborne Campion:	3rd Novice F/C
Noiroche Aquarius:	4th Novice F/C
Wavendon Blackberry:	COM Novice
Warresmere Pedlar:	COM Novice
Tarncourt Rejoice:	2nd Open F/C, 3rd AV Open 24-dog
Bold Bokhara:	3rd Open F/C
Heathland Juniper:	3rd Novice AV
Shopnoller Sarah of Staverton:	1st Novice AV
Leeglen Midnight Lady:	3rd AV
Wemdon Bright Bond of Tarncourt:	3rd A/A AV, COM Open AV 24-dog, COM Open AV 24-dog
Artemis the Huntress:	3rd AV Open

1991

Brown Keston of Varingo:	1st Novice F/C, COM A/A F/C
Bryshot August Sun:	2nd Novice F/C

Valeborn Campion:	3rd Novice F/C
Trioaks Raffle:	4th Novice F/C
Warresmere Pedlar:	COM Novice F/C
Noiroche Aquarius:	COM Novice F/C, COM A/A F/C
Tarncourt Little Oak:	1st A/A F/C
Smiler of Claverdon:	3rd A/A F/C
Shopnoller Sarah of Staverton:	4th A/A F/C, 3rd Open F/C
Heathland Juniper:	COM A/A F/C
Jet of Staverton:	4th Open F/C, COM AV, 1st Open AV
Dawgil Which Wong of Staverton:	2nd Novice F/C, 1st Nov AV
Fenstorm Kyalami:	3rd Novice F/C
Claverdon Dandy:	COM Novice F/C
Wizardwood Dark Legend:	COM Novice AV
Cleovine Gipsy Moth:	COM Novice AV
Emanon Black Satin of Auro:	3rd Novice AV

1992

Twinwood Yes Sir:	3rd A/A F/C
Cleovine Gipsy Moth:	1st Open F/C
Jet of Staverton:	2nd Open F/C
Bold Bokhara:	3rd Open F/C
Exclyst Wild Silk of Collarm:	1st Novice F/C
Trioaks Raffle:	COM Novice F/C, COM Novice AV, 3rd Novice AV
Valeborn Campion:	COM Novice F/C
Kiri Leighwarren at Wolfhill:	1st Novice F/C
Leeglen Enboy:	2nd Novice F/C
Wavendon Loganberry:	3rd Novice F/C
Mr Thomas Traddles of Taurgo:	4th Nov F/C
Ch Riversflight Bobbin:	COM Novice F/C
Heathland Juniper:	COM Novice F/C
Moonlight Padarn:	1st Novice AV, 2nd A/A AV
Goosander George:	2nd Novice AV
Mystic Spirit:	1st Restricted Novice
Riversflight Irthing of Holloway:	4th Restricted Novice

1993

Moonlight Padarn:	1st Open F/C
Shopnoller Sarah of Staverton:	2nd Open F/C
Riversflight Irthing of Holloway:	4th Open F/C, COM Novice F/C, 1st Restricted Novice, COM A/A AV, 2nd A/A AV
Ch Brown Keston of Varingo:	COM Open F/C
Trioaks Raffle:	COM Novice F/C, COM AV Novice, 2nd A/A F/C, 3rd AV Novice
Trioaks Alice of Tunnelwood:	COM Novice F/C, COM A/A F/C and AV, 2nd Novice AV
Valeborn Campion:	COM Novice F/C, COM A/A F/C
Leeglen Enboy:	1st A/A F/C
Riversflight Gwili:	COM A/A F/C
Leeglen Jazz:	COM A/A F/C
Balham Girl:	1st Novice F/C
Leeglen Paris:	3rd Novice
Staverton Tinker:	COM Novice F/C
Highbird Bold Imperial:	COM Novice F/C
Twinwood Yes Sir:	1st Restricted Novice
Kenar Rondo:	2nd Restricted Novice
Hallbent Dorabella:	3rd Novice AV

1994

Twinwood Yes Sir:	1st Restricted Novice
Kenar Rondo:	2nd Restricted Novice
Fossdyke Bronze Justin:	COM Restricted Novice
Leeglen Jazz:	1st A/A F/C
Riversflight Irthing of Holloway:	1st Novice F/C
Trioaks Alice at Tunnelwood:	1st AV Novice
Claverdon Raffles of Collyers:	1st Novice F/C

FT Ch Werrion Redwing of Collyers

Born .8.5.73

Parents	Grandparents	Great-grandparents	Great-great-grandparents	Great-great-great-grandparents
Ch Wizardwood Sandpiper	Ch Tonggreen Sparrowboy FTA	Ch Fenrivers Golden Rod FTA	Ch Woodlark FTA	Ch Waterboy FTW
				Ch Claverdon Tawney Pippet FTW
			Fenrivers Evergreen FTA	Ch Atherbram Pedro
				Alyssum FTW
		Tonggreen Swift	Pewcroft Priam	Pewcroft Pegasus
				Pewcroft Peep FTA
			Rettendon Linnet	Pewcroft Praetor
				Rettendon Plover
	Halstock Jemima of Wizardwood	Halstock Downstream Daniel	Ch Woodlark FTA	Ch Waterboy FTW
				Ch Claverdon Tawney Pippet FTW
			Salrik Donna	Fenrivers Fern FTA
				Blakeholme Waterwitch
		Halstock Julia	Pewcroft Perch	Gaff of Riverside
				Pewcroft Peep FTA
			Halstock Black Jewel	Ryshot Rungles Trademark
				Halstock Dinah
Collyers Juno	Tonggreen Starling	Ch Fenrivers Golden Rod FTA	Ch Woodlark FTA	Ch Waterboy FTW
				Ch Claverdon Tawney Pippet FTW
			Fenrivers Evergreen FTA	Ch Atherbram Pedro
				Alyssum FTW
		Tonggreen Swift	Pewcroft Priam	Pewcroft Pegasus
				Pewcroft Peep FTA
			Rettendon Linnet	Pewcroft Praetor
				Rettendon Plover
	Collyers Skeets FTA	Ch Collyers Blakeholme Brewster FTW	Blakeholme Jem	Sh Ch Pewcroft Pitcher
				Blakeholme Joke
			Rettendon Spoonbill	Arthur of Fizzgigg
				Rettendon Bullfinch FTA
		Collyers Rose	Ch Collyers Blakeholme Brewster FTW	Blakeholme Jem
				Rettendon Spoonbill
			Collyers Christina	Claverdon Skipper FTW
				Collyers Chiffchaff

Int FT Ch Hartshorn Sorrel

Born..3.4.62

Int FT Ch Hartshorn Sorrel	Gen 2	Gen 3	Gen 4	Gen 5	Gen 6
Int FT Ch Hartshorn Sorrel	Teal of Hawk's Nest — Owner.. Brian Farr Esq JP, Worksop Manor, Nottingham.	Gaff of Riverside	Nobby of Riverside FTA	Smoke of Riverside FTA	Wizard of Riverside
					Lassie
				Sheafhayne Gypsy FTA	Atherbram Gunner
					Cemlyn
			Waaf of Riverside	Dusk of Riverside	Ch Atherbram Prince
					Blackdale Hush
				Bryn Asaph Fair Trade FTW	Bryn Asaph Quick Step
					Trade FTW
		Pewcroft Peep FTA	Sweep of Riverside	Dusk of Riverside	Ch Atherbram Prince
					Blackdale Hush
				Bryn Asaph Fair Trade FTW	Bryn Asaph Quick Step
					Trade FTW
			Pewcroft Peg	Atherbram Warrior	Atherbram Gunner
					Atherbram Jetty
				Pewcroft Plague	Pewcroft Puzzler
					Pewcroft Pest
	Nesfield Stratton — Owner..Mr Wilson Stephens, White Hill F'Hse, Pitton, Salisbury. SP5 1DY	Pewcroft Page FTW	Sweep of Riverside	Dusk of Riverside	Bryn Asaph Quick Step
					Trade FTW
				Bryn Asaph Fair Trade FTW	Ch Atherbram Prince
					Blackdale Hush
			Pewcroft Peg	Atherbram Warrior	Atherbram Gunner
					Atherbram Jetty
				Pewcroft Plague	Atherbram Gunner
					Atherbram Jetty
		Sh Ch Claverdon Miss Tinker	Ch Atherbram Nobby	Atherbram Monty	Atherbram Gunner
					Cemlyn
				Atherbram Bridget	Ch Atherbram Prince
					Atherbram Bess
			Claverdon Celest	Revival of Ettington	Technician
					Miss Celeste
				Ch Claverdon Jet FTW	Atherbram Gunner
					Cemlyn

FT Ch Nesfield Michael

Born...17.4.65

Breeder and Owner:
Major H A Wilson

Blakeholme Joiner	Ch Workman FTA	Ch Waterman FTW	Atherbram Simon	Toby of the Hill
				Atherbram Duchess
			Atherbram Meg	Atherbram Gunner
				Atherbram Jetty
		Claverdon Faith FTW	Revival of Ettington	Technician
				Miss Celeste
			Ch Claverdon Jet FTW	Atherbram Gunner
				Cemlyn
	Pewcroft Prim	Denmere Prince	Patch of Sauch	Dusk of Riverside
				Brek
			Dot of Sauch	Bang of Riverside
				Brek
		Ch Pewcroft Pitch	Bryn of Adlington	Rastus of Adlington
				Gwyneth of Adlington
			Pewcroft Peg	Atherbram Warrior
				Pewcroft Plague
Hartshorn Midnight	Ch Woodlark FTA	Ch Waterboy FTW	Ch Waterman FTW	Atherbram Simon
				Atherbram Meg
			Claverdon Faith FTW	Revival of Ettington
				Ch Claverdon Jet FTW
		Ch Claverdon Tawney Pipit FTA	Claverdon Pewcroft Pieman FTW	Sweep of Riverside
				Pewcroft Peg
			Ch Claverdon Powderbox FTW	Ch Waterman FTW
				Ch Claverdon Jet FTW
	Nesfield Stratton	Pewcroft Page FTW	Sweep of Riverside	Dusk of Riverside
				Bryn Asaph Fair Trade FTW
			Pewcroft Peg	Atherbram Warrior
				Pewcroft Plague
		Sh Ch Claverdon Miss Tinker	Atherbram Nobby	Atherbram Monty
				Atherbram Bridget
			Claverdon Celeste	Revival of Ettington
				Ch Claverdon Jet FTW

Ch/Ir Ch Shargleam Blackcap (Hips...Pass) Born...26.6.77

Breeder and Owner:
Miss P Chapman

Ch Dameses Tarquol of Ryshot	Ch Tonggreen Sparrowboy FTA	Ch Fenrivers Golden Rod FTA	Ch Woodlark FTA	Ch Waterboy FTW
				Ch Claverdon Tawney Pippet FTW
			Fenrivers Evergreen FTA	Ch Atherbram Pedro
				Alyssum FTW
		Tonggreen Swift	Pewcroft Priam	Pewcroft Pegasus
				Pewcroft Peep FTA
			Rettendon Linnet	Pewcroft Praetor
				Rettendon Plover
	Hallbent Contessa	Hallbent Woodcock	Ch Fenrivers Golden Rod FTA	Ch Woodlark FTA
				Fenrivers Evergreen FTA
			Hallbent Happy Wanderer	Halstock Bo'sun
				Strathendrick Dawn
		Hallbent Dusk	Sh Ch Stolford Black Knight	Ch Stolford Whinchat
				Ch Stolford Hartshorn Memory
			Strathendrick Dawn	Ch Strathendrick Shadow
				Claverdon Veracity
Ch Yonday Willow Warbler of Shargleam	Kenstaff Whipster FTA	Int Sh Ch Wood Man	Ch Tonggreen Sparrowboy FTA	Ch Fenrivers Golden Rod FTA
				Tonggreen Swift
			Ch Woodpoppy FTA	Ch Woodlark FTA
				Hartshorn Sweetbriar
		Birchinlee Wendy	Ch Coulallanby Remus	Ch Fenrivers Golden Rod FTA
				Halstock Delia
			Ryclose Julie	Black Ace of Yarlow
				Blakeholme Donna
	Claverdon Flapper	Teal Of Hawks Nest	Gaff of Riverside	Nobby of Riverside FTA
				Waaf of Riverside
			Pewcroft Peep FTA	Sweep of Riverside
				Pewcroft Peg
		Claverdon Rhapsody FTA	Black Friar of Yarlaw	Claverdon Sweep
				Ch Pewcroft Prop of Yarlaw FTW
			Claverdon Cindy FTA	Bob of Riverglade FTA
				Claverdon Turtledove FTW

Shooting Dog
Certificate

Introduction

The Shooting Dog Certificate (SDC) was introduced in the 1981/2 season to encourage the breeding of better working Flatcoated Retrievers. Hitherto we had to rely on the few field trial awards and the recommendation of owners as to their dog's prowess in the shooting field for reliable information before breeding from our dogs.

The Shooting Dog Certificate was devised as a yardstick for testing the inherited characteristics that are so essential when breeding a useful working dog: soft mouth, quietness, temperament and game-finding on an ordinary shooting day.

The day

1   Not more than four dogs are tested on one day. This ensures that the day is not disruptive.

2   There are two judges: one from The Kennel Club Field Trial Panel and one from the SDC Organising Committee of The Flatcoated Retriever Society.

3   The four dogs sit by the guns to be tested for steadiness and quietness at a drive. If they show any tendency to run in, they are put on leads.

4   If possible the dogs are required to retrieve from water, but where this is not possible the handler may apply to the Society for a special test at a later date in order to complete their Certificate.

5   Provided that a dog is quiet at a drive he may be granted a 'B' Certificate even if he has to be on a lead. Dogs both quiet and steady may be granted an 'A' Certificate.

6   The handlers are required to keep their dogs under control all the time; not just for short periods when in line.

7   The judges are looking for a good shooting dog that is quiet and biddable and that proves to be a useful companion in the shooting field.

8   It is hoped that by the introduction of this certificate the standards of working Flatcoats will be improved for the good of all shooting people.

Since 1981, 113 dogs and bitches have passed the Shooting Dog Certificate.

Type in Flatcoats
by Stanley L O'Neill

(As it appeared in British Yearbook - 1957)

HEAD TYPE IN FLATCOATS

Dr Laughton asked me to write on the formative years but I feel that the typewriter is again going to run away on to something else. It seems little use writing on the formative years when so many know so little of what was formed.

Some eight years ago it came to notice that a book on Dogs in Britain from a great publishing house stated that the Flatcoat had a wedge-shaped head. This made me choke but Mr Cooke, to my surprise, was indisposed to rush in with a contradiction and thought we had need to go carefully. He surprised me again by saying there were Flatcoat breeders whose motto was 'A good stop and a good square muzzle' - a still more blatantly wrong description. At his age he felt unequal to the task of steering a clear course between Scylla and Charybdis in the event of a controversial storm blowing up. He thought the whole position badly charted and urged me to clear the matter up. He pledged his full support if I would but warned me I should find my authorities hard to come by in case of argument. There was no argument. I made a public contradiction and there were no back-answers from either author or publisher - but those authorities were hard to find!

All writers were agreed that few understood the head; that such understanding was of major importance and very hard to acquire; but none of them ever got down to the job of describing it. Mr Cooke said it was something everyone knew but no-one had defined, knowledge handed down and picked up by contact. He thought there had been some break in the continuity through the decline in numbers and this had become a complete gap in the 1939 - 1945 stoppage. He attributed much of this process to the growth of the commercial outlook which made breeders unwilling to further the true or accepted type where it conflicted with the type of their own dogs. There could be something in this view, but it must be observed that, many years earlier, some forthright critics, like the famous Dick Sharpe, had blamed Cooke himself for not adhering firmly to type. What Cooke certainly did was to give a decided lead to the movement in the middle twenties for reducing size, in itself, I think, a reasonable and sensible aim. However, 'a small dog at all costs' seemed to become an over-riding law, and at the Crystal Palace in 1930, Mr Cooke, after judging, made an open statement that on account of size he had put out of the prizes what he described as 'the best dog in the country if he were only half-an-inch less'. Cooke himself was soon showing a larger dog again, like 'Kiss' and her brothers 'Mate' and 'Kipper' but the effects of the smaller dogs were to be seen in the newer generation. By 1933 the red light was shining clear when a freak like 'Bank Boo' could figure prominently in the prize list. Small, short and plump, with a head like a dab of dough and legs like foreign matchsticks, she resembled nothing so much as the Christmas sugar pigs of my childhood. Just how much of the typical features of the breed were lost in this size-slide will never now be determined but it must be nearly twenty years ago that in a critical assessment of some of the results I remember writing that the proportions of the dog had been changed completely. We could have expected when things had settled down to have lost an inch of height and half-an-inch of head-length, but we had in fact shed at most half-an-inch of height but lost at least a full inch of head. In his report of the first championship show after the War, the judge, Mr Simms, concluded his general remarks with, 'But where have our beautiful heads gone?'

The Standard itself could be more informative and does not always conform to the rules accepted up to the time of its publication in 1924. It must be remembered that the Standards were not then the universally authoritative documents that they seem to be considered to-day and the authors of ours certainly never considered it in that light. Many of the great all-rounders who had so long been the great repositories and arbiters of type were still on the scene. Theo Marples incorporated the Standard in his handbook, 'Show Dogs' but when he asked if any statements in his article contravened it in any respect, he was given to understand that the Standard was meant as a guide to the important features of a working dog. For detail and fancy points people must refer to Marples and his Show colleagues. Ten years after the Standard was published, Harding Cox, a very old man, still stood alone as an entry-puller. In that year, 1934, he did the article on Flatcoats for Hutchinson's, giving his own description and standard of points, without reference to the Associations's Standard. Cox, who owned the 'Black' prefix, probably did more to produce the Flatcoat as we know it than anyone else, Shirley not excepted. In the nineties he was the Architect and the Builder of the Flatcoat which had its Golden Age, on the Bench and in the Field, from 1900 to 1910. It seems a great pity that this distinguished writer, critic, judge and breeder was not consulted in the drafting of our Standard.

Everyone used to know that a Flatcoat should be clean in lip. It is axiomatic: Marples emphasizes it; Cox is definite. It is not a fancy point. In the days when the retriever was being made it was held that a dog hated feathers because he couldn't get rid of them. His method of freeing himself is to rub his mouth and lips on the ground. A clean short lip would allow feathers to be brushed out much more easily than a long heavy flew. Right or wrong - and I believe our grandfathers had the last word in wisdom on the subject - it was the theory in vogue at the time the breed was being formed and was one of the specifications to which it was built. And yet I saw, at one of the more recent annual Festivals in the Olympian Hall itself, the judge make three determined efforts to tug the flews of a particularly clean-lipped bitch well below her lower jaw. His grip slipped twice but at the third attempt, flew gripped between thumb and forefingers and knuckles getting leverage under the lower jaw, he succeeded, to the dog's great discomfort, in doing ... I hope he knew what.

All writers agree that the foreface should be broad at the nostril but none mentions depth. Obviously it will not have the square finish at the tip which the heavier-lipped breeds show but in actual substance and skeletal structure a good Flatcoat foreface is at least as strong and deep as any Gundog breed.

There is nothing of the two-brick formation about the head. It is a one-piece casting. The foreface runs at the sides gradually into the skull, giving a well-filled-up appearance under the eyes. The amount of moulding varies in individuals but Cox's observation that the eyes are placed rather wide is very significant. They are set in the side of the head: definitely not 'front-on'. The upper line of the foreface may also be said to merge gradually into the skull. The nose runs straight back to the top of the eyes and with a slight upward incline between the eyebrows, continues as a diminishing furrow into the general flatness of the skull. The amount of the incline is quite specific: it must be slight, just sufficient to prevent a 'Downface' or 'Dishface'. Townend Barton, who in 1913 wrote perhaps the most valuable article of all on Flatcoats in his book *Gundogs*, makes a point of this furrow. As he had the qualification of MRCVS, perhaps we must grant this furrow some special significance too.

The Standard says ears should be small. Cox says they should be of fair length. Some judges and writers have tried to make a fancy point of this small ear. This is not intended. I am old enough to remember the controversy as to whether the aural organs should be protected by a large heavy flap like a spaniel or whether the flap should be neat and less likely to be caught and torn in rough cover. The sponsors of the Standard declared their agreement with the latter school of thought.

I have always felt in strong sympathy with a famous and forthright old judge of the days when I was learning how to count and spell, named Helliwell, who advised a man to give up dogs if he had to use the span of his hand and the widths of his fingers to measure the proportions of a head: 'Tha'll be carrying a foot-rule wi' thee instead of thy pipe. Tha'll make nowt o' dogs if tha can't measure 'em wi' thy eye.' Nevertheless, one can't fail to note that, whilst most who have written about Flatcoats have told us that the distance from the occiput to the inner corner of the eye should be the same as from the eye to nostril, nobody says a word as to how the breadth of the foreface at any part should compare with its length or with the breadth of the skull or even - what seems quite simple - how the breadth of the skull should compare with its length. We can remember, if we so wish, that for many years Flatcoats and Curlies were judged and bred to roughly the same standard so that the maxim which governed the head proportions was 'long and narrow for the length'.

I once knew a bitch whose head was almost like a brick: skull and foreface fell in almost the same continuous straight line. It was a most striking and handsome head and seemed to me to show tremendous Flatcoat character and expression. The skull was not unduly narrow but the flew was unusually thick. Unfortunately, the rest of her did not live up to her head. A very steep shoulder and straight hind legs precluded the validity of the head being tested in the Show Ring. Her napper impressed judges immensely, but her highest card was a third.

TYPE IN FLATCOATS

In omitting discussion of the back of the skull from the general description of the head, the intention was to treat the occiput, or the lack of occipital peak, from the viewpoint of the effect that it has on the neck. It would be a bold man who would attempt to better the traditional account still printed in Crufts catalogue. This is one of the few really classic writings on the Flatcoat. Although it is most probably anonymous by now, it has been familiar to the oldest breeders seemingly all their lives. I personally associate it almost subconsciously with the catalogue of the old Kennel Club Show, that perfect show, spacious, unhurried, uncrowded, sunny if ever there was sun but otherwise independent of the weather. This was the social event of the Dog year, and when it disappeared forever in the fire that destroyed the Crystal Palace, some touch of dignity, some air of prestige left the Kennel Club and dog breeding generally that has never been regained.

All this was more than twenty years ago and very many people who have cut a broad swathe in dogdom never knew the 'Glass House'. Few indeed will remember the days when the catch phrase of the salesmen at the London Pet Stores in selling pups was 'The mother was shown at the Palace'. Probably the last time I was at the Palace was about 1932 and I can't remember the catalogue description but I wouldn't be surprised if that is the origin of Crufts summary. It reads: 'The occiput is not accentuated, as in some breeds, the skull forming a curve where it joins the neck'. The standard says the neck should be long but one would rarely be struck by the length of a Flatcoat neck or by its elegance.

It has long been recognised by the leading minds in every breed that no amount of reading and learning by heart will give a mastery of a standard: it must be studied carefully in the light of the trends and dogs of the times in which it was drawn up. One must try to discover something of the men who wrote it and what was in their minds at the time if there is to be any success in arriving at the connotation they meant their words to carry. There seems to be a quaint conception abroad that a standard is devised by a divinely inspired body of highly qualified technicians as a guide and compendium to a breed both for the present and for all posterity. Such a thing may be possible and I have thought the sponsors of some Continental breeds could have had this high intention but many of our breed standards are just rough agreements or contracts drawn up between themselves by practical breeders owning no great skill as draughtsmen nor overmuch bothered with visions of the future. Often one sees in the same standard one feature described obviously as it was displayed by some Pillar of the breed who excelled in this point whilst another is described in terms of a hackneyed counsel of perfection, an ideal displayed by no member of the breed, quite regardless of whether it is possible to breed it in, what I call a pious hope.

This latter treatment has consequences, perhaps not foreseen, and, as I have had frequently to point out the dangers underlying certain interpretations of our own standard, it may not be out of place to give an actual instance here. Thirty years ago I was stewarding at a Sanction Show for one of the great old-time All-rounders, the late Frank Butler. Apropos a certain exhibit, he told me he was always hoping to be able to award Best-in-Show to an Alsatian. He had met several which he felt he could have justly put there, dogs of exceptional build in shoulder, back and quarters, but they all fell down at the feet. It was not the fault of the dogs. They had feet up to the average for their breed but they were all of the normal hare-foot type, whereas the Standard of the Alsatian Wolfdog Club, the recognised general standard, said 'Feet should be round and short'.

It would be going too far to say the long neck of ours is a pious hope. It could be that our necks are long, though I question whether the origins of the Flatcoat were such as would produce long necks, but there are some factors which would militate against their appearing long. This curve of the skull to meet the neck means that the junction of head and neck is not clearly defined and that the neck does not have to reach up to the high occipital peak, as in some breeds like the Setters, a reach which always gives an air of length. Another militating factor is the distinct suggestion of mane which should be apparent, more markedly perhaps in the male than the female. From the top of the neck to an inch or two behind the withers, the hair is longer than it is in the flat and small of the back. It varies with the individual but show-goers know how the coat can curve obstinately round the lower part of the shoulder blades to give a coarse and thick look to these important parts and add to the length and generally spoil the outline of the body. Since the removal of the restrictions on trimming and stripping, the temptation to 'clean out' neck and shoulders must have grown enormously. Too many judges to-day have Kennel Club approval but no other qualification for sorting out Flatcoats, and with one thing and another it would not be surprising if we ended up by clipping our dogs out like the exhibits in an American Setter Ring. There may, of course, be nothing wrong in all this in these days of atomic progress but I'm one of those breeders with a perpetually uncomfortable feeling that things are best left where nature put them. The plain fact remains that some of us used no other tools for trimming than finger and thumb with a bit of resin to rub them in. Dogs looked more like dogs and judges looked more and harder at them. My line of argument is that if we allow judges to stress this 'neck should be long' phrase, we are inevitably bound to encourage excessive trimming and shaping of necks and throats into something like what they ain't - and were never meant to be. And when I say 'if we allow', I mean exactly us - the members of the Society. We made the Standard and we are responsible for its maintenance. Nothing can sap the foundations of the Club and bring it into decay so much as the conception that we and our dogs are just marionettes jiggling to the touch of an all-seeing, all-knowing, all-doing Kennel Club. The KC is interested in neither the shape nor the colour of our dogs - that is our business. There would have been no object in the drive to initiate younger and more active members into the administration of the Society had there been nothing to do but conform to a schedule.

Closely related to the neck in its effect on appearance generally, is the brisket. This term in Flatcoats is understood to mean the effect of a breast-bone jutting prominently forward beyond the junction of the shoulder and upper-arm. Of itself it would just seem to be a breed characteristic inherited from the elements on which the breed was built and without any practical significance. One often finds, however, in such cases that its special mention is due to its association with a point of practical utility, and this is no exception. The standard goes on to say that the elbows should work cleanly and evenly on the brisket. The prominent brisket is associated with a long and well-laid back upper-arm, which, in its turn, is the prerequisite for a clean and easy movement of the elbows.

It has always been my impression that the importance of a long, well-raked upper-arm to a clean, straight elbow action was first recognised after the first World War and the theory had percolated through a considerable body of opinion by the time the Standard was drawn up. It must be recorded, though, that another explanation of the well-laid back upper-arm was current: it was contended that it was to prevent the legs catching awkward or badly carried game. Whatever the reason, there was certainly a close connection - if not an absolute confusion - between the prominent brisket and the length and position of the humerus.

The picture of the body to be gained from the Standard is quite clear, even if a little impossible within the space. The chest should be 'fairly broad' and the fore ribs 'fairly flat', that's cautious but consistent. Ribs should show 'gradual spring', be 'well arched' in centre of body but lighter towards quarters. Clear enough again, although the reader could be forgiven for thinking the writers must have thought they had a row of Public Park railings to play about with. If the ribs are to be well arched in the centre then the springing can't be very gradual in the space available. The salient point is that any springing must come behind the shoulder. If the fore ribs are sprung, the shoulder is coarse and almost invariably steep or short, the clean elbow is thrown out of line and the body assumes the appearance of being slung between the legs instead of being poised well over them. There is, in fact, a complete loss of type and the whole build of body resembles another breed. By deep chest we may be sure the Standard means deep in brisket. It should be pointed out here that the dog that corresponds to a deep-chested man is the one that is long in that part of the body that is ribbed.

Sometime during the last War, it seems that the strong, firm, straight back that had characterised the breed was lost and a school of thought grew up just after the resumption of Shows which imagined the remedy for these 'puddingy' backs was to shorten the body and make the dog cobbier. One well-known breeder who started in the middle thirties actually told me that the old dogs were cobby and that the Flatcoat should be cobby. I well remember Mr Warner Hill writing in his column that the term 'cobby' was 'anathema' to Flatcoat enthusiasts, and that about summarised the discussion. I first dealt with the matter of body length in the Press some twelve years ago and it has cropped up once or twice since. Only about three years ago, Harry Wilson made a very forthright contribution to the theme. (Why anyone should think that a dog that needs wind and stamina should have a short body is difficult to understand.) It must have plenty of lung and heart room, plenty of space, in fact, for all the body organs. One has only to think of the whelping and rearing troubles that have overtaken the bitches of those breeds which have cultivated the short body. Possibly a short body has a wider aesthetic appeal to the public. The truth is that, as with everything else, there is a happy mean. I would suggest that a body is too long when the hind legs cannot throw it about in one piece. A short back is different. Its length is influenced to no small degree by the length and rake of the shoulder. In such Flatcoat literature as exists, one repeatedly reads that the build of the dog should show plenty of liberty. Obviously a short body can restrict liberty but a short back in my view can, of itself, only increase it. I take the back proper to be from withers to hip. For the same reason, it seems reasonable to like a long, fairly flat croup, which must give the stifle more play. All these things may be matters of individual taste, however, but my reason for taking a strong line against those who would thrust shortness into undue prominence in assessing merit, is severely practical. However 'short-cast' a Flatcoat may be, it can never, by reason of the prominent breast-bone and the breeching on the hindquarters, give the short, sharp, clean-out impression that certain other breeds can. If we ourselves make a fetish of shortness we shall be judged on that count by outsiders and Flatcoats will be handicapped out of Variety Show Competition before they enter. This is not hypothetical or suppositious; I saw it happen. I remember when a good Flatcoat always scored in Varieties; I saw it drop from favour because it wasn't what it could not be. Breeding is just the same. I saw a great breeding kennel decline to almost nothing through pursuing this false ideal.

Appendix C

Mr Colin Wells once remarked to me that he thought the great dogs of his younger days always showed slope, ie the withers were higher than the croup and the back showed as a straight incline between the two. Dr Laughton has also observed that in some of the old pictures the body outline of the dogs could be compared roughly to an isosceles triangle on its side with the base running vertically through the shoulder. That these two authorities are correct, each from a different angle, there can be no doubt. I think the dogs of the past must have made that impression on me, for I remember being disappointed, when Mr Cooke showed me Woodlark in 1938, that the dog did not display much of this feature, in contrast to his famous dam, Ch Kiss of Riverside, who inherited it from her dam, Ch Atherbram Jet. Jet was by Leecroft Buxton and I would say that the Ashton dogs had it. Nevertheless, I don't ever remember slope being regarded as a point of type, either in conversation or in print. In their more popular days, Flatcoats were notable, even amongst other breeds, for their long and well-placed shoulder-blades and their firm backs. Add to this the deep brisket and the suggestion of tuck-up from hard condition and we quickly get the suggestion of the converging sides of an isosceles triangle. From actual handling for this point, I would say that the straight-backed effect just behind the shoulder was helped very much by the profusion of 'mane'. I was astonished to find one Champion was quite hollow behind his shoulder - his strong back was just a fortunate coat. This slope is much less seen nowadays and the old hands will probably be quite sure they know the reason why.

There have been few good feet on Flatcoats in the last few years. It's not surprising, for people have different ideas of what is a good foot just as they have of what is the desirable height for a dog. Ashton insisted on a lot of hair between the pads, as a protection against the heather. I myself don't care for much hair but I like very close pads as the dog is thus much less impeded in snow and mud. A correspondent in one of the dog papers wrote that all the Riverside dogs he ever saw had large feet. Well, I can assure him that I saw Riverside dogs with smallish, neat feet. The fact is that Riverside had all kinds of feet. It was not a family and its occupants did not necessarily have similar attributes. If anything, history favours the larger foot. If we settle for a good strong foot capable of taking all the stresses of quick turns and rough ground, we shan't be far wrong.

A lot of words - many of them foolish - have been scattered over tails since the War. A man who was in the Breed for some years told me in all seriousness that he had always heard (this is only six years ago) that the most important quality in a Flatcoat was that its tail should be straight and come in a straight line off its back. Now, a tail is just a tail and almost the only thing about it that matters is that it can play an important part in the general appearance of the dog - just how much will depend on the individual looking at it for 'Beauty is in the eye of the Beholder'. The Standard says the tail should be straight. By 'straight' it means 'not hooked or ringed'. It does not mean a poker. If you think it does, just bind your dog's tail to a piece of wood or other narrow, straight object and put it at different angles down from the horizontal. It will look ridiculous. A certain amount of flexibility and a little curve is required below the horizontal and, in my view, also above. If a dog can float his tail straight out in line from his back, keeping it horizontal and gently wagging it, then he is using it most effectively. But how many can? I would say that a man can go through a normal career in the Flatcoat Show Ring and never see it. For one thing, it seems to me almost an impossible feat for a dog with a well built-up loin, which implies a slightly downward trend to croup and set-on (or start-off) of tail, and this almost horizontal set-on has been associated mostly with dogs that were very flat over the loin - one might even say weak, and some would say long. By an odd trick of fate, after my efforts to destroy the cult of this unattainable ideal, there came into my possession the dog who most nearly cocked a snook at all my theories. People still talk of the Specialist tail but of all the tails I have seen I never knew a better than that of Claverdon Pegasus and in his case it was combined with a short, strong, sturdy back, a smooth action but a corky carriage and, that most important factor, the right mental attitude. I never knew him miserable or disinterested, he faced everything gaily and courageously. He wagged his tail at the world, perhaps even at the Liverpool Hook Boat Train that cut off his life at barely two and took something irreplaceable out of mine. In using the term 'straight', the authors of the standard were writing for themselves, it was something they all understood and needed no fancy description. It just meant not 'curled'. In applying the term 'short' to the tail, they were writing in the same vein. We each will have our own ideas on shortness and I myself believe that what suits one dog best may not be the same as another, but this is carrying things to a very fine issue. Many have said the tail should fall exactly to the hock and I have even heard it categorically stated that a tail cannot be too short. Taken literally, of course, this latter could quickly be reduced to absurdity but few of us will be lucky enough to meet a tail that does not want to be trimmed. It does happen, however. Mrs Barwise once showed me a dog on the end of whose tail she had to leave three inches of hair. It was at a big show and the dog, if I remember right, was a good winner. That must have been the shortest I ever saw but I used to leave about an inch on Pegasus and he was a very small dog.

Coat is a very tricky matter. Like size, each wants that which suits his own work and his own country best. I personally like a dog that likes the water and am inclined to grade coats according to how quickly they will dry. I must admit that I was always at variance with Mr Cooke about this. I always thought the coats that were so dense as to be somewhat open, dried much more quickly than the very flat ones and those with a little wave were of stronger texture. I have dogs which have a nice, flattish coat in winter that go very curly in summer with continual swimming. Other people don't worry so much about water because their dogs seldom have it to contend with and they rate most highly the coat which does not pick up burrs or any of the inconveniences which they may contact in cover or other ground they are working. Some like a shorter coat, and some a longer one. To a certain extent we may think extremes are held in check by the over-riding condition that the limbs must be feathered. Let's hope so. In the Ring, at least, a bright coat of good length and feather should score but I am not so sure that denseness gets its due reward or full consideration.

Training the Family
Companion Dog
to the Gun

by Sheila Neary, of the Collarm affix

There are probably as many ideas on how to achieve a well trained companion in the shooting field as there are gundogs. A professional gundog trainer once told me that if you pick up even one tip from each trainer, experienced handler, book, video or article, you can begin to put them all together to develop a method that will suit you, your lifestyle and your dog. I hope, therefore, that there will be something in what follows which will help you to achieve your goal.

The shooting field is not the place for a badly behaved dog. Not only could it be dangerous but it is also unfair to the land owner, shoot captain and his guns, gamekeeper and other members of the team. It should go without saying that a dog who squeaks or has a hard mouth should be left at home however much he may enjoy his job and under no circumstances should a dog with those faults be entered into competition. He will be eliminated at an early stage. In a minority breed such as ours, we must be aware of our responsibilities, not only to ourselves and the other shoot members, but also to our chosen breed for whom we are ambassadors every time we go out on a shoot or enter a field trial.

I believe that a puppy who is going to be trained to the gun but is primarily the family companion comes under a lot of pressure during his formative months because of the inevitable distractions in the home environment. The first step therefore is to decide who is going to work and train him and, that decision having been made, the rest of the family, children included, must tow the line! In other words, if, for example, the trainer gives the dog a command to sit and stay, no-one else must either give him another command or try to distract him in any other way. Choose what commands are going to be used and, even in the absence of the trainer, adhere to those words.

Before you can think in terms of starting gundog training, you have to get the foundation right. Do not be tempted to rush the basic obedience as, along with the stop whistle, it is the king pin of all your future training. If you run before you can walk, you can guarantee that everything will fall apart when the going gets tough later on. It is not a race, and Flatcoated Retrievers are slow to mature.

You will not need much in the way of equipment at first: a puppy dummy or softly stuffed sock, a slip lead and a whistle. A number of people use an Acme black plastic whistle - the 210$\frac{1}{2}$ is a popular one.

Avoid bullying your dog into obedience. The puppy phase of their lives should be fun, and training should evolve without them being aware of it as such. This is why praise at the right moment is so important. At this stage you are not really training so much as conditioning the dog. However you will have to be firm and the iron hand in the velvet glove will help you achieve a well trained dog who **wants** to work for you.

When your dog has had his inoculations, you may enjoy taking him along to the local Dog Training Club for advice and socialisation. It will also be very beneficial to the dog as he has to learn to behave and concentrate on you when there are other people and dogs around.

This is a particular valuable lesson for a Flatcoat to learn because they do tend to think of everyone as a long lost friend who should be greeted warmly. It will also help him to differentiate between work and play which, for the family companion, is going to be vital later on. Your trainer will expect you to do your 'homework' - 10 minutes twice a day is better than one session of 30 minutes, because a young dog's concentration span is limited.

Prefix any command with the dog's name. This will get his attention and help him distinguish what follows from the general background noise of family life.

There are a number of little ways in which you can supplement the basic obedience training that will help encourage steadiness in your dog. Make him sit before you feed him and only allow him to get up on your command. Another is to make him sit before you allow him into the car and again when you open the boot at your destination. This is also much safer.

A word of warning about obedience training: a working gundog should walk to heel calmly but you do not want a dog who wraps himself around your leg. Later on when out shooting, he needs to walk a few inches in front of you so that he has an unrestricted view of where the birds are falling.

A working gundog has to learn to sit promptly on three different commands: verbal, hand signal and the stop whistle. I tend to introduce the stop whistle and hand signal early on so that it is established before the recall whistle is introduced and becomes a totally familiar part of their repertoire prior to starting dummy work. If you are to work your dog properly, he must obey the stop whistle immediately, every time, without exception. Disobeying the stop whistle once is once too often and, from the day you introduce it, you must ensure that he does obey it.

Start off with your dog on the lead walking to heel. Blow the whistle (long pip) and, at the same time, place him into the Sit. Praise him gently, walk on and repeat. Do this regularly as part of your basic obedience training. When he will sit on just the sound of the whistle, introduce it at meal times. You have already taught the dog to sit before being fed so now, in place of the verbal command, blow the whistle and raise your arm straight up over your head with an open palm facing the dog. He should sit! If not, blow the whistle again and make him sit. Praise him. Once he understands what is required of him, you can alternate the Sit commands: verbal and hand, whistle and hand, just hand, or just whistle. Do this initially in the house or a confined area where you can go out to him if he does not sit first time. As he progresses you can try it on a walk, but make sure that you blow the whistle when he is close at hand so that, if he does not sit, you can run out to him, put him on the lead and take him back to where he was when the whistle was blown. Do not say anything to him. Blow the whistle again and make him sit. Remember always to praise him quietly in the early days when he does stop and to vary what you want him to do afterwards. Go out to him sometimes, call him back to you or give the command to 'Get on!' (ie, release him). This will help later on when he is working. When he has mastered the stop whistle completely, you can introduce him to the recall whistle - a series of short pips.

Do not give a command if you cannot ensure it will be carried out; otherwise the only thing the dog will learn is that it does not matter if he does not do as he is told. If the dog does not sit on the first command, repeating the word in rapid succession or raising your voice is unlikely to have any effect either. If for example he does not sit the first time, make him by repeating the command firmly but quietly whilst simultaneously pushing him into the sit, and then praise him.

The recall, or rather lack of it, seems to be a grey area! From the beginning, get into the habit of calling the dog to you when you are in the house or garden and then give him plenty of praise when he comes to you. Nearly all puppies during the first few days in their new home will only be too pleased to come when you call them, so capitalise on that. They will soon learn that coming to you when called is a pleasurable experience, and if they occasionally get a titbit as well, so much the better. So often dogs are only recalled at the end of a walk, and the owner then puts them on a lead. If you think about it from the dog's point of view, he is enjoying himself in the field or wherever and he is called. If he does as he is told, his fun stops; so he ignores the recall. Later on when he is old enough to go for a walk, call him back to you every so often just to say hello. Playing hide-and-seek behind trees or hedges and then calling will teach him to keep his eye on you all the time and not regard a walk as a time when he can do what he wants when he wants. If he does ignore the recall, regardless of how angry you might feel, **never** tell him off when he does come back to you: he will associate being disciplined with returning to you, not with having ignored your commands earlier.

Appendix D

It is not a good idea to throw things for a puppy to retrieve until you are sure that he will come back when called. However there will be times when he runs off with something that he is not allowed to have. If he does, do not chase him or allow anyone else to, but encourage him to come to you by calling him normally or run away from him. If this fails, tempt him to you with a titbit. When he has brought you his 'treasure', take it from his mouth gently with the command 'Dead!'. Please do not snatch it or allow anyone else to do so, however precious it may be. Although you may not feel like praising him, when he gives up what was in his mouth, do just that. It is very important that anything to do with retrieving is handled positively and calmly. Equally, if he picks up something that he is allowed to have, use the situation to your advantage by calling him as above. Once he has given you 'the retrieve', give it back to him for a little while with the command 'Hold!'.

When the day comes that your dog will sit, stay, lie down, come when called and generally conduct himself sensibly, you can begin the journey from raw recruit to seasoned campaigner. It is a journey which is well worthwhile because one of the most satisfying aspect of training a dog is when you begin to reap the benefits of the rapport and respect that develops from the partnership.

In the early days, go on your own somewhere quiet where there are as few distractions as possible. Sit the dog up beside you and throw the dummy a few feet in front. With luck, he will run out, pick it up and return to you. However there are a number of scenarios that could occur:

1. He will not go out to the dummy and/or pick it up. In this case, collect it yourself, call him back and, when you throw it again, go with him and wiggle the dummy around on the ground to attract his attention and then throw it a short distance away and try again.

2. He will not come back to you with the dummy. As before with contraband articles, call him, run away or crouch on the ground. When he does bring it back, praise him and let him hold it for a few moments before giving him the command 'Dead!'. Another way around this problem is to train in a narrow passageway or corridor so that he cannot get past you or out the other end.

3. He drops the dummy on the way back. Collect the dummy yourself and try again, but with plenty of encouragement on the recall. If this becomes a persistent problem, gently put the dummy into his mouth and give him lots of praise with the command ' Hold it!'. It may take a while before he will hold it of his own accord, but never force the issue.

4. He will not release the dummy. Talk to him quietly and, after a while, take the dummy from him by gently opening his mouth. Give it back to hold before throwing again.

Avoid the temptation to do 'just one more' retrieve. Three or four retrievers at this stage are enough.

Once your dog has mastered the early stages of retrieving, you can start to think in terms of keeping him steady, extending the retrieves and introducing the command 'Hie lost!' (ie 'find it'). Sit your dog beside you in the usual way, but place your hand in front of his chest, holding him if necessary, and then throw the dummy. Extend your right arm and point with an open palm in the direction of the dummy. Say the dog's name and let him go. When he reaches the dummy, give him the command 'Hie lost!'. Later on he will know, on hearing that command, that he is in the right area. It is much safer to use the dog's name to send him out rather than generalised terms such as 'Fetch it!' or 'Go for it!' because in a trial, when steadiness is of paramount importance, he will not be so tempted to run in if your neighbour uses the same command. You would have to be unlucky to have dogs on either side of you with the same name as yours!

Build up the distance of the retrieve slowly but aim to remove your hand from in front of him as soon as you think he will sit until sent. If he does run in, try not to let him get the retrieve as it should be regarded as a reward. Run out after him, put him on the lead and firmly take him back to where you were. Sit him up and fetch the dummy yourself. The next stage is to send him only for some of the dummies thrown. Vary which dummies you fetch, otherwise he will soon work out the 'one for me, one for you' routine! It is very important, even at this stage, that he never regards everything thrown as 'his'.

Once he is steady, you can sit him a little way in front of you and throw dummies around him. Praise him if he succeeds, and give a firm 'Leave it!' if he gets up. Retrieve the dummies yourself.

Teaching your dog hand signals is not as difficult as you might think. For this exercise you do not prefix the commands with the dog's name, as in the long term he will be working away from you and will not be able to hear your voice unless you shout. The latter is something that should be avoided! These are the usual signals:

Get Back: Sit your dog in front of you and throw a dummy over his head but slightly to the right. Blow your whistle and raise your arm as in the sit command. Take a small step forward with your right foot and, using your arm as a policeman would to stop traffic, command him to 'Get back!'. When he has mastered that, do the same but throw the dummy over his head but slightly to the left. Use your left arm and left foot.

Right Hand Signal: Sit your dog with his back to a wall, hedge or fence and walk back about 10 paces from him. Throw a dummy up against the wall a few feet from him, to your right. Raise your right arm, as in the sit command, blow your whistle and then lean to the right lowering your arm to shoulder level. Without using his name, tell him to 'Get on right!' and then 'Hie lost!'. I use the words right or left because it does help enforce the command. When he has given you the dummy, praise him, take him back to where he was and repeat.

Left Hand Signal: Do the same as above, but to the left.

When each of these steps have been learnt individually, you can mix them up until you have him sitting in front of you with dummies thrown to the left, right and behind. Do not forget: **sit, throw, blow**. After he has retrieved the dummy for which you have sent him, put him back into position and throw the dummy out to its original place, thus ensuring that there are always three dummies out at a time. However your dog will tend to concentrate on the last dummy thrown, so be aware of this and vary which dummy you send him for first. If he does go out for the wrong dummy, blow your stop whistle and put him back where he was.

As he becomes more competent, increase the distance between you and use an area where the grass is longer so that, although he will see it thrown, he will not be able to see it on the ground. This teaches him to mark and use his nose.

The next piece in the jigsaw is the blind retrieve. This is when you will find out how well the previous lessons have been learnt, as it requires a great deal of trust and respect for your dog to go and look for something that he has not seen thrown. It is a good idea to get into the habit of putting the whistle into your mouth before you send the dog as it can save time later, if you need it quickly, if it is not deeply buried below layers of clothing!

Start off by throwing a dummy out a few feet in front of you into a patch of undergrowth or long grass. Send him as normal. Throw the dummy back into the same place and send him again. Next time, cover his eyes before throwing it as before. Pointing firmly and clearly in the direction of the dummy, send him out for it. If he becomes confused, go with him and show him the dummy. Let him pick it up and then try again. When he reaches the spot where the dummy is, give the command 'Steady!', followed by 'Hie lost!'. Once he can do this, put a dummy out in the same spot before you take him out training next time and do as above. If this goes well, move to another place and follow the same procedure. It will not be long before you can put out a number of dummies before training but remember always to line him up straight with the direction of the dummy, using the wind to help. You can also drop dummies whilst you are walking along beside a hedge or on a path and then send him back for them. As the distance and complexity increases, your hand signals and stop whistle come to the fore. Hopefully he will soon begin to appreciate that the stop whistle is not a negative but a positive command and that, by taking directions from you, he will find the dummy quickly. One of the best tips given to me was to visualise a passageway between you and the dummy when you sent your dog out for a blind and keep your dog within the imaginary lines. You are there to help him find the dummy, so use the wind to the dog's advantage (a dog can pass within inches of a dummy if on the wrong side of the wind) and do not leave him floundering if he is having difficulty.

If at any stage he starts to disobey the hand signals or stop whistle, go back to the beginning and revise the initial lesson.

The swimming phase of the training is rarely a problem as Flatcoats love water, but there are always exceptions to every rule.

A quiet river bank (with no current running) or a pond with a shallow, sloping approach is ideal. Stand on the water's edge and encourage your dog to enter the water. If necessary, wade in with him. Should your dog show no inclination to swim, try going out with another dog who really enjoys swimming, as this often gives the young dog enough courage to take the plunge.

Make the first water retrieves simple. The usual reaction is for the dog to drop the dummy when he first comes out of the water so that he can shake. Stand on the water's edge and command him to hold it as soon as he starts to emerge. Take it from him gently and, as he shakes, give the command 'Shake!'. With perseverance and patience, he will learn to hold onto the dummy, even as you stand further and further away from the edge, and to shake on command.

The final stage of the basic training is to teach your dog to cross a river or ditch and to jump. Set up a small jump in the garden and, just before he jumps, give him the command 'Get over!'. The same with water; throw an easy dummy for him across a narrow river and with the 'Get over!' command, send him. When you are training, look for suitable objects such as fallen tree trunks, narrow ditches or short fences for him to practise jumping. Eventually, as he becomes more advanced, on hearing the command 'Get over!' he will start to look for something to jump or cross and you will be able to incorporate unseen retrieves on the other side of hedges, ditches and water into your training programme.

It can be very frustrating when things do not go according to plan, but dogs can have their off days as can we, so if either of you are not in the right frame of mind, give him an easy retrieve, lots of praise and call it a day. Continuing when not in the mood or losing ones temper does far more harm than good.

I hope that you will have gundog training classes nearby and I strongly recommend that you join them, but do not be disheartened if other breeds are more advanced at an early age. There are so many advantages to attending gundog classes ranging from companionship and support right the way through the training programme to advice as to when your dog is ready to pick up and/or compete.

Good Luck!

Sheila Neary (May 1995)

Bibliography

Books and Articles

BISHOP, Sylvia **It's Magic.** BAS Printers.

CREE, John **Nosework for Dogs.**

CROXTON SMITH, A **Dogs Since 1999.** Dakers.

DAY, Chris **The Homoepathic Treatment of Small Animals**.

DEELEY, Martin **Advanced Gundog Training.** Crowood.

DEELEY, Martin **Working Gundogs.** Crowood.

DE PRISCO, Andrew *and* JOHNSON, James B **Canine Lexicon.** TFH.

DOBBS *and* WOODYARD **Tri-tronics Retriever Training.** Tri-tronics Inc, 1650 S Research Loop, PO Box 17660, Tucson, AZ 85731.

DOBSON, *Dr* Jane **Tumour survey.** Department of Clinical Veterinary Medicine, Madingley Road, Cambridge CB3 OES.

EVANS, J M *and* WHITE, Kay. **The Doglopaedia.** 4th ed. Henston, 1994.

HOLMES, John **The Obedient Dog.**

LAUGHTON, *Dr* Nancy **The Review of the Flat-coated Retriever.**

LEIGHTON, Robert **The Complete Book of the Dog.** Cassell.

LEWIS, Peter **The Working Trial Dog.** Popular Dogs.

PHILLIPS, Brenda *and* KEARTON, Sue **Flatcoated Retriever Directory.** Private publication

RUTHERLAND *et al* **Retriever Working Certificate training.** Alpine Books, PO Box 7027, Loveland, CO 80537, USA.

RUTHERLAND *and* LOVELAND **Retriever Puppy Training.** Alpine Books.

RUTHERFORD *and* NEIL **How to Raise a Puppy you can live with.** Alpine Books.

SCALES, Susan **Retriever Training.** Swan Hill.

SCHEFFER, Mechthild **Bach Flower Remedies.**

WALLACE, Guy **Training Dogs for Woodland Deer Stalking.** Fowley.

WHITE, Angela **Train that Dog.**

WILCOX, Bonnie, *DVM, and* WALKOWICZ, C Atlas of dog breeds of the world. TFH.

WILLIS, *Dr* M B **Hip dysplasia in the Flatcoated Retriever: a report on hip scoring.** 1993.

WILLIS, *Dr* M B **The Progeny Tests for Hip Scores: Flatcoated Retriever.**

Videos

The AKC Flat Coat Video is available through AKC at 919-233-9767-press 2324 or through many sporting and pet supply stores.

HALLSTEAD, John *and* HALLSTEAD, Sandra **Advanced Gundog Training.** HJR Productions, 81 Stoughton Road, Oadby, Leicester LE2 4FQ.

HALLSTEAD, John *and* HALLSTEAD, Sandra **The Drakeshead Method.** HJR Productions.

SEAL, Sam *and* SEAL, JUDY *with* DEELEY, Martin **Training Your Flatcoat.** Paul French Video. (01733 252567)

Useful
Addresses

The American Kennel Club

Tel:919 233-9767

(Press 215 for general information.
General information can only be accessed
between 8:30 am & 6:30 pm Eastern Time,
Monday to Friday.)

Associated Sheep, Police, Army Dogs Society (ASPADS)

Hon Secretary: Mrs R.Jones
5 Hare Street
Grimsby
South Humberside   DN32 9LA

British Association of Homoepathic Veterinary Surgeons (BAHVS)

Hon Sec: Christopher Day
Alternative Medicine Centre
Stanford -in-the- Vale
Farinidon
OXON   SN7 8NQ

The British Deer Society

Oakdene
Mill Lane
Dunsfold
Surrey

Denes Advisory Service

Tel: 01273 325364

Dog World

9 Tufton Street
Ashford
Kent   TN23 1QN

Federation of Dog Trainers and Canine Behaviourists (FDTCB)

Ann Devizio
15 Lightburne Avenue.
Lytham St Annes.
Lancs FY8 IJE

Tel: 01253 722923

Flat Coated Retriever Society of America

Membership Secretary: Miriam Krum
167705 West 327th Street
Paola
Kansas 66071-9517.

Tel: 913 849-3218

The Flatcoated Retriever Club of Scotland

Mrs M Scougal
19 Craigiebield Crescent
Penicuik
Edinburgh   EH26 9EQ

Tel: 01968 73808

The Flatcoated Retriever Society

Secretary: Mrs J E Maude
The Homestead
The Causeway
Mark
Nr Highbridge
Somerset   TA9 4PZ

The Flatcoated Retriever Society

Rescue, Rehousing and Welfare Scheme
Co-ordinator: Mrs Barbara Harkin
Stormwinds
Quakers Drove
Turves
Peterborough PE7 2DR

Tel: 01733 840585

Hearing Dogs for the Deaf

National Training Manager: Claire Guest
Hearing Dogs for the Deaf Training Centre
London Road (A40)
Lewknor
Oxford   OX9 5RY

Tel:01844 353898
(Voice and
Minicom)
Fax: 01483 200509

The Homoepathic Society for Animal Welfare (HSAW)

Co-ordinator: Mrs N J Brook
Newparc
Llanthidrai
Gower
Glamorgan   SA3 HIA

The Kennel Club

1-5 Clarges Street
Piccadilly
London   W1Y 8AB

Tel: 0171 493 6651

(For youth activities, contact The Kennel Club Junior Organisation (KCJO) Manager at the above address)

The Northern England Flatcoated Retriever Association (Proposed)

Secretary: Mrs S Kitching
Sandhills Farm
Crathorne
Yarm
Cleveland   TS15 OAD

Our Dogs

5 Oxford Road
Station Approach
Manchester   M1 8DP

PAT Dogs

4-6 New Road
Ditton
Kent   ME20 6AD

Tel: 01732-872222

Working Trials Monthly

WTM Publishing
16 Hartlip Hill
Nr Sittingbourne
Kent   ME9 7PA

Index

Index

Index

Index

O

P

Index

V

W

Y